Strategy and transaction
in an African factory

Bruce Kapferer

Strategy and transaction in an African factory, 1972.

African workers and Indian management
in a Zambian town

Manchester University Press

HD
8799
Z33
K3
1972

Published by the University of Manchester at
The University Press
316–324 Oxford Road, Manchester M13 9NR
ISBN 0 7190 0434 9

Distributed in the USA by
Humanities Press Inc
303 Park Avenue South, New York, N.Y. 10010

Printed in Great Britain by
Butler & Tanner Ltd, Frome and London

Contents

List of tables and illustrations

Foreword
by J. Clyde Mitchell

For many years Zambia has enjoyed an enviable place in the literature of social anthropology. In the 1930s the then relatively unstudied matrilineal system of social organisation attracted the attention both of ethnographers like Smith and Dale and Melland, and social anthropologists like Audrey Richards. But the establishment of the Rhodes–Livingstone Institute in 1938, under the direction first of Godfrey Wilson and then of Max Gluckman, led to a series of systematic studies of the peoples of the region. These studies have since become recognised as unique in Africa, and they provide a historical foundation for future work.

It was characteristic of the studies which Wilson and Gluckman conducted personally, and which they encouraged in others, that the contemporary colonial and industrial–commercial relations into which the peoples of the region had been drawn were as much a proper subject of anthropological study as the indigenous social systems of the peoples themselves. It is understandable, therefore, that the necessity to study the forms of behaviour and the social institutions of Africans in towns should have been an integral part of the work of the Rhodes–Livingstone Institute. Wilson himself pioneered urban anthropological studies in a remarkable examination of the life of Africans in Broken Hill (later Kabwe) (see Wilson, 1940–41). When Gluckman became Director of the Institute in 1945 and funds for social research became available through the United Kingdom's post-world war II Colonial Welfare and Development Act, he was instrumental in including urban studies as part of the integrated research programme he proposed. It was under these auspices that Epstein, McCulloch and I started work in the towns of Zambia in the 1950s.

Urban studies in Zambia were taken one step further in the period 1960–66 by Peter Harries-Jones, an officer of the Rhodes–Livingstone Institute, and by two Commonwealth Scholars, David Boswell from England and Bruce Kapferer from Australia. All were contemporaries: Harries-Jones working in Luanshya, Boswell in Lusaka and Kapferer in Kabwe. Under the Commonwealth Scholarship scheme young academics from member States of the Commonwealth were able to study at institutions of higher learning in different parts of the Commonwealth. The University College of Rhodesia and Nyasaland (as it was then) was extremely fortunate in being recognised as an appropriate institution in Central Africa, and Boswell and Kapferer—and Long and Fry, who worked in rural areas in Zambia and Rhodesia respectively— came out to Central Africa to pursue studies there.

The Department of Sociology at the University College of Rhodesia and Nyasaland was a new one with a relatively young staff located in a changing and turbulent part of Africa. African movements of protest against the Federation of Northern Rhodesia and Nyasaland were beginning to gather force and we were conscious of the moving times in which we were living. The earlier lead towards the study of contemporary society given by Wilson and Gluckman was now particularly germane. The academic interests of members of the department were particularly oriented towards social change and modern society, and the subsequent studies which the research workers took up reflect this—Kapferer and Boswell on urban studies and Long on individual economic activity. At this stage also we were exploring the potentialities of the use of the notion of social networks to analyse social behaviour. The upshot of these discussions have been published elsewhere, but in this book Kapferer extends the interest which he developed during his early contact with the department in Salisbury, and he demonstrates in a most intriguing way how the notion of social networks can be combined with exchange theory as expounded by Peter Blau.

Kapferer has not dealt extensively with the methods he used to collect field data. Although he knew in advance that he was going to do an urban study he nevertheless spent a full year doing fieldwork in a Bisa community. We knew that the Bisa were a sizeable element in the African population of Kabwe. We also knew that there had been few modern ethnographic accounts of the Bisa. The choice of where Kapferer was to become familiar with the rural background of the migrants to town, to learn the language and generally to acquire the skills of fieldwork, was made in terms of these two considerations. He was able to report on his findings of this 'familiarisation' field trip in a publication entitled *Co-operation, leadership and village structure* (Zambian Papers, No. 1, 1967). In 1964 he started fieldwork in Kabwe. At that time progress towards independent rule in Northern Rhodesia was well under way and in these circumstances a type of fieldwork was feasible which in the colonial period, when Wilson, Epstein, McCulloch and I had done our fieldwork in town, had been impossible. Kapferer and Boswell were able to take up residence in the areas normally occupied by African families and to develop social relationships with Africans which would have been impossible for earlier field workers to achieve. The more detailed urban ethnography that they have been able to accomplish is immediately apparent in their work.

Although in this book Kapferer reports on the material he collected as an observer in one factory situation, it is apparent from his analysis that he had followed the protagonists in the events back into their places of residence and to their places of recreation. He had done the same for a set of workers in the cell room of the lead and zinc mine in Kabwe. But this is only a fraction of the fieldwork he managed to accomplish. He made intensive studies in several beer halls and a tavern, he collected data on the political contacts of the elite, he collected exceedingly detailed information on the conjugal behaviour and relationships of several residents and he made a meticulous examination of the visiting and sociability of a set of residents in a street of an African residential area. These techniques of study required, as did the studies on the factory floor, a very complete recording of inter-personal behaviour and conversation. This indefatigable recorder was able to accumulate a mass of exceedingly detailed observations of what had transpired in the very different social settings in which he was able to be present with people as they went about their daily life.

But in addition to this essential observational material, which most anthropologists would consider to be a *sine qua non* of successful fieldwork, Kapferer was able to organise and conduct two sizeable social surveys—one among the residents of the township in which the mine employees lived, and the other in the general municipal residential area. These social surveys included not only the usual 'fact sheet' variables of sex, age, occupation, religion, and so on, but a detailed mobility and occupational history and a questionnaire on social prestige and the factors associated with it. Some of the findings relating to his survey of the municipal residential area have already appeared (see Kapferer, 1966). Finally, through the courtesy of the mining company, Kapferer was able to consult its records and so build up an appreciation of the historical background of the situation he was describing in Kabwe. In this, of course, he was assisted by Wilson's study some twenty-five years earlier and, to a lesser extent, by the social survey which McCulloch and I had conducted some twelve years earlier. Although Kapferer has chosen, thus, to report on one limited aspect of his fieldwork, it should be appreciated that this study should be set in the context of the variety of fieldwork situations to which he has exposed himself and the different sorts of data he has accumulated to back up his generalisations.

Kapferer elected deliberately to report in the first instance on workplace behaviour. It is a remarkable fact that although the number of studies of Africans in urban contexts has increased considerably in the last twenty-five years very few have concentrated on such behaviour. Yet in a sense the work-place is often the most characteristically urban of the contexts in which African townsmen interact, and it is usually the context in which they spend the greater part of their time. While studies such as those by Hellman, Bell, Glass, Elkan or Van der Horst have, indeed, been of Africans in work-places, they have been based on social surveys or analyses of records and not on the anthropological procedure of direct observation. I conjecture that the paucity of studies of work-place behaviour in Africa is partly because direct access to workers on the shop floor has been so difficult to achieve in the past and that in colonial times the presence of an observer might have changed the situation so as to make it unrepresentative. But it may also be because studies of the kind that Kapferer presents in this book require a meticulousness in recording, an assiduity and a discipline which few ordinary field workers can attain.

Of course, the sort of fieldwork that Kapferer became involved in derived essentially from the sort of problem he was interested in. It is possible that students of African work-place behaviour in the past have used other techniques because, in essence they were interested in problems different from those which interested Kapferer. In his previously published analysis of the cell room and in his analysis of the tailoring factory in this book, Kapferer is interested essentially in small-scale personal interaction rather than in the wider institutional structure of society, a distinction which he recognises (p. 334) and which he appreciates is fundamentally a matter of the level of abstraction at which the analyst is operating.

The emphasis on personal interaction requires detailed systematic recording of the innumerable personal exchanges that take place among the workers on a shop floor over an extended period of time. Given the capability of intense and sustained effort, from a suitable vantage point in the work situation, a field worker like Kapferer, who knows the language and enough about the protagonists to be able to catch the significance of the innuendos conveyed in their exchanges, is able to build up a considerable body of data. But data of course, do not of themselves constitute an analysis: data are the observer's first level abstraction from the totality of behaviour in the situation. Since no field worker, however able and gifted, is able to record everything that is going on, some exchanges or some events have been either excluded or have gone unnoticed. Given, however, the selected nature of the basic field data, the analyst is faced with the necessity of fitting these data themselves into some framework which imparts to them a relevance and a significance.

Initially, influenced no doubt by the ferment of discussion in which he was involved in Salisbury, Kapferer sought to order his material in terms of social networks. But he himself has argued cogently (1970) that social networks do not by themselves constitute a 'theory'. At most the notion of a social network throws the emphasis away from dyadic towards indirect social relationships. At the same time a regimen is imposed upon those who wish to present their material in terms of social networks. This ensures that the analytically relevant categories of information relating to all the actors are systematically recorded. Kapferer was aware before he went into the field that if he wanted to use a network approach to present his material he would need to ensure that he had systematically collected data relating to the interactions of each member of the work force of the factory with every other member. The fact that he was able to compute measures of span, density and multiplexity for each person in the network (see table 5.2, pp. 186–7) demonstrates how successful he was in doing this.

The burden of his argument in chapter 5, where he presents the detailed interactional data, however, is that he must go beyond these data for an adequate explanation of the events he is considering. Specifically, he states subsequently that: 'the various structural measures used for networks, and also the presentation of the interactional relationships in matrix form, do not take account of the changing processes which have taken place within the time period for which the various indices are relevant' (p. 293). To supplement this analysis, therefore, he resorts to two somewhat different though related strategies. On the one hand he uses exchange theory to derive propositions which he is able to examine in the light of his data. Exchange theory thus provides him with a set of logically connected concepts by means of which he is able deductively to arrive at the sort of behaviour he could anticipate from the protagonists. The second strategy is to provide a longitudinal analysis of the sequence of events, through which he is able to trace the unfolding of the relationships between management and workers in the factory. The transactions he records during these events, however, are significant, and presumably these particular events have been selected from a much more extensive set of events of which Kapferer was no doubt aware but which for his argument he considered to be irrelevant. He recorded, I know, extensive data on the conjugal relationships of some of the workers involved in the transactions he recounts. While events relating to these activities would be germane to a paper on marriage and kinship, they were presumably not so for the relationships between management and workers in the tailoring factory. The information relating to the transactions of the workers among themselves and with the manager that Kapferer presents, as in all good analytical writing, is a product of the particular theoretical approach he adopts. In his case he has adopted an essentially interactionist approach towards the interpretation of the development of relationships between workers and management—to which the notion of social networks is particularly germane—and this has determined the sort of evidence he needs to present to back up his arguments.

Theory and data are, as he points out, inextricably interconnected—this is both a strength and a weakness of analytical writing of this sort. But Kapferer is acutely conscious of the extent to which his own framework of analysis has led him to present certain kinds of data rather than other. Accordingly, he has deliberately presented a good deal of detailed descriptive data in the form of statistical tables, the adjacency matrices reflecting the relationships of the workers to one another, the network structural measures (tables 5.1 and 5.2) which he uses in conjunction with the interlinkages in the network to characterise the social relationships in which the protagonists are involved, personal information on each of fifty-seven protagonists (appendix 1) and the chronicle of thirty-five events from June 1965 through to February 1966 (appendix 2). This detailed ethnographic rapportage not only provides evidence to enable a sceptical reader to check the deductions that Kapferer draws from it but will also presumably help an analyst with a somewhat different theoretical orientation to provide an alternative interpretation of the course of events in the factory. One of the laudable features of this book is that although it is essentially about the theory of personal interaction, it is very solidly grounded in actual events so that theory and data have an intimate relationship.

Yet the extent to which an alternative explanation of the events in the factory might be essayed is nevertheless constrained by the very intimacy between Kapferer's particular theoretical bent and the sort of data it necessarily generates. However stimulating and refreshing it may be to be presented with solid ethnographical detail within the framework of a reasonably rigorous theory—a theory that enables the analyst to arrive deductively, on the basis of general processes, at propositions which can then be checked against the course of actual events—those who have been trained in a structuralist framework will almost certainly have an uncomfortable feeling that the events described in the factory as Kapferer describes them appear to be somewhat isolated from events in the wider social, economic and political sphere in which the factory was placed.

This is a problem of which Kapferer is acutely aware. One of the attractive features of his analysis is that he deliberately takes up the bearing of factors outside the factory upon the behaviour of the manager and workers within it. He sees the factory, as he puts it, 'as a setting or locale in which the participants organise resources present in the setting itself and introduce resources external to it in the pursuit of their various interests. A process is isolated whereby individuals and groups representative of such bodies as the trade unions, the political party and government organisation become involved in issues which have their course in the factory floor' (p. 120). To do this he makes use of three concepts. First is the 'general environment', by which he means all the social contexts in which the actors have been involved prior to or during their employment in the factory, other than that of the factory itself. This enables him to take account of the effect of conjugal relationships, recreational activities, kinship and similar circumstances in the lives of the actors on their behaviour on the shop floor. The second is the 'arena', which is composed only of those elements or resources which individuals or groups use or can potentially use in their activity. These elements in the arena may be organised into specific relationships with one another and as such they constitute a field. Thus the third concept is the 'field', which refers either to the actor's perceptions or to his actions. He defines these terms thus: 'By perceptual field I refer to the particular image an individual or group has of the resources in the arena relevant to the achievement of particular interests. It also includes some idea of the way these resources are likely to be organised in relation to each other. In contrast, the action field includes all these resources and interconnections between them which are activated in the course of action' (p. 123). The arena of the events in the factory, therefore, is Zambian society at the time of the fieldwork. The actors were utilising special advantages which they were able to command in this arena in order to better their working conditions at one level and to establish command over their fellows at another.

Thus in spite of the fact that Kapferer is concerned specifically with the social relationships of a small set of workers in a modest factory he

avoids the trap into which so many of those who work within an interactionist framework fall. The behaviour he observes is not completely
abstracted and isolated from the wider social currents which immerse
them. Instead, through his use of notions such as 'environment',
'arena' and 'social field', he is able to expand the context of meanings
in terms of which the workers are ordering their behaviour so as to
include relevant features of the wider society of which they are but a
part. The equivocal stance of the Indian manager at the beginning of
the period of the study is related to the recent political changes in
Zambia, when Africans had assumed political control over the affairs of
the country but were still heavily dependent upon the financial, industrial and commercial skills of non-Africans for the economic welfare
of the country. At the time of the strike the political climate had so
stabilised that the manager was able successfully to use the government
administrative bureaucracy against the workers. The reactions of the
African workers and the behaviour of the Indian manager towards them
may be interpreted in terms of these wider political events which
Kapferer is able to introduce into his analysis through the notions of
field and arena.

The African factory-workers' discussion of the qualities of town life
(pp. 224-5), which Kapferer uses so skilfully to demonstrate the ways
in which leaders who are competing with one another for the esteem of
workers are able to discredit their rivals, has social significance in the
context of the much wider processes of urbanisation and industrialisation in Zambia. Urbanisation, in Zambia in particular, has led to a
marked contrast between general levels of rural as against urban living,
and this lies behind the evaluations the workers are making in their
appraisals of the opinions expressed. These general processes of
urbanisation are not directly germane to the topic which Kapferer is
concerned with but they do constitute a relevant element in the arena
in which the contest among the workers is being staged. Kapferer's
sensitiveness to these wider issues and his location of the particular
network of social interaction of the workers in a much wider perceptual
and action field allows him to demonstrate how these issues impinge
upon the rather narrow scene he is viewing. This prevents his analysis
from being an interesting but futile examination of daily chit-chat on
the shop floor and makes it an exciting and full-blooded account of
people facing real problems in a changing world.

Urban studies have not yet attained the full stature of respectability
in British social anthropology. This is partly because as yet the set of
theoretical tools available to urban anthropologists has been inadequate

for the formidable task for which it has to be used. The pioneers have
been involved mainly in establishing the city as a legitimate field of
anthropological study and of trying to decide what anthropological
questions have to be asked in it. Kapferer's book, I think, marks a stage
in the maturation of urban anthropology, for his brilliant synthesis of
interactional perspectives with sound structural insights, his neat
marriage of theoretical rigour with detailed ethnographic reporting and
his subtle interfusion of small-scale with wide-scale phenomena, all
provide a model which not only urban anthropologists but anthropologists and sociologists in general will be able to use to achieve new
depths of understanding of complex social situations.

J. Clyde Mitchell
January 1972

Preface

This analysis is concerned with social relationships between African workers in an Indian-owned clothing factory in Kabwe (Broken Hill), Zambia. The study of the factory is presented in the general context of the changing social and political relationships of Kabwe and Zambia at the time. Although the study is focused on a specific work place, it is a context from which I attempt to explore various aspects of life in the town and the country generally.

A number of themes are pursued. Two are particularly dominant. First, the significance of processes relating to urbanisation and the social and political changes in the town and country for the relationships of the African workers and their Indian management on the factory floor. Second, the consequences of changing alignments and the process of structural development within the factory for the strategies which the factory employees adopt towards management in bids to achieve wage and work improvements.

Fieldwork was carried out between May 1965 and March 1966. Research in the factory was part of a broader two year study of Kabwe which started in March 1964 after a period of fieldwork in a rural area in Zambia's Northern Province. Before I began research in the clothing factory I had already carried out intensive study into the shop floor and after-work activities of African mineworkers employed in the cell room of the Kabwe lead and zinc mine. I had also completed a large social survey of the African population in the municipal residential areas and two small neighbourhood studies, based on participant observation. Therefore, at the time of my starting this research I already had a relatively extensive fieldwork experience in Kabwe and was broadly familiar with patterns of social activity in the town.

Originally I decided to carry out this study in order to collect research material which would balance, to a certain extent, my knowledge of industrial and work activity in the mining area of the town. The choice of the particular factory in which to do the study was considerably influenced by the fact that I already knew many of the workers employed there. This I felt would ease the difficulties all social researchers must experience when they enter a new field context.

B

Research in Zambia was financed by a Commonwealth Scholarship to the University College of Rhodesia and Nyasaland from March 1963 to March 1966, and administered by the Institute for Social Research (then the Rhodes-Livingstone Institute) of the University of Zambia, Lusaka. Throughout my stay in Zambia I was a Research Affiliate of the Institute. The Institute's administrative staff, under the directorship of Professor A. Heron, gave me every assistance. I am also grateful to the American Friends Service Committee in Kabwe and its director there, Mr Alan Connor, who assisted with a grant so that I could conduct a social survey of the municipality.

Many people have contributed to the shaping of the ideas as expressed in this book. In Africa Professor J. C. Mitchell, then of the Department of Sociology, UCRN, showed great patience in teaching an extremely raw student the methods of fieldwork and the techniques of analysis. He gave of his time, ideas and extensive knowledge with unstinting generosity. This has continued back at Manchester during the writing up of the research and after. Professor J. van Velsen, now of the Department of Sociology, University of Zambia, has also contributed a great deal in the way of detailed criticism and ideas at various stages in my research.

In Zambia and back at Manchester I benefited enormously from the encouragement, friendship and interest shown by Dr Norman Long. He introduced me to my first experience of anthropological fieldwork. Our subsequent joint field ventures and many long discussions late into the night and early morning will live long in my memory.

Mr H. D. Ngwane, Mr Boniface Zulu, Mr Phillip Ngoma and Mr Kenneth Shipota, among numerous others, both extended their hospitality and readily gave their assistance at various times during fieldwork. I am especially grateful to Mr Blackson Mupeseni and Mr Lawrence Mulenga, who guided me expertly through the many complexities of urban life and instructed me carefully in the forms and varieties of urban behaviour which we observed. Of course, for this study the people to whom I am indebted the most cannot be openly named, for that would destroy their anonymity, which I have tried to preserve through the use of pseudonyms in the text. Without the complete co-operation and patience of both management and worker in the clothing factory this study would have been quite impossible.

In Manchester Professor Max Gluckman afforded me every opportunity to discuss my research with him. His broad sociological knowledge, insight and readiness to listen to views and ideas not always in accord with his own have been both invaluable and a major source of stimulation. I am especially grateful to Dr Wesley Sharrock, whose originality, depth of sociological insight and *penchant* for violent verbal disagreement always exposed my research data to new possibilities for analysis and theoretical treatment. Dr V. G. Pons, Dr Don Handelman, Dr Kingsley Garbett and Dr Richard Werbner have spent long hours discussing with me many issues and problems I have pursued in this book, and I am indebted to them. Of course, it is an invidious task to separate out so few from the many who have at various times and stages of research and analysis contributed to the book. Others at Manchester and elsewhere have contributed in various ways to its writing, and they include Professor Michael Banton, Dr Anthony Heath, Dr Bryan Roberts, Dr David Morgan, Dr Martin Southwold, Dr Basil Sansom and Mr David Boswell. My wife, Judith, has helped considerably during the writing of the book. She has read countless drafts and improved as well as she could the grammar and also offered suggestions for improvements in the analysis. Mrs J. Harris did the typing of the manuscript. Finally, my wife and I would like to extend out gratitude to all those in Zambia who looked after us at different periods during the research. Without their friendship and hospitality our stay in Zambia would have been far less enjoyable than it was.

Bruce Kapferer

A note on fieldwork method

I began fieldwork in the factory in early May 1965 and finished at the end of February 1966. As explained in the preface, I knew many of the workers prior to my entry into this research context. However, there were numerous employees I had not, of course, known before, and they as well as management had to adjust to me and I to them. I do not place overmuch weight on the material collected in the first few weeks of fieldwork before June in the factory, although by the time I had started research there I had already experienced over a year's fieldwork in Kabwe which included research among a group of African mine workers. More than anything the early weeks of research covered a period when I familiarised myself with the character and pace of activity on the shop floor and adjusted my techniques of observation and data collection to the circumstances of the particular context in which I found myself. With the help of an African research assistant I noted as far as possible the precise details of interactional activity which occurred at the work place. This was done at the time the activity was going on or immediately upon the conclusion of a sequence of activity. I cannot overrate the importance of my assistant in this research, for he acted as an important check on my observations and I on his. The opportunity to discuss in detail with another person who was observing and recording the same activity in much the same way as oneself was invaluable.

The noting of social activity observed in the factory was generally done in the open presence of the participants. This may come as a surprise to those anthropologists and sociologists skilled in the craft of fieldwork and concerned about such recurrent methodological problems as observer effect. I cannot accurately gauge how much my method of research affected and distorted the behaviour I observed. Irrespective of what method I chose, it seemed to me that some distortion was inevitable. The problem, as I saw it, was to opt for an approach which as far as I was aware created as little distortion and disturbance in the everyday flow of activities as possible. During the initial stages of fieldwork, both in the Kabwe mine plant and at Narayan Bros., I attempted to conduct research without doing any obvious note-taking. In both contexts, during these periods, considerable concern and

suspicion were evidenced over my presence. But as soon as I was
regularly seen to take out a note book or schedule form and write things
down the atmosphere became less tense and, from what I could gather,
concern and suspicion largely disappeared.

I think there are good reasons why this should have been so. While I
was not seen to be taking notes I was in effect limiting the behavioural
cues by which the workers could check my statements of why I was in
the work place against what they inferred from their perceptions on my
activity. I was, of course, giving out a wide array of behavioural information, but to them it seemed undirected and purposeless. I seemed to be
interested in everything without discrimination. To the workers there
was no pattern to my interest. I was neither management nor worker.
My introduction to the factory, and (at first reserved) acceptance by the
workers, had been achieved on the basis that I was a research student,
interested in work behaviour, affiliated to the Institute for Social Research at the University of Zambia. For most workers I was the first
research student of whom they had had experience, and the category to
which I belonged was devoid of meaningful content. Some satisfactory,
accepted and understood definition of my role in the factory was
necessary for them to organise their behaviour towards me and relatively naturally towards each other in my presence. Without some
clear and agreed understanding of my activity the factory employees
had no sense of control over the information they were communicating
to me or sense of control over my interpretation of it. No defence
against my intrusion into their activity could be operated save employ-
ing a virtually complete blanket on the communication of information
to me. This is exactly what they did. Thus, in the early stages of my
research in the work place, as soon as workers became aware of my
presence their conversation came to an abrupt halt. However, once I
began to take notes openly I began to communicate to them a more
patterned idea of the kind of information I was after. Although they
never actually knew what it was I was writing down, they were able to
see that I was responding in the form of note-taking to certain kinds of
activity, while not reacting to others. Furthermore, they could now
check my somewhat abstract, and as far as they were concerned un-
tested, explanations for my presence against their experience of my
behaviour. The hitherto relatively empty category of research worker
assumed a meaning which enabled them to fit me into a fully accepted
place within their scheme of social activity at work. Having a clearer
understanding of the meaning of my presence, the workers operated
their defences more selectively, and as far as I could judge began to act

relatively naturally towards each other. Once I began taking notes openly the workers, in my view, became relatively oblivious to this activity, and the tense and suspicious atmosphere I had encountered early in my research dissolved.

Of course, there are other reasons which could be used to account for the change in behaviour of the workers in relation to my presence. For example, the change can be seen as a function of my increased exposure to their observation the longer I researched in the factory. I do not discount this possibility, but it would not seem to account for the abrupt change in behaviour immediately I started taking notes. Other factors, such as identification with management, may also be an explanation. I do not consider this to be very important here. As a European observer in an Indian-run and -owned factory I was, as far as the African workers were concerned, seen as independent of management. An identification with management was more relevant in my earlier research in the mine plant, where the management personnel were, at the time of fieldwork, mainly European.

The general point, therefore, which I wish to stress is that far from being an obstacle between me and the workers the open taking of notes constituted a way in which barriers to observation consequent on my presence were broken down, and their way eased in a general acceptance and understanding of my activity.

For Robert and Gwen

I   Themes and the urban setting

Anthropologists and sociologists have paid little attention to behaviour at work in the towns and cities of the third world. Although there is a voluminous literature on developing nations which refers to the growth and importance of an industrial working class in these countries there are few detailed studies. Where these exist, most, with some exceptions (Abegglen, 1959; Epstein, 1958; Nash, 1958; Savage, 1964; Sheth, 1968), have concentrated on activities outside the work place or shop floor to the exclusion of a consideration of work activity within the industries and factories.   This is surprising given the research interest of many anthropologists and sociologists in social change. The participation in industrial and factory work has had and will continue to have far-reaching socio-economic and political consequences for the nations in the developing world. To cope with the conditions and privations of industrial and factory work and to safeguard their economic interests urban industrial workers develop and establish trade unions. These in turn, as the political history of many new nations demonstrates, have played significant roles in urban and national politics. The lure of industrial and factory wage employment accounts for huge numbers of migrants every year moving out of the rural areas to swell the ranks of the rapidly increasing urban populations of the third world. Industries and factories impose restrictions, regulations and an order on social activity previously unexperienced in the lives of many of the migrants. It is at work that urban migrants come into frequent contact with individuals and agencies indirectly influential in other diverse areas of their lives. The work place is often the central locus for the expression and experience of major aspirations, disappointments, failures and frustrations of members of an urban industrial class. It is probably on the shop floor that workers most often experience the oppressive bite of the wider social and political systems in which they participate. Here also new forms of consciousness emerge which may override other loyalties not immediately relevant to their involvement in an urban industrial and political system.

While anthropologists and sociologists with broad interests in social change in the urban centres of the developing world might increase

their understanding of such processes by considering more the behaviour of urban dwellers at work, so too might industrial sociologists.
In the sparse field of African industrial sociology, apart from some
isolated examples (e.g. Glass, 1960), explanations of factors relating to
absenteeism, labour turnover, work efficiency etc., have been found in
areas of social activity not directly related to the work context, such as
in ethnic allegiances and the influence of 'traditional' beliefs, customs
and practices (Smith, 1968: 93). The emphasis has been on social
processes originating outside the plant or factory. This is almost the
reverse of the trend in industrial sociological research in the West,
often severely criticised, of explaining work behaviour solely in terms
of the social organisation of the work context itself.

This study focuses on a small group of African workers employed in
an Indian-owned-and-managed clothing factory in Zambia. In the
course of describing the behaviour of the factory employees at work I
will examine certain problems which have been the concern of industrial
sociologists. Indeed one of the general themes which runs through many
of the following chapters relates to the nature of the inter-relationship
between social behaviour observed on the shop floor and broader
processes connected with the overall urban and national environment of
the factory. This problem of the nature of the influence of *external
factors* on the *internal* system[1] of a factory has been a recurrent area of
debate in industrial sociology. Although this theme and other topics
which assume an importance in my description and analysis, such as
absenteeism, labour turnover etc., properly belong in the field of
industrial sociology, this book has not been conceived as simply an
exercise in industrial sociology. The description I present is also intended as a general contribution to research in urban anthropology and
sociology in developing countries.

The factory is a context from which I examine various aspects of
participation in the socio-economic and political life of an African
town. At various points in the analysis I describe processes relating to
the patterns of labour migration, the search for work and the organisation of small-scale trade and business. The operation of one major trade

---

[1] Homans (1951: 90-9, 108-10), in his re-analysis of Roethlisberger and
Dickson's research in the bank wiring room, makes a distinction between the
external and *internal* system of the work group. Broadly, the external system
is conditioned by the general environment whereas the internal system is not.
Lupton, and Cunnison (1964: 103-28), extend critically on Homans' notions,
and refer to *external* and *internal* factors. By external they mean the influence
of factors such as the sex of the workers, the type of product and location of
the industry, and trade union organisation. Internal factors refer principally
to the production process, wage system and the social structure of the factory.

union, and how it is related to the local urban and national political scene, becomes an essential element of my description. In a most important respect this book represents an account of the way a group of African workers organised their work activity and framed their agitation for improved wage and work conditions at a critical time in Zambia's recent history. Zambia had just thrown off the shackles of colonial rule. It had its first independent African government and numerous reforms beneficial to African interests were either in progress or were being mooted. All sections of the population, African, European and Indian, were in the process of re-defining their relationships with each other and amongst themselves. Europeans, no longer in control of government, had to establish new relationships and modify their behaviour accordingly. African workers full of high expectations now felt their position as regards their employers sufficiently strengthened to press all the harder for wage increases, improved working conditions and jobs previously the preserve of Europeans. But African political party leaders in ministerial and civil service posts were now often required to act in a manner contrary to the high expectations of those with whom they were united in pre-independence days. The political party organised in the colonial period to uproot an alien government was now used to order and control the behaviour of the African population in the interests of a wider national unity and well-being. This book, therefore, to a considerable extent, is the story of how management and worker in one small factory tested out their positions *vis-à-vis* each other in the new and relatively untried political order.

The basic analytical approach I adopt develops out of a tradition of urban research established by Gluckman, Mitchell, Epstein and others at the Rhodes-Livingstone Institute (now the Institute for African Studies, University of Zambia) and later at Manchester University. Much of what they have argued and stressed is assumed in the description I make. Thus, above all, I analyse the activities of a group of factory workers not as individuals still guided by the customs, norms and values of 'traditional' rural life and acting within a tribal institutional framework, but as participants in a changing modern socio-economic and political system. The description proceeds in accordance with the view that workers in developing countries are much like workers the world over. I consider that the analytical and theoretical principles that can be applied to understand the activities of workers in more highly industrialised countries can also be used to comprehend the behaviour of workers in the third world.

My analysis also draws extensively on the orientations of decision theory, game theory, symbolic interactionism and the theory of social exchange. Exchange theory incorporates many elements of the other orientations and is most significant for the analysis and description I present. Various exchange theories have recently been put forward (Thibaut and Kelley, 1959; Homans, 1961; Kuhn, 1963; Blau, 1964; Barth, 1966; McCall and Simmons, 1966) and all are to some extent relevant for this analysis. The approach of which I make the most explicit use, however, is that set out by P. M. Blau in *Exchange and Power in Social Life* (1964).

A central concern of Blau's is to explain the generation and emergence of social structures in terms of the basic processes which govern interaction between individuals. In the course of concentrating on and isolating these basic processes Blau focuses his attention explicitly on social behaviour as a process and on social change. He directs attention particularly to the dynamics of status and power in interpersonal relationships and the paradoxes and dilemmas to which individuals become exposed in their social activity. It is the attempt by individuals and groups to resolve these dilemmas which in Blau's view imparts to social life its essential process. Individuals in the course of solving dilemmas which confront them in certain areas of their social life create new dilemmas in other areas. In essence Blau's approach marks a clear return to the Hegelian dialectic of thesis and antithesis. Though synthesis is never achieved society receives its essential processive form and generates the conditions for its own transformation. As the following quotation demonstrates Blau departs from conventional anthropological and sociological structural-functional and institutional approaches which neglect the study of social process and erect models of society which are basically static and unchanging. 'There is a dialectic in social life, for it is governed by many contradictory forces. The dilemmas of social associations reflect this dialectic, and so does the character of social change. To conceive of change in social structures as dialectical implies that it involves neither evolutionary progress in a straight line nor recurring cycles but alternating patterns of social reorganisation along different lines' (Blau, 1964; 336).

Blau's formulations appeared most pertinent to the empirical setting of my study. My mode of research, which involved the detailed observation of the activities of a set of individuals predominantly in the work context but in other contexts as well, impressed upon me the extreme variety and change in their behaviour and the changing way in which behaviour on the factory floor was interrelated with the broader urban and national environment. Furthermore, many of the changes I observed

appeared to be closely connected with the competition between individuals for status and power.

There are other reasons why I have relied most explicitly on Blau's
theory of social exchange. Blau is aware of the tautological nature of
a theory which aims to apply to all social behaviour. His exchange theory
which is not able to explain behaviour resulting from 'irrational push
of emotional forces' and is limited to actions which are 'contingent on
rewarding reactions from others and that cease when these reactions are
not forthcoming' (1964: 6). These strictures of Blau's do not avoid
completely the tautological nature of his approach, as Blau himself
recognises. Whether the approach is tautological, and the real danger to
sociological explanation of this, rests in the empirical use to which such
a theory can be put and its utility in generating hypotheses which can
be tested on observed material.

In common with all other recent exchange theories, Blau's perspective
is based on some assumption of rationality. He himself devotes very
little attention to this assumption, but some discussion is necessary, to
show how it is employed in my own analysis. There are two main ways.
The first involves its use as a strategy for the analysis of empirical data.
Its use here is similar to the role of maximisation in sociological in-
vestigation as seen by Cancian. 'Maximisation is one of the standard
restatements of the *a priori* truth that all behaviour is patterned; that all
human behaviour has a reason. This use of maximisation as a scientific
strategy involves seeking out the norms or motives (or whatever the
investigator sees as the impetus of behaviour) and attempting to rank
order them so as to see the behaviour as the (conscious or unconscious)
maximisation of these things' (1966: 467). Thus rationality is an
assumption which I make in an attempt to discover underlying patterns
and regularities in the behaviour and events which I have observed.

Its second use is as an approximation to the reality of everyday
individual conduct. There are many senses in which individuals can be
understood to be acting rationally (Homans, 1961: 82; Garfinkel,
1967: 262–83).[2] When used to refer to the reality of individual behaviour very little in fact seems to be assumed in the sense that much

[2] The importance of realising that there are many different senses in which a
concept of rationality can be related to individual and group behaviour is
demonstrated in Blau's critique (1964: 234–6) of Downs' (1957) rational model
of political activity. Downs uses rationality as an approximation to the reality
of social behaviour in the restricted economic sense of the concept. Thus Downs
explains political behaviour in terms of the rational calculation of rewards
which individuals and groups derive from governmental activity. This approach
cannot explain, as Blau points out, the growth of minor opposition parties and
neglects other forms of rationality which may influence behaviour. An example,

of human behaviour we observe can be considered rational given the broad spectrum of behaviour which can be classed as rational. Thus Blau, making use of Weber's distinction between *wertrational* and *zweckrational,* emphasises that he includes as rational behaviour that which is oriented towards the achievement of some personal gain and that which is directed towards the achievement of socially mediated goals (1964: 5–6). In addition Blau recognises that the rationality of behaviour may be limited by such factors as limited information, restricted perception, *etc.* The important point which must be stressed is that, given that there are many kinds of activity which can be regarded as rational, one of the aims of Blau's analysis, and certainly my own, is to discover the conditions under which an individual or group may display one kind of rationality rather than another. What, for example, are the circumstances which may lead individuals to value the activity in which they are engaged for the intrinsic qualities of this activity itself rather than for the benefits it may typically bring? Under what conditions will individuals pursue their own self-interest or subordinate this to the wider interests of the group to which they belong?

An important aspect of Blau's approach for my own analysis is that he does not view individuals as independent social actors and he attempts to avoid the dangers of psychological reductionism. Blau never sees individuals acting independently of the opinions, choices and decisions of others. He constantly emphasises the restrictions placed on independent individual activity by investments and commitments in their sets of interactional relationships. It is in his rejection of an individualistic perspective that he introduces a concept central to his theoretical framework, that of emergent property. (1964: 3–4).

Although new structures emerge from the interaction between individuals, these structures cannot be understood simply in terms of their constituent units (i.e. individuals). Structures acquire new properties which are not located in individuals but which feed back into and influence individual behaviour. The social relationship established between two individuals is an emergent property which cannot be understood through reference to one partner in the relationship. Power and status are emergent properties in that they relate to the quality of the interactional relationships between individuals. To view a social relationship as an emergent property demands that it be seen as the joint product of both parties to it, which has the further consequence

for instance, is the value which people may attach to the expressive manifestation of political belief and practice.

that the action of one partner cannotbe und erstood without reference to the action of the other.

The idea of emergent property is a cornerstone of Blau's theory. The introduction of this concept marks a departure from other exchange theories such as those of Homans and Barth which view structural and institutional forms as ultimately reducible to their individual components. In addition this concept recognises that wider structural and institutional processes influence individual action. Blau acknowledges that social behaviour cannot be understood purely in terms of separate individual interests and motives. But he emphasises also that many processes cannot be understood simply through reference to higher level orders of abstraction such as structure or institution. In developing the concept of emergent property, and in his exchange theory generally, Blau tries to bridge the gap between abstract institutional and normative explanations of social behaviour and the psychological reductionism exemplified in Homans' theory of social exchange. The following quotation should clarify Blau's position. I hope it clarifies mine. He states that we must steer carefully between '. . . the Scylla of abstract concepts too remote from observable reality and the Charybdis of reductionism that ignores emergent social and structural properties' (1964: 3).

It is not my intention here to discuss the merits and demerits of the various exchange theories. A number of statements already exist which examine specific aspects of some of the recent exchange theoretical approaches (e.g. Abrahamsson, 1971; Buckley, 1967; Eken, 1969; Heath, 1968a, 1968b; Petersen, 1969; Robson, 1968; Stebbins, 1968). I simply declare openly my preference for one approach in particular and isolate some features of it which I find especially attractive. A deeper understanding of how it is used in my analysis and how I have developed it to suit my own empirical requirements will only be gained by reading the way I apply it to the description and explanation of the social behaviour I observed. This is probably the final test of whether it is justifiable or not for a specific theoretical approach to be employed in sociological analysis. Sociological and anthropological theories have, I consider, value only in the extent to which they permit insight and an understanding of empirical data. They are somewhat arid if their purpose, as it seems so often to be, is only to generate further articles and books of abstract discussion frequently unrelated to the analysis and description of first-hand field material.

Before I turn to a description of the general urban setting in which this study is located it is crucial for me to emphasise that, although exchange theory is at times an important element of my analysis, it is so because I consider that it allows me to present relatively accurately what I observed and to explain this behaviour. The study itself is definitely not viewed as necessarily a justification for adopting an exchange theoretical approach. My first aim is to describe and explain what I recorded in the course of field observations. If some principles drawn from the theory of social exchange appear to be supported by my ethnographic evidence then this is a bonus and secondary to my main aim.

It is also important for me to stress that I was not aware of exchange theory in the form argued by Blau and others prior to my arrival in Manchester upon the conclusion of my fieldwork. But, my interest in 'situational analysis' and the 'extended case method' (Gluckman, 1961; Van Velsen, 1967) and a concern to collect relatively full interactional data for the application of social network analysis resulted in my gathering material sufficiently detailed to enable me to utilise an exchange theory approach.

Kabwe (Broken Hill): history and socio-economic environment

Geographically, Kabwe lies in the heart of Zambia (see fig. 1.1) on the Great North Road, approximately eighty-six miles north of Lusaka, the capital, and 120 miles south of Ndola. The Great North Road branches at Kapiri Mposhi, a small trading settlement forty miles north of Kabwe. One route links Kabwe to the Copperbelt towns in the Western Province and to the Luapula Province via the Congo pedicle. The other route branches in a north-easterly direction and connects Kabwe with the Northern Province and beyond to Tanzania and East Africa.

Like the Copperbelt towns which developed later, Kabwe owes its origin to its mineral deposits. In 1902 lead and zinc were discovered and in 1904 the Rhodesian (now Zambia) Broken Hill Development Company[3] was registered in London and the first furnaces were constructed. The railway reached the town in 1906 and facilitated the development of Kabwe's mining industry. The arrival of the railway also stimulated the growth of commerce and until the railway reached Sakania in the Belgian Congo in 1911, Kabwe was the centre from

[3] This company is now a subsidiary of the Anglo-American Corporation, which controls many of the mines on the Copperbelt. In 1935 the Rhodesian Broken Hill Development Company ran into difficulties caused by the flooding of underground shafts when attempts were made to mine ore below the water table. Anglo-American were appointed as consulting engineers and the difficulties were overcome by the application of a deep-level cementation process.

which settlements as far afield as Mwansa (Fort Rosebery) and
Mbala (Abercorn) received their supplies. The first store opened in
1907 and others soon followed. In 1914 a post office was opened and
four years later the town's first bank began business (*Economic Survey,*
1953: 1–3). Commerce was initially dominated by Europeans but Indian
trading and commercial interests increased particularly after the 1940's

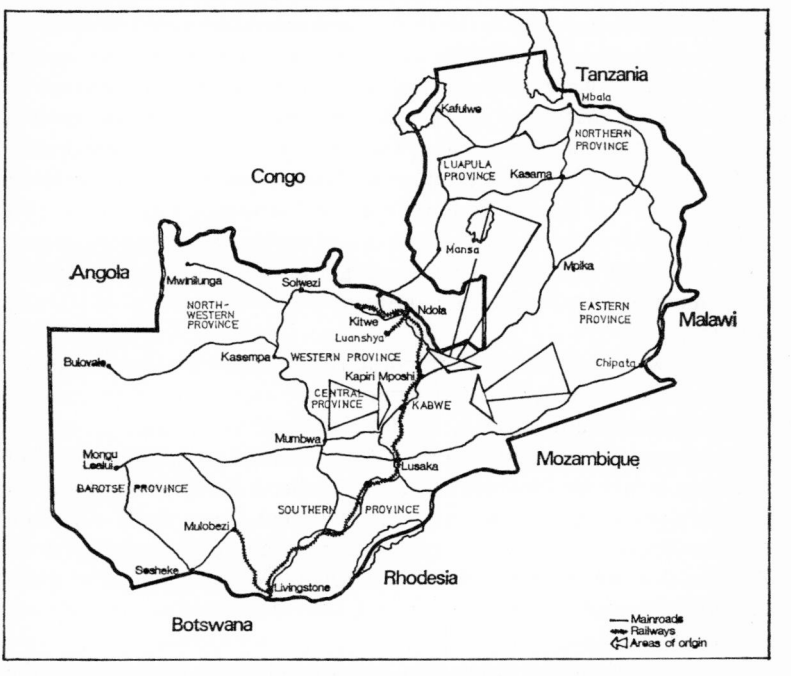

Fig. 1.1   Kabwe and main areas of origin of population

and the hold which Europeans had over commercial activities steadily
declined. The dominant position which Indians established in the
commercial and trading enterprise of the town was symbolised by the
taking over in 1959 by an Indian firm of the largest European owned
department store. In 1954 Kabwe was declared a municipality, with a
municipal council which had jurisdiction over residential and business
areas not on mine property.[4] The mine housing areas are administered
separately by the mine company.

[1] The railway housing areas remained separate until 1949 when they came under
the control of the Kabwe (Broken Hill) local authority (*Economic Survey,*
1958: 2).

c

By comparison with other major towns on the 'line of rail' Kabwe does not give the visitor the impression of thriving prosperity. The tall modern buildings, broad avenues and bustling shopping centres of the Copperbelt towns contrast sharply with the older 'colonial style' buildings, dusty streets and tranquil shopping area of Kabwe. The buoyant and booming atmosphere of the Copperbelt towns owes much to the wealth of the copper mines which are their industrial base. Kabwe's lead and zinc mine, upon which the town's economy largely depends, shows small profits and is constantly exposed to fluctuations in the market and the heavy competition of other lead and zinc mines elsewhere in the world. Moreover, lead and zinc does not bring as good a price as copper on the world metal markets,[5] wages for Europeans and Africans working in the mine are lower than the wages received in the copper mines. Their lower rate of spending, which is a consequence of lower wages, not only reduces their apparent prosperity compared with the workers in the copper mines, but also affects those in commerce, much of whose business consists of trade with mine workers.

Nevertheless, Kabwe is an important town despite its lower degree of economic prosperity when compared with other 'line of rail' towns. Kabwe is the administrative centre for Kabwe district and the provincial headquarters for the Central Province. It is also a communication and transport centre for Zambia. The Zambian head offices of the Rhodesia Railways are located in the town and it is the headquarters of Central African Road Services, the largest road transport organisation in Zambia. Surrounding the town is a relatively prosperous European farming area and it is on Kabwe that these farmers depend for their supplies.

At the 1961 census of the non-African population, Europeans in the town numbered 4,911 and Indians 585 (1965:37). A later census of Africans in 1963 showed that 40,570 were living in Kabwe (1964: 47). The population is largely immigrant, though this is less so than for other urban areas in Zambia. After Livingstone, Kabwe is the oldest major town on the 'line of rail'. Many adult African and European residents were born there and proudly point to the fact. Generally, however, most Africans and Europeans living in the town have migrated to it. Indians, unlike Africans and Europeans, are a relatively recent addition

[5] In 1964, on the London Metal Exchange, where Zambia's mineral exports are sold, lead received an average price of £117·7 per long ton and zinc £100·7 per long ton. Copper, however, fetched an average price of £351·3 per long ton. All the copper mines have a higher productive output than Kabwe (Source: *Mining Industry Year Book*, 1964).

to the population, the period of considerable Indian migration to the town being between 1951 and 1956.[6]

Europeans and Indians, though tending to be residentially separated from each other, live close to the town centre. The main African housing areas, however, are clustered at some distance around the town periphery. (see fig. 1.2).[7] For example, the African mine housing area is approximately two miles from Kabwe post office while the three main African municipal areas (Bwacha, Chimanine and Ngungu) are three miles from the post office.

The residential separation of Kabwe's population reflects some of the basic social and political cleavages which divide the town's inhabitants. Africans, Europeans and Indians, apart from their meeting at work, in the market place or through the course of performing various administrative duties, rarely come into contact on other occasions. The drama society, the mine club and the returned soldiers' club are largely confined to European membership. The Indian community has its own cinema organised by the Kabwe Indian Association, which shows imported Indian films with a Hindi soundtrack.

After Zambia's independence on 24 October 1964 the Zambian Government attempted to break down discriminatory practices shown particularly by Kabwe's European population towards the Africans. The mine cinema and swimming pool, which had been open to all except Africans, now had to admit Africans. However, social separation was still maintained. At the cinema ticket office Africans were sold seats which ensured that they did not sit near Europeans. A membership fee was levied on all who wished to use the swimming pool. This acted as a deterrent to the majority of the town's Africans. It was only among

[6] In 1931 there were seventeen Indians resident in Kabwe; the number rose to 103 by 1946. This number had increased only by sixty-three at the time of the 1951 census. But between 1951 and 1956 there was a sudden influx of Indian immigrants, the number resident in the town by 1956 rising to 510. After 1956 the migration of Indians to the town declined, so much so that by the 1961 census the Indian population had risen only by seventy-five (Source: *Economic Survey*, 1958: 2).

The large influx of Indians to Kabwe after 1951 is consistent with the general pattern of Indian migration to Zambia. Dotson explains this pattern by the attractive economic opportunities presented by Zambia following the boom in the copper industry in the early 1940's and the extension of education in India, which enabled immigrants to overcome the literacy test in English which was enforced in 1915 (Dotson, 1968: 50–1).

[7] This pattern is similar to other Zambian 'line of rail' towns (cf. Epstein, 1958: 7; McCulloch, 1956: fig. 111; Kay, 1967: 596). After independence in October 1964 the Zambian government pursued a policy aimed at breaking down the residential separation on racial lines, and Africans began to move into other housing areas.

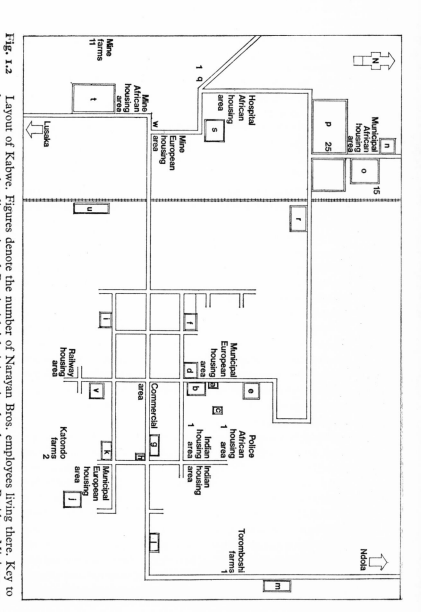

Fig. I.2 Layout of Kabwe. Figures denote the number of Narayan Bros. employees living there. Key to letters: *a* central police station, *b* Provincial Administration headquarters; Resident Minister, *c* labour office, *d* railway head office, *e* Central African Road Services, *f* post office, *g* Narayan Bros.' factory and general store, *h* NUCIW office, *i* UNIP regional and constituency offices, *j* secondary school, *k* municipal offices, *l* Hindu hall, *m* secondary school, *n* Ngungu, *o* Chimaninine, *p* Bwacha, *q* Makololo, *r* messengers' township, *s* hospital, *t* mine African housing area, *u* railway station,

the elite that any regular social meeting took place between members of the different ethnic sections of the population.

The social distance between these ethnic sections, and especially between Europeans and Indians on the one hand and Africans on the other, intensifies their opposition on economic/industrial lines. Europeans and Indians tend to be the employers or superiors of Africans at work. They constitute the wealthier section of the community. Their spacious homes and modern cars are in marked contrast to the crowded housing areas, confined living conditions and bicycles of the African population.

In addition to their social separation there is a tendency for the major ethnic sections of the population to be politically opposed. This political cleavage mostly affects Africans and Europeans. The Indian community has changed its political allegiance according to the group in power. Thus in pre-independence days Indians supported the European controlled government. With the successful emergence of African nationalism and the increased likelihood of an African government, leaders of the Indian community in Kabwe began actively to assist the main African nationalist party.

Kabwe was the headquarters of the United Federal Party and the constituency of Sir Roy Welensky before he became Prime Minister of the Central African Federation in November 1956. In Kabwe during pre-independence days, UFP received most of its support from Europeans. After the victory of the coalition of the two major African political parties at the 1962 elections, UFP changed its title to the National Progress Party. This party continued to have its headquarters in Kabwe and was led by a prominent European farmer on the outskirts of the town. Like UFP before it, NPP continued to receive the staunch support of the town's Europeans.

Opposed to NPP locally and at the national level was the United National Independence Party. This party, after the dissolution of its coalition with the African National Congress and its victory at the 1964 general elections, formed the new Zambian African government.[8] UNIP was supported by most of Kabwe's African population. There were a few members of ANC in the town and these lived mainly in the railway housing areas. By the end of fieldwork the local branch of ANC had disbanded and the local officials had publicly declared themselves to be UNIP supporters.

Each of the main African housing areas has its own UNIP branch, which has authority over a number of party sections based on smaller

[8] Mulford (1967) gives a good account of Zambia's recent political history.

neighbourhoods within the housing area. All the UNIP branches are in turn subordinate to the Kabwe UNIP constituency officials. The Regional headquarters of UNIP are located near the town centre (see fig. 1.2) and these officials are responsible for all party officials and members in Kabwe and its environs.

It is through the political party organisation that local government representatives attempt to control and direct the activities of the town's African population. Thus the Resident Minister, who is the head of the administration for the Central Province and has a seat in the Zambian National Assembly, has two appointed Political Assistants. The main duty of the Political Assistants is to act as liaison officers between the government and the political party.

The description so far has focused on the broad social and political factors which divide Kabwe's population. The broad ethnic categories of Africans, Europeans and Indians can be further subdivided according to the occupational sector in which they work (e.g. government administration, commerce, railway or mining). Other subdivisions, such as religion, wealth and status in the town community, are also relevant and in social intercourse often cross-cut divisions based on occupation.

The African population of the town is heterogeneous. Africans are represented in all occupational sections and are divided on the basis of ethnic background, area or province or origin, religion etc. In the remainder of this section I will limit the description to the broad social and economic characteristics of that part of the African population which is engaged mainly in commercial activities and which lives in the three townships administered by the municipal authority, Bwacha, Chimaninine and Ngungu (see fig. 1.2).

Most of the employees in the clothing factory live in these townships. Nevertheless some live in other African dwelling areas such as the mine farms, Katondo farms and Mukobeko.[9] There is a tendency for the population in these areas to be more stabilized in terms of continuous residence in town than the municipal African population. But from my

[9] The mine farms were established by the mine company for employees who wished to settle permanently in Kabwe. Katondo and Mukobeko were established by the Northern Rhodesian government and the Kabwe municipality respectively for the same purpose. The bulk of the population resident in these areas, however, is composed of migrants to town, most of whom will eventually return to their rural homes. There is a shortage of housing in the main municipal African townships, and many migrants build small mud-and-thatch huts to accommodate them until they can find more suitable housing. A large number, nevertheless, continue living in these areas. One major reason for this is that they do not pay rent, which would be the case if they moved to the municipal townships.

general observations and earlier survey material, the broad demographic aspects of the population in these areas are markedly similar to those of the three main municipal townships.[10] The African population of all these areas is continually changing. The demographic features of the African population generally are subject to the process of circulatory migration whereby Africans move from their rural areas to the towns in search of work, to return to their homes at some later stage in their lives.

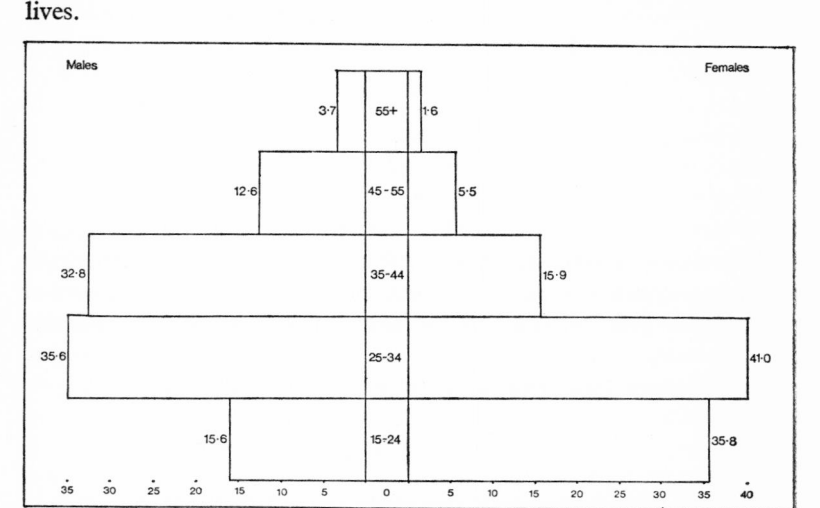

Fig. 1.3   Age/sex structure for African municipal township population: a 1964 sample survey of Bwacha, Chimaninine and Ngungu

Fig 1.3 shows the age and sex structure of the Africans 15 years and over living in the municipal townships. This diagram should be viewed in conjunction with table 1.1, which shows the proportion of resident adult males to 100 females in broad age categories.[11] The age and sex structure indicates that the highest percentage of males is between the ages of 25 and 44, whereas the highest percentage of females occurs within the age categories 15 to 34. This is borne out on table 1.1, where in the 15–29 category there are only forty-eight men to every 100 women. In the higher age categories, however, men noticeably

[10] Survey data on these areas were collected by Professor J. C. Mitchell in 1953. I am extremely grateful to him for allowing me to see his unpublished material relating to these areas.

[11] The data presented in the tables for the municipal population were collected from a 20 per cent random sample survey of these housing areas made in 1964. A more detailed account of the results of this survey, together with a brief history of the townships, can be found in Kapferer (1966).

outnumber women. That the majority of the adult male population is between 25 and 44 years of age is due, as Mitchell stated for the Copperbelt towns, to the migration of able-bodied men and their wives into the urban area at the expense of the rural area (Mitchell, 1954: 4).

Table 1.1   Sex ratios in broad age
            categories, Kabwe, 1964

Age group	Males per 100 females
15-29	48
30-34	168
45-59	205
Effective sample	1,123

Two factors explain the tendency of men to outnumber women in the higher age categories and for women to outnumber men in the lower ages. First, there is a pattern for men to marry women considerably younger than themselves. Second, there is a tendency for women to return to their rural homes after the birth of their children.[12]

Table 1.2   Country and provincial origin of
            adult male and female population

Province	Males	Females
Barotse	3.6	1.8
Central	26.8	41.0
Eastern	28.1	27.2
Northern	17.3	13.3
Southern	5.4	2.2
North Western	3.4	3.4
Luapula	1.4	0.9
Western	2.5	1.8
Malawi	9.4	5.6
Congo (Leopoldville)	0.2	0.4
Portuguese West	1.1	-
Portuguese East	0.4	0.2
Tanzania	0.2	-
Rhodesia	1.8	2.9
South Africa	-	0.4
Total	100.0	100.0
Effective sample	562	561

[12] Other factors are also relevant for an explanation of the age and sex structure of the municipal housing area. For further details see Kapferer (1966: 9–12).

Most of the adult Africans living in the municipal townships were born in rural areas. Inclusive of towns both within and outside Zambia, 12·5 per cent of the adult male population was born in town against 18 per cent of the females. Of these 5·7 per cent of the men were born in Kabwe compared with 7·3 per cent of the females. The population is extremely heterogeneous having its origin in a variety of rural areas inside and outside Zambia and claiming association with a host of different ethnic groups. However, the Central, Eastern and Northern provinces (see fig. 1.1) supply the bulk of the African males resident in the township (see table 1.2). Malawi accounts for most of the population coming from countries outside Zambia. The Eastern Province supplies slightly more of the African men living in the municipal housing areas than the Central or Northern Province. This pattern is slightly different for females where the Central Province supplies the highest population of women living in the township, followed by the Northern and Eastern provinces. An important regularity relating to the migration of men and women to the town is highlighted. There is a marked tendency for men migrating to town from areas distant from Kabwe such as the Northern and Eastern provinces to be unaccompanied by their wives, particularly in the early stages of their urban and labour experience. Many of the men are unmarried when they come to town and there is an increasing pattern for them to marry women who live in the areas close to and surrounding Kabwe. This accounts for the high proportion of women from the Central Province resident in Kabwe. Further evidence for this is given in table 1.3, showing the ethnic composition of the townships.

As is to be expected the ethnic groups which are the most heavily represented in the municipal housing areas come from the rural areas which provide the bulk of the population. There is a larger number of women than men living in the township who belong to ethnic categories such as the Lala and Lenje, whose areas are relatively close to Kabwe. In contrast there is a tendency for men to outnumber women whose rural home areas are distant from the town, such as the Bemba, Bisa, Nsenga, Chewa, Tumbuka, etc.

Despite the extreme heterogeneity of the town, as table 1.3 indicates, many of the ethnic groups share similarities in terms of culture, social organisation and language. Most of the population is formed from the ethnic groups who belong to the Northern matrilineal or Eastern matrilineal categories.

As described by both Mitchell (1956) and Epstein (1958) the broad ethnic identities based on such factors as similarity of culture and

Table 1.3 Ethnic categories (males and females)

Social type	Ethnic category	Males	Females	Distribution
Northern matrilineal	Aushi type			
	Aushi	2	1	Luapula Province
	N'gumbo	1	1	
	Total	3	2	
	Luapula type			
	Kazembe Lunda	2	2	Luapula Province
	Chishinga	1	1	
	Total	3	3	
	Bemba type			
	Bemba	80	73	Northern Province
	Bisa	24	15	
	Tabwa	1	2	
	Kunda	12	14	Eastern Province
	Total	117	104	
	Lamba type			
	Lala	52	67	Central Province
	Lamba	11	12	and Western Province
	Lima	4	3	
	Luano	5	7	
	Swaka	19	40	
	Ambo	6	8	
	Total	97	137	
Central matrilineal	Ila type			
	Ila	2	1	Southern Province
	Tonga type			
	Tonga	23	9	Southern Province
	Toka	1	-	
	Total	24	9	
	Lenje type			
	Lenje	21	56	Central Province
	Sala	1	-	
	Soli	6	13	
	Total	28	69	
Western matrilineal	Ndembu type			
	Ndembu	5	3	North Western
	Kaonde	12	15	Province and
	Other	1	1	Central Province
	Total	18	19	

ial type	Ethnic category	Males	Females	Distribution
	Lwena type			
	Chokwe	2	1	North Western
	Luvale	9	4	Province
	Mbunda	4	1	
	Total	15	6	
	Nkoya type			
	Nkoya	1	1	
lateral	Lozi type			
	Lozi	14	4	Barotse Province
thern rilineal	Nyakyusa type			
	Nyakyusa	1	-	Northern Province and Tanzania
	Mambwe type			
	Mambwe	1	3	Northern Province
	Lungu	1	-	and Tanzania
	Inamwanga	6	3	
	Nyika	-	1	
	Total	8	7	
	Henga type			
	Henga	2	-	Northern Province,
	Tumbuka	20	14	Tanzania and
	Lambya	3	1	Malawi
	Sisya	1	-	
	Kamanga	-	1	
	Other	1	-	
	Total	27	16	
stern trilineal	Chewa type			
	Nsenga	66	77	Eastern Province
	Chewa	53	22	and Malawi
	Nyanja	3	1	
	Nganja	1	-	
	Lakeside Tonga	5	4	
	Total	128	104	
	Yao type			
	Yao	10	8	Malawi and Mozambique
uth-eastern trilineal	Zambezi type			
	Sena	1	-	Eastern Province
	Cikunda	4	1	and Mozambique
	Total	5	1	

Social type	Ethnic category	Males	Females	Distribution
Southern patrilineal (Shona)	Korekore type			
	Budya	–	1	Rhodesia
	Other	1	1	
	Total	1	2	
	Zezuru group			
	Zezuru	3	4	Rhodesia
	Ndau group			
	Zanga	1	–	Rhodesia
	Manyika group			
	Manyika	1	–	Rhodesia
	Ungwe	–	1	
	Bargwe	1	–	
	Total	2	1	
	Karanga group			
	Govera	1	1	Rhodesia
Southern patrilineal	Sotho type			
	Sotho	1	–	South Africa; Ndebele in Rhodesia
	Zulu type			
	Zulu	–	2	South Africa; Ndebele in Rhodesia
	Ndebele	2	5	
	Total	2	7	
	Ngoni group			
	Fort Jameson Ngoni	41	45	Eastern Province and Malawi
	Malawi Ngoni	9	10	
	Total	50	55	

The tribal types have been based on those listed in Mitchell's numerical code for tribes.

language play an important part in the political and social life of Africans living in the urban areas of Zambia. It is on the basis of such broad cultural and linguistic identification that individuals establish social relationships and frame their behaviour to one another. Much of the struggle for leadership and power within the political party at the local branch level was expressed in the idiom of the opposition between broad ethnic and cultural categories. Thus people who classified themselves as Bemba, a category which frequently included members of other Northern matrilineal groups such as Lala, Bisa, etc., opposed others categorised as Ngoni, a category which included the patrilineal but largely Nyanja-speaking Ngoni as well as other Nyanja speakers, who are matrilineal, such as members of the Chewa and Nsenga ethnic categories.

But other factors apart from specific ethnic identity or broad cultural or linguistic affinity are important in the social life of all Africans in Kabwe and other 'line of rail' towns. Prestige and status, based on such considerations as wealth and occupation, associate or oppose individuals. A common way of greeting a newcomer to a drinking group in the beer hall is by addressing him by his occupational status.

Table 1.4 Occupation and age of adult males

Occupation	15-24 years	25-34 years	35-44 years	45-54 years	55+ years	% of total
Unemployed	70.4	8.5	4.3	6.1	10.5	16.7
Unskilled	9.1	37.7	33.0	43.9	52.6	32.9
Semi-skilled	3.4	9.0	10.8	7.6	15.8	8.5
Self-employed	1.1	4.5	6.5	3.0	5.3	4.5
Skilled	8.0	23.6	28.6	27.3	10.5	22.8
Supervisory	-	3.0	4.3	4.5	-	3.1
Police	1.1	3.0	1.6	1.5	-	2.0
Clerical	4.5	7.5	5.4	4.5	5.3	5.9
Professional	2.3	3.0	5.4	1.5	-	3.4
Total	99.9	99.8	99.9	99.9	100.0	100.1
Effective sample	88	199	185	66	19	556

The occupational categories in tables 1.4, 1.5 and 1.6 have been ordered in approximate accordance with the prestige generally given to individuals in the township who belong to these categories. Table 1.4 shows occupation and age. The two occupational categories into which the largest percentage (55·7 per cent) of the male employed population fall are the unskilled and skilled. There is a slight tendency for unskilled occupations to be filled by men from the older age categories. The distribution of men from all age categories in skilled work is fairly even. If anything there is a tendency for men in the younger age categories to be more represented in the skilled and above occupations. This is most noticeable in the police, clerical and professional occupations where most of the adult males are below 44 years of age.

In table 1.5 broad ethnic/cultural categories are shown against occupation. There is no marked tendency for any one ethnic category to

Table 1.5 Broad ethnic categories and representation in occupational categories

Tribes	Occupation Unskilled	Semi-skilled	Self-employed	Skilled	Supervisory	Police	Clerical	Professional	Total %	Total
Northern matrilineal	38.6 -0.7	9.1 -1.4	7.4 +1.6	29.0 +1.5	3.4 -0.2	0.6 -1.8	8.0 +1.1	4.0 +0.1	100.1	176
Central matrilineal	33.3 -6.0	11.1 +0.6	2.2 -5.6	31.1 +2.1	2.2 -1.4	8.9 +6.5	6.6 -0.5	4.4 +0.5	99.8	45
Western matrilineal	62.5 +23.2	3.1 -7.4	6.3 +0.5	9.4 -16.1	6.3 +2.7	6.3 +3.9	3.1 -4.0	3.1 -0.8	100.1	32
Bilateral	54.5 +15.2				9.1 +5.5	9.1 +6.7	18.2 +11.1	9.1 +5.2	100.0	11
Northern patrilineal	31.0 -8.3	20.7 +10.2	3.4 -2.4	31.0 +3.5	3.4 -0.2		3.4 -3.7	6.9 +3.0	99.8	29
Eastern matrilineal	38.5 -0.8	13.9 +3.4	4.1 -1.7	28.7 +1.2	4.9 +1.3	0.8 -1.6	5.7 -1.4	3.3 -0.6	99.9	122
South-eastern patrilineal	50.0 +10.7	25.0 +14.5		25.0 -2.5					100.0	4
Southern patrilineal	38.9 -0.4	5.5 -5.2	8.3 +2.5	27.8 +0.3		5.5 +3.1	11.1 +4.0	2.8 -1.1	99.9	36
Other	18.2 -1.1	9.1 -1.4	18.2 +12.4	45.5 +18.0			9.1 +2.0		100.1	11
% of total	39.3	10.5	5.8	27.5	3.6	2.4	7.1	3.9	100.1	

+ Over-represented.
− Under-represented.

Table 1.6 Occupation and basic monthly earnings

Earnings	Unskilled	Semi-skilled	Self-employed	Skilled	Super-visory	Police	Clerical	Profes-sional	Total
Up to £4 19s	15.0	8.2	38.1	5.5	6.3	-	-	-	10.4
£4 1s - £9 19s	43.3	36.7	38.1	32.8	43.8	9.1	9.8	5.6	34.8
£9 1s - £14	36.7	42.9	9.5	33.6	12.5	36.4	19.4	16.7	32.3
£15 - £19	2.8	10.2	9.5	20.3	12.5	27.3	22.6	5.6	11.2
£20 - £24	2.2	-	4.8	3.1	25.0	-	19.4	38.9	5.7
£25+	-	2.0	-	4.7	-	27.3	29.0	33.3	5.5
Total	100.0	100.0	100.0	100.0	100.1	100.1	100.2	100.1	99.9
Effective sample	180	49	21	128	16	11	31	18	454

Note: percentages enclosed by heavy lines show the median wage
earned by each occupational category.

be over- or under-represented in specific occupational categories. One possible exception is for the bilateral group (Lozi from Barotse Province) to be over-represented in unskilled work and in higher status occupations such as police, clerical and professional work. The sample in this case, however, is too small to attach much significance to these particular results. The pattern for each of the main ethnic categories represented in Kabwe, Central matrilineal, Northern matrilineal and Eastern matrilineal, is very similar especially in the unskilled and skilled occupations. All show a tendency to be slightly under-represented in unskilled work and slightly over-represented in skilled work.

In comparison with other areas in Kabwe—for instance, the Africans employed by the mine and living in the mine township—the residents in employment living in the municipal township generally receive low incomes. Table 1.6 shows that 77·5 per cent of the occupied males in the municipal townships were earning less than £15 a month. As can be expected, those in the higher occupational categories tend to receive the highest wages. The group of factory workers with whom the analysis in the following chapters is concerned is drawn mainly from that part of the population I have classified into the unskilled and skilled occupational categories.

The organisation of the argument

The analysis falls into basically two parts. Chapters 2–4 describe the factory setting and place the processes observed there within the general urban and national context of Kabwe and Zambia. Chapters 5–8 focus more explicitly on the patterns of interaction in the factory and in particular the competition for power and status.

In chapter 2 I describe the factory layout, production process and the wage system. Many of the empirical problems which emerged in the course of fieldwork and the explanations I use to solve them are introduced in this chapter but extended and elaborated in the following chapters. Thus chapter 3 which shows that the factory labour force consists of individuals at different stages in their life and employment careers focuses on factors which generate worker commitment to the work place. Various aspects related to commitment are used in chapter 2 to explain, at least partly, such factors as the variation in wages earned and the propensity of certain categories of worker rather than others to take strike action against management. Chapter 3 also examines other factors not only related to commitment but also to other features of worker behaviour in the factory. The involvement of some of the workers in running their own tailoring businesses in the town is examined, as too are processes of recruitment to factory work, labour turnover and migration. A problem of a more general nature also guides the analysis and description of chapter 3 and this concerns the relationship of factory behaviour with broader social processes affecting the African urban population. This theme continues through into chapter 4. Here I examine aspects connected with Government labour policy, trade union and political party organisation in so far as these impinge on management and worker negotiation over wage and work improvements. The analysis in this chapter, as in the others preceding it, is influenced by a choice/decision-making approach. However, to this orientation I add the concepts of 'arena' and 'field' and through them show how the field of action relevant to worker and management dispute and negotiation expands and contracts over time. Dependent on the expansion or contraction of the field is the extent to which individuals and agencies who do not regularly participate on the factory floor are able to take part in and influence activity centred on management and worker negotiation.

Chapter 5 has a more restricted focus than those preceding it. In this chapter my concern is to examine the structure and change of inter-actional relationships recorded within the factory. Earlier chapters refer to a change in the distribution and structure of interactional relationships to explain partly, among other behavioural features, the preparedness of all the factory workers to unite in strike action against management. Through such concepts as social network and the introduction of major principles drawn from exchange theory I describe the distribution and structure of interactional relationships at two separate time periods. Exchange theory becomes most significant in the analysis for explaining how important changes in the structure of interactional relationships were generated. The discussion in chapter 5 provides an analytical and theoretical frame in terms of which the description in the remaining three chapters is presented. Chapters 6, 7 and 8 examine the dynamics of interpersonal relationships as this relates to the competition for power and status. This competition is seen to have important consequences not only for changes in the structure of alliances, interactional relationships and perceptions of the employees but also for the character of management and worker dispute and negotiation. The description in these last chapters is done largely through a close discussion of a series of events organised in chronological sequence.

D

The clothing factory: production and wage
system

'The Africans of Broken Hill are not a cattle people, nor a goat people,
nor a fishing people, nor a tree-cutting people, they are a dressed
people' (G. Wilson, 1942 : 18). The paragraph from which the above
quotation comes begins:

Every African man of whatever social group tries to dress smartly for
strolling round the town, or for visiting in his spare time, and loves to
astonish the world with a new jacket, or a new pair of trousers of distinguished appearance. Women behave in the same way; and they judge
husbands and lovers largely according to the amounts of money which
they are given by them to spend on clothes.

Fourteen years after Wilson wrote this, Mitchell (1956: 13) emphasised
the importance of dress for the social behaviour of Africans in Luanshya.
Today in all towns along the Zambian line of rail clothing continues to
be a most important item of expenditure and its significance as a symbol
of status has not diminished. In Kabwe the quality of clothing and the
way it is worn is a critical indicator of another's social position and is an
important consideration upon which one individual will base his
behaviour towards another. Many people maintain they can identify a
fontini merely by the clothes he wears. A *fontini* (it is a term of both ridicule and abuse) is a person who is not accustomed to town ways.[1] He
wears dirty and poor quality clothing. If he should wear a tie likely as
not he would wear it outside a pullover.

Much conversation is taken up with the discussion of the quality of
material. Curtains are displayed in house windows with the often
brilliant patterns facing out into the street for passers-by to admire.
Technical words originally confined to types of material have become
more generally applied in town language. 'Terylene'[2] is used by women
to apply to a very popular fish sold in the markets.

[1] The term *fontini* has application well beyond the proper wearing of clothing.
Its use is largely situational and can be used to refer to anyone who is judged
by another not to be behaving in a town fashion. Thus a man who is not able
to open a car door properly may be called a *fontini*, as may a person who rushes
off the side of the road at the approach of a car.
[2] It is said that Terylene trousers are the most popular among men in town.
They are the easiest to keep clean and well pressed. Because, women argue,

Clothing is big business. The busiest and most colourful parts of the markets are those sections where clothes are sold. The traffic in stolen clothing is extensive. Clothes-hawking is a major money-earning activity in all the townships. Clothes form the greatest proportion of the trade in the Indian trading areas and Africans are the most frequent customers of Indian stores. Because dress is such an important part of urban life it seems fitting that the following description should be concerned with one context where people important to the Kabwe clothing industry work. Therefore, in this opening chapter my general aim is to describe the setting of an Indian-owned clothing factory which employs Africans.

History and background of the factory

Narayan Bros., the factory which is the subject of this study, is located on the edge of the main Indian commercial area of Kabwe and is one of the older established Indian business and trading firms in the town. Also, as one of the largest it spans numerous interests. The business is divided into two main parts, the store and the clothing factory. The store has on display goods for sale ranging from foods, which include both fresh vegetables and tinned foods of a wide variety, to clothing, many kinds of hardware (specialising in kitchen and gardening utensils), and bicycles.

In short it is a general store which aims at stocking most of the food and other requirements of all sections of the population of the town and its immediate environs. The success of its appeal is reflected by the composition of its clientele, the store on any day being crowded by Europeans and Africans alike. Most of the Indian stores in Kabwe direct most of their attention towards competing for the custom of the town's African population. There is only one other Indian store which offers similar goods for sale in the town and successfully attracts both Europeans and Africans as its customers.

The business as a whole is controlled by a partnership of four Indians, all of whom were born in India and who belong to the Hindu section of the relatively small but economically powerful Indian community in Kabwe. The present partnership of the firm gained control of it in 1954 when the Indian owner–founder of the business sold up his interests in the establishment and retired to India. Narayan Bros. began originally

the best trousers are called 'Terylene' it is only natural that the finest fish should also be so called.

as a small food and clothing shop but, like many other Indian stores in
the town and generally in Zambia, a few African tailors were hired to
work in the store making up limited amounts of clothing for sale.[3] In
February 1946 a clothing factory was opened and is still in its initial
position behind the main store. It was started by the current factory
manager, Patel, who also became one of the firm's partners in 1954.
Patel recounts with pride how the factory was one of the first of its kind
in Zambia and the first in Kabwe.

Recently another Indian store in the town opened a rival clothing
factory and this new competition has caused some concern to Patel and
his partners. Significantly, the new clothing factory is owned by
Narayan Bros.' main competitor for the European and African trade in
the town. But, in spite of this new competition, the clothing factory
continues to be a lucrative source of income to Narayan Bros. This is
evidenced by the wide variety of clothing which is made and the high
rate of sale of the finished articles. Although the Kabwe mine discon-
tinued an extremely valuable contract with Patel in 1963, Patel still
supplies work clothing on contract to the Kabwe municipality and is
under contract to supply all school clothing for Kabwe district's
primary and secondary schools and, in addition, to the Zambia Youth
Camp eleven miles outside Kabwe. Apart from the clothing contracts
which Patel has established, he supplies much of the clothing which is
on sale in other stores in the town and he appears to have cornered the
market in Kabwe for the supply of uniforms to Europeans and Indians
for their African domestic servants.

The factory premises of Narayan Bros. are small. Most of the
activity surrounding the manufacture of clothing is done in one room
(approximately 40 ft × 20 ft; see fig. 2.1). It is here that the majority of
the clothing factory employees work. A much smaller annexe behind
the main room is used chiefly as a store for the finished clothing, but as
will be described subsequently a few employees do work there. Fig. 2.1
shows that there are three tailoring benches but when the factory first
opened in 1946 there were only two. Apart from the addition of a third
tailoring bench in 1948, up to the time I left the field the clothing
factory had altered its layout little in the twenty years of its operation.
Nor has time seen any notable changes in the types of skill demanded
by the factory. All the sewing machines in the factory are powered by

---

[3] In 1942 Godfrey Wilson observed that many of the tailors in such employment provided their own sewing machines (Wilson, 1942: 36). Most of the
tailors working in the stores during my fieldwork had their sewing machines
provided by their Indian employers. Some, however, did provide their own.

electricity, which was introduced at the factory's inception. With the exception of line 2, most of the sewing machines are similar. On line 2 there is a number of machines designed for specific work and these are: the elasticating machine which puts elastic into waists: the initialling machine which is used for stitching the initials of the ordering firm on specific kinds of work clothing and boiler suits; the joining or overlook machine which double stitches seams in trousers, shorts, boiler suits, etc., and finally the two button machines, one which stitches the button holes and the other which attaches buttons.

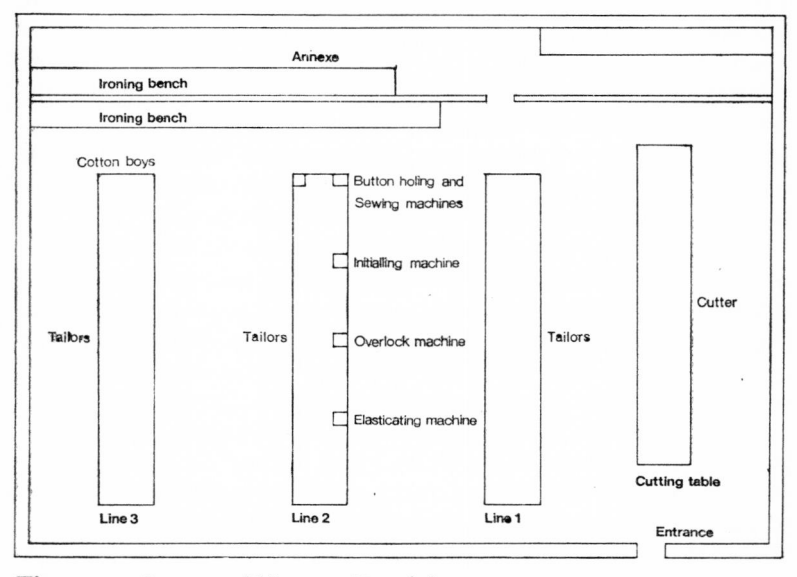

Fig. 2.1   Layout of Narayan Bros.' factory

Working conditions are cramped and an outsider when first arriving at the factory cannot fail to note the extreme difficulty with which the employees move about the room. It is therefore expected that the restriction of their work environment should be a source of continual complaint by the factory employees. Other aspects of their working environment also lead to dissatisfaction being expressed by them. The noise of one sewing machine when combined with twenty or so others becomes, in such a confined space, a clattering cacophony which rages in the ears of the workers, making it difficult for them to talk normally with their friends. To communicate they must shout. The limitation of space also produces other conditions which lead to complaint. With over forty men working in the factory premises it is no wonder that the work place should become unbearably hot, especially considering the inadequacies of the ventilation. Even those who remain seated (such as tailors) throughout most of the working day have sweat stippling their faces. Lighting is also poor. Boxes and material are stacked on the windowsills, blocking much of the normal sunlight and the pale yellow glow of the auxiliary lighting casts insufficient light.

Although no great changes have taken place in the production system, the layout or the type of work demanded of the employees, the wage system has altered. Much of the argument in the following chapters will be concerned with an analysis and explanation of the high incidence of dispute in the factory during the research period, often with reference to wage and work conditions. A brief sketch of the major changes in the wage structure of the factory prior to the start of the research indicates that the uneasiness of relations on the factory floor is not unique to the period of fieldwork but was probably a regular feature of labour relations throughout much of the history of the factory.

In the original wage system workers were paid on a monthly basis with those jobs requiring a greater degree of skill being paid more. Thus when the factory started, skilled workers such as tailors were receiving 25s per month with cotton boys receiving about 6s or 7s per month for a job which demands no skill. In addition to this monthly wage each worker at the end of the year was paid a bonus calculated at $12\frac{1}{2}$ per cent of his monthly wages. The early 1950's saw considerable agitation among Patel's African employees who were demanding improved work and pay conditions. In 1954 after the change in management of Narayan Bros., which followed on the retirement and return to India of the founder of the firm, the African workers in the factory staged a nine-day strike with the expressed purpose of achieving some improvement in their conditions. The strike was ineffectual and Patel's employees returned to work with none of their demands being acceded to by either Patel or his new partners in the management of the firm. Nevertheless agitation in the factory for improved work conditions continued, marked by short walkouts and small disturbances. Possibly as a result of the pressure built up from this continued agitation the wage system was changed in 1960 from a monthly to an hourly system. All workers were expected to work a $9\frac{1}{2}$ hour day and were paid a flat rate regardless of skill of 1s per hour. The end of the year bonus scheme was also withdrawn. Patel had conceded to his employee's demands for higher wages but at the same time had extracted some concessions from his workers. Although all workers stood to gain from the wage increases some workers benefited more than others, in particular the unskilled employees. With the exception of the African supervisory staff and a handful of the more senior and skilled employees, who were on a marginally higher hourly rate, all workers, despite differences in skill could theoretically earn the same wage. Moreover, the discontinuance of the monthly pay system saw the introduction of the hourly system, a scheme Patel considered would curb the loss to production incurred by absenteeism. The hourly scheme is invidious as any time lost even through idle conversation can be docked from a worker's pay, though this is rarely done. Lateness to work, even through no direct fault of the employee concerned, can also result in lost wages. In brief the introduction of the hourly wage system produced much resentment among Patel's employees. Finally, the factory employees had lost the bonus scheme largely because Patel considered that with the wage increases it would be uneconomical to run.

What follows will be mainly a presentation of the production and wage system of the factory. In the first section I examine the various kinds of work expected of the employees and the way this relates to the production process. This is followed in the second part, with a detailed examination of the factory wage system. But the purpose of this description does not end here. My principal aim is twofold. In the first place I set the description of the production and the wage system in the overall context of management–worker relations. Second, I examine how various factors emanating from the production process and the wage and working conditions influence the behaviour of the factory employees and affect the way they perceive themselves and others in the work place. Towards the end of the chapter I examine the prestige ranking of some of the occupations and it is here that the disparate aspects of the analysis will be drawn together.

The production process and occupational structure

Broadly the occupations in the factory can be classified into two categories, skilled and unskilled, but can be sub-categorised as: supervisory, tailors and non-tailors. Within each occupational category there are differences in skill which distinguish the members of a category from each other and associate some of them with members of other categories. The supervisory category consists of the head tailor, lead tailor and the cutter; the tailor category consists of all those working on lines 1, 2 and 3 in the factory, with the exception of the two button machine operators;

and the non-tailor category which consists of the button machine operators, the ironers and the cotton boys. The non-tailoring occupations are concerned with the various supplementary tasks to the major work of making the clothing done by the tailors. All the above occupations and the skills included in their performance will now be discussed in relation to the production process in the factory. However, before this description it must be emphasised that my account of the duties and responsibilities pertaining to the various occupations is not derived from any set of written rules or regulations drawn up by the management. These do not exist. The following description is derived purely from my observations in the factory. Consequently, it is important for the following analysis to realise that the duties performed by many of the employees are not merely the property of a particular occupational position but very much relate to the qualities of the individual incumbent of that position and to that individual's position in a set of social relationships which extend throughout the factory and beyond it into the outside community.

Supervisory Although I have classified the head tailor and cutter as supervisory occupations, both the nature of their work and the nature of their supervisory duties vary.[4] However, these two positions are critical both for the production system and for the general work and social relationships in the factory. Of the two, the head tailor is more important. At the start of work in the morning it is the head tailor, acting on instructions from Patel, the factory manager, who delegates to each tailor the type of clothing he must work on during the day. During the working period he moves about the factory, directing his supervising energies mainly towards the non-tailors. The head tailor's main supervisory concern is to inspect the work of the tailors to see that it matches up to the required standards set by the management. But, no less important, the head tailor's other duties include teaching the recently hired and often inadequately trained tailors tailoring skills which their new work demands as well as assisting those workers in the factory who are uncertain how to make specific articles of clothing. Finally, with the cutter, the head tailor is an important intermediary between the factory manager and the employees. Not only does he intervene in disputes between them but he serves a necessary function of explaining to the

[4] For the purpose of presentation I discuss the position of the lead tailor when I come to deal with the work of tailors in the production process. Unlike the head tailor, for example, the individual who occupied the position of lead tailor for most of the research period was involved in the machining of clothing.

parties concerned each one's particular grievance. This is all the more significant as the manager can only communicate with his employees through the medium of *chilapalapa*[5] and does not have sufficient knowledge of any of the local dialects. Furthermore, the head tailor often advises the manager on possible recruits to the factory.

The cutter's main task is to operate the machine which cuts bulk material to a required pattern prior to its being distributed among the tailors for machining. The use of the machine does not demand any particular skill. The only part of the process which does, being the marking out in chalk of the clothing pattern on the material. Throughout most of the research period in the factory the marking out was done by Patel, the head tailor, or the lead tailor. At the end of November 1965 the person who had hitherto occupied the cutter position left, his tasks being taken over by the lead tailor. With this change the task of cutting and marking out the pattern was combined in the activity of one man. The supervisory duties of the cutter are mainly directed towards the non-tailors but when this position was taken over by the lead tailor later in the year there was a greater orientation towards the tailors. As with the head tailor, one of the most noticeable activities of the cutter is to mediate between the manager and the employees. However, this feature of the cutter's activities diminished with the assumption of the cutter's duties later in the fieldwork by the lead tailor. One of the most important duties of the cutter in relation to both management and the African employees is his recording of instances of absenteeism in the ledger kept on the cutting bench. Two record books are kept. In one are noted the days and half-days absent from work and the reason for the absence, whether it be absence without leave, absence where leave has been granted or absence due to illness. In the other are recorded the hours worked by each employee per month. The number of hours worked is calculated from information recorded in the previous book combined with a noting of any time lost of half an hour or over spent by an employee during work hours outside the factory.[6] For the recording of this information the cutter generally acts on the advice of Patel and occasionally the head tailor. Finally, like the head tailor, the cutter assists Patel in the recruitment of new employees to the factory.

[5] *Chilapalapa* is a pidgin language incorporating African, Afrikaans and English words. It is most commonly used between Indian or European employers and their African employees, most frequently domestic servants.

[6] Workers who lose time through extended conversation or frequently go outside during the work period are often threatened by Patel that the time lost will be deducted from their monthly pay. In practice only periods of half an hour or more are recorded against an employee. However, there are other factors which affect whether such information is recorded. These will be discussed later.

Tailors There are basically two production processes in which the factory tailors can be engaged. Either a tailor will make an article of clothing from start to finish or he will, with other tailors, be assigned the task of making part of a complete garment. Following Sheila Cunnison (1966:42– 45) I shall call the former process the *make-through* method and the latter process the *section* method. Throughout the observation period some tailors were employed in each of the two processes, with most normally being occupied in the latter. However, at any one time the number of tailors working in each process varies according to the size and type of the clothing orders placed with the factory manager. Large orders which have to be supplied to the customer within a limited period of time involved nearly all the tailors in the section method of production. This is more efficient than the make-through method as a greater quantity of finished garments can be completed in a shorter time. But there are exceptions. Certain types of clothing, such as petticoats, aprons etc., are simple in design and easy to make and nothing is gained in productivity by distributing sections of them among a number of tailors. In such cases simplicity both in design and in the making of the article reduces the advantage of parcelling out parts of the garment to be tailored separately and the make-through method tends to be employed. The make-through method is also preferred for small orders and in particular where the garments required are difficult to tailor. Other factors also influence a preference for the make-through method and these are related to the expectations of specific customers. If the customer places emphasis on quality in the clothing he has ordered or if the manager wishes to maintain a customer's patronage against the pressures of outside competition, the make-through method is used as this ensures a better quality. In most cases the section method ensures higher productivity but because the work is spread among a number of tailors of varying expertise there is some loss in quality. Apart from those cases where the garments are simple to design and make, which often results in tailors of all degrees of skill being employed in the work, those tailors who regularly employ the make-through method are the most skilled in the factory. The lead tailor is regarded by both the factory manager and employees as most skilled. Until his assumption of the cutter's duties later in the fieldwork due to the departure of the previous incumbent of that position, he worked on line 1. The lead tailor always uses the make-through method and is generally occupied by the manager in making garments which require highly skilled work such as suits and sports clothing. The lead tailor still continued to do specialised work for the factory manager after taking over the cutter's position towards the end of 1965. Besides his specialised tailoring work the lead tailor also assists the factory manager in the marking out of patterns on the cloth and the taking of measurements from the customers. Throughout the research period the lead tailor also was used by Patel to assist with the supervision of the employees.

As the foregoing description suggests, skill is an important factor which differentiates tailors from one another. Skill is relevant in determining both the type of task on which a tailor is employed and his work position in the factory. Thus tailors on line 1 tend to be more skilled than those on line 2 and those on line 2 more skilled than the tailors on line 3. An indication of the line 1 tailors' greater skill is that they are more frequently involved in the make-through method of production. In addition, when working according to the section method they are apportioned the most difficult work. The tasks less demanding of skill are distributed among the line 2 and 3 tailors.

Clothing produced by the section method, unlike that produced by the make-through method, passes through a number of different machines before it is completed, such as the overlock machine, the elasticating machine, the initialling machine and the button holing and sewing machines. The overlock machine operator is central to the production process based on the section method. Most clothing made by this method passes through his hands and in many cases must do so before other operations such as cuff and sleeve turn-ups can be done. It is thus essential to the efficient working of the section method that the overlock machine operator should complete work quickly and skilfully, for his failure to do so can slow down production severely. At different periods during the time of observation one tailor who was relatively highly skilled was employed on line 2 as the overlock machine operator. The overlock machine operator during the early period of my observation was later transferred to line 1 and placed at an ordinary machine as his increasing absence from work was slowing down the rate of production. He was replaced by a more constant worker from line 1. As well as operating the overlock machine, the particular tailor concerned usually operates the elasticating machine, though other tailors, frequently those engaged on make-through work, may also use it. The initialling machine requires considerable skill and only the head and lead tailors are sufficiently skilled to operate it. Both the button holing and the button sewing machine are operated by non-tailors and their work will be described subsequently.

In concluding this section it can be noted that the tailors employed in the factory are differentiated according to skill. The differences in skill are generally reflected in the part of the production system in which they are more regularly involved, whether they are working according to the make-through or the section method: the type of task and the degree of expertise required for its fulfilment on which tailors are occupied; and finally the line on which a tailor is employed.

Non-tailors All the non-tailors in the factory are occupied in the various subsidiary tasks connected mainly with finishing the garments once they have passed through the main tailoring process. The non-tailors include the button machine operators, the cotton boys and the ironers. Garments which require button-holing and button stitching after completion by the tailors pass to the button machine operators. Some skill, although not as much as for tailoring, is required for this work.

Garments which have passed through the button holing and stitching process then pass to the cotton boys who work at the end of line 3. This work is completely unskilled, the main activity being the removal of loose cotton ends from the clothing. In addition to this task cotton boys also fill bobbins with cotton for use by the tailors. On occasions cotton boys can be occupied in a diverse number of other activities which range from doing small errands for the factory manager and making tea for break, to sweeping out the factory. In October 1965 the factory manager employed six girls[7] who did some of the work previously done only by the cotton boys, such as the picking of loose cotton ends off the finishing clothing. However, even with these new employees, the cotton boys still continued in this work. Once the loose cotton ends have been removed the clothing goes to the ironers for pressing. This is done by electric hand iron and the work, though arduous, is unskilled. The completed garments are then stacked in the annexe for distribution to various market outlets or for collection by customers.

The description has emphasised that skill is a basic differentiating factor among the factory employees. But other points, essential to an understanding of the factory context, also emerge from the preceding discussion. Both the variety of clothing made in the factory and the two methods of production mean that the tailor's work and the type of garment they make varies from day to day. On one day, for example,

[7] The six girls who joined the factory are excluded from the study. They associated very minimally with the other employees and I was unable to subject them to a systematic observation as the other workers. Generally they played little part in the events to be recounted later.

shorts, shirts, petticoats, nuns' habits and overalls were being made. The tailors producing shorts, petticoats and overalls were using the section method, while the tailors making the shirts and nuns' habits were using the make through method. On another day only trousers and skirts were being made and all the tailors were working according to the section method. The constant changes in the kind of garments being made and the alternation between production methods produces a continual uncertainty among the tailors about the nature of their daily work. Moreover, the factory manager presents to the tailors no clearly defined set of output expectations on which they can base their own behaviour, beyond that of expecting the tailors to work hard and with as few breaks as possible. This leads to 'sweat shop' conditions, with the factory manager continually urging the tailors to maintain a fast rate of work and threatening to dismiss those who slacken the pace. Many of the tailors view Patel as an unreasonable task master. In the words of one tailor, 'God made a bad mistake to create such an employer.' Patel's expectations towards other occupations in the factory are also ill-defined, especially towards the cotton boys who can be called upon to perform a wide variety of tasks some of which are not remotely connected with the manufacture of clothing.

One final point important to the ensuing analysis must be emphasised. The different occupations in the factory are of varying significance to the production process. Some occupations are more important than others, the most critical being those of the head and lead tailors, the cutter and the tailors on all three lines, but especially the line 1 tailors and the overlock machine operator.

The wage system

During normal working hours the employees are paid according to an hourly rate. But at peak periods when there are urgent orders to fill which cannot be completed in normal working hours Patel approaches his workers to do extra work. On these occasions he pays them overtime rates (i.e. double the normal hourly rate). Alternatively, Patel asks them to do piece-work. Generally, everyone in the factory is given the opportunity to work overtime and the production process is the same as when the employees work normal hours. In contrast, piece-work is usually parcelled out among the more skilled tailors, and even then only to those who have their own sewing machines at home. Under the piece-work system material is given to a tailor, who is asked to make certain items of clothing in his own time. Piece-work rates vary according to the type of clothing being made but usually it works out at approximately 10s per dozen garments finished. For Patel the agreement of his employees to work overtime is preferable to their working according to the piece-work system.[8] However, Patel often does not succeed in achieving the agreement of his employees to work overtime. This is usually the result of the refusal of most of the line 1 and 2 tailors to work overtime, for without them the production process is virtually rendered inoperable. The tailors state that their refusal to work overtime is in direct response to Patel's refusal to act on their demands for improvements in the wage and work conditions. But this refusal works less in the interests of some of the factory employees than others. The majority of the line 1 and 2 tailors have their own sewing machines and so have the opportunity to recoup their losses because of such action by doing piece work which Patel is then likely to offer them. The line 3 tailors, button machiners, ironers and cotton boys are less fortunate as they do not have their own machines (see table 3.3). Therefore, the point is made that the action of one set of individuals at work will produce an effect which is opposed to the interests of others. This will be a recurrent theme in the following description of the wage system and the differing employee reaction to it. First, however, I will describe in more detail the wage system which normally operates.

The starting rate for all the employees with the exception of the cotton boys is 1s per hour. The rate on which the cotton boys start varies according to their age. New employees who are considered by Patel to be very young and who are generally entering their first job are employed at the rate of 6d per hour. Patel is often supported by senior workers in the factory in his employment of these people at this rate for they consider that unskilled workers just out of school (which in fact is often the case) are worth little more. But it must be stressed that employment at this rate is at Patel's discretion. There is no generally accepted ruling which states that job applicants below a certain age will be employed at such and such a rate. Therefore, despite the pattern for

[8] Some qualification is needed here. If there is a small number of clothes required to be made which demand some skilled workmanship, then the piece-work system is preferable. But it is the large orders which Patel feels the most urgent need to meet in the specified time. The larger orders tend to be more lucrative, and Patel is concerned that he could lose valuable custom should he fail to complete the order in the time agreed. When the overtime system operates, being, as it is, an extension of the normal production process, he has some control over the speed of work. But with the piece-work system much of the control over the rate of work is transferred from him to the employee.

Table 2.1 Average monthly earnings before and after September
(includes workers employed for both periods only)

Name	Occupation	Time 1 Hourly rate	June-August 1965	Time 2 Hourly rate	September-January 1966	Wage higher or lower at time 2 than at time 1
		s d	£ s d	s d	£ s d	
Mukubwa	Head tailor	1 6	14 1 6	1 7	13 5 11	−
.Hastings	Lead tailor	1 9	15 15 0	1 10	15 4 1	−
Chisokone*	Cutter	1 3	12 1 5	1 4	6 2 3	−
Line 1 tailors						
Nkoloya	Line 1	1 3	11 14 10	1 4	10 12 0	+
Nkumbula	Line 1	1 3	11 1 8	1 4	8 12 10	+
Abraham	Line 1	1 3	12 7 1	1 4	12 1 1	−
Zulu*	Line 1	1 3	11 17 1	1 4	8 14 0	−
Lyashi	Line 1	1 0	9 10 4	1 1	8 9 5	−
Chipata	Line 1	1 0	9 1 10	1 1	10 8 11	+
Kamwefu	Line 1	1 0	8 9 4	1 1	8 17 0	+
Ibrahim*	Lines 1 and 2	1 0	8 8 4	1 3	10 14 1	+·
Kalamba	Lines 1 and 2	1 0	9 4 0	1 1	9 16 0	+
Chilwa	Line 1	1 0	10 15 7	·1 0	8 16 3	−
Lwanga	Lines 1 and 2	1 0	9 2 0	1 1	9 15 10	+
Seama	Line 2	1 0	8 4 10	1 0	8 15 6	+
Enoch	Line 2	1 0	9 10 8	1 1	8 17 4	−
Paulos	Line 2	1 0	9 10 8	1 1	10 0 0	+
Macdonald*	Line 2	1 0	6 14 6	1 0	9 6 8	+
Mulondo*	Line 2	1 0	5 18 0	1 0	9 1 6	+
Kalundwe	Line 3	1 0	8 15 8	1 0	8 16 7	+
Zakeyo	Line 3	1 0	8 15 8	1 0	8 6 6	−
Sign*	Line 3	1 0	8 19 8	1 0	9 3 0	+
Nyirenda	Line 3	1 0	9 11 8	1 0	10 6 1	+
Ben	Line 3	1 0	9 11 8	1 0	9 8 7	−
Mateo	Line 3	1 0	8 19 8	1 0	8 18 10	−
Mpundu	Line 3	1 0	9 14 8	1 0	9 0 5	−
Meshak	Buttons	1 0	9 14 8	1 1	10 10 0	+
Adrian	Buttons	1 0	9 1 0	1 1	9 3 0	+
John	Ironer	1 0	9 3 10	1 0	9 8 0	+
Chibale	Ironer	1 0	9 10 8	1 0	9 6 11	−
Isaac	Ironer	1 0	9 6 0	1 0	9 1 6	−
William	Cotton boy	1 0	9 10 3	1 0	9 3 8	−
Henry	Cotton boy and line 3	1 0	7 7 0	1 0	9 10 11	+
Kalonga	Cotton boy and ironer	1 0	9 7 8	1 0	8 3 4	−
Joseph	Cotton boy and line 3	1 0	9 15 0	1 0	8 13 3	−
Mubanga	Cotton boy and ironer	1 0	9 17 8	1 0	9 8 10	−
Michael	Cotton boy	1 0	9 17 8	1 0	9 7 8	−
Chilufya	Cotton boy	1 0	9 17 8	1 0	9 6 11	−
Christian*	Cotton boy	1 0	8 0 0	1 0	8 14 6	+

* Chisokone and Zulu left during the post-September period and therefore
the drastic reduction in their wages at this time has no importance to
the argument or the table. Similarly, Macdonald, Mulondo and Chipalo
joined the factory half-way through August, so little meaning is attached
to their average wage in the first period. Ibrahim was promoted to overlock machine operator, so his wage rose 4d in the hour, which accounts
for his substantial rise in wages. Sign and Christian worked for only one
month of the second period.

older men like Paison (who is 35) to be employed as cotton boy at the
1s rate while younger men like Lundazi and Mpande (19 and 16 years
respectively) are employed at 6d, it is difficult to give a convincing
reason why Mulenga, who is 21, should be employed at the 6d rate whereas
Nelson (22) is employed at 1s. After a period of time, again at Patel's
discretion, a cotton boy who has been employed initially at the 6d rate,
may receive an hourly increment of 6d.

Until the beginning of September the employees worked a 45 hour
week. On week days work commenced at 7.30 a.m. and continued
through to 3.40 p.m. when work ended, with a ten minute tea break at
11.30 a.m. Employees also worked on Saturday morning from 7.30 a.m.
to 12.30 p.m. Two factors brought about a change in this set of conditions. In September 1965 the Zambian National Assembly passed a bill
which ruled that all African employees should be paid for a 40 hour,
five-day working week.[9] The purpose of the new Act was to improve
the poor work conditions which many Africans in employment suffered.
Apart from the influence the Act may have had on the factory manager's
subsequent action he had been under continual pressure from his
employees to change the wage system. This agitation culminated in a
walkout of the factory workers and resulted in some of the more skilled
and/or longer served employees receiving an hourly increment of 1d.
The most active participants in the walkout were the line 1 and line 2
tailors, and it was mainly workers on these lines, in addition to the
supervisors, who received the 1d increment. But Patel with his award
of the 1d increment to some of his employees now stopped Saturday
morning work. This change resulted in the employees losing money
rather than gaining it. For example, assuming that a worker on the
previous system works a 45 hour week he would earn £2 5s 0d for that
period. On the new system an employee could work the full 40 hour
week but even assuming that he received the hourly 1d increment,
which many employees did not, he would earn 1s 8d a week less than on
the previous system. Some of the workers who expected to benefit more
from the wage increase in fact benefited less. For example, Mukubwa,
Hastings, Abraham and Lyashi had for the months September to
January inclusive earned on average a smaller wage than for the months
prior to their receipt of a wage increment. There are other reasons

[9] This was the Employment Act of September 1965. It applied only to those
Africans employed on monthly contract and was not strictly applicable to
Narayan Bros.' employees. For a more detailed account of the Employment
Act with reference to the process of events in the factory, see chapter 7,
pp. 275 ff.

which contributed to this fall in their average earnings and to these I will return in a later section.

The point which must be emphasised is that although more money per hour is received by those who gained the increment the length of the working week was cut. Thus in fact, to receive an increase in monthly earnings it is necessary for the employee to make more use of the working hours available and to reduce, if possible, the time he might lose through lateness or absenteeism. Hitherto, I have been discussing briefly the plight of the workers who received an increment, but the position of those who did not receive an increment was aggravated to a greater extent. For not only was their working week cut but also, unlike those discussed above, they did not receive an increment to offset the loss in wages incurred by them as a result of the reduction in working hours. An important effect of this was to create an increased awareness for many of those workers (particularly the tailors on lines 2 and 3) of the disadvantages of their working conditions, which in turn led to their taking more active part in factory politics. This development is important for an understanding of the changing leadership patterns in the factory and will be pursued in more detail in later chapters. Let it suffice for the present discussion that the shortening of the working week and the loss in hours it caused was a major underlying factor explaining much of the conflict in the subsequent process of management–worker relations.

Moreover, the change in wages and in working conditions did not alleviate the dissatisfaction which many of the skilled workers felt concerning the lack of a clear definition of the basis of wage differentials between workers with varying lengths of service and different skills. Though some of the most skilled and/or longer serving employees (notably Hastings, Mukubwa, Zulu, Chisokone, Nkoloya, Nkumbula) were on higher hourly wage rates, there were others in the factory (for example, the remainder of the tailors) who could claim a higher wage rate at least because of their skill, if not for their length of service. The situation was substantially altered with the award of the increment. It did, for instance, heighten aspects of social differentiation within the factory.[10]

In the main those who benefited were the line 1 tailors, who considered themselves vastly superior in skill and experience to the rest of

[10] All the employees who were previously on higher wage rates received the further 1d increment. In addition, Lyashi, Chipata, Abraham and Mumba also were given a 1d increase. Paulos, Enoch and Kalamba of line 2 were given increases, as were the two button machiners and William, a cotton boy.

E

the tailors and often behaved accordingly. But the award of the increment did not reduce the force by which most of the workers expressed their grievance with the lack of skill and length of service wage differentials. Those who did receive an increment remained dissatisfied, largely as a result of the cut in working hours described above, and continued to press for further increments as did many of the employees who received no such increment but nevertheless felt entitled to one.

Related to the foregoing point is the lack of a clear criterion for the award of increments to employees. All the workers who received an increment were entitled to it, on the basis of skill and/or length of service. But equally, in terms of one or both of these criteria, others in the factory who were less fortunate could have received an increment (in particular in the case of Mpundu, who was a line 2 tailor and had been working at the factory for thirteen years; Nyirenda, a line 3 tailor and employed continuously for over eighteen months; and Chilwa, a line 1 tailor who had been working at the factory for more than two years). Indeed, it appeared to many of the workers that Patel's awards were either to persons who were his 'favourites' or were an attempt to buy off some of the major trouble-makers in the factory. Notwithstanding appearances, the feeling of injustice generated among some of the workers was to affect the pattern of leadership in the factory. In addition, it was to lead to renewed pressure on the management by the workers for a clarification of the principal criteria upon which wage increases were to be assessed.

Even from the brief discussion above it should be clear that management's reaction to worker pressure exacerbated the state of tension which existed in their relations. Agitation in general increased against what the employees considered to be low wages and the inequities of the hourly system. In February 1966 the factory employees went on strike and negotiations for further changes in the pay and work conditions were still under way when I left the field.[11]

Together with their monthly pay, employees are permitted three days sick leave and provided they have been employed in the factory for at least a year, twelve days' paid holiday leave per year. Workers who live in the municipal African townships have the choice either of the factory manager's paying the municipal council their house rent or paying the rent themselves. Employees who make the former choice have the rent deducted from their pay.

[11] See the account of 'The February strike' in chapter 8.

Factors explaining the variation in hours worked[12]

In the preceding description I drew brief attention to the agitation of
the factory workers for increased wages and improved work conditions.
I now discuss some of the factors which account for the variation in
hours worked by the employees. The pattern of worker militancy is
related to differences in the hours worked each month by the factory
employees. Militancy and variation in hours worked are subject to
explanation by a common set of factors. These are (a) commitment and
the distribution of investments, (b) position in the production process,
and (c) placement in a set of factory-located social interactional relationships. But before these factors can be examined a more detailed understanding of the problem is required.

Table 2.2 indicates a clear difference in the number of hours worked
by skilled and unskilled workers. October excepted, the cotton boys
tended to work the longest hours of all the factory workers.[13] This
contrasts with the tailors. Whereas the cotton boys worked consistently
in excess of both the mean and median number of hours worked in the
factory as a whole, the tailors recorded hours either slightly above or
slightly below the mean and median hours worked each month in the
factory.

Most time, and therefore money, is lost by being late for work, sick
or merely absent because of an involvement in some other activity
elsewhere.

Lateness to work and illness[14] are the most common ways the workers

[12] Concern with explaining variation in working hours and the argument
employed here is nothing new to industrial sociology, and is usually discussed
with reference to restriction of output. Roethlisberger and Dickson (1941:
chapter 18) were the first to subject this problem to detailed examination.
Homans (1951: 299–301) elaborated further on the findings of Roethlisberger
and Dickson. There is an extensive amount of later literature which examines different aspects of the restriction of output, for example, Roy (1952),
Lupton (1963: 3–8).

[13] A similar tendency is evidenced for the ironers but this is less marked than
for the cotton boys.

[14] The taking of a 'sicky', which is a commonly found form of institutionalised
behaviour in certain work contexts in most industrialised societies, is not less
a regular form of behaviour at Narayan Bros. The highest proportion of
entries in the record book states that most of the absences from work are due
to illness. But my own independent checking of many of these entries showed
that very few of the absences are due to illness. I consider that giving a reason
for absence as being due to sickness is very closely associated with the 'indulgency' system which operates in the factory. Of course, Patel uses his
discretion in accepting an explanation of sickness for absence, but it gives
him a ready rationale in terms of which he can exercise leniency. If he

Table 2.2 Working hours for each occupational category at Narayan Bros.

	Mean for occupational category	Deviation from mean for factory	Number above mean for factory	Number above median	Number in category
June					
Supervisory	196.0	+10.1	2	2	2
Tailors 1	176.9	-9.2	7	2	12
2	190.8	+4.7	5	2	6
3	180.0	-6.1	5	3	8
Buttons	196.0	+10.1	1	1	2
Ironers	190.7	+4.6	2	2	3
Cotton boys	195.6	+9.5	9	8	9

Mean for factory 186.1
Median for factory 195

	Mean for occupational category	Deviation from mean for factory	Number above mean for factory	Number above median	Number in category
July					
Supervisory	190.5	-7.5	1	1	2
Tailors 1	187.7	-10.3	2	4	13
2	171.2	-26.8	0	1	5
3	188.3	-9.7	2	4	8
Buttons	186.5	-11.5	0	0	2
Ironers	195.7	-2.3	1	3	3
Cotton boys	199.2	+1.2	7	9	10

Mean for factory 198
Median for factory 193

	Mean for occupational category	Deviation from mean for factory	Number above mean for factory	Number above median	Number in category
August					
Supervisory	183.5	+0.7	1	0	2
Tailors 1	183.9	+1.1	6	5	11
2	182.6	-0.2	5	5	7
3	176.3	-6.6	2	2	8
Buttons	196.0	+13.2	1	1	1
Ironers	174.2	-8.6	1	1	3
Cotton boys	189.4	+6.6	7	6	8

Mean for factory 182.8
Median for factory 187

	Mean for occupational category	Deviation from mean for factory	Number above mean for factory	Number above median	Number in category
September					
Supervisory	87.5	-83.3	0	0	2
Tailors 1	173.2	+2.4	8	5	11
2	177.1	+6.3	3	3	5
3	171.2	+0.4	4	3	6
Buttons	158.5	-12.3	1	1	2
Ironers	178.5	+7.7	2	0	2
Cotton boys	182.2	+11.4	8	7	10

Mean for factory 170.8
Median for factory 180

decides to be lenient he overlooks a worker's absence, which in effect means accepting illness as an explanation. In these instances he will refrain from severely rebuking the culprit—which can introduce tension into his relationships not only with the person concerned but also with others in the factory —and will not sack, or threaten to sack the offender.

Table 2.2 concluded

	Mean for occupational category	Deviation from mean for factory	Number above mean for factory	Number above median	Number in category
	October				
Supervisory	182.0	+0.7	1	1	2
Tailors 1	183.5	+2.2	6	6	10
2	179.9	-1.4	5	4	9
3	184.5	+3.2	4	4	6
Buttons	168.0	-13.3	1	1	2
Ironers	177.4	-3.9	1	1	4
Cotton boys	182.8	+1.5	5	5	9

Mean for factory 181.3
Median for factory 184.5

	November				
Supervisory	171.5	-5.7	1	0	2
Tailors 1	164.2	-13.0	4	5	8
2	178.4	+1.2	6	5	8
3	179.1	+1.9	3	2	6
Buttons	171.5	-5.7	1	1	2
Ironers	174.3	-2.9	2	2	3
Cotton boys	191.0	+13.8	9	6	9

Mean for factory 177.2
Median for factory 184

	December				
Supervisory	199.8	+14.6	2	2	2.
Tailors 1	183.3	-1.9	7	4	11
2	184.6	-0.6	3	2	9
3	180.2	-5.0	4	4	7
Buttons	196.0	+10.8	2	1	2
Ironers	176.0	-9.2	2	2	4
Cotton boys	195.0	+9.8	4	4	5

Mean for factory 185.2
Median for factory 190

	January				
Supervisory	162.0	-4.3	1	1	2
Tailors 1	167.3	+1.1	7	6	12
2	165.8	+0.5	4	3	8
3	164.2	-2.1	4	4	7
Buttons	146.5	-19.8	1	1	2
Ironers	164.1	-2.2	3	3	5
Cotton boys	171.0	+4.8	4	4	5

Mean for factory 166.3
Median for factory 167

lose time. The management records indicate that generally the more skilled employees (i.e. supervisors, tailors and button machiners) lost more time in these ways than did the unskilled employees (i.e. cotton boys and to a lesser degree ironers).

Commitment[15] and position in the production process are the main factors I examine in explaining this pattern. Position in the production process requires little explanation and should become clear during the analysis. However, some statement is needed of the meaning I attach to the term commitment and how this relates to the third factor I discuss, placement in a set of factory-located social relationships. By commitment I refer to the extent to which an individual, as a result of the nature of the current distribution of his investments, is restricted from pursuing various alternatives. Fundamental to this meaning of commitment is the assumption that an individual is restricted from pursuing alternatives if the costs he incurs from the pursuit of these alternatives would outweigh the possible gains. Also important to my view of commitment is that individuals will be constrained from seeking alternatives not just in terms of the way they may independently view the costs to their current investments but also by the extent to which their pursuit of alternatives will affect the investments of others with whom they come into association. It is here that my use of the term commitment is closely connected to the third factor, individual placement in a factory-located set of relationships. I suggest that an individual will be constrained from pursuing alternatives when his action will involve costs to others with whom he is involved in a close-knit set of interactional relationships. Should such an individual attempt to pursue an alternative course of action the other individuals concerned are likely to exert pressure on him through their social relationships in order to constrain him. Obviously, however, the success of their

---

[15] My use of the term 'commitment' follows closely Blau's definition (1964: 98–9, 160–5). Blau uses 'commitment' in association with other terms such as 'investment' and 'attachment'. He states that an individual, for instance, will invest time and resources in another individual, group or organisation. The extent to which he invests in some individual, group, organisation, etc., to the exclusion of others is an expression of his commitment to them and results in a differential degree of attachment. Thus an individual will be more attached to some rather than others, because of his differential investments. 'Strong attachments prevent individuals from exploring alternative opportunities and taking advantage of them to increase their rewards and improve their positions —from turning to a better consultant, taking a more promising job, moving to a more desirable community, or switching to a more profitable occupation' (*op. cit.*, p. 161). See also Becker (1960) and Schelling (1960). In the next chapter I develop further my particular use of the terms 'commitment' and 'investment' in relation to labour turnover.

constraining pressure will be dependent on their ability to make the result of the pursuit of alternatives by the individual concerned appear more costly than beneficial to his interests.

Most of the cotton boys are characteristically target workers.[16] Employment at Narayan Bros. is often their first labour experience and they freely state their intention to move on to another job once they have earned a reasonable amount of cash, learnt a skill or have been presented with another more attractive job opportunity.[17] Their move from one job to another with its attendant risk of a brief period out of employment is not hampered by familial obligations as in the case of the older and more skilled factory employees. Various aspects of these points will be pursued more extensively in the following chapter; all that must be stressed at present is that, as target workers, cotton boys wish to receive the greatest cash reward in the shortest possible time. They are prepared to work within the present system and any additional cash rewards in excess of the maximum which they can earn in the context of their current employment are achieved by changing their place of employment. This seems a better course of action to them than attempting to change the system of work and wage conditions to their benefit. Such action (which most often entails some process of collective action like a strike) will sacrifice the certainty of immediate rewards to the uncertainty of some future gain.

An added explanation for the tendency of cotton boys to work the highest number of hours derives from the very fact of their lack of a skill. For employers, people with a skill are scarce but those without are plentiful.[18] As those employed as cotton boys, largely because of

[16] I have used the word 'target worker' in reference to the cotton boys for want of a better term. My usage of it is not in strict accordance with its more usual application. The normal meaning of the term is that labour migrants who are target workers have a fixed cash sum in mind and will return to the place from which they have migrated once their target has been met (see Baldwin, 1966: 114). Berg (1961: 468–92) surveys critically the literature connected with this view. One of his arguments is that the target set by the migrant before his entry into the labour market changes when he begins work. In my application of the term 'target worker' I do not necessarily imply that the individuals referred to either have a fixed target in mind or will return to the area from which they have migrated. All I mean to imply is that a target worker is an individual whose actions are affected by mainly economic motives, and that various other social considerations will play a subordinate part.

[17] A few of the unskilled workers stated that one of their express purposes in joining Narayan Bros. was to learn how to operate a sewing machine.

[18] This is not strictly accurate. Jobs on the mines and railway, for instance, can be classified as unskilled work but in fact do demand some training and expertise. High labour turnover in these jobs can cause the authorities in-

their few investments in other areas of their social experience, are able to change jobs frequently, so this frequent job changing produces no real problem for the employer as the jobs vacated can be quickly filled with other unskilled workers. The position of the cotton boys is thus insecure and the failure to carry out the manager's demands as well as regular absence or lateness to work exposes them to the threat of dismissal—a threat with which Patel continually harasses them. So as to attain their objective they must avoid the risk of other factors which might intervene and threaten the attainment of their objective; such risks are dismissal and the loss of pay through absence and lateness. To avoid these risks they must conform to the wishes of their employer.

A further effect of this lack of skill and the cotton boys' generally weak position in relation to management is that it permits the manager and the factory supervisors to exert stricter and more constant control over their working behaviour than they do over most of the other factory workers. Greater and more frequent exposure to manager supervision will alone have some influence on the cotton boys to work longer hours.

The basic principles of commitment and position in the production process of the factory also account for the much lower number of hours worked by the tailors. Whilst cotton boys evidence a tendency to be target workers, tailors have generally reached a more stable period in their labour experience. In the former case I argued that the 'target worker' pattern is produced by a lack of commitment, but in the instance of the tailors it is the presence of a commitment to continued work in the factory which explains this particular aspect of their work behaviour. This commitment, engendered as it is by factors both external and internal to the factory, induces the tailors frequently to choose a course of action, in seeking to improve their wage and work conditions, which aims to change to their advantage the present factory system. Their intentions to remain for an extended period of employment in the factory are expressed in statements on their future labour movements, most stating that they will continue working at Narayan Bros. for periods of two years or more (see table 3.15). Because the tailors often opt for action which is intended to change their wage and work conditions they are prepared to delay the achievement of immediate benefits for the sake of an eventual change in wage and work conditions. This kind of action at times demands collective action such

---

volved considerable concern. However, as I described in an earlier section of this chapter, no skill is required for the job of cotton boy and the expertise required for it can be quickly picked up by a newcomer to the job.

as a strike or walkout. But more pertinent to this discussion is their preparedness to come late to work or to miss complete working days (see table 2.2) in order to cut production and so bring pressure to bear on Patel. Agitation for the improvement of wage and work conditions occurred throughout most of the fieldwork period. In the months prior to the September wage increase the majority of the tailors fell below the mean number of hours worked in the factory or barely exceeded it. With the September awards, those who received the 1d increment show a marked increase relative to the rest of the factory in the number of hours they worked. However, in the subsequent months the pattern evident before September reasserts itself with the realisation by many of the employees that they stood to lose rather than gain and the development once more of worker agitation for improvement.

The risk incurred (of loss in pay and dismissal) is to a large extent reduced by other factors not relevant to the unskilled factory employees. Many of the tailors, and in particular those on lines 1 and 2, have small tailoring businesses in which they are involved at home after work. The income derived from these enterprises compensates for a loss of income caused by their absence from factory work. In addition, tailors are relatively scarce. There is not a surplus of skilled tailors readily available for work in the factory. While Patel is not particularly concerned to stabilise his unskilled work force he is interested in reducing any turn-over among his tailors. Connected to this interest is the fact that even though a tailor new to the factory knows how to work a sewing machine he frequently does not have the expertise to do the variety of work which Patel will demand of him. Most tailors on taking up employment at Narayan Bros., therefore, receive a certain amount of in-service training. For them to leave the factory results in a loss for Patel of the benefit he gained from investing time in training them.[19]

I have been discussing what I consider to be the main principles underlying the general variation in hours worked between skilled and

[19] A similar argument is used by Elkan (1956: 24), who explains the greater support of the semi-skilled employees in the Kampala factory of the East Africa Tobacco Company for strike action in contrast to the lesser support given it by the clerical, skilled and unskilled factory workers. The clerical, skilled and unskilled workers have the opportunity of improving their wage and work conditions by moving to alternative places of employment. However, the semi-skilled have been trained specifically for work in the tobacco factory. If they moved they would not be able to find similar alternative employment and would be exposed presumably to a loss in wages. The semi-skilled tobacco factory workers received their training in the factory and also, therefore, by their moving they would incur a cost to the factory, which would have to train new workers to fill their places from scratch.

unskilled factory workers with reference to the wage conditions in the
factory. But I also argue that the factors of commitment to the work
place, which can be produced by processes external to it, such as involvement in familial responsibilities, and position in the production process,
will affect the number of hours worked and the variations among
individuals in the hours worked within the two broad categories of
skilled and unskilled employees. Within the skilled category there is
considerable variation in the number of hours worked, particularly
when some of the line 3 tailors are compared with tailors on other lines.
It might reasonably be expected that the factors of commitment and
work position will be applicable in explaining these variations. As
described in an earlier section it was stated that the line 3 tailors are
generally less skilled than those on lines 1 and 2. Moreover, many of the
line 3 tailors are among the younger workers in the factory and like
most of the cotton boys evince target worker characteristics and/or are
still at an early stage of their labour experience. This general lack of
intention to remain for any extended period of time in the factory is
freely voiced. These effects are the result of a relative lack of skill which
accounts for their position in the production system and low value to
Patel, coupled with the short time they expect to remain working in the
factory. A low skill exposes them to greater supervisory control from
Patel and his supervisors. This exposure is largely conditioned by their
need for additional training and therefore means more control over
their work behaviour. In addition their lack of skill results in insecurity
among them as they are more open to the risk of dismissal by Patel.
Both these effects influence them to work longer hours. The third
effect relates to their being target workers. This means that the defer-
ment of immediate rewards for some future gain does not appeal to
them as a worthwhile course of action. Furthermore, the type of
behaviour it entails such as the withdrawal of labour through absenteeism introduces factors which would jeopardise the attainment of
immediate rewards. For they would suffer a reduction in wages and
expose themselves to the threat of dismissal.

   Although I consider that factors relating to commitment and position
in the production process largely explain the variance in hours worked
between categories of workers as well as many individual variations,
within these categories too heavy an emphasis on them could obscure
others.

   One factor, referred to earlier, which should be considered in conjunction with those already described relates to the placement of
individuals within a factory-located set of social relationships. Two

cotton boys, Peter and Kalonga, for example, were often late and failed to turn up for work. They are related by kinship to the cutter, Chisokone, and it was largely through the latter's good offices that they were employed in the factory. Furthermore, all three men are regular companions after working hours. Chisokone had extensive personal influence with Patel. This was largely due to his critical position in the process of factory relations as well as his considerable political importance generally in the Kabwe community. Chisokone did use this influence to protect the interests of Mulenga and Kalonga in the factory against the threats of Patel. Mulenga and Kalonga's relationship with Chisokone and also their involvement in other sets of factory-located relationships influenced much of their work behaviour and reduced some of the risks attendant on their withdrawal of labour. At the centre of this other set of relationships are many of the line 1 tailors who also play a dominant role in the sphere of factory politics generally. It is these tailors who place pressure on individuals to conform to standards of work behaviour which the tailors concerned consider will operate eventually in their best interests.[20] Such pressures to conform have the effect of reducing the hours of many employees. At this stage it is necessary to describe briefly the term *chichawa*.

Broadly, the word *chichawa* means informer, and it achieved wide currency during the years of political conflict leading to independence. It was specifically used by Africans to apply to any of their fellows who conveyed information to Federal government officials concerning the activities of African nationalist leaders. At Narayan Bros. the word is used by employees towards others whose behaviour indicates that they are in league with the management in a way which could be interpreted as detrimental to the interests of their work companions. In effect almost anyone who is seen by others to benefit from the existing factory system by conforming to Patel's general expectations of his workers, and/or contributes to the continuance of the factory system by his actions, is referred to as *chichawa*. The word has a wide area of application and most workers at one time or another have been branded as such. But some workers, largely because of their position in the

---

[20] Although this will be discussed more fully in later chapters, it is realised that in order for one person to exert pressure on another to conform to a specific form of behaviour there must be the threat of the withdrawal of certain benefits which the former furnishes the latter. Most of the line 1 tailors have control over services which some of the younger and less skilled workers require and use. Such services include some protection against the possibility of Patel's carrying out his direr threats and the provision of tuition free of charge in the skills of tailoring.

production process and/or their approach to employment in the factory, appear to others to be almost continuously cast in the role of *chichawa*. These employees include the head tailor Mukubwa, the cutter Chisokone and the lead tailor Hastings. Their work involves closest association with Patel and often demands that they assist him in supervisory duties and/or do special work for him.[21] Cotton boys are also regularly referred to as *chichawa* because of the large number of hours they work relative to others in the factory.

The workers who most frequently use this word are the more skilled employees and particularly the line 1 tailors or those who are involved in the web of their social relationships and whose interests are similar. However, it is pertinent to the current analysis that part of the explanation for the regularity with which the cotton boys and the supervisors are accused of being *chichawa* is the inability of others to exert pressures on them through their social relationships to conform to behaviour more consistent with others' interests. This receives support from the fact that prior to September the supervisors and the cotton boys tended to be isolated from the sets of relationships dominated by those who wished to exercise control over their working behaviour.[22]

This was also the period when *chichawa* was the most common epithet used in reference to the cotton boys and supervisors. After September workers in every occupation in the factory became more united in an effort to change the factory wage and work conditions. This greater unity was facilitated by the expansion of social relationships cutting across many of the divisions along occupational lines which existed before September. In accordance with this expansion was the more widespread ability of some of the workers to exert influence through their social relationships which led, I consider, to a greater conformity of the junior workers, like the cotton boys to their standards of work behaviour.[23] The effect of this widespread influence

[21] These men are in an intercalary or interhierarchical position (Gluckman, 1949; 1969). As employees of Patel they are in much the same position as the other workers. At times they are used by the latter to represent their interest to Patel. But more often than not they must by their actions further the interests of Patel often against the interests of their fellow workers.

[22] This is not so true for those engaged in supervision, a more accurate explanation for them being that although they had numerous relationships with such workers as the line 1 tailors, the latter had few services which the former required. This meant that before September line 1 tailors could exert little control over the behaviour of their immediate superiors.

[23] The relationship of productive output to the degree of group cohesion has been examined by Seashore (1954), who found that the more cohesive the group the more the individuals concerned conformed to the same output

and acceptance is clearly evidenced in the marked falling off in the number of hours worked in every occupational category. It is significant also, that with the general change in the pattern of social relationships in the factory after September the frequency with which the supervisors and cotton boys were branded as *chichawa* declined.

I have described three factors which appear to account for the variations in the number of hours worked each month by the factory workers and these are position in the production process, degree of commitment to the work place and urban context generally, and the extent and way in which people are tied into the sets of social relationships in the factory. Although I consider these factors to be the principal ones in understanding patterns of behaviour in the factory this does not discount the importance of other factors. For example, one explanation why some of the more skilled workers work fewer hours than unskilled workers could relate to the wage rate on which they are employed. If they are on higher wage rates than others in the factory then they still do not need to work as many hours as the latter to earn a higher monthly wage.[24] However, my evidence does not appear to support this argument.

Many of the individuals on the higher wage rates for the most part exceeded the mean number of hours worked in the factory and also quite frequently the median. Moreover, those whose behaviour could be seen as explicable in terms of the argument, such as Mukubwa and Chisokone who worked a low number of hours, would seem to be better understood in terms of the principles outlined earlier. This behaviour of Mukubwa and Chisokone can be more satisfactorily explained in terms of the conflict between their interests connected with regular work at the factory and their interests outside the factory. Thus, of all the tailors, Mukubwa had the most extensive trading and tailoring commitments outside the factory and this consumes much of his time.[25] Because of his high value to Patel at the work place, Patel permitted Mukubwa considerable time off. The explanation for Chisokone is similar to that put forward for Mukubwa. During

---

norm. For a detailed description of the extension of social interactional relationships to involve senior and junior workers in a common set of relationships, see chapter 5.

[24] This applies to Mukubwa, Chisokone, Hastings, Nkoloya, Nkumbula, Abraham, and Zulu. After September more are added to this list, but as their increments are small I would tend to play down the significance of their inclusion for this argument.

[25] Patel even takes an interest in Mukubwa's business and advances him large sums of money. At one time Patel had advanced as much as £30 to Mukubwa.

September Chisokone became heavily involved in an outside commitment for he was negotiating with the Zambian government for a £10,000 grant for a recently formed farming co-operative of which he was an important organiser.[26] His outside involvement, which used up much of his time, often caused him to be late or absent for work. Although Chisokone did lose pay, Patel could not bring any pressure to dismiss him, largely because he feared Chisokone's very influential political contacts. At any rate, as previously described, when present at the factory Chisokone was extremely useful as a mediator between Patel and his employees. Thus both Mukubwa's and Chisokone's critical positions in the production system allowed them to use these as a lever with Patel so that they could pursue alternative opportunities outside the factory.

But whereas Mukubwa's involvement in his township business was closely connected with his factory work (a total withdrawal of his labour from the factory would result in a cost to his township business as money earned in the factory is crucial to its operation). Chisokone's outside involvement had little connection with the factory. For Chisokone cash earned at the factory was used to see him over the risky transference period when he was withdrawing from his involvement in one context to launch himself on an alternative venture.

This short discussion of the above two cases illustrates the utility of such considerations as position in the production process and commitment in the explanation of work behaviour in the factory. But if I have suggested the analytical usefulness of these considerations as well as the necessity for examining other factors such as the sets of relationships in which the factory workers are involved, how do such factors influence the employees' perception of their work context?

The following section discusses, with particular reference to occupational prestige, some of these factors and attempts to evaluate the way they affect the factory employees' perceptions.

Occupational prestige

Many of the features which appear to the observer as important for an understanding of behaviour in the factory are also important in the eyes of the employees who participate in it and are used by them to give meaning to their own position and that of others in relation to them.

[26] One partner of Chisokone in the farming co-operative was Zulu. With the likelihood of the receipt of the government grant, Zulu took over many of the organising responsibilities of the co-operative and left the factory altogether.

Table 2.3 Occupational prestige and occupational category (December 1965)

Rank	Occupation	Mean score	Rank	Occupation	Mean score
Prestige ranking by forty-two employees			**Ranking by supervisors** (2)		
1	Head tailor	3.7	(5) 1	Button machiner	4.0
2	Cutter	3.5	(4) 2	Tailors, line 1	3.5
3	Overlock machiner	3.5	(3) 3	Overlock machiner	3.5
4	Tailors, line 1	3.1	(1) 4	Head tailor	3.0
5	Button machiner	2.8	(2) 5	Cutter	3.0
6	Tailors, line 3	2.2	(8) 6	Cotton boys	2.5
7	Ironers	2.2	(6) 7	Tailors, line 3	2.0
8	Cotton boys	1.4	(7) 8	Ironers	1.0
Ranking by tailors, line 1 (12)			**Ranking by tailors, line 2** (8)		
(1) 1	Head tailor	4.0	(1) 1	Head tailor	3.3
(4) 2	Tailors, line 1	3.6	(2) 2	Cutter	3.3
(3) 3	Overlock machiner	3.5	(3) 3	Overlock machiner	2.3
(2) 4	Cutter	3.4	(5) 4	Button machiner	2.3
(5) 5	Button machiner	2.5	(4) 5	Tailors, line 1	2.0
(6) 6	Tailors, line 3	2.3	(7) 6	Ironers	1.7
(7) 7	Ironers	1.9	(6) 7	Tailors, line 3	1.5
(8) 8	Cotton boys	1.2	(8) 8	Cotton boys	1.5
Ranking by tailors, line 3 (6)			**Ranking by button machiners** (2)		
(1) 1	Head tailor	4.3	(1) 1	Head tailor	4.0
(2) 2	Cutter	4.3	(2) 2	Cutter	3.5
(3) 3	Overlock machiner	3.8	(5) 3	Button machiner	3.0
(5) 4	Button machiner	3.7	(4) 4	Tailors, line 1	2.5
(4) 5	Tailors, line 1	3.3	(7) 5	Ironers	2.5
(7) 6	Ironers	3.3	(6) 6	Tailors, line 3	2.0
(6) 7	Tailors, line 3	2.8	(3) 7	Overlock machiner	1.5
(8) 8	Cotton boys	1.5	(8) 8	Cotton boys	1.0
Ranking by ironers (5)			**Ranking by cotton boys** (7)		
(3) 1	Overlock machiner	4.5	(3) 1	Overlock machiner	4.0
(1) 2	Head tailor	3.6	(2) 2	Cutter	3.5
(2) 3	Cutter	3.6	(1) 3	Head tailor	3.4
(4) 4	Tailors, line 1	3.0	(4) 4	Tailors, line 1	3.2
(6) 5	Tailors, line 3	3.0	(5) 5	Button machiner	2.5
(5) 6	Button machiner	2.5	(7) 6	Ironers	2.4
(7) 7	Ironers	2.3	(6) 7	Tailors, line 3	2.0
(8) 8	Cotton boys	1.3	(8) 8	Cotton boys	1.4

The following analysis of the prestige rankings of the occupations in the factory will not only illustrate this but also will provide some index of the relative value which the factory workers place on the control of or access to certain resources which individuals in the various occupations have.

The information presented in table 2.3 is the result of a questionnaire administered to forty-two factory workers in December 1965. The respondents were asked to rate eight factory occupations recorded on the table according to a five-point scale. The responses were then scored; five points were given to a 'very high' response, four to 'high', down to one for 'very low'. The mean score for the total responses given to the prestige rating of each occupation was then calculated, and the occupations were then placed in rank order. Those which achieved the highest mean score appear highest in the rank ordering. The individuals to whom the questionnaire was administered were also asked why they rated each occupation the way they did. I have used these responses to this additional question in the analysis.[27]

Factors connected with control over others at work, skill, importance in the production process were frequently mentioned as standards by which the workers accorded high prestige. For example, a line 1 tailor ranked the head tailor high 'because he is the man who controls all of us'. Most of the workers accord the highest prestige to the occupation of head tailor, who is highly ranked in terms of these three dimensions. This occupation is followed in prestige by that of the cutter and overlock machiner. The former occupation demands supervisory responsibility and is important to the production process while the occupation of overlock machiner is critical to the production process and requires skill. The remaining rank ordering of the occupations can be explained by the extent to which these qualities are requirements of the various jobs.[28] But other aspects associated with the work conditions in the factory are also given as reasons. Thus a frequent explanation given for rating the cotton boys low in terms of prestige was the lack of any precise task definition in their job. 'Patel can ask them to do anything,' was a regular response.

[27] Although the questionnaire was administered to line 2 tailors working in the factory at the time, no one was asked to give a prestige rating for this occupational group. At the time I gave this questionnaire I was concerned to reduce the interview time as much as possible. Given the small amount of time saved, this was undoubtedly an error in research design, an error which I did not fully realise until I was in Manchester analysing my material. Nevertheless, I doubt if this error reduces to any great extent the value of the results and the analysis based on them.

[28] The ranking of the overlock and button machiners would appear to be slightly anomalous. Most of the tailors for most of the time are engaged in working according to the section method which places the overlock machiner, as they see it, in a critical position in the production process. It is expected, therefore, that most factory workers would rank the overlock machiner above the line 1 tailors—with the exception of the latter. In terms of skill there is very little between the line 3 tailors and the button machiners. It could be argued, however, that the button machiners have more importance for the production process.

This latter type of response points to a more general factor influencing the workers' prestige ranking of the factory occupations, which is that the ranking is most often made in reference to the benefits which seem to accrue to a particular job and the general form of behaviour in the factory which a certain job appears to permit and/or demand. The form of benefit accruing to a job most often mentioned in relation to prestige ranking was the monthly wage derived from the respective jobs. The relatively high monthly income of the supervisory workers and the overlock machiner was the reason stated by many of the employees in according these occupations high prestige. Similarly, some workers tended to devalue the prestige of many of the line 1 tailors because their wage was at the same level as the line 3 tailors and cotton boys. Another regular aspect which influenced the prestige ranking was the extent of freedom from managerial control as well as the heaviness of the work demanded by a particular occupation. Ironers, for example, were often ranked higher than expected because, it was stated, of their seeming freedom from continual supervisory contact with Patel or one of his supervisors. Tailors were ranked high by some respondents because their work let them sit down and did not involve the constant and tiring movement around the factory which is the lot of the cotton boys.

So far I have discussed occupational prestige in the factory in general terms and have excluded from the analysis important points of reference which are significant for prestige ranking. Table 2.3 shows that the prestige ranking of the occupations by the respective occupational categories in the factory evinces considerable variation. I suggest that for this variation to be explained the occupation must not be treated as divorced from the incumbent. Individuals when asked to give a prestige ranking to an occupation will draw on their knowledge and experience and it is expected that their ranking will be very much affected by those whom they know in these occupations. In such cases it can be expected that the prestige ranking they give is likely to be based on qualities (such as age, the way a person dresses, important position in a political party) in addition to those associated with the particular occupation. Prestige ranking in accordance with factors not directly connected to the occupation is to be particularly expected in such a context as Narayan Bros., where the majority of the workers know each other. Moreover, each respondent will be affected in his assessment of the prestige of an occupation by the nature of his relationship to individuals who work in the various occupations and the way he sees himself in relation to such individuals.

Many employees, for example, ranked some occupations high because

F

the persons employed in such work were senior workers in terms of the length of time they had worked in the factory. This underlies the high prestige given to the button machiners and the line 1 tailors by the supervisors (the head tailor and cutter). It is into these groups also that the supervisors have developed most of their friendship ties and it is possible that this influenced the prestige ranks they gave. Their contact with the cotton boys, line 3 tailors and the ironers is largely supervisory and the somewhat peculiar rank order given by them to these occupations could be explained by a tendency of the supervisors to see the incumbents of these occupations as relatively undifferentiated, as they are all placed in markedly subordinate positions in relation to themselves. The explanation the supervisors gave for ranking their own work lower than would be expected (given their general high ranking by the other employees) referred to the difficult position in which their work placed them. They see themselves as caught between the crossfire of abuse occasionally levelled at them and frequently at their fellow workers by Patel, and the counter accusations levelled at them and Patel by their work companions.

In contrast to the supervisors the line 1 tailors give themselves high prestige and this is very much related to their conception of their own importance in the sphere of factory relations. This is most regularly reflected in the eagerness with which some of the line 1 tailors attempt to assume leading roles on the many occasions of dispute which are a constant feature of life in the factory. In the course of emphasising their high prestige in the work place in relation to the low prestige of many of the others they are quick to point to the lack of urban experience or education of the more junior workers.

This analysis of prestige has a significance beyond merely illustrating the way different workers perceive occupations and their incumbents in relation to the factory context. One feature which has emerged from this discussion is that the prestige accorded individuals in the respective occupations is related to their access and control over various resources. If prestige, which in itself is a resource, can be used as an indicator of the value attached by the respondents to these resources then some index has been presented of the general ways members of the various occupational categories value the resources which others in the factory have access to and control over. Some such index is important for analysis in later chapters, where I argue that the pattern and structure of interactional relationships and the change in these relationships among the factory workers is related to the value of various resources used in transactions.

It is important here to emphasise that prestige is only an index. Not all resources which individuals have access to or control over will necessarily be reflected in the prestige ranking of occupations. For example, with reference to the changing pattern of interactional relationships in the factory, cotton boys became a valuable resource for the senior tailors in their struggle to differentiate between each other in terms of power and status and to increase their bargaining position *vis-à-vis* the factory manager. The increased value of interaction with the cotton boys did not, according to my observations, increase the prestige of the occupation of cotton boy in the eyes of the tailors. However, it is possible that my observation of the increased frequency of interaction between line 1 tailors and the cotton boys did reduce the prestige of the former occupational category in the eyes of members of other categories who were closest to them in terms of such factors as skill and importance for production. The information recorded on table 2.3 was collected in December 1965 during a period when the line 1 tailors had begun to extend their set of interactional relationships into the ranks of the unskilled. A consequent reduction in the prestige accorded them by other skilled workers may be reflected in the lower ranking given line 1 tailors by line 2 and 3 tailors relative to the way the former were ranked by members of the other occupational categories.

Not all aspects of occupational prestige in Narayan Bros. have been dealt with here and in subsequent chapters the topic of occupational prestige and prestige in general will be referred to again. Further analysis would obscure rather than add to the general points which I wish to emphasise here. These are, first, that many of my analytical points of reference in describing the factory context are also used by the factory workers, though often expressed in differing forms, in their perception of their work place. Second, I also suggested that the 'perceptual world' of the factory contains features relevant to behaviour in it which are not a product of it but of the general urban environment of which it is a part. This was illustrated with reference to occupational prestige where it was indicated that factors like education and degree of urban experience influence prestige rankings.

At the outset of this chapter I stressed the inadequacies of the work environment, and showed how they are exacerbated by the lack of a clear definition by management of work expectations, beyond Patel's general requirement that employees should work quickly, efficiently and hard. 'Sweat shop' conditions prevail and the dissatisfactions these produce among the factory workers are increased by the disadvantages for them of the hourly wage system, low wages and the lack of any adequate guide from management as to the basis upon which individual workers can expect to receive wage increments. Therefore, an overall system exists in the factory which appears to favour management to the disadvantage of the employees. It follows that the almost continuous disputing which is such a feature of the factory must be seen in the context of a struggle between management and worker all trying to wrest a greater benefit to themselves from the situation.

However, although towards the end of the fieldwork period there was the development of a more clearly expressed polarization between the interests of management and workers, for much of the early period all workers could not be seen as opposed to management. Management and worker generally behave with reference to a common set of values. This is the basis of their dialogue. Management seeks to get the greatest cash benefit and sees the importance of skilled workers in achieving this goal. Like management the factory workers also value skill and seek to earn as much as possible. But the factory workers have basically two choices open to them by which they can increase their earnings. Either they can work according to the current factory system and maximise to the limit the system will allow or else they can change the system. The first choice is consistent with management interests, the second, as seen by the management, is against its interest. The degree to which the factory employees take either one of these choices is dependent on their skill and/or importance in the production process. If an employee has one of these attributes he has control over a resource which is valuable to management (more so because it cannot easily be replaced) and a degree of security from the threat of dismissal. Those who have neither of the above qualities are disadvantaged in relation to management. As can be expected the former tend to be involved in action which seeks to change the system, whereas those to whom the latter applies behave in a manner consistent with the system.

Action oriented towards changing the system often means delaying immediate rewards in the interest of possibly achieving greater rewards, while action consistent with the system gives immediate return for effort. Commitment to the factory is important. To many workers, some future and uncertain increase in benefits is not attractive. Target workers and others who are not committed to the factory, if they wish to improve their wage and work conditions, would tend to move to another job rather than engage in such action. However, there is an additional complication to the argument which affects the behaviour of even those uncommitted to the factory. This is the nature of the set of social relationships in which the factory workers are involved. Should an unskilled and uncommitted worker be isolated in his social relationships from, for instance, skilled workers committed to the factory who are interested in changing their wage and work conditions, it is likely that his behaviour will conform to most of the expectations of the factory manager. But for such a worker to be caught in the social relationships of workers who are skilled and committed gives these the opportunity to control some of his behaviour, particularly behaviour which would normally operate against the interests of those employees interested in changing the factory system.

Although the factory workers act within a common framework of values the degree of importance given to some values in preference to others is dependent on the position from which they view the context. This factor along with others already applied in the preceding discussion was shown to be evident through an examination of the occupational prestige rankings in the factory. However, the discussion of the way in which the employees perceive the context as in the discussion of commitment before it, demonstrated the relevance of other factors not necessarily produced by the factory in order to arrive at an adequate analysis of processes within it. Each worker evinces various social characteristics which influence his behaviour in all contexts and not least in the factory. It is part of the aim of the following chapter to examine some of these social characteristics and the way they relate to the factory.

The description of the social composition of the factory in this chapter does not derive from any preconception regarding what should be included in an adequate monographic analysis. Many monographs leave me with the impression that their authors, upon completing the description of the basic social composition of the environment they have studied, have heaved a sigh of relief at the way at last being cleared for the more interesting work of analysis and explanation. To allay a similar reaction in the minds of my readers I emphasise that my description of the social composition presented here is both an extension of an argument of the preceding chapter and is fundamental to the development of the analysis in subsequent chapters.

The social composition of the factory is continually changing because of the regular movement of individuals in and out of employment. Broadly, I consider that the changes emerge as a result of the operation of the interconnection of three main sets of factors. First, it is a product of factors associated with the different points individuals have reached in their life, migratory and job careers, second, of the structure and content of the sets of interpersonal relationships of the employees within and without the factory context; third, of the general properties of the contexts (e.g. wage and work conditions in the factory context) in which the employees participate as these contexts are defined by them.

In order to demonstrate this I am confronted with a technical problem. How can I describe the changing social composition of the factory without introducing a considerable element of unwanted stasis into my description? A partial solution is to show the major social attributes of the factory employees at three separate points of time during the period of observation; at the end of the months of June, September and January. These points of time correspond approximately with the start of my observations in the factory, the end of a period during which there had been considerable worker agitation against the management which did not receive the unified support of the workers, and a point in the development of worker militancy when the unified support of the workers against management was achieved. But the principal solution lies in the form of analysis.

My orientation is essentially one which employs concepts of choice and decision-making. It is directly related to my conception of the social composition of the factory as being an emergent property from an ongoing social process. I view the clothing factory as a social organisation which straddles a number of life, migratory and job careers which are at different points of development. Its social composition at any given time is viewed as emergent from a set of individual choices and decisions subject to a variety of constraints. These constraints are of four major kinds: first, by the choices and decisions which an individual has already made in the past and which he expects to make in the future;[1] second, by the degree to which an individual organises his choices and decisions according to a set of multiple objectives and the nature of the interrelationship between these multiple objectives;[2] the third, closely connected with the second, relates to the extent to which the choices and decisions made by an individual in one context will affect, as he perceives them, the expected outcomes from choices made by him in other contexts, fourth, the particular placement of an individual in a set of social relationships of varying content and structure in a number of contexts and not just the context to which the bulk of the descriptive effort is directed.

The use of a choice/decision-making orientation implies that individuals have clearly worked out plans of action, but this is not assumed. Individuals are frequently unclear about the objectives

[1] The relation of past and future choices to current choices and decisions is likely to be different. A choice or decision, once made, is difficult to go back on and thus its consequences are likely to have a continuing effect. This is not to state that the effect of past choices and decisions on subsequent action cannot be altered or made null by a later set of choices and decisions. All I wish to emphasise is that a past set of choices and decisions establishes the frame for those that are made subsequently, whether they seek to nullify or to confirm the pattern established by an earlier set of choices and decisions. In contrast, expected future choices will continually be exposed to the possibility of re-definition in response to that set of choices and decisions currently being made. The constraint on current action imposed by future expected choices and decisions can simply be altered by a redefinition of those types of choice and decision which an individual expects to make in the future.

[2] It is fundamental to this position that statements relating to the choice behaviour of individuals cannot be made on the basis of the expected pay-off from the achievement of one objective considered independently of other objectives which an individual is oriented towards achieving. Rather, I suggest, an individual is more likely to choose between one alternative than another on the basis of the extent to which the pay-off from this choice is likely to increase or reduce the expected outcomes from other choices in which an individual is currently involved. The approach adopted here is closely related to that developed by Simon (1956: 127) with reference to his concept of 'satisficing'.

towards which their actions are directed. More often than not individuals appear to direct their choices in accordance with the rules of tactics rather than those of strategy. In my terms an individual is pursuing a strategy when he organises his choices on the basis of his total understanding of the context in the way that current opportunities relate to future opportunities and objectives. When an individual pursues a tactic 'he does not take into account the whole of the situation, but proceeds according to a criterion of optimality that is applied locally stage by stage' (Schutzenberger, 1954: 99). Instead of assuming that individuals proceed according to well defined plans of action, I direct my attention to the *conditions* which induce individuals to organise their behaviour in accordance with rules of strategy rather than those of tactics or vice versa.

The four major kinds of constraint on individual choice behaviour isolated above are open to restatement in propositional form, they thus acquire the status of statements which must be demonstrated and tested through the examination of empirical material. They cannot be regarded as mere orientational assumptions. Treating the four constraints as propositions I hope to show how the change in social composition of the factory and the differential behaviour of the factory workers is a function, first, of the specific ways past and future expected choices relate to current choices in terms of the different points individuals have reached in their life, migratory and job careers; second, of the degree to which the employees organise their action according to a multiplicity of objectives and the nature of the interrelationship of these objectives; third, of the extent to which the choice behaviour of the workers in one context is constrained by their choices in other contexts; and, finally, of the extent to which the workers' placement in a set of social relationships of varying content and structure, extending across a number of contexts, affects their behaviour.

The particular nature of the approach and the way it organises my view of behaviour in the factory context directs me to examine the interrelationship of the factory with the general environment in which it is located. This general environment is seen as composed of all the other contexts in which the employees have participated prior to and during their employment in the factory. The relationship of organisation to environment is a recurrent theme in the literature of industrial sociology (Warner and Low, 1947; Walker, 1950; Gouldner, 1954; Lantz, 1958). These studies generally treat the organisation and the environment as 'wholes', separate but interdependent. Two major difficulties arise from such an approach. First, the organisation and its environment are conceptualised as being in a one to one relationship. Little account is taken of the fact that individuals are incorporated in different ways into both the organisations and general environment. In my approach, organisations are related to their environment through individuals. It follows that the relationship of the organisation to its environment will vary in accordance with the differential incorporation of individuals into them. Second, it is difficult to specify in any exact way how the behaviour of individuals is affected by the general environment, or by the organisation, or is a product of the interaction between the two. The approach adopted here is an attempt to overcome these difficulties.

The chapter is broadly divided into three parts. In the first section I consider factors which have been influential in channelling the careers of the factory workers, and in particular of the tailors. How did they choose tailoring as a career? What combination of factors enabled and directed them to make such a choice? What set of conditions led them to choose certain modes of employment rather than others? This is followed by a section on the various factors which influence certain processes of recruitment to the factory. Recruitment to factory work is subject, it will be shown, not only to the preferences exhibited by the manager for specific kinds of worker but is controlled by the influences which certain of the workers exert on his decisions. The final section on migration and labour turnover examines the processes which explain why certain sections of the labour force experience different rates of stability and change.

The analysis in each of these sections is directed to exploring the problem of the way the factory is related to the general environment in which it is set. I demonstrate that the social composition of the factory is not simply a product of processes general to the environment but that processes specific to the factory context mediate and control the extent to which general environmental processes influence its emergent social composition. That the social composition of the factory is not just a simple product of processes general to its environment can be illustrated briefly by reference to the age structure of the factory as it compares with that for the municipality.

The age structure of the factory employees (see fig. 3.1) is broadly similar in shape to that of the adult male population of the Kabwe municipal townships. The latter assumes the shape it does because most of the African inhabitants of the municipality were born in rural areas and migrated to town and most are able-bodied males between the ages of 25 and 44. The factory as a place of work must by definition

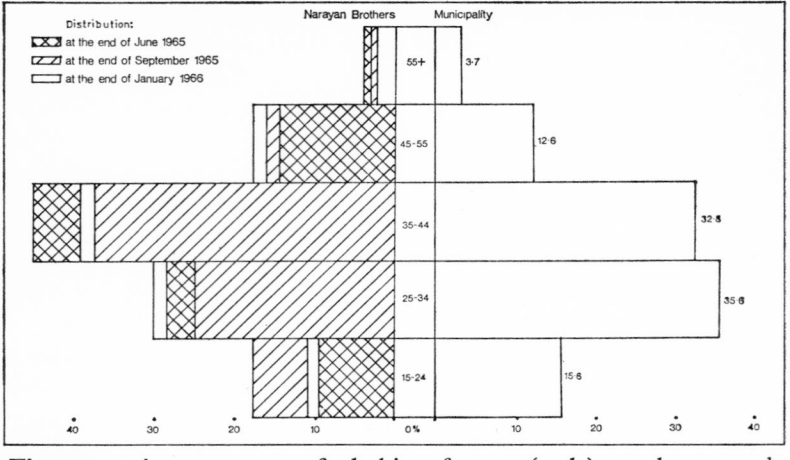

Fig. 3.1 Age structure of clothing factory (male) employees and municipal townships (males)

employ able-bodied males and it draws from the population resident in the town but this does not in itself demand that the factory population should have the age structure it does. Although most of the factory employees were born in rural areas (only three workers were born in town) and are in the 25–44 age category, the broad similarity between the age structure of the factory and municipality ends here. For in contrast to the general pattern in the municipality age structure, there is a greater tendency for the factory workers to be drawn from the older (35+) age categories than would normally be expected had the shape of the factory's age structure fitted exactly with that for the municipality.

It would seem that the difference between the age structure of the factory and the municipality is a consequence of the fact that work in the factory is largely skilled and, as table 3.1 shows, skilled workers in the factory tend to be older than unskilled workers. This tendency persists over time despite the continual turnover of personnel. Thus, for each of the periods represented on table 3.1, the mean ages for supervisors, tailors and button machine operators (semi-skilled work), tended to be above the mean age for the factory as a whole. Exceptions are found among the line 2 tailors whose mean age in June fell below the mean age for the factory, and the line 3 tailors whose mean age in January fell below the mean age for the factory. These lines experienced the greatest change in social composition due to both internal mobility and tailors' either leaving or newly arriving in the factory.

Table 3.1 Occupation, age range and mean age of employees
(June, September and January)

Occupation	June			September			January		
	No.	Range	Mean	No.	Range	Mean	No.	Range	Mean
Supervisory	2	41–44	42.5	2	41–44	42.5	2	44–56	50.0
Tailors 1	12*	33–56	43.2	12	31–56	42.3	12	26–50	42.4
2	6	31–48	36.8	8	26–48	37.8	8	31–47	37.4
3	8	32–53	40.1	6	35–53	42.5	9	25–53	35.4
Buttons	2	36–39	37.5	2	36–39	37.5	2	36–39	37.5
Ironers	4	21–42	32.0	4	21–42	32.0	6	21–42	30.5
Cotton boys	8	19–36	25.6	12	16–36	23.4	6	16–35	21.8
Mean total			37.0			35.5			35.9
Total	42			46			45		

* Hastings is counted as a line 1 tailor for June and September.

Why are skilled employees in the factory older on average than unskilled employees? This pattern is not consistent with the tendency represented generally for the municipal African residents where skilled workers are in the main younger than unskilled workers. Furthermore, the unskilled workers in the factory are considerably younger than would normally be expected should the age structure of the factory be identical with that of the Kabwe municipal areas as a whole. It would thus seem that processes connected with the factory are operating to select certain types of employees rather than others for unskilled work. Some suggestions as to what these processes are will be discussed in later sections of this chapter.

Tailors: opportunity, choice and career patterns

A tailor's skill does not only allow him to 'exploit' the employment opportunities offered by the Indian companies such as Narayan Bros. It also enables him to participate in the township clothing trade which is dominated by Africans. Many of the tailors employed by Narayan Bros., in fact have their own small businesses in the townships (see table 3.5). Because tailors can and do participate in wage employment and run independent businesses of their own they constitute an occupational category quite distinct from those other skilled workers (e.g. in the mine and railways) whose incomes are more exclusively made up of wages.[3]

[3] Some skilled and unskilled workers in wage employment do have side business ventures in addition to their regular occupations. For example, a study I made in another industrial context in Kabwe where the workers were employed in

Why do people become tailors? What are the benefits accruing to a skilled tailor? The acquisition of skill as a tailor ensures some security in a competitive employment market and permits the individual concerned to make choices concerning his future action, which appear most attractive to him at the time. By security here is meant the ability of an individual to control to some extent the nature of his employment and income which in turn allows him a degree of independence in the planning of his subsequent social action. Attention is drawn to this by Godfrey Wilson (1942, Part II: 36–7), writing of Kabwe (then Broken Hill) in 1942. He records the case of a Bemba railway employee who, on suffering a leg injury which resulted in his discharge from work, bought himself a sewing machine and set himself up as a tailor. This enabled him to continue living in town rather than make the other choice open to him at the time, which he considered unattractive, of returning to subsistence farming in his rural area. Tailoring is a skill which offers security because the control over its operation lies largely in the hands of its owner and it can be separated from the place of employment. Most tailors in commercial employment own their sewing machines (see table 3.5) and can make a living from cash earned in private business.

Self-employment, which is capable of providing a gross income at least comparable with an income earned[4] in commercial employment, also permits an individual tailor to escape poor employment conditions when they seem intolerable.

Although most tailors in the factory are in the older age categories, the majority entered tailoring early in their employment careers. Table 3.2 shows that of the thirty-seven tailors who were employed at Narayan Bros. over the research period, thirty-one first entered employment as tailors before the age of 30. Of the twenty-three tailors over the

---

the Cell Room of the Mine plant revealed that some of the employees financed small business concerns with their cash earned from the Mine (see Kapferer, 1969). Normally, however, the supplementation of a regularly earned income with cash earned in side business ventures is not common.

4 I have no figures which could more adequately demonstrate this point. But from my general observations among self-employed tailors occupied in the mine and municipal markets they can earn in gross terms more cash than in commercial employment. This, however, is largely offset by the expenditure which the self-employed tailor must incur in buying cloth and cotton. He is also much more exposed to the fluctuations of market demands. Therefore, as Wilson implied in 1942 (op. cit., p. 38), self-employment should not be viewed as an equivalent alternative to commercial employment. I suggest that it should be seen as such only when other factors, such as poor wage and work conditions, reduce the attractiveness of commercial employment. This is discussed more fully on pp. 80-2.

age of 35, nineteen had started tailoring before 30 and twelve before the age of 25. The tendency for men to enter tailoring at an early stage in their urban experience suggests that a desire for security is not necessarily related to either increasing age or to working experience. A need for a steady income and some certainty of employment can enter at any point in a man's working life and may be due to numerous factors such as those provided by the demand to support a wife and children or a wish to become settled into a town life.

Table 3.2 Present age and age when first employed as a tailor

Age employed as tailor (five-year age groups)	Present age (in ten-year age groups)				Total
	25-34	35-44	45-54	55+	
15-19	2	2	3	1	8
20-24	8	6	-	-	14
25-29	3	5	2	-	10
30-34	1	2	2	-	5
Total	14	15	7	1	37

Note: Laurent, a tailor, left soon after I arrived, so I have no information on him.

Once a man has embarked on tailoring as a major occupation he tends to remain in it. Only seven out of the tailors at Narayan Bros. had worked in other jobs after being first employed as tailors, and six of these reported having had only one intervening job which required different skills. The early age at which tailors commence employment in their skill means that they have had little experience of other occupations. Of those who were in other kinds of employment prior to becoming tailors, most were employed in unskilled occupations in the commercial sectors of the towns to which they had migrated even though these towns offered opportunities for employment in the mines or on the railway.

Why do tailors learn and become employed in their trade at an early stage of their occupational lives? Among the most influential factors are those already discussed such as the need for security which includes an individual's wish to stabilise his income and exert a greater control over his employment chances.

But other factors influence an individual's choice of occupational career. Two are of particular importance. First, the employment sector (e.g. domestic service, commercial, mining, railway) of the urban economy which a migrant initially enters will structure his perception of the employment opportunities which are open to him; and will expose him to an experience which, in the first place, may lead him to an awareness of a need for security and a wish to exert a greater control over his job chances in the urban economy. Second, a migrant's involvement in a set of social relationships with other individuals who have specific experiences of the urban employment market are also influential on the pattern of migratory careers and occupational choice. Moreover, the type of skills which these other individuals have (and the extent to which they can transfer knowledge of these skills)[5] and the kind of assistance they provide will influence the direction of a migrant's occupational choice.

An examination of the points in their careers when migrants enter tailoring provides evidence for the first factor. For example, those individuals who first entered employment in the commercial sector, but not as tailors, tended to choose tailoring as a career sooner than those whose initial point of entry was the mining sector. Thus the mean period spent by workers in commercial employment before becoming tailors is 3·2 years (median three years), while the mean is eight years for those whose point of entry is mining (median eight years). Relative to other employment sectors mining provides high wages, reasonable conditions of service (such as cheap house rents, good welfare facilities, electricity) and opportunities for job advancement.[6] In Zambia the mineworkers have the support of a strong union which protects their interests against management. This is in contrast to the weak and frequently ineffective unions representing the workers employed in the commercial areas of the towns. Another factor which can explain the quicker entry of migrants into careers such as tailoring if their initial experience is in the commercial sectors of the towns, is the fact that in these sectors migrants have a greater likelihood of coming into social contact with individuals in these occupations than in other areas of the urban economy.[7]

[5] By this I refer to the fact that trade skills like plumbing, tailoring, carpentry, etc., can be transferred from one place of employment to another. Skills learnt in railway or mining work, however, are often job-specific and are difficult to transfer to other centres of employment outside these sectors.

[6] In Kabwe the mining company also had a retirement scheme which enabled workers at the end of their able-bodied lives to live in houses provided by the mine on mine property.

[7] This argument that a migrant's occupational career is influenced by the em-

The general point which is being made here is that an individual's choice to enter wage employment in either the commercial or mining sectors of the urban economy affects the rate of his choice to enter other occupations, in this case tailoring. In discussing labour migration, Mitchell (1961: 271) draws a distinction between rate and incidence. Rate refers to the broad patterns of movement whereas incidence refers to the variation between individuals as to the timing of their choices. This individual variation is disguised in the general rate. An explanation of incidence or the reasons why and when individuals make the specific choices they do, e.g. why an individual should choose to leave the relative security of mine work and take up tailoring, would require an examination of the specific range of factors which relate to these particular individuals.

The importance of the second factor, that of a migrant's involvement in a set of social relationships with other individuals, in influencing the pattern of migration and occupational choice can also be demonstrated with reference to the tailors. I begin by outlining the main ways tailors learn their trade. This will be followed by a discussion of the influence played by relatives and friends in the structuring of migration careers and occupational choice, largely through reference to three occupational histories.

Learning to be a tailor Individuals become tailors in any one of three ways. These are: (1) learning to tailor from a relative or friend in the rural home area prior to migration to town; (2) learning to tailor in the town from an experienced tailor, often a relative or friend, after some other occupational experience; (3) learning to tailor while in the employ, typically, of an Indian storekeeper or factory owner. All three ways by which an individual comes to learn the trade usually entail some period of apprenticeship.

Table 3.3 shows that more tailors have learnt their skill at their rural home or in town, usually from a relative or friend, than have learnt in stores or factories. It is the tailors who learn privately who are the most affected by 'apprenticeship'. If the trade is learnt privately the learner tailor normally works as an assistant to his teacher in return for which he acquires skill but usually receives no wage.[8] In fact the normal

ployment sector he initially entered has been extended and discussed generally in relation to migration behaviour in a recent paper (see Garbett and Kapferer, 1971).

[8] An assistant's duties include measuring clients for fittings, cutting loose cotton ends off clothing and numerous other small tasks and errands. Later on in his apprenticeship he will do some tailoring work.

pattern is for the learner tailor once he considers himself competent to
pay his teacher some money on leaving. During the apprenticeship the
learner earns no money and must depend on the support of relatives
and friends for his sustenance. Although some stores and clothing
factories may not pay learner tailors a wage (I have one case where the
learner tailor in fact paid his Indian employer money for teaching him
his trade), most of the tailors who were employed while learning, whom
I encountered during my research, received wages.

A few who were employed as learner tailors were paid half the normal
wage rates for the duration of their apprenticeship. For the majority of

Table 3.3 Where and how skill as a tailor was learnt

| Where | Number | Learnt from | | |
		Store	Friend	Relative
In rural area prior to move to town	5	0	2	3
In town: privately from another tailor	14	0	5	9
In town: on the job, skill learnt while in employment	15	18	0	0
Total	37*	18	7	12

* Information on one tailor was unrecorded.

those who learnt while in store or factory employment, and who were
not hired as learner tailors but as cotton boys or shop assistants, apprenticeship was uncommon or at least did not involve the same kind of
difficulties encountered by those who learnt while unemployed. For
instance, some learners apprenticed themselves to a tailor they had met
while in store or factory employment and learnt in their spare time.
Others, like Joseph and Henry at Narayan Bros., acquired their skill
while engaged as cotton boys in the factory. Understandably, to learn
the skill while in employment is considered preferable to being unemployed and apprenticed.

Of the thirty-seven tailors who were employed in Narayan Bros. over
the course of my fieldwork, five had learnt their skill preparatory to
coming to town in search of employment (see table 3.3). Although one
of these, Mateo had some previous urban experience, after three years

working in town he returned to his home village in Malawi, learnt the trade and then returned to town where he found work as a tailor. Three of these five tailors learnt from a relative who was a tailor, the remaining two from friends. Only two of the tailors in this category, Mateo and Chipalo, did not pay cash to their teachers. In both cases the teachers were relatives, a sister's husband and a father respectively. But it cannot be inferred from this that because an individual learns from a relative he need not pay his tutor. One man, Chilwa, who was taught by a kinsman, an elder brother, paid him £5. The remaining two men, Ibrahim and Joshua learnt their trade from friends in the rural area, the former paying £19 and the latter £5. Chilwa paid his teacher after he had found employment in town but Ibrahim and Joshua were assisted in their payments by relatives in their rural homes.

In all cases the acquisition of the skill before leaving their home areas involved an expenditure at the very least in time, and for some, in cash, not only for those being taught but for the friends and relatives who assisted them in acquiring their trade. Commenting on the labour migration of the Lakeside Tonga of Malawi to towns in Central and Southern Africa, Van Velsen states,'. . . migration to the urban centres has become a part of Tonga culture . . . they [the Tonga] see Tongaland as a training ground for the young and a place of retirement for the old. Young men consider their stay in the village before they can go off to the towns as a period of marking time' (1961: 236). As other studies (Watson, 1958; Mayer, 1961) have shown, Van Velsen's observations are generalisable to many other areas in Central and Southern Africa, as are his further elaborations on the connection between town and country for the Tonga. He emphasises the dependence of rural kinsmen on the remuneration of cash and clothes from their relatives working in the towns and the reliance in turn of urban workers on their rural kinsfolk to keep alive their political and economic interests in the home areas to which they will eventually return. That five of the tailors received their training in their rural home areas before leaving for town illustrates the way in which the rural area prepares young men for urban employment.[9] That other people in the rural areas, particularly relatives, have invested time and money in these tailors is a form of

[9] All the five tailors discussed maintained their contacts with their rural homes. Chilwa, for example, regularly sends clothing and cash to relatives in Malawi. During 1965 he sent over £10 in postal orders to his mother and a younger sister. In addition he sent two pairs of long trousers, two pairs of shorts, seven shirts and three pairs of shoes to his two younger brothers. Chipalo, a Bemba, has sent money, amounting to over £15 to his relatives at home near Kasama in the Northern Province via kin who have visited him in town.

G

insurance that they will maintain their ties with their home area and send money, clothing and other gifts home.

But it is not only rural kin who assist and direct relatives in the achievement of a skill; friends and relatives from home living and working in urban areas are also influential in determining the kind of work, as well as the place of employment, which new migrants choose. Many of the factory workers, and particular tailors, are 'incapsulated' in a set of ties which originate in an individual's home area and which radiate through various centres of employment.[10] It is their dependence on them which reinforces both their commitment to friends and relatives in their rural homes and in the towns and which has an important influence on the pattern of their employment career. A clear example of this dependence on relatives and friends from the home area and the influence it has on the pattern of employment and urban migration is seen in the labour career of Chilwa.

Occupational history 1: Chilwa

Chilwa is a Lakeside Tonga from Nkhata Bay, Malawi, and was born in 1925. In 1932 he left school after completing only two years. In 1940 his elder brother Dickson returned home after a period of work as a tailor in Luanshya, and it was he who first gave Chilwa tailoring lessons. A few months after his return Dickson again left for town, but before doing so he put Chilwa in contact with a Chewa friend of his who was working as a tailor in Blantyre. He apprenticed himself to this man in late 1941, and by the middle of 1942 Chilwa considered that he was sufficiently skilled. He found employment in a small store in Blantyre, and with the assistance of some of his relatives and the cash he saved each month out of his monthly wage of £5 he paid his teacher the £12 the latter was demanding. After approximately four months in Blantyre as a tailor he heard that a relative of his owned a small store near Kabwe and had work for a tailor. Upon arrival in Kabwe he discovered that his mother's father's younger brother owned a store at Mkushi, so he journeyed there and was employed at £6 per month—£1 more than he had been earning in Blantyre.

In 1957 Chilwa left Mkushi and again went to Kabwe, where he stayed with his father's younger brother, who works as a medical orderly in the Kabwe hospital. He soon found employment at the Indian-owned syndicate store in the town, where he was placed on the same wage as he had received in Mkushi. But his work conditions were poor and the store's proprietor did not find him housing or pay him a housing allowance, so in 1959 he moved to Luanshya. His elder brother, Dickson, by

---

10 The studies of Mayer (1961) and Gutkind (1968) demonstrate the influence of similar factors in urban areas elsewhere.

this time had left Luanshya for another town but Chilwa was able to contact a friend who came from a neighbouring village in Malawi, and stayed with him. He was again successful in finding employment, this time in a store run by a European.

Unfortunately, later in 1959 the store owner went bankrupt and so Chilwa was once again thrown on the employment market. This time Chilwa went to Choma, in the Southern Province, where he knew Banda (married to his elder brother Dickson's daughter) was working. He stayed with Banda and while there found a job as a tailor—at a considerably higher wage than he had been employed at before. Although he was satisfied with his work conditions, his wife, whom he had married at home in 1941 and brought with him to town, became ill. Her illness was diagnosed by a *nganga* (African doctor) as *ngulu* (possession by a nature spirit) and Chilwa suspected that someone in the area had bewitched her. In late 1963 he left work and returned to Kabwe. He rejoined his father's younger brother at the hospital and was employed in one of the local stores as a tailor.

Although his wage was the same as at Choma he did not receive a housing allowance and so in 1964 he decided to leave his job and set himself up as a self-employed tailor at the Bwacha market. Although he was doing well, fear of witchcraft drove him away from his market stand. His suspicions had been aroused one day when he found a small tree root with beads wound round it in a box where he kept his sewing materials. In addition he found the bone of a small animal and a small bottle of Vaseline in which had been mixed some crushed tree roots. Chilwa believed that another tailor was jealous of his success and so he thought it wise to leave the market premises. In July of the same year he was taken on by Narayan Bros. He had been relatively isolated in the set of factory social relationships, and in September 1965 he was the only line 1 tailor who did not receive an increment. Insult was added to injury when at the beginning of January, Patel, who was dissatisfied with Chilwa's workmanship, demoted him to line 3. Two days after this Chilwa left employment and joined a friend tailoring at the mine market.

The importance which kinsmen play in Chilwa's employment and urban experience is to a large extent repeated in the following labour histories. However, the major point of difference between the labour history which follows and that of Chilwa is that it is concerned with the employment and urban experience of a man who learnt his trade in town and who, although he was introduced to his teacher by a relative, was taught by a man to whom he was not tied by kinship.

Occupational history 2: Lyashi

Lyashi was born in 1923 in the Bemba village of Mwansabamba in Chief Nkula's district. He had no schooling and in 1937 he travelled to Shiwa

Ngandu,[11] where he was employed as a labourer. He was only employed for three months and soon returned to his village. In 1939 he left for Tanzania, where he found employment as a sisal cutter. Between 1939 and 1946 he went from job to job as a sisal cutter, and in 1946 he returned home, where he married. The following year he left with his wife for Mindolo, Kitwe, and stayed with his mother's younger sister's daughter. After a few months of unemployment he secured a job as a lorry boy but the pay was so bad that in 1948 he joined the mine as an underground worker. But in 1950 he suffered an accident and was given £150 compensation. He then left town and returned home for two and a half months. But he soon left again for Kitwe and the mine where he was employed as a township labourer. In 1951 he was fired because he fought with his foreman. However, in the same year his mother's elder sister's son introduced him to a Luvale tailor who taught him his trade. It took Lyashi almost a year to learn the trade, and he paid the Luvale tailor £14 tuition fees. While learning tailoring he stayed with a fellow Bemba, Brown, whom he had met at Mindolo in 1948 while attending the regular *mbeni*[12] dances.

In 1952 Brown and Lyashi (Lyashi had sent his wife home while he was learning to tailor) left for Livingstone, as they were both unemployed, and stayed with Chisenga, a Bemba, and a friend of Brown. Lyashi managed to secure a job as a tailor in a Livingstone factory, but Brown was unsuccessful and so he left for Rhodesia in search of a job as a driver. Soon after the friends had parted, Lyashi also left Livingstone and went to Kabwe. Other forms of employment and other towns followed, including a brief time mining at Wankie and two months, when unemployed, as a fish seller. In late 1953 we find Lyashi back in Kabwe, where he was joined by his wife at his mother's brother's government farm on the outskirts of the town. Lyashi again went through a succession of jobs, as a tailor, a general labourer on the mine and a clothes hawker, until in 1964 he joined Narayan Bros. in his present job as a tailor.

The third occupational history I give concerns a tailor who learnt his trade while employed in a clothing factory. A noticeable feature of this case is the reduced dependence of this labour migrant on the support of relatives, a dependence which is a more prominent feature of the two previous labour histories.

Occupational history 3: Nkoloya

Nkoloya, a Kunda, was born in 1924 in Katemwa village in the Chipata (Fort Jameson) district of the Eastern Province. His education finished

[11] This was the estate of Sir Stewart Gore-Browne, a man who figured prominently in the early and relatively recent political history of Zambia, and is located in the Northern Province.

[12] *See* Mitchell (1956: 10–11) for an account of *mbeni* and its relation to the *kalela*.

after three years' schooling in 1934 and three years later, in 1937, he left for Kitwe on the Copperbelt. When he reached Kitwe he found the house of his mother's elder brother, Yolam, who was working at a local butchery. Nkoloya remained with Yolam for over two years but it was only towards the end of this period that he found employment. When he first arrived in Kitwe he was a little over thirteen years of age and his extreme youth, despite numerous attempts to find work, prevented him from achieving much success. Nevertheless, he was eventually taken on as a cotton boy in a local Indian clothing factory and was paid 12s 6d per month. This first job experience was to prove useful to Nkoloya later in his career for a fellow cotton boy in the factory at the time was Mukubwa, the head tailor at Narayan Bros. In 1940 Nkoloya's mother's brother died and Yolam's wife decided to return home to her rural village. With no place to stay and earning a relatively meagre wage Nkoloya decided to leave for Wankie in Rhodesia where he had heard there was available work at the colliery. There were no kinsfolk he knew of living at Wankie and he slept for two days in the open. But he was successful in finding a job and he was employed at 25s per month in the mine township as a sweeper. While living in Wankie he found a few Kunda also working there. In particular he became friendly with Boniface, who came from a village, he discovered, very close to his. Nkoloya went to live in Boniface's house. Boniface at that time was working as a cotton boy in a clothing factory, and he convinced Nkoloya of the opportunities which awaited him in the clothing industry. Nkoloya left his job at the mine—not, however, before Boniface had secured him a job as a cotton boy at the factory where he was working.

Although by taking this job Nkoloya reduced his monthly earnings from 25s to 15s, it was his intention through his work at the factory to contact a tailor and learn the trade. He managed to find a Bemba tailor who was willing to teach him, and Nkoloya received his instruction both at the factory when time could be spared during working hours and after work in the township. Nkoloya spent more than a year acquiring his new skill, and at the end of this period he paid his teacher £8 for his services from the money he saved from work.

In 1947 he left his job at the clothing factory, where he had since been promoted to tailor. His main reason for leaving was that he had heard that a home friend, Oscar, had recently arrived in Livingstone. Nkoloya and Oscar had been in almost constant correspondence and although they were not related they were firm friends. As he now had a skill Nkoloya foresaw no difficulties in securing gainful employment, so he left Wankie to visit his friend. Moreover, Oscar too was a tailor and upon Nkoloya's arrival in Livingstone Oscar told him to contact some friends of his who were working at the United Clothing factory. Nkoloya not only received a better wage in Livingstone than he had been paid in Wankie but it was also the town where he met his wife, Rosemary, to whom he was shortly married, who lived next door to him and is a Bemba from Kawambwa.

After Livingstone other towns followed. In 1953 Nkoloya went to Ndola. Although he had no relatives here, with the assistance of a letter of recommendation from his previous employers he secured a tailoring job at an attractive wage. But, again, in 1956 he left work and came to Kabwe. He had no relatives in Kabwe that he knew of at the time, and for the first few nights in the town he and his family camped at the railway station. However, while on the Copperbelt he learned that his old friend Mukubwa now had an important job at Narayan Bros. Nkoloya quickly contacted Mukubwa and was willingly taken on by Patel, who was impressed by Nkoloya's experience and Mukubwa's assurances that Nkoloya was highly skilled.

Although he was at first pleased with his new work, Nkoloya soon discovered that there were disadvantages. For example, no housing was provided and he was forced to go searching for a house on his own. Eventually he was given permission by a retired miner living on one of the mine farms to erect a house on the farm plot. Nkoloya still lives there, and as a result of contacts which he has established in the mine area has built up a flourishing tailoring business, which he operates from his tailor's stand in the mine market. The income derived from this business supplements what he considers to be the poor wages he receives at the clothing factory.

The case histories I have presented emphasise the importance of kinsmen and friends from home for influencing a migrant's urban moves, choice of work and securing of employment. A similar pattern obtains for most of the other tailors employed in the factory.

Other evidence, not restricted to workers in the clothing trade, indicates the general importance of kinsmen and home friends in the process of urban and employment experience. To have kinsmen or friends from home in the clothing trade is an invaluable asset to the individual who wishes to enter the industry and at the very least will be considerably influential in determining the career of those who have not as yet so clearly made up their minds. Not only is it fortunate for the aspiring tailor to have relatives or home friends who are skilled in the trade, for it is from them that an individual can himself learn the trade, but they are also the major channels, particularly if the person is unskilled, by which entry can be gained to the stores where clothing is made. At Narayan Bros. many of the unskilled workers were sponsored in their employment by other employees, who are relatives or friends from home, at the factory (see table 3.5).[13]

The importance of store employment Once an individual has made the decision to embark on tailoring as a career, other choices become relevant. These choices relate to his successful pursuit of tailoring as a

[13] In chapter 2 I emphasised that relatively few of the unskilled workers have any intention of working for any extended period of time in the factory (most being target workers), and only a small number of those entering unskilled work intended at the time to learn the tailoring trade.

career, in the sense of his ability to secure gainful employment as a tailor, and to his new status in an economic environment which brings him into competition with others involved in the clothing business. The choice either to enter or not to enter store or clothing factory employment constitutes a decision which is likely to have considerable consequences both for an individual's successful pursuit of tailoring as a career and for his competitive position in the clothing business.

From the perspective of an individual who has just chosen tailoring as a career, stores and clothing factories are more than mere places in which to learn his trade or to gain employment. It is significant that tailoring, unlike other trades such as carpentry or plumbing, is not taught at technical schools. An advantage of learning a trade in a technical or trades school is that upon completion of the course a diploma or certificate is awarded. This gives official recognition that the individual concerned can adequately practise his trade and is therefore of considerable value to someone competing with others for job opportunities in a highly competitive labour market. A tailor, because he does not learn his skill in an establishment providing official recognition of his ability, must receive recognition in some other way if he is to compete successfully for work against his fellows. By finding employment at a store or clothing factory not only does a tailor gain greater experience in his skill, but he receives more widespread recognition of his ability. Moreover, on leaving his work at the store or clothing factory he asks his employer (usually an Indian or a European) for a letter of recommendation. This is his diploma.[14] For this reason alone stores and clothing factories are the most attractive places in which to learn the trade. This information also partly explains the general tendency for tailors who did not learn their skill in a store or clothing factory to receive work experience in either one of such places shortly after acquiring their new skills.

Obviously, however, other factors in addition to a desire to achieve wider recognition of skill lead to a tailor's decision to enter store or factory employment. In order to isolate these factors the advantage of securing employment in these places must be examined in relation to the other major alternative which is open to tailors—that of self-employment. First it should be stressed that it is impossible to choose

---

[14] Letters of recommendation, particularly from Indian or European employers, are highly prized possessions. Men in search of employment in any sphere will present letters of recommendation for almost anything, including the ability to wash a car, the right to beg, etc. Anyone who has travelled in developing countries where there is gross unemployment cannot fail to notice the extreme importance attached to such letters.

self-employment as an alternative if the tailor does not own a sewing machine or have regular access to one through a friend or relative.[15] Many tailors, and nearly all those who have recently learnt their skill, do not own or have access to sewing machines, and these must find employment in stores or factories where sewing machines are provided. Only when a tailor acquires a sewing machine (generally at a later period in his employment experience) does self-employment present itself as an alternative to store or factory employment. But whether it is a *viable* alternative to store employment depends on a number of other considerations.

The circumstances of self-employment are fraught with uncertainties. The self-employed tailor is thrown into open competition both with

Table 3.4   Age at which tailoring was learnt and present age

Age first employed as tailor	Present age				Total
	25-34	35-44	45-54	55+	
15-19	2	2	3	1	8
20-24	5	6	-	-	11
25-29	5	5	2	-	12
30-34	2	2	2	-	6
Total	14	15	7	1	37*

* Information on one tailor was unrecorded.

other self-employed tailors and with the clothing factories and stores, the latter being able to produce large quantities of clothes more cheaply. The competition is perhaps greater with other self-employed tailors for the competition is spread over all aspects of their business. There are two sides to the business of a self-employed tailor, that of the making of new clothes and the repair of old clothing. In both these aspects of the business a self-employed tailor competes with his fellows for custom. An outcome of this is the reduction of charges to prospective customers for services and the willingness to accept credit. Both these types of behaviour are responses to the competitiveness of the economic sphere

[15] Whether or not a person who has recently learnt how to tailor owns a sewing machine depends on the amount of savings and previous employment experience he has. Some tailors, but none included in this study, have learnt their trade late in life, once they have earned sufficient money to buy a sewing machine on which they teach themselves the skill or are taught by someone else; viz. an instance reported by G. Wilson (1942: 36–7).

in which he participates and can cause a tailor to operate his business at a sub-economic level. By this is meant that a tailor's expenditure on cloth, cotton and the maintenance of his machine is not offset by his income from his trade. Because of low charges and a large number of outstanding debts it is difficult for a self-employed tailor to maintain a profitable business.[16]

In contrast to store or factory employed tailors, the self-employed tailor must attract his own custom and find his own market outlets. In addition he is constantly exposed to fluctuations in market demand. By and large, these are not problems for the store or factory tailor who transfers such risks as he encounters to the employers. In the context of open competition in which self-employed tailors are placed it is not surprising that competition between them becomes intense (especially at the markets where they are grouped together in a part specially set aside for them) often manifested in witchcraft and sorcery accusations as is evidenced in Chilwa's labour history. Thus it is to be expected that the majority of tailors prefer work in stores or factories to the problems of self-employment.

Nevertheless, it is possible for the self-employed tailor to exert some control on his economic environment and to make his business profitable. To do this he must build up an extensive network of trading ties, which provides him with market outlets and customers.[17] The lynchpins of the trading networks are clothes salesmen who are the middlemen in both the attraction of customers and the distribution of finished work. But the building of an effective network of trading ties takes time and at the early stages of self-employment a tailor will run the risk of being forced out of business before he has established a profitable trading network.

The above analysis shows how self-employment as a tailor is unattractive when taken as a straight alternative to employment in a store or clothing factory. Self-employment is a reasonable choice only if it is not possible to secure work as a tailor in a store or factory or if factors connected with store or factory work make it less attractive in relation to self-employment. Factors which can make employment in a factory or store less attractive—and that of self-employment correspondingly

[16] Outstanding debts can be a problem even to the moderately successful tailor. Nkoloya, for example, who runs a profitable business after working hours spends a considerable amount of valuable time in debt collection.

[17] I do not deny the existence of other ways by which self-employed tailors can reduce the disadvantage of the circumstances in which they are placed. For example, some tailors co-operate with one or more other tailors, but this appears to be the exception rather than the rule.

more attractive—range from the nature of the work and wage conditions
to the individual's position in the set of social relationships in the factory
or store context. Thus Chilwa left Narayan Bros. after he was the only
tailor on line 1 who did not receive the September wage increment and
after the manager had reduced his status in the eyes of his fellows by
'demoting' him to line 3. But other considerations could explain
Chilwa's action. As his labour history shows, he had been self-employed
in Kabwe before joining Narayan Bros. and, according to his own
statement, was successful. Also, despite his taking of employment at
Narayan Bros., he had continued in his private tailoring business, though
not at the market. Because of this he had maintained many of his ties
into the township clothing trade and self-employment was therefore a
reasonable alternative.

So far this discussion has presented some of the advantages of store
or factory employment in contrast to self-employment. However, I
do not wish to imply that these are the only alternatives open to a
tailor. In fact, a tailor can best exploit his economic environment by
utilising one form of employment to complement the other. Assuming
that people in urban employment wish to maximise their earnings (i.e.
they prefer more cash to less cash), the best strategy which a tailor can
adopt is to utilise his skills and opportunities in as wide an economic
sphere as his skill permits, while at the same time not exposing himself
to unnecessary risk. In these terms the most effective line of action for a
tailor is to maintain a secure base in a factory or store while simultaneously 'raiding the town' for the other economic benefits which it
presents. Of the thirty-seven tailors who worked at the factory over the
period of the study, twenty owned sewing machines (see table 3.5) and
all of these supplemented their income in varying degrees by engaging
in private business outside factory hours. Some distinction must be
made, however, between the factory tailors who derive a regular income
from private business and those who use their skill outside factory
hours only occasionally as a means towards obtaining extra cash. Table
3.5 shows that twelve tailors out of the twenty are engaged in regular
business outside factory hours. These are the two supervisory workers,
six of the line 1 tailors, three line 2 tailors and one line 3 tailor. None of
the remaining tailors earns cash regularly from outside tailoring.

A regular wage from factory work is not only supplemented by
outside work but the regular income is often used to support a tailor's
private business.[18] Thus many tailors use part of their pay to buy cotton

---

[18] One tailor, Mulondo, used his wages from factory work to support both a
private tailoring business and to support a fish trading business. He is in the

Table 3.5 Ownership of sewing machines and tailors who run private businesses

Name	Date present machine bought	Cost of machine	Business after work
Supervisors			
Mukubwa	1965	£45	Full-time
Hastings	1954	£48	Full-time
Line 1 tailors			
Nkoloya	1962	£33 10s	Full-time
Lyashi	1958	£58	Full-time
Chipata	1965	£33 10s	Full-time
Chilwa	1963	No information	Full-time
Abraham	1955	£53	Full-time
Kamwefu	1964	£42	Part-time
Nkumbula	1952	£50	Part-time
Mumba	1964	£33 10s	Part-time
Zulu	1962	£48	Part-time
Lwanga	1960	£60	Full-time
Line 2 tailors			
Mulondo	No information	No information	Part-time*
Kalamba	1964	£55	Part-time
Ibrahim	1965	£50	Full-time
Mateo	1965	£67	Full-time
Seama	1965	£55	Part-time
Paulos	1966	£71	Not yet but intends to
Mpundu	1961	£36	Full-time
Line 3 tailors			
Sandford	1965	£33	Full-time

*Also runs fish-selling business.

and material. Furthermore, Patel takes an indirect interest in their business affairs. He allows tailors to take material and cotton from the factory (although the cost of this is generally debited to them and accrues as debt) and on occasions lends large sums of money some of which is used for their private business.[19] Mukubwa, the head tailor, is

fish business with two other men, who operate from the nearby Lukanga swamps, do all the fishing and market the catch in Kabwe. Mulondo is regarded as the senior partner, as he has used money earned at Narayan Bros. and elsewhere before joining the factory to buy crucial goods such as nets and canoes.

[19] Not all money borrowed from Patel is necessarily ploughed into the business, nor is the borrowing of money restricted to tailors, although it is generally the tailors who are the heaviest in debt.

most heavily in debt (£30 7s 3d) to Patel. A large portion of this debt is attributable to the size and extent of the private business which he runs. Mukubwa has hired two young men to whom he pays £2 per month to sell the clothes which he makes and to measure customers for fittings. His expenditure on materials is often considerable (one month it was £8) and he is frequently not paid for some months after completing the order. This problem is not confined to Mukubwa; Chipata and Nkoloya among others, are constantly faced with the difficulty of bad debts.

The relative security of a regular income and the opportunity to borrow money from Patel permit the tailors concerned to compete favourably with self-employed tailors in the townships. They can afford to allow a degree of credit which might otherwise force out of business a self-employed tailor who does not have the backing of regular cash earned in a store or factory. Another aspect of Patel's extension of credit facilities to his employees (and in particular to those tailors engaged in private business) is that, in their eyes, it gives them an opportunity to save. A general attitude prevails among the factory workers that if an individual wishes both to accumulate savings and to keep these savings relatively intact it is better to go into debt to Patel than to break into his savings. The presence of this attitude explains the pattern recorded for those tailors who have quite large amounts of cash in savings bank accounts to prefer becoming indebted to Patel rather than drawing on these savings.[20]

Debt facilities and the system of debt relationships in which many of the factory employees are involved with management and, with special reference to the tailors, the symbiosis of store or factory employment with other economic activities in town has other consequences for factory behaviour. These other consequences will be discussed later in the chapter. The important point at present is that the combination of factory employment with private business allows tailors to exploit their economic environment to their best advantage.

The factors which shape the career pattern of the tailors are also influential for the unskilled workers in the factory. Like the tailors, both ironers and cotton boys are dependent in their urban moves on kin and home friends, these latter being no less important, as in the case of the tailors, for the securement of employment. But there are also marked differences. Unlike many of the tailors, the unskilled workers do not

[20] Arensberg (1959: 168–80) describes how shopkeepers, through extending credit, are able to bind their customers to them. In the same way Patel, by placing some of his employees in his debt, binds them to the factory. This has some consequences for labour turnover and will be discussed in a later section of this chapter.

participate in other areas of the urban economy. Undoubtedly this is connected with their lack of skill, but even so it is possible for unskilled workers to participate in other economic ventures in town which do not require skill, such as fish trading, clothes-hawking, etc. Basically, the unskilled factory employees are on the same wage rates as the other workers; however, Patel is not willing to extend them large amounts of credit (except for Chisokone, who is unskilled but in a supervisory position) which is perhaps one of the factors preventing them from becoming involved in other economic ventures. At this point it is only fair to state that this also applies to some of the tailors, especially on lines 2 and 3.

There are two main principles which operate in the factory which induce Patel to advance credit. The first relates to the degree of trust which exists in Patel's relationship with a possible debtor. Trust is connected with the extent to which Patel can expect some future repayment of the debt and such an expectation is stronger between Patel and those workers who have been employed in the factory for a relatively long period of time. Secondly, Patel's advancing of credit is influenced by his dependence on certain workers for the production system in the factory. This dependence is related to two considerations, one being the degree to which a worker because of his skill and/or task is critical to the production process, the other being the extent to which Patel requires their support in his attempts to control the work behaviour of the other employees. For example, Patel often relies on the support of Chisokone and Meshak when he is drawn into dispute with some of his employees. His advancement of large sums of credit to them is one way by which he attempts to secure their support. Furthermore, Patel is disposed to give more credit to those workers who are important to the production system because the bestowing of such benefits binds the worker to the factory by increasing the advantages of his current work place relative to other job opportunities. The implications of this argument will be discussed in greater detail in the section on labour turnover but, generally, as is expected from such an argument, those who are not so critical to the production system, such as ironers and cotton boys, and who have generally worked in the factory for relatively short periods of time, if advanced credit at all, have only small credit allowances given them.

But other factors apart from the degree to which a person can depend on credit facilities will influence an individual's choice to extend his interests into other areas of his economic environment. The profitable establishment of other business enterprises, as I have previously argued, takes time and therefore the non-involvement of the unskilled worker (as well as some of the more skilled employees) in outside cash ventures will relate to the length of time he has been in the job and in town—which affects the extent to which the necessary business ties have been built up—and the degree to which he wishes to commit himself both to the job and to the town. Most of the unskilled employees and many of the skilled workers have not been in the town and/or employment long enough for them to have established the necessary ties for them to embark on outside business. In addition many of them do not wish to commit themselves to their job or the town for any extended period of time and, particularly in the case of the cotton boys, are continually on the look out for more attractive job opportunities. Investment in outside business ventures results in a feedback in terms of commitment. For if an individual tends to try his fortune in other jobs either in Kabwe or elsewhere the time he expends in building up the necessary contacts and the cost of the initial capital outlay will be wasted.

The analysis, directed mainly towards the tailors, has traced the various factors which influence individuals to choose tailoring as a career and then lead them to choose between the alternatives of wage employment or self-employment or to combine both. A general point which has emerged is that the current employment of the tailors as well as the unskilled factory workers is a consequence of a set of previous choices and decisions. These choices and decisions become relevant and are made in accordance with the particular set of socio-economic conditions and social relationships in which the individuals concerned are or become involved. I then turned to a discussion of the credit facilities which are open to certain tailors. At this point the analysis changed from a concentration on the processes which are general to all those who choose tailoring as a career to an emphasis on the particular aspects of the factory context which influences career opportunity and choice. I continue this emphasis in the next section with a closer attention to particular aspects of the factory social composition.

Recruitment to the factory

The argument I now present is that particular features of the social composition of the factory are related to two main factors operating in the work context. These are (a) the attributes looked for in prospective employees by the factory manager, and (b) the control over recruitment exerted by certain of the employees. First, however, I will outline some

Table 3.6 Proportional representation according to age and occupation (June, September and January)

Age	Supervisory June	Supervisory Sept.	Supervisory Jan.	Skilled June	Skilled Sept.	Skilled Jan.	Unskilled June	Unskilled Sept.	Unskilled Jan.	Totals June	Totals Sept.	Totals Jan.
15-24							100.0 4+	100.0 8+	100.0 6+	4	8	6
25-34				50.0 6-	50.0 6-	76.9 10+	50.0 6+	50.0 6+	23.1 3-	12	12	13
35-44	10.5 2+	11.1 2+	5.9	68.4 13+	66.7 12+	64.7 11+	21.1 4-	22.2 4-	29.4 5-	19	18	17
45-54				100.0 6+	100.0 7+	100.0 8+				6	7	8
55+			100.0 1+	100.0 1+	100.0 1+					1	1	1
% total	4.8 2+	4.3 2+	4.4 1+	61.9. 1+	56.5 1+	64.4	33.3	39.1	31.1			
Total	2	2	2	26	26	29	14	18	14	42	46	45

+ Indicates that this age category is over-represented.
- Indicates that this age category is under-represented.

Table 3.7 Proportional representation according to occupation and province of origin (June, September and January)

	Supervisory			Skilled			Unskilled			Totals		
	June	Sept.	Jan.	June	Sept.	Jan.	June	Sept.	Jan.	June	Sept.	Jan.
Central Province	9.1 1+	8.3 1+	7.7 1+	36.4 4-	41.7 5-	46.2 6-	54.5 6+	50.0 6+	46.2 6+	11	12	13
Luapula Province				100.0 1+	100.0 1+	100.0 1+	100.0 1+			1	1	1
Western Province							100.0 1+			1		
Northern Province	9.1 1+	9.1 1+		54.5 6-	36.4 4-	75.0 6-	36.4 4+	54.5 6+	25.0 2+	11	11	8
Eastern Province				90.0 9+	75.0 9+	76.9 10+	10.0 1	25.0 3-	23.1 3-	10	12	13
Southern Province							100.0 1+	100.0 1+	100.0 1+	1	1	1
Malawi			16.7 1+	100.0 5+	85.7 6+	66.7 4-		14.2 1-	16.7 1-	5	7	6
Tanzania							100.0 1+	100.0 1+	50.0 1	1	1	2
Mozambique				100.0 1+	100.0 1+	100.0 1+				1	1	1
Total outside Zambia			50.0 1+	23.1 6+	26.9 7+	20.7 6+	7.1 1-	11.1 2-	14.3 2-	7	9	9
% total	4.8 2	4.3 2	4.4 2	61.9 26	56.5 26	64.4 29	33.3 14	39.1 18	31.1 14	42	46	45
Totals	2	2	2	26	26	29	14	18	14	42	46	45

+ Indicates that province of origin is over-represented.

Table 3.8 Proportional representation according to ethnic category and occupation (June, September and January)

	Supervisory			Skilled			Unskilled			Totals		
	June	Sept.	Jan.	June	Sept.	Jan.	June	Sept.	Jan.	June	Sept.	Jan.
Northern matrilineal	8.7 2+	9.1 2+	4.8 1+	52.2 12-	45.5 10-	61.9 13-	39.1 9+	45.5 10+	53.3 7+	23	22	21
Central matrilineal				33.3 1-	33.3 1-	50.0 1-	66.7 2+	66.7 2+	50.0 1+	3	3	2
Eastern matrilineal			6.7 1+	83.3 10+	73.3 11+	66.7 10+	16.6 2-	26.7 4-	26.7 4-	12	15	15
Northern patrilineal				50.0 1-	50.0 2-	60.0 3-	50.0 1+	50.0 2+	40.0 2+	2	4	5
Southern patrilineal				100.0 2+	100.0 2+	100.0 1+				2	2	1
South-eastern patrilineal						100.0 1+						1
% totals	4.8	4.3	4.4	61.9	56.5	64.4	33.3	39.1	31.1			
Totals	2	2	2	26	26	29	14	18	14	42	46	45

+ Indicates that tribal category is over-represented.
− Indicates that tribal category is under-represented.

of the major social characteristics of the factory population. An examination of these social characteristics establishes some empirical problems which can be explained through reference to the recruitment process.

Tables 3.6–10 show that the workers are disproportionately represented in the factory, generally and in specific occupations, according to age, ethnic category and district and province of origin. This is not explicable by general reference to the demographic structure of the Kabwe population from which the factory labour force is drawn.

Table 3.9   Proportional representation of employees according to ethnic c

Age	Northern matrilineal			Central matrilineal			Eastern matrilineal	
	June	Sept.	Jan.	June	Sept.	Jan.	June	Sep
15-24	75.0 3+	62.5 5+	50.0 3+	25.0 1+				25. 2-
25-34	50.0 6-	33.3 4-	30.8 4-	8.3 1+	8.3 1+	7.7 1+	33.3 4+	41. 5+
35-44	57.9 11+	55.6 10+	58.8 10+				26.3 5-	27. 5-
45-54	50.0 3-	57.1 4+	50.0 4+	16.7 1+	14.3 1+	12.5 1+	33.3 2+	28. 2-
55+							100.0 1+	100. 1+
% total	54.8	50.0	46.7	7.1	4.3	4.4	28.6	32.
Total	23	23	21	3	2	2	12	15

+ Indicates that tribal category is over-represented.
- Indicates that tribal category is under-represented.

Table 3.6 shows that tailors are over-represented in the 35+ age categories while those in unskilled work are over-represented in the age categories 34 and below. This tends to be the same for all the three time periods indicated. Both these patterns are a departure from what can be expected if specific processes operating in the factory are not considered. If the social composition of the factory reflected that of the municipality then we could expect a more equal proportion of unskilled workers in the 34 and below categories to those in the 35+ age categories. Survey information on the municipal African residents indicates an even distribution of males in all age categories through all kinds of unskilled work. With reference to the tailors we could also expect a higher proportion of tailors in the age categories 34 and below. Nearly all the tailors 35 years and above entered the factory after their 35th birthday.

This is not because, as discussed earlier in this chapter, the factory tailors learnt their skill at a late stage in their employed life. Neither is it because tailors tend to enter store or factory employment at a later stage in the practise of their trade. Moreover, my general observations in Kabwe indicate that there are more tailors in the 34 and below age categories than would appear to be so from my Narayan Bros. data.

Tables 3.7 and 3.8 show the degree to which the factory work force is over or under-represented according to place of origin and according to

(June, September and January)

n neal		Southern patrilineal			South-eastern patrilineal			Totals		
Sept.	Jan.	June	Sept.	Jan.	June	Sept.	Jan.	June	Sept.	Jan.
12.5 1+	16.7 1+							4	8	6
8.3 1-	14.6 2+	8.3 1+	8.3 1+					12	12	13
11.1 2+	11.7 2+	5.3 1+	5.6 1+	5.9 1+				19	18	17
							12.5 1+	6	7	8
								1	1	1
8.7 4	11.1 5	4.8 2	4.3 2	2.2 1			2.2 1	42	46	45

the major cultural categories. The problem which arises here does not relate so much to the general representation of the workers according to these categories (for it will be clear in the description that this representation follows broadly the pattern for the municipality) but rather why the workers in these categories should be disproportionately distributed in the various age and occupational categories. Thus, as is the case for the municipality as a whole, the majority of employees at all periods have come from districts close to Kabwe in the Central Province. The other areas which provide the bulk of the remaining work force are the districts in the Northern and Eastern provinces of Zambia and districts in neighbouring Malawi.

The preponderance of employees in the factory from the Central, Northern and Eastern provinces and from Malawi explains the ethnic origin of most of the workers (table 3.7). The majority of the employees

Table 3.10 Proportional representation according to province and age
(June, September and January)

	Zambia							
	Central			Luapula			Southern	
Age	June	Sept.	Jan.	June	Sept.	Jan.	June	Sep
15-24	25.0 1-	25.0 2-	33.3 2+					
25-34	16.7 2-	16.7 2-	15.4 2-				8.3 1+	8 1
35-44	31.6 6+	38.9 7+	47.1 8+	5.3 1+	5.6 1+	5.9 1+		
45-54	33.3 2+	28.6 2+	25.0 2-					
55+								
% total	26.2	28.3	31.1	2.4	2.2	2.2	2.4	2
Total	11	13	14	1	1	1	1	1

belong to either one or the other of the two broad cultural categories formed by the Northern and Eastern matrilineal peoples. Broadly, the Northern matrilineal peoples can be distinguished from the Eastern matrilineal both linguistically and in their forms of social and economic organisation. Within the Northern matrilineal category the ethnic groups most represented in the factory are the Lala, Bemba and Bisa. For the Eastern matrilineal peoples employees who regarded themselves as Nsenga are the most heavily represented, the remainder of the employees in this category belong to the Chewa, Nganja, Lakeside Tonga and Yao ethnic groups.

Workers from the Central Province show a clear tendency (for each of the months taken) to be over-represented in the older age categories between 35 and 54. In comparison, employees from the Northern and Eastern provincial areas, although this does vary for each of the months taken, tend to be over-represented in the 15–34 age categories and in the 45 and over age categories with a marked under-representation in the middle 35–44 age category. The other important place of origin for many of the factory workers, Malawi, indicates a similar pattern to that for the Eastern Province. The Northern matrilineal peoples appear to be evenly distributed through all age categories but in fact are under-represented in the 25–34 age category. This is not the case for employees who belong to the Eastern matrilineal groups who are clearly over-represented in the 25–34 age category but under-represented in the 35–44 age category.

Not only, in accordance with the above description, are certain ethnic

Western			Northern			Eastern		
June	Sept.	Jan.	June	Sept.	Jan.	June	Sept.	Jan.
25.0			50.0	37.5	16.7		25.0	33.3
1+			2+	3+	1-		2+	2+
			41.7	33.3	30.8	25.0	25.0	23.1
			5+	4+	4+	3+	3+	3-
			21.1	11.1	5.9	15.8	16.7	17.6
			4-	2-	1-	3-	3-	3-
			16.7	28.6	25.0	50.0	42.9	50.0
			1-	2+	2+	3+	3+	4+
2.4			28.6	23.9	17.8	23.8	23.9	26.7
1			12	11	8	9	11	12

Concluded overleaf

and broad cultural categories over- or under-represented in both the factory generally and in particular age categories, but the factory workers, insofar as they are represented in each of the ethnic and cultural categories, are disproportionately distributed in skilled and unskilled occupations in the factory. Employees from the Central and Northern provinces contribute significantly to the work force (together with the Eastern Province and Malawi). They are under-represented in skilled work but over-represented in unskilled work. The pattern is reversed for workers from the Eastern Province and Malawi, who are over-represented in skilled occupations (see table 3.7). This marked tendency continues to be evidenced in the differential distribution of the various ethnic categories in skilled and unskilled work. To achieve some understanding of the disproportionate representation of the employees according to the aspects just discussed I now turn to a consideration of the main factors influencing recruitment to the factory.

Patel's main effort in controlling the recruitment of employees is directed to the hiring of tailors. The basic attributes he looks for in a prospective employee are skill and experience in the trade. The best evidence for Patel of a tailor's skill and experience is previous employment in an Indian- or European-owned store or factory. But Patel also frequently seeks the advice of Mukubwa, Chisokone or Hastings in the hiring of new workers. At least one of these workers always assists him in the interviewing of job applicants. Mukubwa or Hastings are regularly consulted by Patel in hiring tailors, while Chisokone's influence on Patel is mainly confined to the employment of unskilled workers.

Table 3.10 concluded

| Age | Outside Zambia | | | | | | | | | Total | |
| | Tanzania | | | Malawi | | | Mozambique | | | | |
	June	Sept.	Jan.	June	Sept.	Jan.	June	Sept.	Jan.	June	Sept.
15-24					12.5 1-	16.7 1+				4	8
25-34			7.7 1+	8.3 1-	16.7 2+	15.4 2+				12	12
35-44	5.3 1+	5.6 1+	5.9 1+	15.8 3+	16.7 3+	11.8 2-	5.3 1+	5.6 1+	5.9 1+	19	18
45-54										6	7
55+				100.0 1+	100.0 1+	100.0 1+				1	1
% total	2.4	2.2	4.4	11.9	15.2	13.3	2.4	2.2	2.2		
Total	1	1	2	5	7	6	1	1	1	42	46

The basis for either Mukubwa or Hastings' advice is not unbiased. Other factors not related to an applicant's skill such as his membership of a certain ethnic category or origin in a specific district or provincial area are important considerations affecting their advice. Related to this, however, and possibly of greater importance for the recruitment patterns to the factory is the knowledge communicated through kinship and friendship ties (*viz.* the case of Nkoloya, above), that Hastings, Mukubwa and Chisokone have senior work positions at Narayan Bros. This influences the type of person who applies for work, the applicants to the factory generally coming from the ethnic categories and rural areas of the three senior men on the factory floor.

The significance of kinship and friendship ties to men who have some control or influence in the finding of work, or common membership of ethnic or other social categories with these individuals, is clearly evidenced in the institution of sponsorship. Many of the employees were sponsored for their job by a friend or kinsman already employed on the premises. Mukubwa, Hastings and Chisokone most frequently act as sponsors. But other employees also act as sponsors, the degree of notice which Patel takes of their advice depending on their skill and/or the prominence which they have assumed in the sphere of factory political and social relationships. Thus (see table 3.11) Lyashi, Chipata, Nkumbula, Kamwefu and Meshak have all acted as sponsors for other workers being recruited to the factory. All, with the exception of Meshak, are skilled workers employed on line 1 and all, excepting Nkumbula, have some prominence in the political and social relationships of the factory. Table 3.11 shows the factory workers who

Table 3.11 Sponsors and the employees sponsored

Sponsor	Occupation	Sponsored	Tribe	Occupation	Province /country of origin
Mukubwa	Head tailor	Chipata	Ngoni	Tailor, line 1	Central
Lala		Mumba	Nsenga	Tailor, line 1	Eastern
(Central		Nyirenda	Tumbuka	Tailor, line 3	Malawi
Province)		Nkoloya	Kunda	Tailor, line 1	Eastern
		Iyashi	Bemba	Tailor, line 1	Northern
		Zakeyo	Nsenga	Tailor, line 3	Eastern
Hastings	Lead tailor	Mateo	Nganja	Tailor, line 2	Malawi
Chewa		Kalamba	Yao	Tailor, line 2	Malawi
(Malawi)		Ibrahim	Yao	Tailor, line 2	Mozambique
		Chilwa	Lakeside Tonga	Tailor, line 1	Malawi
		Lundazi	Nsenga	Cotton boy	Malawi
		Mpande	Nsenga	Cotton boy	Eastern
Chisokone	Cutter rel.	Henry	Bisa	Cotton boy and tailor, line 2	Northern
Bemba		Joseph	Bisa	Cotton boy and tailor, line 2	Northern
(Northern Province)		Peter	Bemba	Cotton boy	Northern
		Kalonga	Bisa	Cotton boy and ironer	Northern
		Chilufya	Bemba	Cotton boy	Northern
Chipata	Tailor, line 1	Mulondo	Lala	Tailor, line 2	Central
Ngoni (born in Kabwe)		Mabange	Nyakyusa	Ironer	Tanzania
(Eastern Province)		Nelson	Tumbuka	Cotton boy	Eastern
Iyashi	Tailor, line 1	Chipalo	Bemba	Tailor, line 1	Northern
Bemba (Northern Province)					
Kamwefu	Tailor, line 1	Seams	Kabende	Tailor, line 2	Luapula
Bisa (Northern Province)					
Nkumbula	Tailor, line 1	Meshak	Ambo	Button machiner	Central
Soli (Central Province)					
Meshak	Button machiner	Adrian	Nsenga	Button machiner	Central
Ambo (Central Province)					
Former employer		William		Cotton boy	
		Christian		Cotton boy	

were sponsored to the factory and the employees who sponsored them. In most of the cases the sponsor is a kinsman, friend and/or fellow tribesman. An illustration of the process where an individual gives his sponsorship is shown in the case of Chipata's sponsoring of Mulondo.

The sponsoring of Mulondo

Mulondo is a Lala who comes from Serenje district in the Central Province. All his employment experience has been in Kabwe, although this has been punctuated by short visits to see relatives at his home village and to other urban areas such as Wankie (Rhodesia), Lusaka and the towns on the Copperbelt. Prior to his arrival at Narayan Bros., Mulondo had had only one previous job, which was at another Indian store in Kabwe, where he entered employment as a tailor in 1944. Consequently it came as a shock to him when he was laid off when, as his Indian employer stated, the store could no longer afford to pay his wages. The loss of employment was an even greater blow to Mulondo, for it was with his earnings in the store that he had been able to finance a small fish trading business based in the Lukanga swamps. Although he fell back for a few months on the income derived from this small business, it was not enough to sustain him in the type of life style to which he had grown accustomed before his dismissal. Expenditure on various fishing requisites was often considerable (such as on nylon line, nets and hooks) and the profit fluctuated. This made it difficult for him to pay his house rent, which in fact went unpaid as early as the first month after he had left employment. Furthermore, his partners in the business lived in the Lukanga swamps and used his house as a place to stay on arrival in town with fish for sale. It was imperative, therefore, not only in order to maintain his current living standard but also for the business that he should find another job.

Among Mulondo's acquaintances in town was Chipata, with whom he had worked at the Indian store and who had left of his own accord some eighteen months previously. Knowing that Chipata worked at Narayan Bros., Mulondo decided to ask Chipata whether he could assist him in finding work there. On the occasion he visited Chipata at his home Chisokone was also present. Mulondo drew Chipata outside and asked him whether there was work at Narayan Bros., and Chipata replied that he thought so, but that they had better return inside and ask Chisokone, as he was the important man. Chipata introduced Mulondo to Chisokone and told him that Mulondo was looking for work. Chisokone remained aloof, saying that he had known Mulondo many years earlier. He followed this up with the statement 'I am the branch secretary of UNIP, and I have never seen you at party section meetings.' Mulondo hurriedly offered excuses, saying that he had been away visiting relatives and was unable to attend. He was visibly embarrassed, for he is a member of the Jehovah's Witness sect, which forbids participation in political party activities. Mulondo lives in the township (*Bwacha*) where Chisokone is an influential official, and Chisokone was well aware of Mulondo's religious affiliation. Chisokone took no further notice of Mulondo's excuses and left the house for his home.

Although Chipata was also an influential political official, his friendship with Mulondo established at their previous work place overrode such political/religious opposition as could have damaged their relationship. Chipata, despite Chisokone's obvious antagonism, promised to raise the matter with Patel. The following morning at the start of work Chipata arrived at the factory accompanied by Mulondo. Patel was then told by Chipata that a friend of Chipata's would like to work at the factory, and at Patel's request he told him where he had been working. Patel then came and spoke with Mulondo and, apparently satisfied, hired him.

In the above case ethnic affiliation did not play a part in Chipata's sponsoring of Mulondo (the former is a Ngoni while the latter is a Lala);[21] the influential factor was their friendship, based on their having previously been co-workers. One other aspect which arises from this case is related to the way Chisokone used Mulondo's non-affiliation to the political party as a basis for not giving his support in his quest. Although Chisokone did not prevent him from joining the factory, Chisokone's behaviour does highlight the way influential employees in the work context affect the selection of new employees to the factory.

The role of all those mentioned above in influencing the selection of new recruits, both tailors and non-tailors, into the factory partly accounts for the preponderance of employees from certain ethnic categories and rural areas in the factory generally, and in certain occupations. It is noticeable that all those who assist Patel in the recruitment of new employees or who sponsor them come from those ethnic groups and rural areas which supply the bulk of the factory work force. That these men also come within the higher wage categories certainly influences, in relation to the tailors at least, the tendency for people employed in skilled work to belong to the high age categories as well. But this does not explain the problem of the reverse pattern for unskilled work where there is a marked tendency for workers to be drawn from the lower age categories.

As for tailors, sponsorship plays a part in the recruitment of employees into unskilled work. Chisokone's role as a sponsor as well as his influence with Patel for the employment of workers into this category is clearly demonstrated in table 3.8, where a very high representation of employees from Northern matrilineal groups is evident.[22] The falling by January of employees in unskilled occupations from these ethnic groups was due to turnover, and to a limited extent promotion, as also the fact that Patel did not wish to hire more people to fill the vacancies created. This was largely because in September Patel hired six girls,[23] who assumed some of the duties of the cotton boys, the occupation which had accounted for most of the employees in unskilled work.

But in addition, although not influential for the ethnic composition,

[21] Although I have no clear evidence in this instance, it is possible that their friendship was established on the basis of an institutionalised tribal joking relationship. In town Ngoni recognise an institutionalised tribal joking relationship with those they categorise as Bemba; Mulondo is a Lala, a tribe which is generally categorised by Ngoni as being Bemba.

[22] Chisokone, in fact, was able to obtain employment in the factory for a number of his own junior relatives, Peter, Kalonga, Henry, Joseph and Chilufya.

[23] Mukubwa and Hastings supplied all the cotton girls from the ranks of their relatives.

the tendency for Patel to prefer young people in unskilled work is important for explaining the relative youth of unskilled employees. Patel's preference for hiring young men to unskilled work is mainly restricted to the cotton boys and does not include the ironers. The work of cotton boys demands no previous experience, and Patel feels it desirable to employ young men whom he believes are likely to be respectful of authority, and whom, initially at least (depending on such factors as the degree of their youth), he can employ at half the normal hourly rate.[24] Patel's selection of employees to unskilled work on these terms explains much of the general pattern in age which those in unskilled work display.

It is expected that the factory would assume many of the broad social characteristics of the population represented in Kabwe, for it is from this population that the factory draws its labour. Nevertheless, the above discussion has shown that various selection processes operate. In particular, the emphasis lay in showing how some of the senior workers in the factory influenced Patel in making his selection from various job applicants and themselves sponsored workers to employment in the factory. This process of selection is related to the structure and organisation of the factory in at least two important ways. First, the selection is largely controlled and influenced by employees who have important positions in the factory work structure, such as supervisory employees and line 1 tailors, and/or who are of long service, relatively highly skilled and experienced, and are influential in the sphere of factory political relations. Second, the nature of these workers' influence in the selection process has implications both for the relationship between the respective employees and Patel and for these employees' relationships with other workers in the factory and amongst themselves. Thus, as with Patel's advancement of credit discussed earlier, that Patel encourages and allows certain of his workers to assist him in recruiting employees is an indication of the degree of trust in his relationship with them and can be used to create stronger bonds between these employees and himself. An example of the latter process is provided by Chipata. Prior to August, Chipata had not been important in the area of factory politics but, for a variety of reasons described in subsequent chapters, he later became more prominent. During this latter period it became increasingly apparent that Patel was entering

[24] Some evidence of this latter aspect being an important part in Patel's hiring preferences is his employment of the cotton girls. These had just left school and were unmarried and his employment of them at 6d per hour met with no disapproval from the other workers, such a wage being regarded as a fair one for girls who were both young and unmarried.

into more frequent contact with him (in an effort to win his support), one feature of this being his seeking of Chipata's assistance in the hiring of new employees. Moreover, the influence which senior workers have in the selection of new employees (exemplified by Mukubwa, Hastings and Chisokone) has the effect of consolidating their positions of authority and power in the work context. By influencing Patel's decision to recruit certain applicants and not others and by sponsoring new employees each builds up a body of workers who are personally indebted to him for employment and who, because of this, may be obligated to support their sponsor at times of crisis. Of course, various social processes which operate in the factory context may reduce the likelihood of a particular worker's supporting his sponsor. But it is important towards the understanding of later analyses in subsequent chapters that some of the alliances and coalitions which form in the factory in relation to specific events and disputes are based on relationships established at the very outset of or even before an individual's entry to the factory.

So far the above discussion has focused on the several processes which affect the selection of workers to the factory but what are the factors which induce employees to remain in or move out of it?

Labour migration and factory turnover I stated at the beginning of this chapter that labour turnover accounts for the continual change in the social composition of the factory. My aim in this section is to isolate the main factors which relate to turnover. In so doing the analysis will be primarily directed towards ascertaining the extent to which factors general to all urban migration or factors specific to the factory context influence this pattern of labour turnover. One theme should become clear as the analysis progresses. This is that general factors which direct and influence the pattern of decisions in relation to migratory and job careers have their effects increased by the operation of factors specific to the factory context. Related to this theme is the proposition that factors general to the migratory and job careers of all migrants establish a set of conditions which determines the way factors specific to the clothing factory operate differentially on the employees.

Table 3.12 shows that over an eight-month observation period (June 1965 to February 1966) the turnover was 38·7.[25] Thirty of the

---

[25] The turnover index for the factory was calculated in accordance with the following formula:

$$TI = \frac{\text{Accessions} + \text{Separations}}{\text{Size of plant at start of period} + \text{Size of plant at end of period}} \times 100$$

Workers who during the fieldwork left or went on leave for periods of up to

forty-two workers employed on the premises at the start of the study were still working there at the end. Workers who left the factory were replaced by new recruits, the mean number of male employees for the eight month period being 42·9. Two general patterns can be discerned when the rate of turnover for the factory is examined. First, the highest

Table 3.12   Number of factory workers leaving and starting employment over an eight-month period

Occupation	No. employed in June 1965	No. leaving between June and January	No. starting between June and January	No. employed in January
Supervisors	2	1	–	2
Line 1 tailors*	12	3	1	12
Line 2 tailors	6	2	4	8
Line 3 tailors	8	3	4	9
Button machiners	2	–	–	2
Ironers	4	2	2	6
Cotton boys	8	5	8	6
Total	42	16	19	45

* These figures include individuals who left employment and were re-employed during the eight-month period.
The lead tailor has been included on line 1 for June, where he was then working.

Turnover index:

$$\frac{\text{Accessions} + \text{separations}}{\text{Size of plant at start of period} + \text{size of plant at end of period}} = \frac{19 + 16}{42 + 45}$$

therefore percentage turnover = 38.7

rate of turnover occurs in the unskilled worker category and in the age categories 35 years and below. Although eight of the sixteen workers who left the factory employment during the fieldwork period were skilled, data on the length of service of the employees (table 3.13) indicates that the skilled workers have been employed continuously in the factory for the longest periods of time. The value of this observation is increased

a month were not counted as leavers (or separations) in the calculation of the index. Hartshorne, in his classic article (1940), was the first, to my knowledge, to suggest the use of this turnover index. Chaplin (1968: 75–8) submits this index to some criticism and suggests refinements but nevertheless uses it in his own calculations. A thorough discussion of turnover indices in an African context is given by Bell (1963) in a study of a Rhodesian manufacturing industry. In association with Mitchell, Bell develops a method which takes account of the differing rates of turnover over time. The number of workers employed at Narayan Bros. is too small for such an analysis to be very meaningful.

Table 3.13 Occupation and length of continuous service

Occupation	Number	Less than one year	Years 1-4	5-9	10-15	15+	Total
Supervisors	3	-	-	-	1	2	3
Tailors 1	15	4	5	2	3	1	15
2	9	5	3	-	1	-	9
3	11	8	3	-	-	-	11
Buttons	2	-	-	-	2	-	2
Ironers	6	4	2	-	-	-	6
Cotton boys	10	9	1	-	-	-	10
Total	56	30	14	2	7	3	56

These figures are based on the length of time workers were employed in the factory up to the time I left the field or they left work.

when the attitudes of the employees towards remaining in or leaving employment is taken into account. Table 3.14 shows that it is the skilled workers who voiced attitudes which indicated their intention to stay, whereas the unskilled employees expressed attitudes to the effect that they would shortly leave employment. The rate of turnover correlates with age in a way similar to its correlation with skill. Eight of the sixteen

Table 3.14 Attitudes to continued employment: a December 1965 survey of employee attitudes

	Unstable	Temporary	Stabilised	Total
Supervisory	-	1	1	2
Line 1 tailors	1	2	9	12
Line 2 tailors	-	2	6	8
Line 3 tailors	3	1	1	5
Button machiners	-	2	-	2
Ironers	-	1	2	3
Cotton boys	6	3	1	10
Total	10	12	20	42

'Unstable' includes all responses which indicated that the individuals concerned would leave within a year.
'Temporary' includes all responses which indicated that the individuals concerned would leave within one to four years.
'Stabilised' includes all responses which indicated that the individuals concerned would remain in employment for at least five years.

workers who left employment over the period of observation were
under 35 years of age. This is further supported by the evidence
contained in table 3.13, where it is shown that the workers employed
continuously for the longest periods of time in the factory are those in
the 35 and above age categories. A second pattern which is clear when
the rate of turnover for the factory is examined is the tendency for most
workers to leave the factory after only a relatively short period of
employment in it. Nine of the sixteen workers who left had been employed in the factory for less than a year. The mean length of employment for those who left the factory was 1·63 years (median 0·5) which
contrasts with the mean length of employment for those workers who
remained of 3·2 (median 2·5).

This pattern of labour turnover must be explained. I regard this as
necessary in order to demonstrate to the reader that the patterns I
observed for one point in time are likely to be repeated over time,
assuming that the conditions which prevailed during the period of my
observations remained constant. It is also necessary because such an
explanation should enable me to predict which sectors of the work force
are likely to be most subject to turnover in the future. An assumption
which underlies my general argument is that the behaviour exhibited by
individuals in the factory will be affected by the extent to which they
expect to participate in it in the future.

Central to the following discussion is the view that processes underlying labour turnover and the general process of migration behaviour
are closely related. Both, therefore, should be subject to explanation in
terms of the one analytical framework. The analytical model I use
constitutes a departure from the static 'push–pull' models commonly
applied by those interested in migration studies.[26] Most studies of
migration 'have too frequently called for no more than description of the
characteristics of migrants *at one point or another in time* while on the
move. They fail adequately to describe the experiential chains, or
chains of events rather than single factors, that account for decisions to
move' (Shannon, 1969: 37). The approach I adopt is one which views
the choice or decision of an individual to move at any one point in time
as a consequence both of the choices and decisions he has made in the
past and the choices he is oriented towards in the future. Two concepts
are of particular importance to the analytical model I use. They are
commitment and *investment.*

In chapter 2 I defined commitment as a function of the degree to

[26] A general criticism of so-called 'push–pull' models of labour migration has
been made by Garbett and Kapferer (1970).

which the investment of an individual in a set of social relationships reduces the attractiveness of investing in an alternative set of relationships. Defined here, investment simply refers to the expenditure which an individual has made in time, energy, emotion or things of a more material kind. The degree of commitment can be measured according to the extent to which the possible gains from investing in an alternative set of relationships exceeds or is less than the costs incurred from relinquishing the benefits received from current investments, as the individual perceives these. Translated to the problem of migration, commitment to a particular town exists when a migrant has invested in a set of socio-economic and political relationships so much so that the gains of pursuing other opportunities, which would entail his movement to a rural area or another town, would not exceed the costs such a move would involve.[27] In other words the probability of a move would be high if the perceived gains exceeded the perceived costs and the probability of a move would be low if the perceived gains were less than the perceived costs. It follows from this argument that the probability of a move would be even if the gains from the move are equal to the costs. However, it is highly unlikely that individuals can assess precisely gains against costs. Experience in Kabwe suggests that in so far as individuals do assess gains against costs they do this in vague and general terms. I consider, therefore, that individuals would only contemplate a move if the gains, from their perspective, *clearly* outweighed the costs. There is an added reason why this should be so, provided it can be assumed that individuals organise their behaviour along lines which minimise risk and uncertainty. Given this assumption, the more gains obviously exceed costs the lower the risk and uncertainty to which an individual would be subject.

The value accorded to investments is of fundamental importance in arguing costs and gains. Before I proceed with the analysis it must be emphasised that the value of investments need not remain constant over time and cannot be adequately assessed if the value of each investment is assessed separately from the other investments. The value of investments and consequently the degree of commitment changes over

[27] The model proposed here bears a marked resemblance to the money-income models used by some economists to explain migration. An example is the one developed by Sjaarstad (1962). Models such as Sjaarstad's, which emphasise only money costs and benefits of migration, have been severely criticised by other economists for their neglect of more sociological considerations. An extremely interesting critique of such an approach is that by Nelson (1959). It should be evident to the reader that my analysis is not confined to investments which can be subjected to relatively easy measurement, i.e. money costs and gains.

time. For example, time itself constitutes an investment and can lead to increased commitment. Thus the length of time an individual spends in one urban centre can have the effect of increasing his commitment to this urban centre. But the value of time as an investment may decrease after a labour migrant has passed the mid-point of his able-bodied career and the possibility of making other investments, which at one time were regarded as low in value, have their value correspondingly increased. Thus the more a migrant approaches retirement age the lower the value he is likely to place on the time which he has invested in the urban centre of his migration.

As the value of investments can change over time, so the value of one investment cannot be assessed in isolation from others. For example, the value of an individual's investment in his job may be dependent on other investments such as having a wife and children.

Factors relevant to the point migrants have reached in their life, migratory and job careers permit inferences to be made as to the likely distribution and type of their investments and the value they are likely to place on these investments. These factors are age, the point an individual has reached in his urban and labour career, marital status, skill and education. Although some of these factors constitute investments in themselves (e.g. marital status, skill and education) I have isolated them because on the basis of my own and others' field experience in Central and Southern Africa they allow a relatively accurate statement to be made as to the distribution and type of a migrant's investments.[28] But the factors selected have another significance. Because these factors are relevant in varying ways to the migration behaviour of all migrants they facilitate an assessment of the extent to which factors underlying the general migration process also explain the differential rate of turnover in the factory.

Some of the factors I have selected are closely interrelated. Thus the age of a migrant has some connection with the length of time he has been on the labour market, his marital status and frequently the level of his education. For example, men between the ages of 15 and 24 are more likely to have just entered on their urban labour careers and are more

[28] Mitchell (1959: 693–711; 1969c: 470–93) discusses various indices of stabilisation. The indices which he considers are in fact indices of urban commitment. Mitchell found that the degree of stabilisation was associated with such factors as marital status, education, skill, etc., which are some of the characteristics I have considered in the above analysis. It is of interest that Hanson and Simmons (1968) have developed a technique using graph theory which should enable a more rigorous examination of the factors related to the life careers of migrants which affect their migration behaviour. A later article by Hanson and Simmons (1969) further extends on aspects of this approach.

likely to be unmarried than those men 25 years and above. However, there remain some aspects which are independently associated with these factors and which are important.

A migrant's age can affect both his ability to maintain a current set of investments and the value of these investments. As a wage labourer nears retirement age (from the age of 45 onward), the more likely it becomes that he will explore hitherto unattractive opportunities in his rural home. A migrant's continued residence in a town is largely dependent on his being able to participate in its economy. Retirement poses a threat to his continued participation unless he has invested in a small business of his own and/or escapes such recurring exigencies as rent by living in a shanty area on the outskirts of the town where he can also cultivate food for his subsistence requirements. There are no well developed pension schemes or welfare services for the aged either in Kabwe or other Zambian towns (I am referring here explicitly to the municipal and commercial areas of the towns and not to the mining areas some of which do have schemes for retired workers): it being, at the time of fieldwork, a standard administrative view that the socially and morally more healthy environment (as contrasted to the town) of a migrant's home village and network of kin best serve the function of a developed welfare service. Towns in Zambia are considered by the authorities as being places of work and not places for retirement.

Although the decision of migrants to move is generally affected by changing conditions relative to their advancing years this factor bears little relation to the pattern of migration and turnover of the factory employees. Many of the workers could be expected to be affected by such a factor and particularly the tailors, some of whom are in their late 40's and early 50's. In interviews with these older workers only one employee, Hastings, who was 56, stated that he was considering leaving work for his home village. An obvious reason why the advancing years of these older tailors was not likely to affect their migration behaviour relates to the fact that all had small businesses of their own in Kabwe and had a skill which increased in value to Patel with age and experience rather than decreased.

The length of time an individual has been involved in an urban labour career is connected in two ways with the likely distribution and type of his investments. First, individuals who have just entered the employment market are more likely to be subject to influence and pressure through a set of social relationships in which they have invested in their rural homes since birth. Second, and correspondingly, they are likely to have invested in few relationships which are town

Table 3.15. Length of time in town, years in employment, years
tailoring, and age

Age group		Number of years		
		in town	employed	tailoring
15-24	Mean	3.6	1.6	-
(10)	Range	8-1	3-1	-
	No. above median	0	0	-
25-34	Mean	8.96	7.88	3.16
(13)	Range	17-2.5	15-2.5	11-0.16
	No. above median	4	2	0
35-44	Mean	17.56	15.78	10.43
(16)	Range	35-7	26-7	25-7
	No. above median	10	13	10
45-54	Mean	26.54	25.45	20.77
(11)	Range	39-14	39-14	36-8
	No. above median	9	11	10
55+	Mean	37	37	37
(1)	Range	-	-	-
	No. above median	1	1	1
	Mean for factory	14.95	13.11	19.43
	Median for factory	14.5	13	12

rooted. I described earlier in this chapter that the introductory experience of migrants to work and town life in general is largely through
relatives and friends from their home areas. Such experience, at the
early stage of their migratory careers, is likely to increase the effect of
influence and pressures emanating from the rural area on their urban
and migration behaviour. The incapsulation of a migrant in a set of ties
rooted in his rural area explains the widely observed pattern for migrants who have just started their urban careers to work for relatively
short periods of time in the towns. Closely related to this phenomenon
is the pattern for such migrants to experience frequent job changes,
although this may not always be associated with a move back to a rural
area. The short experience of urban life which the recent migrant has,

often means that he has few investments in the town of his migration other than that of his job. A lack of other investments means that the recent migrant is not subject to the same degree of constraint on his action which is often the case with other migrants who have had considerable employment and urban experience.

Eight of the employees who left the factory had just started their urban careers and also, as described earlier, had only worked for a short time in the factory. Not only did they have few investments in Kabwe but also they had developed few social relationships in the factory itself which could have acted as a constraint on their decision to leave employment. Most of the young workers (below 35 years of age), as table 3.15 shows, are still in the early stages of their urban and labour careers and in the terms of this argument may be expected to provide the bulk of the factory leavers in the future. I suggest that because these younger workers are likely to have few other investments in the town they will be subject more to the rules of tactics than of strategy as these were defined at the beginning of the chapter. Employees who are well into their urban and employment careers, because they are likely to have a number of town rooted investments, must more carefully consider the effect of a job change on their other investments. The tendency for older workers to organise their action in relation to a change in employment with reference to their total set of investments can be demonstrated through examining the factors behind the decision of four of the older workers to leave their jobs in the factory.

These four workers were Chisokone (12 years), Zulu (7 years), Lenard (7 years) and Chilwa (2½ years) and had been employed, as the figures in brackets after their names indicate, in the factory for some considerable time. In each case the change of job which these workers experienced did not greatly threaten their continuing investment in other relationships in Kabwe. Both Chisokone and Zulu became involved in the organisation of a farming co-operative for which they had received a substantial government grant. The farm which they acquired was on the outskirts of Kabwe and they considered that they would be able to run it without giving up their residences in the municipal housing areas. Both men were important political party officials and had their children at school in town. It was largely because they did not wish to lose their political status—which would have been threatened if they had given up their houses in Kabwe—and their wish to give their children a good education (better obtainable in Kabwe than in a rural area) that they resisted government attempts to place them on a farm in Mkushi district, some fifty miles away. Only when a suitable farm was acquired near Kabwe did they leave their employment at Narayan Bros. Chisokone's and Zulu's departure from the factory and the timing of their move were occasioned by the emergence of an alternative opportunity which in their view did not involve a cost to their other investments in the town.

The decisions to leave work by Lenard and Chilwa were not so much occasioned by the appearance of more attractive opportunities elsewhere but were brought about by a deterioration of their position in the factory. Nevertheless, like Chisokone and Zulu, they only made their decision to move once they were clear that such a choice would not adversely affect their other sets of urban investments. Lenard left employment following a dispute with Patel concerning the quality of his work (see 'The case of the badly stitched trousers', chapter 6). He did not leave, however, until he had secured work in another clothing factory in Kabwe. Chilwa left a few weeks after he was demoted to line 3 and not given a $1d$ increment in September along with his former work companions on line 1. Chilwa returned full-time to his small tailoring business on which he had relied prior to his finding work at Narayan Bros.

The presence of a migrant's wife and children in town affects the consequent pattern of his migration and job movement. Migrants who have wives and children with them make fewer inter-urban moves and moves back to their rural homes than single migrants. In many cases this pattern is a consequence of the fact that some migrants have married after they have become well advanced on their urban labour careers, and have entered a more stabilised period of urban residence. Indeed the timing of a migrant's decision to marry or his choice in bringing a wife and children from his home village to join him in town is often an indication of his having begun a more settled period of his urban labour career, in the sense of more prolonged periods of continuous residence in a town. However, irrespective of these considerations, the presence of a migrant's wife and children in town further increases his tendency to become stabilised in urban residence. This is evidenced by my observation that single migrants just beginning their urban careers experience more inter-urban moves than married migrants accompanied by their wives and children who have also just embarked on their migration experience.

Housing is an important factor which differentially affects single and married migrants not only in terms of the frequency in changes of urban residence but also their propensity to change jobs. Lodging is both easier to find and cheaper for single migrants than married men. Single migrants find that relatives are more prepared to support them as house residents during periods of unemployment while searching for a job than the same relatives are prepared to support married men accompanied by their families. Single migrants can also take advantage of the single quarters provided by the municipal authorities at cheap rents. Married men with families are barred by the authorities from lodging in single quarters. This restriction is often disregarded by married migrants but they must resort to all kinds of subterfuge to disguise their status in order to avoid the risk of summary ejection. The municipal authorities employ special police, one of whose specific duties is to eject migrants who are not complying with municipal housing regulations. The waiting lists for married quarters are long and once a house is found migrants are loath to give up their lodging, which would occur if they left town. This reduces the frequency with which married men are likely to leave one town in search of work in another.[29]

In general, therefore, I contend that married men are more likely to leave one job for another when the alternative employment does not necessitate a change in urban residence. For married men the choice to remain in current employment or to seek alternative employment in the same town is preferable to seeking alternative employment in another town. This is because the costs of movement, transporting their families and giving up housing for which they have at the very least expended considerable time in waiting, would exceed the possible gains from new employment in another town.[30] It is significant that the

[29] I have written only in general terms of the aspects which are likely to constrain a married migrant from changing his town of residence. There are clearly many other aspects connected with a migrant's marriage which can constrain him from moving to another town. For example, for many migrants, wives play a significant role in the decisions which the husbands make. Wives, like their husbands, also can build up considerable investments in town, and the prospect of moving to another town can place these at risk. When Chisokone was presented with the opportunity of moving to Mkushi his wife played an active role in discouraging him. Like her husband, she also held high status in the local branch of the political party and was concerned for the education of her children. Furthermore, a considerable number of her close kin are resident in Kabwe and she did not look forward to the possibility of being separated from them. This example well illustrates that a married migrant can be constrained in his decision not only by his own set of investments but also by the set of investments in which his wife is involved.

[30] At this point it is worth noting that the costs of a move are greater at certain stages than others. In searching out alternative opportunities, migrants often experience periods when they have no cash income. It stands to reason that the costs involved in moving a family and finding new housing are likely to be higher during these periods than once the migrant is firmly established in his new job. Given this, it is possible that these short-term costs may deter migrants from pursuing alternatives, even though these may bring increased

only married men accompanied by their families in town who left Narayan Bros. during my research, the four mentioned previously— Chisokone, Zulu, Lenard and Chilwa, found alternative employment which did not involve a change in urban residence.

Although the above discussion explains the general pattern for single men to experience more inter-urban moves than married migrants, it does not necessarily allow us to expect that married migrants would exhibit a lower rate of job changes than single men. We could only expect such a pattern if married migrants because of their greater commitment to the town of their current residence also had fewer job alternatives open to them. For example, it is possible that a married migrant who is skilled may have just as many employment opportunities in the one town as a single migrant who is unskilled but yet relatively free to search for work over a wide number of towns.

Here the factor of skill is relevant to the discussion. Survey data and general observation indicate that migrants who are skilled experience fewer rural–urban or inter–urban moves than unskilled migrants. Although this pattern tends to be the same for all migrants, the reasons for the pattern vary according to the type of skill concerned. For migrants whose skill is detachable from their place of work, like tailors, plumbers, carpenters, drivers, mechanics, etc., in the competition for work the ratio of men to jobs in the one town is lower than for unskilled migrants.[31] The highest proportion of unemployed men in all the towns of Zambia is in the unskilled categories. It follows from this that unskilled migrants in their search for employment may have to range over a large number of towns whereas skilled workers may be able to restrict their moves to a more limited number of urban centres.[32] So far I have discussed only migrants whose main participation is in the commercial

---

advantages in the long run. Many married men who did explore alternative opportunities in other towns reduced high short-term costs incurred as the result of brief interim periods of unemployment by leaving their families in the towns of their previous employment during this time. However, it must be emphasised that, relative to single men, they were still exposed to high costs. For example, they still had to provide for the subsistence requirements of their families and pay rent, if due.

[31] It should be noted here that there are more jobs available for certain skills than others. Carpenters, for example, relative to other skills, have comparatively fewer job opportunities. During my fieldwork I encountered many men trained as carpenters who had to make do with low-paid unskilled jobs because of the lack of opportunities for carpenters.

[32] In 1964 I conducted a survey of occupational prestige in the municipal and mine areas of Kabwe. Many of the respondents accorded high prestige to skilled occupations because they considered that men in these occupations could pick and choose their jobs.

sector of the urban economy. In the railway and mining sectors of the towns skills are often highly specific to the place of work, e.g. shunters, engine drivers, rock breakers, furnace operators, etc., and cannot be easily transferred to another place of work. Because of this skilled workers in these sectors are likely to evince stable periods of urban residence. If they sought work in another town they would risk lower rates of pay as a consequence of their skill acquired in the previous place of work not being recognised in the new town of their employment. In the terms set by this discussion skilled workers in the railway and mining sectors of the towns can be expected to exhibit both a lower rate of inter–urban mobility and job turnover than skilled workers in either these sectors or in the commercial sectors of the towns. The pattern of movement between skilled workers in the commercial sectors compared with the other sectors can be expected to be similar only in terms of their movement in and out of towns and not with respect to their pattern of job mobility. The skill of commercial workers, because of its detachability from the place of employment, in contrast to skilled workers in other sectors, may not reduce their propensity to change jobs but in some cases could even increase it.

A general point emerges from the above discussion. As a migrant's skill can lead him to spend more time in the urban centres of his migration it can be expected that this additional aspect will lead him to invest more heavily in other socio-economic and political relationships in the town than unskilled migrants. This will have a feedback effect further increasing his commitment to the town relative to other possible centres of investment. Most of the senior branch and constituency officials in the main political party represented in Kabwe, the United National Independence Party, are skilled workers. This feature, of course, is not just a consequence of the amount of time they have invested in Kabwe whereby they were able to build up a considerable amount of local support leading to their recognition as political representatives of the Kabwe population. The nature of their skills as carpenters, tailors, etc., itself leads to the development of an extensive network of relationships which is likely to influence their recognition as local political leaders. This is supported by the fact that even in the mining area of Kabwe, for example, party leaders tended to be men with skills such as carpentry or tailoring and although living on or adjacent to mine property were not employed by the mine company.

The factors discussed so far have all been presented in terms of the extent to which they are connected with patterns of inter–urban and rural–urban migration and labour turnover. I consider that education

Table 3.16   Occupation and education

Occupation	Educational standard					
	Nil	I-II	III-IV	V-VI	Form 1	Form 2
Supervisory (3)	0	1	2	0	0	0
Tailors 1 (16)	7	5	4	0	0	0
2 (9)	3	1	4	1	0	0
3 (11)	5	0	5	1	0	0
Buttons (2)	1	1	0	0	0	0
Ironers (6)	1	2	1	2	0	0
Cotton boys (10)	2	2	1	4	1	0
Total (57)	19	12	17	8	1	0

bears a closer connection to expected patterns of labour turnover than it does to general patterns involving changes in urban residence. No specific pattern of migration appears to be connected with the different educational achievements of migrants. To the extent that education is a factor associated with particular patterns of urban movement it is dependent on its combination with other factors such as white-collar work and the stage migrants are at in their urban and labour careers. My specific interest in the factor of education here is its connection with the range of prospective alternative opportunities which a migrant sees before him. In other words the way a migrant's education is likely to influence the way he conceives of his career in employment and how this in turn will affect his decision to leave or remain in current work. Migrants who have a standard VI education and above (individuals who have attained this level normally can read and write both in English and the vernacular) tend to view their occupational careers in white-collar work. This career orientation is most evident among migrants who have just entered the labour market. An orientation towards white-collar work was not so clearly evident among those migrants who were relatively highly educationally qualified, who were well advanced on their labour careers and who had learnt through bitter experience that education was not the only qualification for getting a white-collar job. I knew many standard VI school leavers who preferred to stay unemployed to taking an unskilled job which they considered did not fit in with their career expectations. Many of the young unskilled workers in Narayan Bros., who were standard VI and above in education (table 3.16), felt that their current jobs were inconsistent with their educational achievement and expressed their intention to leave the factory in search of white-collar work. This orientation was particularly entrenched in the minds of young migrants, largely as a result of the political climate of the time. Zambia had just achieved its independence and many white-collar jobs previously the preserve of Europeans were now becoming open to Africans. In addition, young school leavers felt assured that their government would give them every assistance in helping them attain their career expectations.

A general conclusion which can be drawn from this discussion of education is that migrants who are relatively highly educated, who have just started on their urban and labour careers, and who are in work inconsistent with their career expectations as educated individuals, can be expected to engage in frequent job changes. Furthermore, this can be expected to persist until their career objectives are met or they re-define these objectives in terms more in line with the realities of their growing experience.

With the exception of education all the factors I have discussed relate, both separately and in their interrelationship, to the distribution and types of investment migrants have in the particular centres of their migration. The extent to which a migrant has invested in a specific centre of his migration will affect his commitment to it and hence the likely pattern of his subsequent migratory behaviour. Aspects connected with one factor will have their effect on the pattern of migration increased or decreased dependent on the nature of their interrelationship with aspects connected with other factors. Thus the expected frequency of inter–urban or rural–urban movement of a migrant just embarked on his urban and labour career will be reduced if he is accompanied on his migration by his wife and children and is in skilled work.

I now return explicitly to a general problem which began this section. This concerned the extent to which factors which explain specific patterns of migration behaviour also explain specific patterns of labour turnover. Dependent on the susceptibility of patterns of migration and labour turnover to explanation by a common set of variables, namely those which are applicable to all urban migrants irrespective of their specific places of employment, is the extent to which an explanation of the current pattern of turnover in one specific place of employment and a prediction of future trends can be made simply by reference to these factors. Earlier I stated that the highest rate of turnover in the clothing factory occurred among the workers in the younger age categories, who were unskilled and who had only worked for a short period of time in the factory. This is consistent with and predicted from the discussion of the general factors influencing the pattern of migration behaviour. Thus those workers who left also tended to have just started on their urban and labour careers, to be unmarried and to be relatively highly educated although in unskilled work. However, from a discussion of the general factors influencing migration we cannot predict the relative stability in factory employment of many of the other workers, particularly those older employees, who are well advanced on their urban and labour careers, who are married, and are skilled. Although it can be predicted that they would be relatively stabilised in their urban residence it cannot be deduced from this that they would be stabilised in employment. Indeed, the very fact of their skill would lead us to expect that they could explore many other employment opportunities in Kabwe. At the time of fieldwork there was another clothing factory in Kabwe which was expanding both its business and the number of skilled personnel it employed. Furthermore, there were a considerable number of stores willing to employ tailors on their premises.

Clearly, there are other factors relevant to the work context itself which influence the pattern and expected future trend of labour turnover in the factory. I shall now argue that the general factors which relate to different patterns of migration affect the way in which factors specific to the work context are likely to operate differentially on the factory workers. This will afford a more complete understanding of the patterns of labour turnover as well as the nature of the factory's interaction with its general urban environment.

I propose that the tendency for an employee to leave one place of employment for another is dependent on the extent to which the set of investments he has made in his place of work indicates and affects his set of investments in the general urban environment. It is also dependent on the perceived value which a worker in the factory is likely to accord his investments there, relative to alternative possibilities.

The factory manager is largely instrumental in involving the older and more skilled workers in a set of investments in the work place. These investments attain an increased value because they interrelate closely with other investments these workers have made in the urban environment arising from aspects already described. Patel is anxious to stabilise the skilled section of his work force, which is critical to the production process. For example he is prepared to allow them certain side benefits such as credit. Patel used the existence of a debt relationship with specific workers to remind them that they are dependent on him and he emphasises to his debtors that they cannot move to another work place, however much they may grumble about their wage and work conditions, until their debts are paid. Credit is also used by Patel both to reward workers who have assisted him in his dealings with their fellows at work and in an attempt to 'buy' the allegiance of specific workers who appear to him as influential in factory politics. Thus, Mukubwa, Hastings, Chisokone, Chipata and Meshak, all of whom can be viewed in either one of the above ways, have incurred the largest debts to Patel.

Whatever the reasons are behind Patel's advancing of credit, once a worker is caught in such a relationship he is bound more closely to his place of work. First, he is under an obligation to pay the debt and should a worker indicate that he will shortly leave the factory, Patel subtracts the amount owing from his monthly wages. This is a cost which few workers can afford. Second, employees in debt to Patel are dependent on the credit facilities open to them for the running of their private businesses in the townships and/or to safeguard their savings. Should they leave employment at Narayan Bros. an unwanted cost to these other investments could be incurred, for it is uncertain whether they would be able to establish such advantageous debt relationships elsewhere. Finally, many of the workers exceed in their monthly expenditure their income derived from working in the factory and are thus partly dependent on their ability to borrow from Patel to tide them over difficult periods. To leave the factory, therefore, can result in a loss of security.[33]

The value accorded to present investments is also a function of the extent to which the benefits from them can be increased in the future. Thus it can be expected that workers who have the opportunity of increasing their benefits by continuing to invest in a current set of relationships at their place of work are likely to evince a greater stability of employment than those workers who can increase their benefits only by pursuing alternative investments elsewhere. Workers who are skilled, because of Patel's dependence on them, are more likely to accrue further benefits from continuing to work in the factory than those who are un-skilled. In chapter 2 I described with specific reference to management–worker bargaining that it is the skilled workers who negotiated most successfully for wage increments. It is also these workers who are able to absent themselves from work or arrive late with a reduced risk of

[33] Patel does run a risk when he advances credit. Workers can leave employment without giving him notice. However, if a worker did this Patel could limit the man's opportunity of finding employment elsewhere in Kabwe. Most of the Indian traders who employ tailors are known to Patel, and he can warn them strongly against the hiring of such a man. Patel also uses the threat of court action against any worker who might attempt to escape his debt obligations.

reprisal and thus can devote time to other remunerative activities outside the factory. All that is being stated here is that skill is a strong bargaining resource which permits the workers who possess it to expect to achieve more benefits from continuing to work in the factory. It is analytically separate, to some extent, from the problem of why skilled workers should devote their activities to bargaining for rewards in the factory in the first place. Obviously, skilled workers also have the opportunity of increasing their rewards by finding alternative employment. Generally, this alternative is less attractive than pursuing increased benefits in the factory because, as indicated above, many of

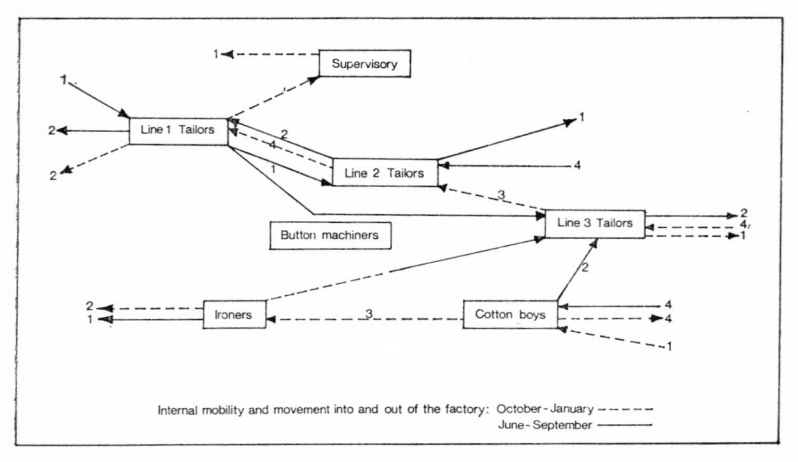

Fig. 3.2   Mobility between jobs and movement into and out of the factory for two time periods

the skilled workers' investments in the general urban environment are bound up with their participation in Narayan Bros. It is conceivable, for example, that they could develop credit facilities in another place of employment but this can take time which could result in their experiencing short-term costs which may reduce the value of any possible long-term advantage gained from their movement. This is particularly so as it is uncertain for the skilled workers that the value gained in the long term from a change of jobs would outweigh the long-term advantages possibly to be gained in their current place of work, for example, as a result of agitation for improved wage and work conditions.

Most unskilled workers have little expectation of gaining many further benefits from continued work in the factory. Indeed, as explained earlier, because of factors associated with the stages they are at in their life and migratory careers they are more likely to explore alternative opportunities in other places of work. Even in the instances where unskilled workers, and particularly cotton boys, have shown an interest in acquiring a skill, a factor which might indicate preparedness to remain working in the factory, Patel shows reluctance to afford such workers either the opportunity to learn or the chance to be promoted if they have in some way learnt tailoring. Even if an unskilled employee should learn tailoring at the factory, Patel prefers to hire tailors who already have some experience in the trade. Fig. 3.2 shows that although there is mobility within the unskilled and skilled categories there is very little mobility across the skilled/unskilled division, the majority of tailors being drawn into the factory from outside.

This discussion of the factors affecting turnover has concentrated largely on the extrinsic and material benefits to be gained by workers from their set of investments. One factor I have not discussed is the increased value a worker may place on a set of investments as a result of their more intrinsic and less easily assessed immaterial quality. I would suggest that the form and content of the sets of relationships established at the work place and the way these overlap with relationships carried on after working hours will affect a workers' propensity to change employment. In chapter 5 I examine in more detail the sets of social relationships which the workers have developed in the factory context. However, it is sufficient for present purposes to note that the skilled workers tended throughout the fieldwork period to be enmeshed in a more closely knit set of relationships than the unskilled employees. These relationships were characterised by a content often expressive of close friendship. Furthermore, these friendships formed at work were cemented by regular contact after work in their homes and the beer halls. In contrast with the skilled workers, the unskilled workers tended to have few relationships at the work place. These also tended to be loose-knit, lacking in intensity and separate from the other relationships they had established out of work. This difference in the structure and content of the relationships between the two categories of workers is largely a consequence of the longer time the skilled workers have spent in Kabwe and the factory. The types of relationships in which the skilled workers are enmeshed constitutes an important investment from which they benefit not only in terms of friendship but also in the assistance they can expect to receive through such relationships at times of crisis. By leaving the factory a skilled worker risks a considerable loss in the form of these investments, whereas the unskilled worker with few relationships does not.[34] The more senior workers (gauged according to whether they are supervisors, line 1, 2 or 3 tailors, button machiners, etc.) tend to have the greatest investments in Kabwe and the factory and are therefore the least likely to change their urban residence or to seek alternative employment. This pattern more firmly establishes the observation made in chapter 2 that the unskilled workers are less prepared to expend their energies in agitation for improved wage and work conditions than the more senior and skilled workers, because they see greater benefits accruing to them from pursuing alternatives outside this particular place of work.

The factory as an organisation straddles a number of individual life, migratory and job careers. In accordance with this orientation, I view the social composition of the factory at any one time as being an emergent property of a number of individual choices and decisions subject, progressively, to a variety of constraints. The changes in the social composition of the factory and the regularities in these changes are a product of these choices and the constraints on these choices. These choices and constraints emerge both in the course of an individual's life career and are part of the social fabric of the variety of contexts in which he participates. This chapter, in so far as it illustrates this process, has set the factory against the background of the broad demographic, social and economic aspects of its urban environment. The chapter also represents an attempt to specify the nature of this inter-relationship or the way in which processes specific to the factory mediate and modify processes which influence the choices and decisions which eventually confront most urban migrants to Kabwe.

The next chapter concentrates on the role of the trade union and the influence of other political factors on the behaviour of the Narayan Bros. employees. Problems already discussed, such as the nature of the

---

[34] The reasons are, perhaps, obvious why an employee—and particularly a skilled worker with a set of relationships of the type described above—can expect a considerable cost in terms of his investment in his set of social relationships. Nevertheless, some of the reasons why this can be expected may be briefly outlined. The intensity of a relationship increases with the number of contexts in which the same partners to the relationship participate. This is so because of the greater amount of shared experience on which they can base their everyday interaction. In many ways the work place provides the greatest source of shared experience for the workers. (After all, the bulk of the workers' waking hours is spent in the factory. Furthermore, aspects which have a direct bearing on their lives outside the factory originate there.) It follows that should a worker leave the factory for another job he would remove himself from this source as well as from the location which gives the most regular opportunity to interact with his friends. Leaving work, therefore, may be expected to lead to a reduction in the intensity of the relationship.

interrelationship between the factory and Kabwe in general, will again guide the analysis. Finally, the description in the chapter will be cast in terms of management–worker relations which was the particular emphasis of chapter 2.

4   The arena of industrial dispute and fields of action

> Society is an arena (or 'field') in which men compete for prizes: to control one another; to achieve command over property and resources . . . and, negatively, to avoid being controlled by others and to retain such resources as they already possess—F. G. Bailey (1960: 10)

> . . . we required a model that would permit focus upon *the organisation as an arena* in which ideologies are put into operation, clarified, modified and transformed—A. Strauss *et al.* (1964: 14)

The general aim in this chapter is to describe the various resources present in the factory setting and in the overall context of Kabwe which are available to both management and worker in their bargaining, negotiation and politicking over industrial interests, namely wage and work conditions. The factory is treated as a setting or locale in which the participants organise resources present in the setting itself and introduce resources external to it in the pursuit of their various interests. A process is isolated whereby individuals and groups representative of such bodies as the trade union, the political party and government organisations become involved in issues which have their source on the factory floor. Because these outside individuals and groups are pursuing interests and policies which lead them to compete and co-operate in a variety of overlapping activities their introduction into the course of bargaining and negotiation on the factory floor leads to consequences which often militate against the interests of the factory workers. A major aspect of my argument, therefore, is to show how this relates to the changing perceptions which both management and worker have of the various bodies located in their environment and the changing use they make of them as bargaining resources. One feature of the description I make is of the way worker and management come to alter their perceptions and the inferences based on them of what resources in the environment in which the factory is set are relevant to the process of their negotiation on the factory floor. The argument presented is in some respects a continuation of that set out in the previous chapter in so far as I am concerned with examining the relation of the factory to its general urban environment as this emerges from the participation of the actors not only in relationships centred on the factory but also in relationships in the town generally.

Arena and field

My definition and use of the concepts of 'arena' and 'field' differ in some important respects from their use in the studies of Bailey (1960) and Strauss (1964), from which I quoted at the head of this chapter. Indeed, as should become clear subsequently my use of these concepts is more in line with recent developments in the definition and use of them by Swartz (1969). Nevertheless, my application of these concepts, as also with Swartz, stems from an analytic concern which I hold in common with Bailey and Strauss. Both Bailey and Strauss used these terms in an attempt to overcome some of the limitations of conventional normative structural–functional analysis. For Strauss the Chicago psychiatric hospitals of his study were arenas where a number of professional careers converge, e.g. psychiatrists, psychologists, physicians, nurses and social workers; all these subscribe to different standards which derive from their commitments outside and inside the hospitals. Social life in the hospital is seen as a process of continual negotiation between the various individuals and groups within the hospital arena, who, according to such factors as the profession to which they belong, have different perceptions of the way hospitals should be run and how they should perform their duties. This process of negotiation within the arena is not only one of modifying and transforming the way individuals perceive the nature of their positions and tasks within the hospital but also one of continual creation, interpretation and reinterpretation of rules and agreed bases of conduct. According to Strauss the notion of arena forces us to look at the way the outside world impinges upon the specific locales we study in terms of the way elements in this outside world are organised by the processes of negotiation which occur within the locale as an arena. It must here be emphasized that Strauss uses the term arena within the general context of an argument which stresses that unlike normative structural-functional arguments which allow for rules of agreed conduct to be stretched, broken or selectively applied, rules of conduct can them- selves be negotiated and new rules emerge.

Bailey developed his own use of field in a way similar to that of other anthropologists before him such as Gluckman (1947) and Epstein (1958). These other anthropologists, like Bailey, were concerned to overcome some of the difficulties they encountered with conventional structural- functional analysis particularly as applied to rapidly changing modern contexts.

This concern of those anthropologists who originally used the concept of field in their analysis continues in the more recent literature directed

x

to the development and application of the concepts field and arena. Thus
Nicholas finds it 'necessary to abandon the conception of social structure
as a coherent whole in which institutions are necessarily interconnected
and consistent with one another' (1969: 297). Later writing—and I
refer specifically to the articles contained in the volume *Local-level
Politics*, edited by Marc Swartz (1969)—has not developed the orientation underlying the original use of the concepts to the same extent as it
has refined their definition.[1] The way in which field and arena are to be
defined is not at all clear in the early work.[2] As Swartz notes (1969: 9),
even in later writing there is a lack of agreement as to how they should be
used, although he does go to considerable lengths himself to clarify
them definitionally.

According to Swartz, arena is a concept which has auxiliary value to
the concept of field. The arena is the environment in which field-organ-
ised activity occurs. It also has a structure though all aspects of this
structure may not be relevant to the activity defined in the field. Swartz
states that 'The arena would consist of the individuals and groups
directly involved with the participants in the field but not themselves
involved in the processes in question. The contents of the arena would
include the resources, values, and rules of the constituents of the arena
but not in use in the field and the relationships of the members of the
arena to each other and to the resources would be its structure' (1969: 12).
A field, in Swartz's usage, is the boundary around social activity
defined by the interest and involvement of a particular set of participants.
Its content includes only those values, meanings and resources contained
in the arena employed by the participants in their activity and in the
pursuit of their interests. Over time the boundary of a field can be seen
to expand and contract as different or new meanings, values and resources are excluded or included in the activity.

Both in orientation and definition my use of the terms 'arena' and 'field'
is similar to those discussed above. I define the arena as the environment in which fields of activity are seen to emerge and intersect most
regularly. An arena is composed only of those elements or resources
which individuals and groups use or can potentially use in their activity.

[1] More recent applications and definitions of the concepts have shown greater
concern to develop them for the analysis of social process. Also in line with
general orientational and theoretical shifts in anthropology as a whole some
anthropologists have shown a preparedness to draw on the work of scholars in
other disciplines. The use which Turner (1969: 136) makes of Kurt Lewin's
field theoretical approach is an example.
[2] Mitchell (1966: 57) draws attention, for example, to the difference in Barnes'
definition of field (1954) from that of Epstein (1958).

The boundary of the arena is established on the basis of analytical convenience and is, therefore, to a considerable extent arbitrary. I conceive of the resources or elements in the arena as having a number of relational properties. That is, each element or resource can be viewed as multi-faceted, presenting a number of different ways it may be interconnected with other resources in the arena. I stress this because I wish to escape an implication contained in Swartz' definition of arena that the elements contained within it stand in a particular relation to each other. Resources within an arena are continually being organised and structured in relation to each other in constantly altering and perhaps new ways.

The organisation of the elements within an arena into a specific relation to each other is in my terms the property of a field. I distinguish two kinds of field—*perceptual* and *action* fields. By perceptual field I refer to the particular image an individual or group has of the resources in the arena relevant to the achievement of particular interests. It also includes some idea of the way these resources are likely to be organised in relation to each other. In contrast, the action field includes all those resources and the interconnections between them which are activated in the course of social action.[3]

Perceptual fields and the action fields which emerge are not necessarily identical. Individuals and groups acting together with reference to certain issues and interests often have different perceptual fields. The action field which becomes relevant thus may emerge from a process of negotiation, bargaining, etc. Even when individuals and groups are agreed as to what resources should be included those that become activated in the action field may not be in line with this agreement. The inclusion of specific resources may unintentionally lead to the introduction of others which lie outside the perceptual fields of those who initiated the action.

Fields (perceptual and action) vary in the degree of their expansion or contraction across arenas. A field is expanded when a relatively large number of resources or elements in the arena are organised into relation with each other and contracted when relatively few elements included in the arena are involved. The process whereby a field expands or contracts has I consider, the consequence of altering the relation of the various elements or resources to each other, which in turn may affect the specific outcomes which the participants who initiated the action

---

[3] The distinction I make between perceptual and action fields is similar to Lewin's distinction between subjective and objective social fields (1964: 195–8).

originally expected to achieve. Therefore I conceptualise Kabwe as an arena across which action fields continually expand and contract, relating various elements and resources in particular ways to one another. The important aspect of field as defined here is that in the course of its emergence certain elements in the arena are activated and made relevant to the course of social action and not others.

The use the factory management and workers made of the various resources available to them in the Kabwe arena and their preparedness to act within expanded or contracted fields of action must be understood in terms of the general political context of the time.

When I began research in Kabwe, Zambia was passing through a period of considerable socio-economic and political change. Independence had just been achieved and Africans for the first time assumed a dominant part in the socio-economic and political affairs of their country. A plethora of expectations which Africans had built up over the period of political struggle were now, in view of most, close to realisation. With an African government in power it was felt that the promises which had been made with reference to the improvement of wage, work and social conditions generally would now be put into operation. Africans in employment considered that whatever action they took to further their own economic interests would be looked on favourably by the government they had elected. If they felt certain that the end of colonial rule would bring them benefits, their Indian and European employers—and I refer mainly to those in commerce—were less certain of the benefits[4] they (i.e. the Indian and European employers) could wring from the changed political circumstances.

Furthermore, in the immediate post-independence period the inhabitants of Kabwe (including the workers in Narayan Bros.) perceived a number of elements or resources which had been relevant to their social action in the pre-independence period in a new light. Such resources as the labour office and the district administration were now seen as agencies which would be more effective in the furthering of their interests. To these were added other organisations such as that of the political party which they had supported and which in turn had supported them in the colonial period and could now be expected to continue in this

---

[4] The European mine management at the zinc and lead mine in Kabwe had reason to believe that, except for a few concessions, the new African government would act in the interests of the European management. For a considerable period prior to independence the mine management had been at pains to establish links with the now ruling United National Independence Party and had been reorganising the mine structure in the light of their expectation that the then Northern Rhodesia would come under African rule.

vein with increased effectiveness. But the efficacy of these various resources, in the arena as perceived by the workers, as avenues for the
pursuit of their interests, was largely untried. Thus much of the social
action in the immediate post-independence period can be seen as a
process of exploration whereby individuals participating in the arena
tested the accuracy of their perceptions. Through this process aspects of
their position *vis-à-vis* these agencies were either upheld or re-defined.

Many of the strategies and tactics which the Narayan Bros. employees adopted in their disputes with management for the improvement of
wage and work conditions must be seen in the context of the employees'
perceiving themselves to be in a strengthened position—as compared
with pre-independence days—and the management to be correspondingly weakened. But a great many other factors also affect the process
of social action in terms of management–worker relations. These relate
to the production system and the organisation of social relationships in
the factory described in chapter 2, and the nature of the employees'
participation in the general context of Kabwe, which was examined in
chapter 3. The process of management–worker dispute and the fields
which are activated as a result of the various strategies and tactics
adopted by either party will be discussed in a later section of this
chapter.

I begin with an examination of the role played by the National Union
of Commercial and Industrial Workers, hereafter referred to as NUCIW,
the union which purports to represent the interests of the factory
workers. This proceeds from a discussion of the union at the broadest
national level to a description of it at the level of Kabwe and the factory.

The trade union

The national level The NUCIW was formed in 1958 from an
amalgamation of three unions: the Factory Worker's Union, the Shop
Assistants' Trade Union and the Food and Soft Drink Workers' Union.
Some branches of the unions party to the amalgamation did not join at
first, and it was not until 1961 that the branch of the Factory Workers'
Union at Kabwe led by Paul Kalichini,[5] to which most of the Narayan
Bros. employees belonged, was absorbed into the new union.

[5] Among many long-term Kabwe residents Paul Kalichini is an almost legendary
figure, not only because of his trade union role as a defender of African workers'
interests but also as a political leader. It was Paul Kalichini, among others such
as Mainza Chona, who formed the African National Independence Party in
1958 at the time when the leaders of the banned Zambia African National

As the title of the union suggests, the NUCIW incorporates as members employees in a diverse number of firms and with a wide variety of interests. Not only does it represent workers in concerns such as cement manufacture at Chilanga, eleven miles outside the capital of Lusaka, but also in the various grain-milling factories, tobacco and cigarette factories, clothing factories and drink and food manufacturing plants. Furthermore, it purports to represent workers in the numerous small commercial and retail trading firms throughout the country. It is, therefore, not surprising that a union which spans such diverse areas of employment which vary both in their structure and interest should be beset by organisational problems. These organisational problems are manifested in two ways. First, in the continual threat of a split in the union and a hiving off of a section of both leaders and members to form a rival union; second, in the difficulty which the union has in attracting a membership and maintaining the support of its members. As I have already suggested, these two problems are caused by the varying nature of the employment and work contexts of the union members. The union cannot be uniformly successful in its negotiations on behalf of its members in the various industrial and commercial sectors it represents. This success depends on the attitude of the employer and the degree of unity and support given to the union by the workers. Many employers refuse to sign recognition agreements with union officials, and this alone produces difficulties for union representatives to negotiate on behalf of their members or to attract new membership. Most important, however, is the amount of support and unity among the workers. If union officials can demonstrate to the employer that a considerable number of his employees are union members the employer is likely to be more willing to sign an agreement with the union. This is even more likely if the workers have been able to organise successfully against the management, for the union then holds out to the employer a hope for equitable solutions to his problems. Furthermore, under the Trade Unions and Trade Disputes Act of 1965,[6] if the union officials can demonstrate to an employer that at least 60 per cent of his workers belong to the NUCIW, then the employer must agree to placing his employees on the check-off system.[7] The check-off ensures a regularity in the payment of union dues, and the

Congress were in restriction. When these leaders were released the African National Independence Party was reconstituted as the United National Independence Party under the presidency of Kenneth Kaunda.

[6] See *Republic of Zambia Government Gazette*, Acts, 1966.

[7] In accordance with this system an employer must deduct from his employees' pay his monthly union dues and pay them into the local NUCIW branch organising secretary.

more firms which agree to it the greater the economic strength of the union, which in turn strengthens it as an organisation. For example, it is able to increase its staff and pay its officials higher salaries, both of which are likely to lead to a greater efficiency. Because the existence of a check-off system implies worker unity it means that worker action for improved work conditions would be more successful than in firms where the check-off system does not obtain. Moreover, because the union does not wish to lose its check-off agreement through a loss in membership, it is likely that the union officials concerned will work harder to arrive at agreements with the employers which are satisfactory to their members. Therefore, the NUCIW will be most successful both in attracting membership and in defending the interests of its members in firms where there is a high degree of worker unity.

But what are the conditions which produce a high degree of worker unity? Obviously these are legion, but perhaps the most important include such factors as the degree of labour turnover and mobility within the employment context, the divergency of interests relating to their employment among the workers and the degree to which these are likely to conflict, and residential propinquity. A high degree of labour turnover and mobility within an employment context would impede the development of relatively stable social relationships between the workers and thus the growth of some unity among them. The same would apply to a context where the employees were divided among themselves according to divergent and conflicting interests. Finally, should the employees be scattered residentially over wide distances, this would prevent the establishment of social relationships between them outside the work context, which might result in a weakening of their unity *vis-à-vis* their employer. Evidence from other contexts where the workers have been closely residentially grouped[8] has shown them to have a high degree of unity.

[8] Epstein (1958) describes the unity and strength of the African Mine Workers' Trade Union compared with the unions in the commercial areas. Two major factors promoting this unity were the residential propinquity of the mine workers and their involvement in a unitary structure by which their relationships with the mine management covered other areas of social activity outside work such as welfare, health and medical care, township amenities, etc. Kerr and Siegal (1954: 191) suggest that workers occupied in particular industries who live together and are separated from individuals working in other industries are likely to resort to strike action more often than those workers who are intermixed with others working in different industries. The research of Gouldner (1965), Walker (1950) and Dennis *et. al.* (1965) indicates the importance of common participation in a range of activities extending beyond the work place and related to residential propinquity for the forging of unity among the workers in opposition to management.

Some employment sectors will benefit more from the services of the union than others, and the resulting dissatisfaction among the latter produces both dissatisfaction with the union at local and national levels and the tendency for sections of the union to hive off and establish themselves as rival unions. Officials at local and national levels exploit these fissive tendencies in the union. Thus in 1963 a new union, under the name of the Shops and Factories Workers' Union, attempted to compete with the NUCIW for membership. However, by January 1964 this threat had been overcome, with the incorporation of many of this rival union's officials and staff into the NUCIW. But towards the end of 1964 the acting president of the NUCIW, who had previously been a leading official in the Shops and Factories Workers' Union while other NUCIW head officials were abroad, had misappropriated NUCIW documents and money and unsuccessfully attempted to revive his old union.

That a high-ranking official of NUCIW should be involved in activities so threatening to the union is symptomatic of the organisational difficulties of the union as a whole. Because the union is not wealthy it cannot afford to pay high wages to officials and staff. Generally, it must be content with attracting, as officials, relatively uneducated men who, although well intentioned, are often not fluent enough in the language of the employer to negotiate successfully and are not sufficiently trained or experienced in the clerical duties which are a necessary adjunct of their work. Those who do have the education are attracted into more lucrative places of work and leave the union's employment. Some officials are so burdened by their own domestic and financial difficulties that they are not able to devote their full energies to union work. Such is the case with the Kabwe organising secretary of the union, who succeeded both to his predecessor's position and to his numerous debts in September 1964. Arriving in Kabwe, he and his family could find accommodation only in the single quarters section of the municipal African township, and he was faced with paying £8 10s 0d in back rent to the municipal housing authority incurred by his predecessor. It was only by threatening the NUCIW head office with his resignation that his position was alleviated, the debts being paid off and proper living accommodation found. Other officials, either through clerical inefficiency or intentional misappropriation, have mislaid union funds. Such occurrences are not infrequent, and at a general meeting of officials for all branches at the head office in Kitwe in July 1965 it was stated by the acting General Secretary of the union that the handling of funds by the branches was causing some concern. As an additional reason for extending the check-off system the acting General Secretary said that it would 'avoid issuing individual receipts to members as many organisers were collecting money from members without issuing receipts'.[9] He continued to state that although many of the union organisers were inefficient, the misappropriation by some of them of the union funds was not necessarily 'a sign of moral weakness on the side of the organisers' but could rather be viewed as 'temptation put in a good man's way'.[10] Again in August of the same year the head office of the union found it necessary to circulate all union branches with a statement which contained the following clause: 'Remit all money, there is a tendency that some organisers feel that they have access to the money collected from members not on check-off. All cash collected is the money for the union and it must be centralised through the Head office, from which the branches will receive their requirements . . .'[11]

The union attempts to compensate for the dissatisfaction within its ranks and its general organisational inefficiency by appealing to nationalist ideals and values. This is apparent both at the national and local levels. Moreover, the union emphasises its close affiliations with the ruling United National Independence Party. Union officials are not loth to state that from their ranks are drawn one Minister of State for Health and the mayors of Kitwe and Luanshya. The association of the NUCIW with UNIP and the government is well exemplified on the occasion of one visit I made to the head office. During my visit countless party and government officials came on business to the union office, including the mayor of Kitwe, who had been made a trustee of the union. Later, when the union officials left for their respective homes, all gave the symbolic UNIP *chisokone* hand wave before leaving each other's company. At the time of fieldwork the NUCIW saw the stress on and the maintenance of close ties with UNIP and the government as providing it with an opportunity to achieve its aims of improved work and wage conditions for its members in spite of employer opposition and poor organisation.[12]

Apart from the union's close affiliation with UNIP and the government, the NUCIW claims a large membership of approximately 16,000 members[13] and it is one of the dominant unions on the Zambia Trades

[9] Minutes of the Central Council of the National Union of Commercial and Industrial Workers, held at Ndola on 17 and 18 July 1965.
[10] *Ibid.*
[11] *Ibid.*
[12] Likewise, the party and government stood to gain by the association, as it afforded greater control over the union's more militant and, as far as the government was concerned, undesirable actions.
[13] Annual report of the Department of Labour, 1965, table 9, p. 66.

Union Congress. The head office of the union is situated at Kitwe, on the Copperbelt, and is the headquarters for the union's senior paid officials. In addition to the head office the union has a paid official or organising secretary at each of its branches along the line of rail as well as in Mbala (Abercorn) in the Northern Province and Chipata (Fort Jameson) in the Eastern Province. The entry fee as a member of the NUCIW is 3s, and membership costs 2s for each month thereafter.

The major points can be summed up as follows: the NUCIW draws its membership from a wide variety of firms and work contexts. The union is not effective as a negotiator for all its members, its effectiveness varying according to the extent of employer co-operation and the unity and support of the employees it represents. Furthermore, the union administration is beset by inefficiency and corruption. Some of the obstacles to its effective organisation the union sees as being partly overcome by the maintenance of a close affiliation with UNIP and the government. But as will be shown in general terms in the next section, with specific reference to Kabwe, the interests of the union and government are to a large extent opposed.

The union at Kabwe   In Kabwe the NUCIW did not secure a firm foothold until it absorbed the Factory Workers' Union, led locally by Paul Kalichini, in 1961. Kalichini resisted the previous attempts of the NUCIW at amalgamation but when it did eventually occur he left to form the Kabwe Municipal Workers' Union. What appears to be true for the union nationally is also true for it at the local level. Although it is the only union in Kabwe which represents Africans employed in factories and commerce, it has difficulty in securing a large and stable membership. The record books of the Kabwe branch of the NUCIW show that up to and including August 1965 the union had 366 members drawn from fifty firms. As Table 4.1 shows, these firms were involved in a diverse number of industrial and commercial activities ranging from maize milling to small retailing. Excluding the six firms which have signed check-off agreements with the union, and which account for 150 of the members on the union books, ninety-eight of the remaining 216 members were paid up to the end of September. Moreover, of the remaining forty-four firms from which the union purported to draw its membership, only twenty-six had fully paid-up union members on their staff.

It should be noted at this stage that I regard the union records as highly inaccurate. For instance, no records were made of the number of union members who had left their employment. It is also conceivable,

Table 4.1 Firms and NUCIW members in Kabwe
          (includes period up to end of September 1965 only)

Industry or business	Number on union's books	Number paid up
Maize milling		
National Milling Co.	64	Check-off
Kabwe Milling Co.	20	Check-off
Dairying		
Dairy Produce Board	29	0
Brewing		
Heinrich's Syndicate	24	Check-off
European butcheries		
Evergreen	2	1
W. Harding	9	9
Greenfeast's	6	1
Heslop's	14	1
Other European stores		
Premier Bakery	1	0
Holdsworth, chemist	14	9
Parmer & Parmer	4	0
E. Hochstein	4	0
Indian stores and businesses		
A B C Stores	12	Check-off
D. H. Patel department store	21	Check-off
B. M. Patel	9	Check-off
Centenary Store	12	11
Zinc Trading	8	7
D. Raskilal	3	0
Syndicate Store	1	1
N. C. Desai	3	2
Kapidi Trading Co.	8	8
Binesh Mart	2	2
Patel & Das	2	2
Kant Store	2	2
Arpe & Co.	1	1
Cash and Carry	3	0
Ishvarlal	2	0
Family Shoe Repairer	3	0
Govindji & Sons	2	1
Galaxy & Sons	3	1
Eastern Trading	2	2
Patel Bros.	2	0
Western Trading	3	0
Kabwe Bazaar	1	1
L. M. Patel Store	1	1
Eastern Bazaars	5	0
Victory Outfitters	2	0
Mangalal & Co.	1	1
Desai Furnishers	1	0
D. N. Patel	1	1
Zambialand	5	2
Young Trading	3	2
Sombhai & Co.	1	0
Naranji & Sons	3	0
Ragha	1	1
Davey Trading	1	0
Raojibhai & Co.	1	0
Victory Clothing	8	0
Panama Trading Co.	5	0
Narayan Bros.	31	28

	European	Indian	Totals
Firms	12	38	50
Number of members on union books	191	175	366
Number on check-off	108	42	150
Number paid up	21	77	98
Number not paid up	62	56	118

judging from the complaints expressed by officials at the head office, that union dues were collected from members but not entered in the books. Nevertheless, the information presented here was drawn from a report sent by the area organising secretary to Kitwe at the office's request. It was on the basis of this report that head office was to assess the ability and efficiency of its organising secretary. For this reason I would have expected a tendency on the area organising secretary's part to over-emphasise the effectiveness of his activities rather than to under-emphasise them. Therefore, while accepting the inaccuracy of the records, I would suggest that they support my general impression of the union in Kabwe as being weakly organised and largely lacking in active support.

This general impression is further borne out by the poor attendance at union meetings. Following the area organising secretary's report to head office at the beginning of September 1965, the union president visited Kabwe to see for himself the problems which faced the branch. A general meeting was organised at the Bwacha welfare hall which was to be addressed by the president. Despite the added attraction of the union president, only slightly over fifty members attended. The president was visibly annoyed with the poor attendance and at the opening of his address to the meeting stated:

It seems that everyone is happy with their jobs and their wages. If this is not the case then all the union members would have turned up and we should have discussed what was to be done about working conditions. The lack of people here just shows how solid we are. We are not solid. It is therefore of no use to be saying, 'Solidarity, solidarity for ever.'[14] I am not the union, the people are the union.

Clearly, the factors which continually impede the effective national organisation of the union, as might be expected, are also evident at the local level. The diversity of work, and consequently conditions, from which the union draws its members and the number of different employers with whom it must negotiate are well reflected in the topics under discussion at the meetings. Thus in the general meeting referred to above the subjects covered ranged from the low wages in the clothing factories, the increased wage of shop assistants, the existence of separate toilets for African employees apart from those used by Europeans and Indians in a large Indian-owned department store, to the union's demand for a wage increment for workers in the milling industry. The emphasis at meetings is placed mainly on the success of the union in righting the grievances of its members but it is clear that not all workers

[14] This is the slogan which opens and closes every general or branch committee meeting.

have benefited from the union's activities, and there is considerable dissatisfaction among the rank and file members. In Kabwe this dissatisfaction is vented against the area organising secretary. At committee and general meetings criticisms as to his inability to effect equitable agreements with employers are openly expressed by branch officials and members alike. There is some truth in the frequent accusations that the area organising secretary is responsible for many of the union's difficulties in the town. His records are badly kept and his control of English is negligible, a fact which continually hinders his dealings with employers.

But much of this dissatisfaction is inevitable, as the union must negotiate with numerous employers whose attitudes to the union differ. An agreement reached with one employer on wage rates, for instance, will not necessarily influence the action of employers in other kinds of business. Basically, the focus of an employee's interest rests at his specific work place and, naturally enough, should his participation as a union member not assist him in the righting of his grievances he is not likely to have much sympathy with the plight of other workers in other work contexts. Many of the union organisers recognise this and are continually involved in trying to make their members conscious of a common identity, as they believe that this is the only way to build a strong union. The broadest basis upon which this can be achieved is their common position as workers, whose interests are in opposition to those of their employers. As expected, it is by frequent reference to this factor that union officials attempt to rally the support of their members. But one of the principal factors which divides the union members is their variety of interest related to their participation in very many different kinds of work. The organisers at both the national and local levels are aware of this. However, the employers with whom the union deals are either Indian or European (see table 4.1) and can be seen as having interests which are politically opposed to those of their African employees. In the progress towards independence considerable political unity was generated among the African population, and it is this unity, which was directed towards political ends, that the union organisers seek to exploit in strengthening their union. Thus an appeal to a common identity among the union members is made along the line of their common position as employees *vis-à-vis* employers and their political opposition to their employers. These lines of opposition conveniently coincide with their membership of different ethnic categories; the union members being African whereas the employers are either Indian or European.

These factors are clearly evident at union meetings. At one meeting, for example, the branch chairman maintained that the poor working conditions in Kabwe are directly related to the fact that the town was the headquarters of the United Federal Party, the party which protected the interests of Europeans against those Africans. Another meeting saw the hostility being directed against the Indians of the town, who, it was stated, not only act against the interests of their African employees at the work place but also carry out their business to the detriment of the Kabwe African community. Considerable time was spent in levelling accusations against the business practices of Indian store-keepers, who, it was alleged, mark up items of clothing and then slash the prices, giving people a false idea that they are getting a bargain. Further accusations included the preparedness of Indian store owners to lower prices for European customers, only to raise them again for Africans, and that Indians, by smuggling money out to their relatives in India, were refusing to help the country.

The question of the truth or falsity of such statements as these detracts from the more immediate concern of illustrating how the union officials and organisers draw on social and political factors common to the experience of their members to build a shared ideology capable of strengthening the union despite the diversity of interest of union members and the union's administrative difficulties. This ideology they perceived as consistent with that held by the political party and the new government. Other statements, such as the one below made by the union president, served to emphasise the union's alignment with ideals regularly expressed by party and governmental leaders on the political platform.

Dear comrades, let us all here in Zambia know that we are a nation and let us unite to destroy tribalism. Tribalism in African society has divided some nations on this continent. The political party and trade union movement should be still one as it was. We should not think of ourselves as apostles of old trade union ideologies of colonialism and imperialism. This should now be discarded, and we should develop a national consciousness, thoughtness [*sic*] and interest in Zambia. We must discard the old reactionary role in order to join hands with the popular forces in Zambia. Comrades, our struggle has not ended, it is still cruel and fierce. As long as we remain talking about tribalism and remain divided, unable to weld our national solidarity as an organic nation, capable of playing our role, we shall continue to suffer at the expense of those interested in dividing us.[15]

---

[15] Extract from the president's opening address to the second Extraordinary Congress Meeting of the National Union of Commercial and Industrial Workers held on 17 and 18 March 1965. Copies were circulated to all branches.

The purpose of much of the address was to reaffirm the union's support of party and governmental policy in the face of many internal grumblings from officials and members alike that the government was not living up to their general expectations of it. The union president continually emphasised that now independence had been achieved the country must enter a period of consolidation and that union members should not be like 'some of us in this country, who are so short-sighted that they believe that what can only be given them in a week should be granted in a day'.[16]

The union saw its relationship with the party and with those now in government as an extension of their pre-Independence relationship, all the organisations concerned having common interests and aims. In accordance with the way the union perceived its relationships with the political party and the government were its efforts to maintain close ties with officials in UNIP and the government. It was by the manipulation of ties into these bodies that the union officials considered that the most effective pressure could be applied on employers to improve wage and work conditions. The union officials were not alone in this view, the same opinion being held by ordinary union members as well as those who did not belong to the union. It was a regular pattern for people in employment to try and win the support of party and government officials in their claims against employers rather than to seek the assistance of their trade union, which many considered the least likely to achieve results for their claim. At the time of fieldwork the party and those now in government were trying to disentangle themselves from matters relating to complaints against employers, and in the process were attempting to define what were the respective areas of interest of the political party, the government and the trade unions. Thus in March 1965 the two Political Assistants to the Resident Minister for the Central Province stationed in Kabwe summoned various leading trade union officials[17] in Kabwe to their offices to emphasise to them that labour disputes were a matter to be dealt with by the trade unions and not by political party officials, the Political Assistants or the Resident Minister.

But in practice it was difficult to define the different areas of interest of the party, government or trade unions. Employees in lodging complaints against their employers often phrased them in political terms. Thus, workers in order to exert pressure on their employers would

[16] *Ibid.*
[17] These were the trade union officials from the Railway Workers' Union, the Plantation and Agricultural Workers' Union, the National Union of Commercial Industrial Workers', the Public Service Workers' Union and the Local Authority Workers' Union.

often allege that their employer had insulted the President of Zambia or in some way had been acting in a racially prejudiced manner. Both types of behaviour were considered as the domain of political party officials or government politicians. Much of the general trade union movement was organised in terms of improving wage and work conditions which were based on some form of racial discriminatory practice. The NUCIW president's address to union members in Kabwe discussed above echoed one of the major objectives of the union—to remove racial discriminatory practices in industry. In these terms alone it was not easy to separate the interests of the trade union from those of the political party or government, especially when in the immediate post-Independence period the employment conditions of most Africans could be viewed as still resting on some premise associated with racial prejudice.

Moreover, government—and this was repeatedly expressed in public pronouncements by government politicians and political party officials—was interested in ensuring industrial stability in the country. In the eyes of the government industrial unrest could only produce economic instability and its policy was directed towards reducing as much as possible the threat of industrial unrest, and particularly the recourse to strike action by African workers. Government saw the improvement of employment conditions as a gradual process and was well aware that this conflicted with the expectation held by most African workers of immediate betterment in their wage and work conditions. The unions, therefore, were perceived by the government as the major organisations through which some measure of control could be exercised over those in employment in the wider national interest—economic stability. Government exerted pressure on union leaders to restrain their members. The president's address to the second Extraordinary Congress of the NUCIW in March 1965, from which I have already quoted, was heavily laden with exhortations to union officials and members to exercise restraint. In Kabwe pressure was brought to bear on the unions largely through officials in local administrative posts, especially the two Political Assistants to the Resident Minister, and through local senior UNIP officials.

Therefore, despite attempts by government and party officials to delineate the boundaries of their interests in relation to the trade union's, these boundaries were inevitably blurred. The sphere of union activity was also of interest to the government and political party, and representatives of these latter agencies regularly intervened in the area of labour relations, either indirectly by bringing pressure on the unions, or, directly, by entering into negotiations with employers and employees. What is of greatest importance for the general argument is that like the trade unions, and with special reference to NUCIW, the government and political party saw the need to maintain close links with the unions in order to preserve their interests. But government and political party interest were not the same as, for instance, the interests of the bulk of the NUCIW officials and members. The former wanted a gradual process of improvement in wage and work conditions whereas the latter wanted immediate rewards for their labours in the fight for independence, which, as they saw it, were partly responsible for the present government's achieving power.

Caught between the opposed interests of government and the bulk of union officials and members was the NUCIW leadership stationed at Kitwe and its paid officials or organising secretaries in each of the union's local branches. These were the men who were subjected to the greatest governmental and political party pressure to restrain their union members from militant action against employers. At the same time they were exposed to continual pressure from local branch officials and members for immediate and dramatic results in the improvement of wage and work conditions. Such was the difficulty of the NUCIW area organising secretary in Kabwe, who, in addition to his lack of administrative ability and the other problems connected with union organisation discussed earlier, was continually subjected to these opposing pressures.

The NUCIW in Kabwe has a membership which is dispersed over a large number of industrial and business enterprises. This produces a divergency of interest among the union members, a varying degree of success for the union in its negotiations with employers and a lack of unity among union members. The union leadership, in an attempt to weld a greater degree of unity and support for the union among members, appeals to their common economic and political opposition to their employers. Furthermore, continued allegiance to the ideals of the government and the political party is expressed and considerable effort is made by the union to maintain close links with them. This is encouraged by the government and political party but is largely motivated by interests which can be seen as opposed to the interests of the majority of local union officials and members.

The government and its various administrative agencies, such as the labour office, the political party and the trade unions, are brought into a relationship with each other through the actions of individuals and groups. Thus on the occasion of industrial disputes, the actions of the employees—most of whom are members of the political party and trade

L

union—and the employers can cause these various agencies to be brought into relationships with each other, some conflicting, others complementary. The degree to which they are brought into relevance through the extension of the field of action across the social arena will determine the extent to which the relationships these agencies have are conflicting or complementary and the pay off which the initiators of the various actions can expect. In the following section the analysis is focused specifically on Narayan Bros., and it will be shown how the management and employees have different perceptions of the arena in which they participate and differing expectations of the outcome of certain actions. Thus a major emphasis will be to show how the various parties to dispute attempt to control the extent of the field of action relevant to their behaviour. I begin the discussion with a continuation of the description of the trade union, this time in relation to the factory.

The union at Narayan Bros. Action through the union is one avenue by which the Narayan Bros. employees can seek to improve their work conditions. All the employees engaged in supervisory work, most of the tailors and both the button machiners belong or have belonged to the union. The majority of non-union members are found among the ironers and cotton boys. These workers have the lowest stake in the factory and can be expected to have little interest in union participation. That they have little stake in the factory is explained by their lack of commitment to it, produced by the short periods of time in which they have been employed in the factory and the likelihood of their leaving the work place in search of employment elsewhere. Many of the ironers, and particularly the cotton boys, have just embarked on their employment careers and at this early stage they are unlikely to remain for extended periods in any one place of employment. However, this lack of stake in or commitment to the work place does not mean that they do not have any complaints about their work conditions. All that is implied is that they are unlikely to express their dissatisfaction with their work conditions by leaving their current employment, whereas those workers who are more skilled and committed to the factory are more likely to express their dissatisfaction through union or other action.

For union members the support of the union, and their actions in terms of it, are extremely variable and are conditioned by factors both specific and external to their work context. Factors which are specific to the work context include management's attitude towards the union and the effectiveness with which the union has met employees' demands for the improvement of their work conditions. The approach of management (which includes Patel and his three partners) to the union is not favourable. Unlike the manager of the other clothing factory in Kabwe, Patel has not agreed to 'check off' in his factory. When the area organising secretary does make a call at the factory a common form of greeting is 'I see you are here to cause trouble again'. Negotiations are entered into with union officials only when they are likely to benefit management. Thus in a case of work stoppage either through a walk-out or strike, management will immediately enter into negotiation with union officials. Once Patel's employees have returned to work, however, negotiations with the union almost invariably break down. Thus management uses the union to its own advantage and in effect against the interests of its employees, an additional factor which produces dissatisfaction among the workers towards the union. This gives the impression to the employees that the Union officials are 'in the pocket of management'.

Worker dissatisfaction with the union find its most open and unanimous expression at times of severe management–employee conflict. This is evidenced in the refusal of union members in the factory to pay their union subscriptions. Thus in the months leading up to the September walk-out[18] all the factory union members withheld the payment of their union dues. This was a period when the factory employees were considerably agitated over the failure of the union to negotiate speedily with management for a wage increment and the introduction of a lunch break. The workers perceived the withholding of union dues as acting as a spur to the union officials to secure an equitable agreement. Following the September walk-out, management agreed to a wage increment and the introduction of a lunch break, and the factory's union members paid their subscriptions for September and October. However, by November considerable dissatisfaction with the new conditions of employment had once again developed and in December and the months following leading up to the February strike union dues were again withheld. Employees gave as their reasons, their dissatisfaction with the agreement which the union had arrived at with management. Although, as on the previous occasion, this could be interpreted as action designed by the union members to spur their union representatives on to attaining a more acceptable agreement with management, I regard it as an additional indication of a general process, evident at the time of the walk-out concerning the 'Five-day working week dispute';[19] that is, of a movement away from participation as union members in their attempts to reach a settlement with management.

[18] See chapter 7 for an account of this walk-out.
[19] See chapter 7 for a full description of this dispute.

But it is an essential theme of my analysis of social relations in the factory that continuous dispute is endemic. Furthermore, the organisation of work and the type of conflict over interest and the continuous dispute which it generates will produce dissatisfaction with almost any agreement and the means or instrument by which it is achieved (whether it be by collective participation through the union or the offices of a particular individual) between the workers and the management. An important finding for the ensuing argument, which emerged from the analysis in the previous chapters, is that while the factory workers are differentiated and distinguish between each other on the basis of such factors as skill, occupation and length of service, with some exceptions most of the workers receive the same flat hourly rate. The differences in wage rates which do exist between some of the employees are slight. There are no generally accepted rules, mutually agreed to by both management and workers, upon which an employee can receive a wage rise, this being left to the personal discretion of the factory manager. Factors such as variations in skill and length of service produce differing interests and grievances among the factory workers. Long-term workers like Hastings, Mukubwa, Meshak, Nkumbula and Abraham feel that a length of service differential should be introduced into the wage system. These workers also consider that a pension scheme should be established, and in this they are joined by many younger workers such as Mubanga, Henry, Kalamba and Paulos. Yet others feel that there should be differential payment according to skill, whereby those who are more skilled in their work relative to others should receive more per hour. Mukubwa, Lwanga, Chipata, Nkoloya, Lyashi, John, Edward, Mpundu and Mumba are among those who feel that such a basis for the calculation of wages should be introduced.

There are two related aspects of these opinions which are significant for the analysis. First, these opinions, as might be expected, tend to be expressed only by factory workers who stand to benefit from such changes. Thus only the older and longer-serving employees stress the need for a length of service differential, the same applying to those who would like the introduction of a pension scheme. A similar pattern obtains among those who feel that a wage system based on a skill differential is necessary. Only the tailors express the feeling for such a change, and even then only those tailors whose skill is demonstrably greater than others in the factory. Thus, for example, Lyashi, Nkoloya, Chipata and Mumba because of the nature of the work they are asked to do by the manager consider that they should receive markedly more than, for instance, tailors who work on line 3. Likewise, line 3 tailors feel that because they employ a skill in the factory they should not be on the same rate as ironers or cotton boys. Second, because of their diversity, arising from vested interests in the work place, their opinions are not likely to have the same degree of appeal to all the factory workers. Thus whereas the two supervisors, Mukubwa and Hastings, and the line 1 tailors have all remarked at some time or another on the necessity for the introduction of changes such as those discussed above, relatively few of the tailors working on the other lines have voiced similar opinions. Indeed, with the possible exception of a skill differential, most of them would be unaffected by the introduction of a length of service differential or pension scheme. But perhaps the most unaffected would be the ironers and cotton boys.

The employees who press the hardest for changes in the factory work conditions and who present themselves before both management and the other workers alike as the major spokesmen on behalf of the factory employees' interests are Lyashi, Nkoloya, Abraham, Lwanga and Chipata. At times others also play a dominant part in factory politics and these tend to share certain characteristics, such as a relatively high skill and an above-average length of service in the factory in relation to other factory employees, with those individuals already mentioned. Other factors are also common to those who tend to play a militant part in the factory and include the tendency for them to work on line 1 and to have a certain commitment to continued employment in the factory. Suffice it for present purposes to state that those who influence much of the process of worker–management dispute in the factory are motivated by interests such as the attainment of skill and length of service differentials, which do not have the same degree of appeal to the majority of the other factory employees. Nevertheless, they are aware that unless they have the support of most of the other factory workers and are able to threaten Patel with a complete stoppage of production through strike action, their ability to elicit an agreement from Patel for the improvement of any work conditions will be considerably reduced. To achieve this they must mobilise support on the basis of issues which have a more generalised appeal. Throughout the period of research the most commonly expressed grievance, voiced by most of the employees, concerned the lowness of the wages and the inequities of the hourly pay system. At other times also complaints, such as the lack of lunch break in the months prior to September and Patel's shortening of the working week after the introduction of a lunch break in August, received widespread currency.

A fundamental dilemma in management–worker relations is revealed by the need of the factory's main leaders first to derive support from the other employees on the basis of these generalised grievances and, second, once this support has been achieved, to present their case to management in terms of these grievances. I do not wish to imply that these grievances are minor; the reverse is probably nearer the truth. But it must be emphasised that those individuals who assume leadership positions have grievances specific to their position in the factory and these are additional to the more generalised grievances of *all* the employees. Furthermore, these specific grievances are an underlying factor in the active participation of those men in factory politics. Because these individuals in order to bring effective pressure on management must appeal to grievances common to all workers, and in fact enter into negotiation with management on this basis, their own specific grievances are usually ignored. In addition, the leaders concerned, as well as those others who share their more specific complaints, are the more stable members of the work force in terms of the length of time served and the expectation of continued employment in the factory. Since the more specific complaints are never adequately dealt with, there is continual pressure on the leaders to negotiate with management. But their lack of success in having their more specific demands met is one factor which produces the continual change of leadership which is a feature of social behaviour in the factory. Also it is a factor which produces dissatisfaction with the union officials. For they enter into negotiation with management on the basis of the more general grievances and do not discuss those specific complaints which lie at the root of much of the process of management–worker dispute.

The part management plays in negotiations also exacerbates the ever-present tendency for dispute to be endemic and the dissatisfaction which most workers have with the union. The management and organisation of the factory appears to be built upon the principle of the maximum return for the lowest cost. Patel and his partners hold the view that the granting of any concession to the factory employees must have the effect of increasing production costs and reducing their profit margin. Acting on this belief is probably more expensive than if they did grant concessions, for production is frequently broken by stoppages and many of the more skilled employees refuse, as a protest against their working conditions, to do overtime or piece-work after working hours.[20] The frequent work

[20] There are other reasons, too, for their refusal to work overtime and to do piece-work, such as the poor rate of pay for such work and their involvement in other activities and business ventures outside the factory, which consume much of their after work hours. However, it is still important that it is the

stoppages, the regular refusal to work overtime or piece-work and the tendency of employees to work fewer hours than is desired of them by management, contribute to the difficulty Patel has, on occasion, of meeting orders placed by customers. Nevertheless, when the management does negotiate with union officials some concessions are apparently made, but so as to maintain as much as possible the previous advantageous position of management, Patel presses for additional changes to be made in the organisation of work in return for his granting certain concessions to the union and his employees. The additional changes are not the basis upon which the negotiations were originally instituted and are designed by Patel to balance the loss he and his partners envisage being caused by agreeing to concessions. For example, in an earlier chapter I described the move of the factory employees for an increase in their wages in 1960. This was eventually agreed to, but Patel also changed the wage system from a monthly to an hourly basis and at the same time cancelled his bonus scheme. Patel's change of the wage structure in fact probably broadened the basis for complaint in the factory as well as having the effect of reducing the wage increase below the level of the employees' expectations. Therefore, through its action management not only maintains much of its position but also ensures—and indeed, promotes—a continuing condition of dispute in the factory. Moreover, it is significant for this argument that, largely out of the machinations of management, the union emerges from the negotiations with a settlement which does little to improve the working conditions. Thus, as might be expected, the union is discredited in the eyes of the employees as an effective force in their interests. But not all the blame for this can be laid at management's feet. The union officials, and in particular the area organising secretary, who plays the major union role in the negotiations, have very little knowledge of the work context. Once negotiations have begun they maintain very little contact with the factory workers and do not sound out the employees' opinions on the progress of the negotiations.

Other factors undoubtedly reduce the effectiveness of the union as a bargaining agent and increase the dissatisfaction about its activities felt by the factory workers. These include the difficulty which the area organising secretary and other officials have in communicating in English, the language in which the negotiations are held; the general inefficiency of the Kabwe branch of the union; and, the pressures

poor working and wage conditions in the factory which the employees concerned give as their reasons, which are expressed to Patel, for their refusal to do overtime or piece-work; their main argument being that if Patel can afford to pay them for overtime and piece-work he can afford to increase their wages.

brought on the union officials by the labour office and other government and political party officials to reach a speedy agreement, often to the advantage of the employer.

For example, the negotiations are held in the labour office, behind the provincial and district administrative headquarters, where the two Political Assistants and the Resident Minister have their offices (see fig. 1.2). Thus the venue of negotiation and the proximity of the government and political officials, given the government's worry about economic stability and its anti-strike attitude, place the most militant union official at a disadvantage. This is particularly the case as the labour office works in close co-operation with the Political Assistants and Resident Minister and often requests their participation in the negotiations.

The major points which have emerged from the above analysis relate to the general dissatisfaction of the factory workers with the union. It is argued that to a large extent this dissatisfaction is inevitable for constant dispute is endemic. The core of the analysis is that the requirements of political mobilisation essential for presenting management with a real threat of strike action demand that the appeal for support be made on the basis of generalised grievances. This process reveals a basic dilemma, for the individuals who assume leadership positions and play an active part in the mobilisation are largely motivated in their action to rectify grievances which are specific to themselves and to others who are placed in the same position. But because they mobilise on the basis of generalised grievances and present their case in these terms to both management and the union, the ensuing negotiations are only concerned with these grievances. The result then is that any agreement reached between management and union must fall below the expectations of those leaders who precipitated these negotiations as well as those who are placed in similar positions to them. That those individuals who assume leadership positions are drawn from the ranks of the more skilled and longer employed workers (as well as generally the more committed to continued work in the factory) ensures the constant recurrence of dispute along the patterns described.

Management's role in the factory also adds to the dissatisfaction with the union. Although management agrees to concessions during negotiations so as to continue to derive, as management sees it, maximum benefit, it incurs in the bargaining with union officials the responsibility for other changes in the work and wage structure of the factory. These other changes often offset any benefit which the factory workers might reasonably have expected from their action. This has the effect of diminishing the effectiveness of the union in the eyes of the factory employees. Also the action management takes serves to maintain if not increase a high degree of tension between itself and its employees.

Finally, to involve the union in dispute either at the request of management or of the employees usually leads to the participation of other agencies and individuals in the dispute. Pressure is brought on the negotiators, and particularly the union, to influence the factory employees to agree to the conditions and concessions pressed for by management.

Other strategies for action

Given the general ineffectiveness of the union and the dissatisfaction which the factory employees have with it, it is predictable that the factory workers would explore other avenues through which they could voice their protest and bring pressure to bear on management to improve their work conditions. Basically, there are three courses of action which the factory workers perceive as open to them, other than action through the union. Although all the courses of action can occur simultaneously, for clarity of presentation I shall discuss each separately. The first involves some kind of collective action such as a strike or walkout and does not, initially at least, involve union participation. The second is to utilise their ties in the political party in such a way as to bring pressure on management either in their own individual or sectional interest or the collective interest of all the employees. The third course is to bargain directly with Patel in the context of the factory. This has some affinity with the first course, except that it is only done to further individual or sectional interest and does not involve strike or the threat of strike action.

Collective action (such as a strike) involving all the employees, which seeks to restrict the field of management–worker contest to the factory, has a number of distinct advantages for the employees. First, the intention behind such action which is expressed by many of the workers is to exclude Patel's business partners, the union, the political party and the labour office and other government officials from interference in an event which is regarded by the employees as purely an affair between themselves and Patel. Its rationale is that most avenues through which pressure could be exerted to their disadvantage are removed. Many of the employees have experienced the detrimental effect of the participation of individuals, representative of these various bodies, in management–worker disputes. Indeed, I have demonstrated the factors which influence the union and party and governmental officials to act, intentionally or otherwise, against the interests of the factory employees. Related to this is the important fact, also openly declared by some of the workers, that by limiting the field of action to the factory the employees would retain greater control over the process of bargaining and negotiation and also would be able to exploit to the full their relationship with Patel developed at work. Although Patel is regarded as a tough taskmaster, many workers believe that he would be more sympathetic to their demands than his partners and even consider that his interests are complementary to theirs. They can produce evidence to support their views. While at work Patel frequently engages some of them in conversation and the subjects range from the domestic problems of his employees to the events of the previous evening at the beer hall. It is Patel who gives them credit when they are short of cash. In brief, Patel is aware of much of their activities, even intimate ones, after working hours, and he of all people, it is stated, should be aware of the difficulties many of them face on their current wages. Moreover, it is additionally believed that Patel's major interest in the factory is not so much to earn money but to keep production going—witness his continual exhortations to his employees to work harder and his fury should a worker leave his bench for more than a few minutes. His poor dress at work (open necked shirt and baggy trousers) also betrays his lack of interest in money. It is thought that Patel's wish to keep production going is complementary to the workers' interest in increasing their wages. Opinions are frequently expressed by the employees which indicate that, should Patel raise wages, less production time would be lost by them in talking to friends or going outside to the toilet for a cigarette. More especially it is felt that in the case of a strike Patel's interest in production would win the day and a settlement for the improvement of wage and work conditions would be made, with little production time lost through days of pointless negotiation and the refusal of either side to reach a compromise. According to the factory workers, Patel's three partners have quite the opposite qualities to him. They have little contact with or knowledge of them at the work place and they are more concerned with money than production. Evidence of the latter is their wearing of smart suits every day to the shop, a way of dress which contrasts with Patel's. It was even remarked by some of the workers that, compared with his partners, Patel looks like a *fontini* or a man ill-versed in the ways of town behaviour.

So far I have discussed a course of action and the reason why some of the workers consider it to be feasible, only from the perspective of the employees. But a strategy which to them appears to be potentially beneficial may not appear so to the other player. In this case the other player is Patel, who holds most of the trump cards and makes the decision on how to play them. These decisions, when taken, influence the ability of his opponents to hold effectively to the line of action they initially choose.

Patel's employees are certainly partly correct when they say that he is interested in production. As I mentioned in an earlier chapter, he continually complains about the laziness of his employees, and on one occasion, as if in wry mockery of the Weberian thesis, he produced a copy of the *Bhagavad Gita* from his back pocket and explained that the major teaching of the book is that one can achieve spiritual salvation only through hard work.[21] But despite his poor dress Patel is also concerned with profit and to him the maintenance of a high rate of production keeps his profits up. Moreover, although he is often concerned with the difficulties encountered by his employees and has sympathy with them and is also interested in establishing regular amicable interaction with some of them at the work place, his interest in the extrinsic benefits derived from his association with them outweighs any intrinsic satisfaction he may receive from his personal relationships with them. Nevertheless, at times of dispute Patel does realise the importance of maintaining as much as possible his personal relationship with his employees. If he does not, it could impair work relations at more peaceful times. This leads Patel regularly to adopt a course of action which allows him to bring the maximum amount of pressure to bear in his advantage while, at the same time, involving other individuals or agencies on to whom some of the hostility expressed by his employees at his success can be displaced. As Patel benefits from maintaining a relationship with his employees, so do his employees benefit from maintaining such a relationship with Patel. Most of the employees many of whom assume leadership positions in the factory depend on Patel for such benefits as the advancement of cash on credit and leave of absence at times of personal crisis. There also is an element of 'contingency planning' in the need of the factory workers to maintain their relationship with Patel even at times of dispute. For example, should collective action fail many employees fall back on manipulating their personal relationships with Patel to secure wage increases or promotion.

Bearing this is mind, Patel has at least two alternatives open to him.

[21] This, of course, very much depends on one's reading of Weber (1930). Patel's attitude to this religious text and its teaching can be viewed as very much in line with Weber's analysis, for if I read Weber correctly it is not so much what is contained in the text as the particular interpretation given to it which is important.

Both of them were used during the period of fieldwork and both worked to his advantage and to the disadvantage of his employees. First, he can agree to limit the dispute to the factory context and by so doing exclude the participation of other parties in the dispute. Second, he can refuse to play the game according to the strategy initiated by his employees, and by various means extend the field of action in which the dispute takes place beyond the immediate factory context. The first alternative involves the most risk. Here Patel agrees with the leading representatives of his workers to consider their requests on condition they return to work. Nothing is then done, Patel giving as his reason that no agreement is valid unless reached in the presence of both an official from the labour office and a trade union official. This strategy has the effect of discrediting the employees' representatives in the eyes of the factory workers. But it does involve a risk to his relationship with his employees, for a considerable degree of hostility is generated towards him. The second course of action open to him incurs the minimum cost. He calls in his partners to negotiate with the factory workers (they are as interested as Patel in the maintenance of factory production). Once they enter into the dispute Patel withdraws into the background, often keeping up a private banter between himself and his employees. Patel's partners can then be relied upon to call the labour office and the union into the negotiations. As explained earlier, because the results of the ensuing negotiations invariably fall below the workers' expectations the various bodies and the individuals representative of them become easy scapegoats for the failure of the workers to attain their goals. Patel even assists in stoking the fire by remarking caustically to those workers who happen to be near him 'What good is your union now?' or 'What else can you expect from your government?' In addition, by removing himself from the process of negotiation, he maintains his relationship with his employees and assists in perpetuating the myth that things would have been better if the dispute had been limited to the factory context.

Before I describe the other opportunities for action which the factory employees see as open to them, a number of points relevant to the above discussion and important for subsequent analysis must be emphasised. If the field of action extends across the arena involving other individuals and agencies not working on the shop floor, it is difficult to see the factory workers operating a winning strategy, for, as previously explained, the outside individuals and agencies in the main have interests which are opposed to those of the factory workers. The effect of this is to strengthen, not weaken, Patel's bargaining position. For example, in the move whereby Patel withdraws from openly negotiating with his employees and draws in his business partners to take over the role of negotiation, other agencies and individuals such as the union, the labour office and other government officials inevitably become involved. The relevant field of action is thus extended, to the factory employees' disadvantage. Should Patel tacitly agree with his employees to restrict the field of action relevant to the dispute to the factory, however, Patel can and did claim the non-involvement of union and government officials in the negotiations as reason enough for the non-implementation of an agreement. The contraction of the field of action, therefore, as in its extension, can lead to the thwarting of the factory workers' aims.

But I do not wish to imply in this broad discussion of management–worker strategy in dispute that it can be interpreted in the terms of a simple two-person 'zero sum' game where one player wins and the other loses. The outcome of a strategy which Patel adopts towards his employees and they to him involves a cost to all those involved as well as a gain, although with reference to the above discussion Patel is able to benefit most from the various strategies pursued. Nevertheless, in the negotiations he often grants some concessions even though he will try to balance out the cost incurred by them in some other way. At best he will endanger some of his personal relationships with his employees, the maintenance of good personal relationships with certain of his workers being essential to the production process. Furthermore, the outcome of a dispute which is seen by the workers as beneficial to Patel and not to themselves results in the resort to other action such as their reduction in the hours they work and the refusal to work overtime and to do piecework.

Finally, rather than the 'zero sum' game being taken as the model for analysis, Schelling's notion of the 'mixed motive' game has provided part of the framework for the above discussion, as it will continue to do for further analyses. Basically, strategies seen in terms of the 'mixed motive' game approach emerge from the social perceptions which the actors have of the context in which they act and the kinds of relationships they have with each other.[22] Such considerations as these are not

[22] Schelling puts his position, as against that of the 'zero sum' strategist, brilliantly in the following words: 'In a zero-sum game the analyst is really dealing with only a single centre of consciousness, a single course of decision. True, there are two players, each with his own consciousness, but min–max strategy converts the situation into one involving two essential unilateral decisions. No spark of recognition needs to jump between the two players; no meeting of minds is required; no hints have to be conveyed; no impressions,

essential to analyses in terms of the 'zero sum' game model. In Schelling's terms, 'mixed motive' refers not, of course, to an individual's lack of clarity about his own preferences but rather to the ambivalence of his relation to the other player—the mixture of mutual dependence and conflict, of partnership and competition (Schelling, 1963: 163).

Thus, for example, I have attempted to illustrate in the preceding description how the workers in trying to restrict the field of action to the factory context organise their strategy in terms of what they perceive to be beneficial to both themselves and to Patel. Naturally, it is expected by the factory employees that, if their action and demands are presented in such a way that they also appear to Patel as providing benefits for him, then they have a strong likelihood of achieving their aims. Patel, as I have shown, does not perceive the action and demands of his employees in the same way as they do; but nevertheless, he does orient his strategy with reference to the relationships he has with his workers. The action by which Patel withdraws from open dispute with his employees, drawing his business partners into these negotiations, enables him to impart the impression to his workers that he feels with them, but that the action surrounding the dispute is out of his control and in the hands of his business associates. This behaviour, well managed, permits him to reduce the danger of breaking close personal relationships with his employees. It also has the added effect of perpetuating the belief among the factory workers that action which excludes other agencies and individuals who are outside the area of shop floor relations has a strong possibility of success.

I now turn to the second course of action which the factory employees see as open to them in an attempt to secure improvements in their wage and working conditions. Given a UNIP government in power, it is reasonable to expect that the factory workers should perceive such links as they have with the political party as potentially advantageous to them. A number are political party officials and they see themselves, and are seen by other employees who are not officials, as having useful contacts in the party and government which can be used to bring pressure on

images or understandings have to be compared. No social perception is involved. But in the mixed-motive game, two or more centres of consciousness are dependent on each other in an essential way. Something has to be communicated; at least some spark of recognition must pass between the players. There is generally a necessity for some social activity, however rudimentary or tacit it may be, and both players are dependent to some degree on the success of their social perception and interaction. Even two completely isolated individuals, who play with each other in absolute silence and without even knowing each other's identity, must tacitly reach some meeting of minds'—Schelling (1963: 163).

Patel. It must be emphasised that use of political ties can be used in the pursuit of collective, sectional and individual interests, these latter two aspects, in addition to the manipulation of specifically political party ties, distinguishing this course of action from the preceding one. But, as in the foregoing, the following analysis will suggest that the utility of political party associations varies according to the field of action in which they are seen as relevant. However, before this aspect is tackled some description is essential as to who are the employees who have political links and which among them use their political ties in their own interests and/or are appealed to by others to act on their behalf and why.

Four UNIP section officials, Mukubwa, Abraham, Chipalo and Isaac, and three UNIP branch officials, Chisokone, Chipata and Zulu, worked or were working in the factory during the period of observation.[23] Section officials are the lowest in the party organisational hierarchy and their power and influence are generally restricted to the small neighbourhood areas within the various townships, each of the major African housing areas having a number of sections. The branch officials, however, who represent the major African housing areas, there being separate branches for each of the main municipal townships of Bwacha, Chimaninine and Ngungu, have more widespread power and influence in the social and political life of Kabwe. They are the major points of connection through which information and directives from the government, UNIP headquarters in Lusaka, the UNIP region and the constituency flow to persons living in the various local areas. Likewise, branch officials are the major representatives of local interests both to higher authorities in the party and the government.[24]

[23] Mukubwa is a section chairman in Chimaninine. Abraham is a section chairman in Bwacha and Chipalo and Isaac are section trustee and section publicity secretary respectively in Bwacha. Chisokone is the branch secretary of Bwacha branch (but at one time as an acting constituency official for Kabwe) and Chipata and Zulu are Chimaninine branch treasurer and secretary respectively.

[24] In political terms the major cleavage is between, on the one hand, the branches, including their sections, and on the other, the constituency and region. It is the branches which express the interests of the local population, which are often opposed to the interests of the officials in the higher organisational levels of the political party, who are placed in the position of protecting the national interests of the party and government. These interests often conflict with those specific to local conditions.

The position of the constituency officials is more ambiguous than I have presented here. Until early 1965 the constituency offices and the Bwacha branch UNIP offices were contained in the same building in Bwacha township. During 1964 the constituency officials worked in close co-operation with branch officials, and especially the officials of Bwacha branch, and competed with the regional officials, who have their offices in the centre of the main

The Kabwe African residents come into contact with their branch officials in a wide variety of contexts. Local branch officials, for instance, take an active part in the organisation of funerals and the collection of money to assist relatives in the buying of food consumed at the funerals of their members. Domestic disputes between husbands and wives are frequently taken to the branch offices to be settled and the branch officials attempt to protect the interests of their members in their dealings with the municipal housing authorities. In comparison, section officials are far less influential than the branch officials to whose authority they are subject. Because of the branch officials' connections into the higher levels of the political party organisation and into government, and because of their considerable influence in the lives of the township residents, it is expected that the factory workers would look more towards their support. The seeking of the support of the branch officials working in the factory would present Patel with the threat of political intervention, and offers the factory workers an opportunity to use the officials' political and governmental connections to pressure Patel into acceding to their demands.

In fact the expected pattern prevails, and Chisokone, Zulu and Chipata who are all branch officials, are frequently approached by the factory workers to use their political status on their behalf. At no time were those employees who were section officials approached to use their political status in this way.[25]

---

commercial area of the town, for power and influence over the Kabwe African residents. The success of constituency and branch co-operation was to erode much of the power and influence which the regional officials may have had. Their function was reduced to that of introducing visiting politicians and other dignitaries to the Kabwe residents and acting as liaison officers between the government officials and local leaders. The government saw the constituency and branches as producing a threat to its interests, specifically with reference to the implementation of government policy. A highly effective political machine which had been built up in the progress towards independence, was now seen in the post-independence period as a liability to the general national interest. Following October 1964, when independence was finally recognised, and throughout 1965 a number of programmes were mooted whereby the strength of the political officials in the lower reaches of the party could be weakened. A change which was effected was the moving of the constituency offices to the Kabwe region headquarters in the town centre. The result of this was to weaken the previously strong association between the branches and the constituency and to bring the latter officials under the close control of the region. This change, in addition, not only weakened the position of the constituency officials but also reduced the power and influence of the branch officials. Finally, the constituency officials, by their removal from their old offices in Bwacha township and their closer association with the region, were placed in a position of opposition to the branches.

[25] This does not mean that the political status of section officials is not im-

There are two ways whereby the branch officials in the factory can bring pressure on Patel. The first is the use of their political status by the branch officials to threaten party political action. The second is to exploit their ties into the political party and the government to exert pressure on Patel to accede to their wishes. The change-over to African government and the uncertainty of employers, Patel included, as to the attitude which the new government would take towards them, gave them no reason to doubt in the early stages of independence that their employees' general expectations of government policy would not, in fact, be pursued.[26] This degree of uncertainty provided enough support for such threats for Patel to be worried enough to consider his employees' demands. Thus in August 1965 Chisokone, Zulu and Chipata were among the main representatives of the factory workers in placing before Patel the workers' demands for a wage increment and the introduction of a lunch break. In making their representation they threatened to take the matter before the Resident Minister should Patel not consider their demands. Patel agreed to a general $1d$ increment for all workers and the introduction of a lunch break. However, although the lunch break was introduced, despite repeated assurances from Patel the end of August saw no wage increment. The threat, therefore, needed more teeth than those provided by the political uncertainty of the time. This became clear when Patel stated that no settlement could be reached without the participation of the union and the labour office in the negotiations. The three branch officials, acting on their threat, now went to see the Resident Minister. All were aware of the change in political party policy by which employer–employee disputes should be dealt with by the labour officer and the relevant union; their complaint was therefore, presented to the Resident Minister in political terms. The complaint was that Patel was discriminating against Africans in his wage and work conditions, and cited his alleged refusal to hang a portrait of the Zambian President in the factory and to remove those of Nehru and the Queen.[27] On this occasion the Resident Minister listened

---

portant in the personal relationships which such an official may have with his fellow employees. All that I wish to stress is that the factory workers do not consider that the support of a section official presents a big enough threat to Patel for the latter to consider the employees' demands.

[26] This uncertainty was due to a large extent to the employers in the commercial areas having a general lack of information as to the nature of the political process currently at work.

[27] At the time there was a concerted party campaign to pressure the various European and Indian store owners into hanging portraits of President Kaunda in their premises. In other words, they were expected to recognise symbolically the fact that Northern Rhodesia had passed from its colonial

M

sympathetically to their grievances but took no action, referring them to the labour officer.[28]

The use of a political threat had some effect, though limited, influencing Patel at least to go through the motions of appearing to agree to the workers' demands; but when the employees were forced into extending the field of action to include the Resident Minister, no support for their threat was forthcoming.

One more example demonstrates the relative ineffectiveness of political ties extending beyond the factory floor in achieving the workers' aims—one moreover, showing a result completely the reverse of that expected by the political official concerned when he attempted to manipulate his ties into the party and the government to the general benefit of the factory workers. The occasion was the February strike of 1966, when a stalemate had been reached in the negotiations with the factory management, both sides refusing to yield the slightest concession. Largely because of pressure from his fellow workers, Chipata (Chisokone and Zulu at the time being absent from the factory) decided to break the deadlock by asking the Resident Minister to intercede on behalf of the factory employees. To Chipata's surprise, the Resident Minister lectured him on the irresponsibility of his and his fellow workers' action, stating that strikes were not the solution to employment difficulties. Later Chipata and some of the other leaders in the strike action were summoned to the office of the Political Assistants, where Chipata was warned that unless he used his influence to bring the strike to a halt he would run the risk of being stripped of his political office. Further meetings with the Resident Minister and the Political Assistants followed, including both representatives from the employees and the management.[29]

This incident does show the inability of political officials to operate effectively to their benefit ties to more important officials in the party and the government. On the contrary, it demonstrates the utility of ties to such higher officials for bringing pressure to bear on lower officials to preserve the interests of government as they were seen at the time.

Political party connections then have most effect when confined strictly to threats. I have suggested that should Patel push the workers into the position where they must act on their threat, given the current

state owing allegiance to the Queen to its independent state of Zambia, according allegiance to the President. Also implicit in this was the demand that Europeans and Indians should eschew their various 'tribal' connections.
[28] See chapter 7, p. 276 for a more detailed account of the strategies employed by the workers on this occasion.
[29] See chapter 8, p. 316.

governmental attitude towards industrial unrest, the outcome is likely to be completely the reverse of that intended by them. However, it is understandable that the workers should expect to be able to manipulate successfully political party connections. Generally, as the factory workers perceived it, the political party which they had supported and which had struggled for and achieved Zambia's independence stood for their interests. In addition, they had important local officials of the party working in the factory.

It is conceivable that political party connections used as a threat are likely to gain the most beneficial results when they are used to support the demands for wage claims of particular individuals or sections of workers. Thus in September 1965 a wage increment was finally awarded to that section of the employees to whose ranks the three branch officials belonged.[30] I assume that the threat of political action was enough to influence Patel to introduce wage improvements for a small section but not for all the workers, the cost being too great. To obtain better general wage and work conditions generally the workers would have to secure the support of outside political and governmental agencies, or convince Patel that they could mobilise further support in the form, for example, of collective strike action. However, I now suggest that other resources available both to the branch officials and to those in the sections of the work force to which the officials belong, may be more effective.

I now come to the third course of action whereby factory employees can bargain privately with Patel either in their own individual or sectional interest. This is a viable proposition only for those workers who are crucial to the production process or who are important to the smooth running of the factory. Therefore, those who see themselves as being in a position strong enough to bargain with Patel are those employees who are in supervisory work or engaged in tasks which are viewed as important to production both by themselves and Patel, e.g. the line 1 tailors and some of the tailors on line 2. Patel conveys his own perception of their importance through such actions as his willingness to advance credit, the seeking of their assistance in settling minor disputes between himself and other workers, or by giving them more difficult work. Patel considers it to be in his interests, for instance, both for the productive output of the factory and the stabilising of his more skilled employees, to give some of his workers additional wage benefits.[31]

[30] With the exception of Isaac, who is an ironer, all the UNIP section officials were occupied in the more skilled occupations in the factory.

[31] For a more detailed description of Patel's interests and how these affect his relationships with his employees, see chapter 2, pp. 49–54, and chapter 3, pp. 83–6.

According to my informants, prior to my entry to the factory Hastings, Chisokone, Mukubwa, Zulu, Nkoloya and Abraham had all negotiated privately with Patel for their higher wage rates (see table 2.2) on the basis of their skill and importance to the general running of the factory. When in August 1965 Ibrahim was promoted to operate the overlock machine on line 2 he at first received no increased hourly rate above the normal 1s per hour. It was only when he pointed out that Zulu had been paid 1s 3d per hour and that the job involved skills which previously Ibrahim had not utilised that Patel increased his wage to 1s 3d per hour.

In bargaining, the degree of success depends considerably on Patel's 'magnanimity'. To threaten to leave work opens a worker to the risk that Patel might accept the possibility of his departure, irrespective of that worker's importance to him. However, Patel's awareness that a worker can drum up support from his co-workers for his claim may induce him to grant a worker concessions before the threat eventuates. For should additional support be mobilised not only does Patel expose himself to the risk of a disruption of production but also to the risk of granting concessions to a number of workers and not merely to one. Much of the competition between tailors particularly on line 1 for leadership over the factory workers (this will be described in detail in chapters 6, 7 and 8) can be seen in the light of specific workers' attempting to impress Patel with their power and influence. Nkoloya, for example, declared that he was only on a higher wage rate because he was one of the major leaders in the factory. Hastings' dramatic change of behaviour towards the end of fieldwork is demonstration of an employee trying to impress his power and influence on Patel in order to give support to his own claim. Hastings had been negotiating unsuccessfully with Patel for a retirement pension. Patel's knowledge that he would shortly be leaving employment anyhow influenced his continual refusal to grant him a pension. Hastings who prior to this had been an outstanding supporter of Patel in the latter's dealings with his employees suddenly began to compete with the line 1 tailors for the leadership of the factory workers. In fact during the February strike [32] he consistently, to all the workers' surprise, put forward more radical proposals for action than any of his fellows had, at the time, suggested.

Individuals use or try to establish influence and power over others in the factory, among other things to impress Patel with their political importance which in turn can be implemented in threat against him in a bid to win further benefits from him. But obviously the potency of the threat will depend on the individuals over whom a person has power

[32] See chapter 8, pp. 311–17.

and influence. Thus the threat to Patel will, for obvious reasons, be less if it comes from a man who is an influential and powerful figure among the cotton boys and ironers than from one influential and powerful among the line 1 and 2 tailors.

The focus on individuals should not obscure the importance of coalitions which form in the factory whereby a number of workers combine and present a joint threat. As in the case of individuals, the coalitions with the stronger bargaining power are those which contain employees who are important to the production process and organisation of the factory. Thus a regular coalition which forms, evidenced in the September walkout for instance, is that composed of the line 1 tailors and some of the tailors on line 2. The workers who constitute such coalitions have more interests in common and bargain with Patel for wage improvements which will affect their own sectional interests and which are not bargained for on the basis of general wage improvements for all the factory workers.

Although for present analytical purposes I have treated each of the three main perceived lines of action separately, both in threat and in the course of action all three may be interwoven. Throughout the period of observation threats, whatever the nature of their support, were relatively ineffective. Whether the threat was one of general collective action (e.g. a strike) by all the employees, of political party and/or governmental intervention, or of action by individuals or a number of workers but not all, using their importance in the production process and organisation of the factory, or combined elements of all three, Patel, when it was a question of wage and work improvements, remained unmoved. This does not mean that threats such as these were not effective in other forms of dispute; for example, when some of the line 1 tailors threatened Patel with a walkout if he did not withdraw his threat to sack Lenard. On this occasion Patel climbed down.[33]

The types of threat used by the workers correspond to different degrees of escalation in management–worker relations. Thus threats which are based on the disruption of the production process by specific individuals or by a coalition of employees are of a different order from threats of political party or governmental intervention and general strike action. They are of a different order because they refer to different fields of action. That which is restricted to individual or sectional bargaining with Patel limits the field of action to the more senior and/or skilled factory employees such as the supervisory and line 1 tailors. Threats of political and governmental intervention extend the relevant

[33] See chapter 6, p. 343, 'The case of the badly stitched trousers'.

field of action to include individuals and agencies not part of the work context. Because of their reference to fields of action of varying extension, threats differ in the degree of sanction appealed to. Threats of political party or governmental intervention as perceived by the factory workers involve more secure sanctions as do threats of general strike action, than threats based on the support of a small section of the work force.

Obviously, the kind of threat used will be dependent both on the scale of threat which a worker or a number of employees perceive as necessary to induce some consideration by Patel of their demands, and the resources which the workers see at the time as being successfully mobilised to their benefit. Therefore, although I regard threats as being representative of different degrees of escalation, this does not mean that the overall process is from small-scale threats to large-scale ones. For instance, the first type of threat I saw used was related to political party and governmental intervention, and in terms of my analysis was a comparatively large-scale threat. Even allowing for the fact that I entered the factory only at a particular stage in an overall developmental process in factory relations which dates from the establishment of the clothing factory, I would maintain that workers would use those threats they perceive at the time, however mistakenly, as being the most likely to succeed and which appear to contain the most substance. The threat of general strike action was resorted to towards the end of fieldwork not only because other threats and other courses of action had failed but also because for the first time employees perceived overall common areas of interest with each other. This had not been apparent at the times when other courses of action had been resorted to. In addition, the employees were aware of the existence of expanded sets of social ties spanning a number of workers of different skill and experience in the factory. The ability of some of the employees to influence the behaviour of other workers which developed at this time was discussed in chapter 2 with reference to the increased control which senior workers, particularly on line 1, had over the work behaviour of the less skilled employees such as the cotton boys and ironers. Owing to factors such as these it was reasonable for some of the workers to expect that they had enough control over others in the context to support the threat of strike action.

But irrespective of the type of threat, Patel often supported by his business partners, remained unbending. His response, therefore, to the threats of his employees forced them into the position of acting on their threats. However, a threat or combination of threats when translated into action did not generally achieve the desired aims expected of them by the employees. Further examination and demonstration of this pattern will be presented in the following chapters. For the present I suggest that it emerged from the false consciousness of the workers of the strength of threats based on an extended field of action including various agencies outside the immediate work context, and the ability of Patel and his partners to extend the field of action in their interests even against the will of the factory employees. Towards the end of the fieldwork period the factory workers became increasingly aware that their best course of action was to restrict the dispute to the factory and to exclude individuals representative of various agencies. But even here the employees' strategy could be circumvented since Patel, with the assistance of his business partners, could himself appeal to outside agencies and so extend the field of action to the detriment of the workers' interests.

One final point must be emphasised and this relates to the notion of the 'mixed motive' game, an approach made relevant in the foregoing section but pertinent equally to the whole chapter as well as to later analysis. With reference to the strategies pursued in management–worker dispute each party to the dispute is influenced by his perception of the arena in which he competes. Each 'player' not only orients his strategy in terms of the single stake about which the dispute revolves, in this case wage and work improvements, but also considers other aspects relating to his relationship with the opponent as well as to other individuals who may form part of the same coalition at that time. This latter aspect which emerges from a 'mixed motive' game approach will be examined in some detail with reference to the general competition for leadership and status in chapters 6, 7 and 8.

Two major themes have run through this chapter. The first was concerned with setting the factory and those who worked there in the general political context of Zambia and Kabwe at the time, and, second, examining the strategies and tactics pursued by the management and workers in relation to demands placed by the factory employees for wage and work improvements. Both these themes were linked analytically by the use of the concepts of arena and field.

Fields emerge in the course of social action and extend or contract across an arena in which are contained various resources or elements. These resources are relevant or irrelevant for social behaviour according to whether they are included in the field of social action. The broad implication revealed by this analytical approach is that certain aspects, for instance, of the general political context in which the factory is placed, may not always be relevant to the course of social process which occurs in and emanates from the factory. However, a dominant pattern of management–worker contest centres on a struggle between management and worker as to what resources in the arena in which they compete shall be made relevant to their field of action. Three main courses of action which they perceived and acted upon were isolated. These were collective action such as a strike, the manipulation of political party and governmental ties in the collective, sectional or individual interest, and the action by individuals or a section of workers but not all, on the basis of their importance in the production process and the general organisation of the factory. In the first and third courses of action the workers perceived their field of action as restricted to the factory, whereas in the second, the manipulation of political party and governmental ties, the field of action, as when the union was involved in dispute, was seen as extending beyond the factory. It was shown that the more extended the field of action the more events tended to work to the detriment of the factory employees. Although the workers began to see that they had better chance of success if they restricted their action to the factory, Patel did not see it their way. Patel's tendency to stand firm in the face of threat forced his employees to act on their threats. This gave Patel the opportunity to circumvent the various strategies of his workers and to draw in representatives of outside agencies, thus extending the field of action to his benefit.

The change-over to African government raised the expectations of the factory employees. This led them to attempt courses of action which were largely untried. Some of these strategies—particularly those which involved political party and governmental intervention—were exploratory, and in a sense just as exploratory for Patel as for his workers. By forcing his employees to 'try their hand' Patel was in fact able to test the strength of his workers' political connections. Through experience the factory employees learnt that their political links were not as strong for their purposes as they had expected and other courses of action were turned to in preference.

No clear indication has as yet been given of the way the various strategies at any one point in time interconnect, nor of the process by which specific strategies become preferred and the workers' perceptions of the effective lines of action change. These problems will be dealt with when a series of events which occurred in the factory are analysed in temporal sequence. Furthermore, a focus on dispute in reference to management and in terms of the attempt to gain wage and work improvements has neglected other aspects as to how the workers decide to pursue specific strategies. To a considerable extent the strategies taken emerge out of the competition for leadership and status which occur between the workers. Agreement is reached among them as to what action will be pursued and which of their co-workers will assume the responsibility of leadership and the representation of their interests. In later chapters, I shall make an intensive examination of case material and the process whereby the workers compete for power and leadership. Only when this has been done can the complete nature of the relationship between management and worker and the process of their disputes be understood. My immediate task, is to examine the structure of the factory workers' personal networks and the broad patterns of interaction between them in the work context.

5   Patterns and processes of interaction

One general aim of this chapter is to support with evidence some of the broad statements made earlier to explain features of worker behaviour. It will be recalled, for example, that in previous chapters I referred to the involvement of the factory workers in a relatively dense set of factory-located interactional relationships as a partial explanation for some of the differences in their behaviour from the less skilled and junior employees. Furthermore, in chapter 4 I gave as an explanation for the development of united strike support the extension of interactional relationships cross-cutting many of the bases of division and opposition among the factory workers. Through the presentation of evidence for statements such as these other broad objectives which guide the analysis and description in this chapter will be achieved. These are, first, some indices will be derived of the potential of specific individuals relative to others in the factory to exercise power and influence through their sets of interactional relationships. This is important for the analysis in later chapters, where I focus in some detail on the individual competition for power and status. Second, it is my aim to explain major changes in interactional relationships over the fieldwork period through the application of certain abstract principles drawn from the theory of social exchange. By so doing the reader will be introduced to some concepts and principles central to my use of exchange theory which will be extended through a closer attention to case material in the chapters to follow.

The chapter begins with a discussion of the main ways I present the interactional data I collected for the factory employees. The material will then be analysed with reference to important changes in worker activity between the close of the two time periods, into which the period of my field observations has been divided, in relation to strike action. The central thesis of the chapter, as stated earlier, is that the support by all of the factory employees of strike action at the close of the later time period, in contrast to only limited support for similar industrial action at the close of the time period preceding it, is related to an extension of interactional relationships cross-cutting and modifying major divisions of interest. A description of the changes in interactional relationships between the close of the two time periods is then supplemented by an explanation, using some exchange theoretical principles, for the emergence of and change in the interactional relationships recorded.

Data, methods of categorisation and analysis

I present the sets of interactional relationships in which the factory workers are involved in two ways. The first and main mode of presentation is in the form of matrices. This enables each factory worker to be placed in the total context of all the factory-located interactional relationships. Second, I rank the individual factory workers according to the main structural features of their personal networks. One form of presentation supplements the other.

The interactions of the factory workers were observed by me each day and immediately recorded on a schedule. The factory premises were small enough for me to observe most of the interactions between the workers, though I by no means claim that all were recorded. As far as possible I noted precise details, for example of conversation, and of other activities such as the giving of cash, help at work and assistance in learning a skill. The methods I have used to categorise this material, were adopted after the data had been collected, not used, as in other studies of small group interaction patterns (Bales, 1950), as a method of data collection in itself.

By interaction I refer to continuous uninterrupted social activity involving the participation of at least two persons. A unit or sequence of interaction defined in this way can be broken down into a number of components. Thus any one sequence of interaction may involve, for example, casual conversation, the sharing of gossip, help at work, etc. These components of interactional sequences I refer to as transactions[1]

[1] The term 'transaction' as defined here refers to a unit of activity and its content directed by one individual to his partner in an interactional relationship. I use 'transaction' cognisantly to distinguish it from another term, 'exchange', often used synonymously (e.g. Kuhn, 1966: 269). The distinction between the terms 'transaction' and 'exchange' reduces the ambiguity contained in the usage of both these terms. Thus Blau (1964) uses 'exchange' to refer to both the process of transaction between two partners, as I define it above, and to the emergent property of an interactional relationship as this relates to a particular patterned flow of transactions within it. An exchange relationship, for example, is typically one where the transactions are reciprocal and the obligations balanced. It is, in Blau's analysis, to be distinguished from power relationships, where the transactions are unilateral and the obligations imbalanced. This critical distinction which Blau makes between exchange and power relationships as emergent phenomena from a process of

and I distinguish between transactions which were sociational or instrumental in content. I have classed as transactions which were *sociational* in content those where the activity was markedly convivial such as general conversation, the sharing of gossip and the enjoyment of a drink together. Examples of *instrumental* transactions are the lending or giving of money, assistance at times of personal crisis and help at work.

The distinction I make between sociational and instrumental content in transactions is similar to that Blau makes between transactions which are intrinsically or extrinsically rewarding (1964: 35–8, 95–6). Thus I have categorised as instrumental transactions those which are essentially detachable from their source and are means to ends rather than ends in themselves. Those which are ends in themselves and not detachable from their source I have classified as sociational. 'The basic criterion is whether individuals are oriented towards an association as a means to some further end, as when they request a neighbour's help, or as an end in itself, as when they simply socialise with him' (*op. cit.*: 58). Clearly to make neat categorical distinctions presents methodological problems. For example, is the sharing of gossip which may involve the communication of information vital to the furthering of the interests of those individuals participating in the interaction to be categorised as sociational or instrumental or both? Is assistance with his work by an individual's close friend to be considered as an instrumental transaction or merely representative of an opportunity to socialise and thus a symbolic expression of their close friendship? I have attempted to overcome such difficulties by categorising a transaction as sociational or instrumental on the basis of what I considered to be its dominant element, according to my general knowledge of the nature of the relationships between the individuals engaged in the interaction.

The separation of instrumental transactions from sociational transactions permits some assessment of the extent to which transactions are unilateral or reciprocal and the degree to which the interactional relationships which these transactions comprise are characterised by a

---

transactions is a good deal more complex than I have room to illustrate here. Blau's book on the subject, as it relates to this point and to others in this chapter and those to follow, should be consulted. For present purposes I have restricted the term 'exchange' to that meaning ascribed to it by Blau in his distinction between exchange and power relationships. My usage of 'transaction' must be distinguished from other definitions, notably Barth's (with whose general orientation I am in accord), who defines transactions as 'those sequences of interaction which are systematically governed by reciprocity' (1966: 4). Transactions for me are the basic units of interactional relationships from which, according to their patterned flow, are derived the structural form of interactional relationships.

balance or imbalance in obligations. The development of unilateral transactions and an imbalance in obligations is held to be a necessary condition for the differentiation between individuals in terms of power and status. It is crucial, therefore, for the analysis in this and later chapters where I focus on processes relating to the distribution of power and status that some index is achieved of the degree of unilaterality or reciprocity and imbalance or balance.

An interactional relationship tends to be unilateral when over a specified period of time the transactional inputs of one partner are regularly greater than that of the other, and to be reciprocal when they are more or less equal. The unilaterality or reciprocity of transactions refers strictly to the *rate* of transactional input.[2] In contrast, the extent to which an interactional relationship is characterised by a balance or imbalance in obligations is dependent on the perceived value of the transactional input made by the partners to the interaction in relation to each other. An interactional relationship represents a balance in obligations when both partners regard each other's transactional input as more or less equal in value. It is characterised by an imbalance when the partners recognise that one is making a transactional input of greater value than the other. In general, I consider that an imbalance in obligations is most likely to occur where transactions are unilateral. But this is not necessarily the case. It is also possible for such an imbalance to occur in an interactional relationship characterised by reciprocal transactions, where one partner is transacting with resources considered by the other to be unequal to those received in return.[3]

[2] It should be stressed here that I use 'rate' purely in the sense of the amount of transactional input of one partner in an interactional relationship relative to the other. It is not what Homans refers to as the 'rate of exchange' (1961: 55) or the amount of activity which another has to emit in order to receive some valued activity in return within a limited period of time.

[3] I should emphasise that I have attempted to distinguish clearly between reciprocal–unilateral transactions and balance–imbalance in obligations. My use of these terms is more restricted than that of Blau, whose lead I generally follow but who never, as far as I am able to discern, makes clear the distinctions in his usage (1964: 25–30). Blau also states that the terms balance–imbalance are drawn from the 'balance' theory of social psychology (Heider, 1958; Newcomb, 1961) and closely related theories of cognitive dissonance (Festinger, 1957). I can see only a very tenuous link between these theories and Blau's use of these terms. One connection is Blau's use of the same general assumption of the balance of theorists that all systems tend towards balance (or consistency) and that an imbalance in relationships will set up processes leading to a balancing out of relationships. Other exchange theories, but not that of Blau, may bear a closer connection with the balance theory of social psychology. Taylor (1970), in a survey of various balance theories indicates, for example, that the exchange theory of Homans (*op. cit.*: 293–4) suggests propositions that have a close relevance for those on balance theory.

It is difficult to identify sociational transactions as unilateral or reciprocal, particularly for the purposes of classification and measurement. Conversation and gossip for example are virtually by definition reciprocal. But reciprocity and unilaterality can be distinguished for instrumental transactions. Where reciprocal instrumental transactions were recorded by me, this is broadly indicative that the relevant interactional relationship was characterised by a balance in obligations. The reverse applies for unilateral instrumental transactions. I make this inference because of the high value which the factory workers placed on those transactions I have classified as instrumental, and the fact that their value is relatively independent of the individual who distributes them. Because of these factors the reciprocity of instrumental transactions provides general standards in terms of which the partners to interactional relationships can judge their relationships to be in a state of balance or imbalance. It is one of the features of a recognised imbalance in obligations that individuals in order to balance out their obligations (which they may be under pressure to do for no other reason than failure to discharge their obligations may risk a discontinuance in the supply of valued benefits and services) may have to comply with the will of another or else defer to his status. Whether an individual will react in either or both of these ways is dependent on other conditions being present. The major point which I wish to stress at present is that an individual can escape obligations incurred through transactions by simply not recognising that he is obligated. But where the imbalance in obligations is established through transactions which have a widely recognised value, then I suggest that an individual would be restricted in his ability to escape obligations incurred. This is so because he would be limited in the degree to which he would receive agreement and support from others participating in the same context for a definition of the nature of his relationship with another which would enable him to escape his obligations.

A summary of the interactional data recorded in the factory is included on matrices 1 and 2. The data which are presented refer only to transactions which were not directly occasioned by the production process and thus not voluntarily entered into by the partners to the interaction. I have excluded, therefore, from the matrices and the network structural measures which follow later, transactions such as supervision or the passing of cloth between tailors engaged in the make through method of production. However, I have not excluded transactions which might emerge indirectly from the working of the production process. For instance, the engagement in conversation regarding township life by a supervisor of a worker who he has just instructed to perform some specific task. By excluding transactions not voluntarily entered into (i.e. transactions directly connected with performance in the production process) I have restricted my analysis to a consideration of that transactional activity with which the exchange theory I apply is largely concerned.[4] Nevertheless, despite this restriction the analysis of the interactional data presented will be used in this and later chapters to gain insight into the behaviour enjoined on the workers in the performance of their various duties and tasks in the factory.

The data on the matrices apply to two separate time periods and this applies also to tables 5.1 and 5.2, in which the measures for personal networks[5] are presented. The two time periods will be referred to in subsequent analysis as time 1 (matrix 1 and table 5.1) and time 2 (matrix 2 and table 5.2) respectively. Time 1 includes the period beginning in June 1965 and ending in the last week of August 1965. Time 2 covers the period beginning in September 1965 and ending in the last week of January 1966. The close of each time period coincides approximately with observable changes in the behaviour of the factory employees. Thus time 1 ends at a period when some of the more senior workers were mobilizing militantly against management evidenced in their resort to walkouts in a bid to secure their demands for wage and work improvements. Although meeting with some initial success, overall their efforts met with failure. One factor which explained this was the inability of the senior workers to secure the support of the less

[4] Blau's theory of social exchange, upon which the analysis I present is heavily dependent, is limited in the main to those social relationships voluntarily entered into by individuals. Blau defines 'social exchange' as 'the voluntary actions of individuals that are motivated by the returns they are expected to bring and typically do in fact bring from others' (1964: 91).

[5] Network as an analytical concept in anthropology was first used by Barnes (1954) and later developed by Bott (1957). Since the studies of these two scholars the concept has been defined in different ways by numerous authors, and these are surveyed and assessed relatively fully in Barnes (1969), Mitchell (1969, 1971) and Bott (1971). Although a debate still continues as to what is an adequate definition of the concept, I follow the egocentric definition argued, I consider, most convincingly by Mitchell. Much anthropological literature has tended to see network analysis as some kind of theoretical breakthrough and not simply for what it is, a technique of data collection and analysis. I have argued elsewhere (Kapferer, 1970) that for network analysis to be of any real value in explanation it must be tied more explicitly to a theory. Network analysis, I consider, can be best used within the theoretical framework provided by exchange theory. This has also been recognised by others such as Katz (1966), Garbett (1970), Boissevain (1971). Leik et al. (1968) and Emerson (1969) have developed exchange theory in relation to a concept of network but their usage of the concept does not appear to derive from any knowledge of the literature referred to above.

skilled and unskilled workers for militant walkout action. But at the end of time 2 the factory employees again became involved in militant action against management. This time the workers were united in their opposition to management and the internal divisions which had impeded their unity had on the surface largely disappeared. This unity continued through into the early weeks of February 1966 and reached its most dramatic expression in a strike in which all the employees participated.

Only those transactions which regularly[6] occurred between interacting partners are recorded on matrices 1 and 2. For each matrix sociational transactions appear above the diagonal and instrumental transactions below the diagonal. An entry of 1 in a matrix cell indicates that the transactions over the time period taken were reciprocal whereas an entry of 2 or 3 indicates a unilaterality of transactions. I have distinguished only between unilateral and reciprocal transactions in the case of instrumental transactions, for reasons discussed earlier. Reading across the rows of the matrices from left to right, an entry of 2 in a cell of an individual whose row it is indicates that the individual concerned is giving out more benefits and services than he receives. An entry of 3 in a cell row indicates the reverse. However, if the matrices are read down the columns for the same individuals whose cell rows have been considered, then an entry of 2 has the same meaning as an entry of 1 in a cell row. For example, in the case of Mukubwa (20) on matrix 1, reading along his row it can be seen that he gives out more benefits and services than he receives (indicated by entries of 2) in his interaction with Abraham (3), Zulu (13), Lwanga (15), Nyirenda (16) and Chisokone (17). Reading down the column for Mukubwa (20), we can also see, for instance, that he gives out more than he receives in his relationships with Ibrahim (26), Ben (25) and Mpundu (30) (indicated by entries of 3). If the entries in these column cells had been 2, then this would have indicated that Mukubwa received more than he put out.

I have indicated on the matrices the major clusters of interactional relationships. Each cluster consists of a set of individuals whose interactions are mainly distributed among each other. I have derived these clusters by using a method for clustering sociometric choices in a matrix devised by Beum and Brundage (1950). Their method involves rearranging the columns and rows on a matrix so as to reveal the areas of greatest clustering in the matrix. Thus through the use of this method

---

[6] By 'regular' I refer to repeated transactional activity. That is transactional activity which I recorded between individuals which occurred more than once and from my data appeared as a relatively frequent aspect of their interaction.

the individuals who tend to form a common interactional set are clustered together on the matrix.

The information presented on the two matrices provides the basis for the measures of personal networks shown on tables 5.1 and 5.2. There are three structural properties of personal networks which I have measured and these are span, density and multiplexity. The measures I use have only been applied to what Barnes terms an ego's primary or first order zone (1969: 59) and thus only refer to an individual's direct (one step) interactional relationships with others and the interactional relationships between these individuals.

The three network structural properties[7] of span, density and multiplexity are, I consider, useful in deriving an *index*, additional to that inferred from an examination of the matrices, of the degree of power and influence which individuals in the factory could possibly wield.

A general assumption, upon which the selection of these structural properties of networks rests, is that individuals in order to achieve the support of others must be able to manipulate and exert pressures through their set of personal interactional relationships. *Span*, therefore, is concerned with the extent to which an individual encompasses the existing sets of factory interactional relationships within his own set of relationships. It is assumed that individuals with an extensive span of relationships will be able to mobilise more individuals to their support than individuals who in comparison have a limited span to their relationships. *Density* relates to the degree to which an individual is involved in a closed or open set of relationships. Here the assumption is that on the occasion of a confrontation or dispute between two individuals requiring the mobilization of support, if one individual relative to the other is placed at the centre of a more dense set of relationships, then the former will be most likely to achieve the greatest success in the mobilization of support. This can be expected because a dense set of relationships indicates that pressure will be exerted on individuals to support another not merely through their interactional relationships with the individual concerned but also indirectly through their relationships to one another. Moreover, where an individual is involved in a dense set of interactional relationships it may be inferred

[7] These structural properties and the measures of them were initially developed and applied in Kapferer (1969). I have not examined all the structural properties of networks here, or indeed used all the possible measures which could be used for the type of properties I investigate. Other measures which could be applied in relation to those aspects with which I am concerned have been dealt with by Mitchell (1969), Garbett (1968, 1970) and Niemeijer (1971).

that this is so because the individuals concerned share many interests in common. For this reason alone an individual who is at the centre of a dense set of interactional relationships may expect greater support than an individual who is at the centre of a more loose-knit set of relationships. However, the extent to which density is a predictive index of behaviour is dependent on the factor of span. That is, if one of the competitors is involved in a slightly less dense set of relationships but has a markedly higher span to his relationships then I would argue that his higher span would lead to a greater likelihood of his chances of success in the competition. For instance, in chapter 6, I discuss aspects of the competition between the head tailor, Mukubwa, and Lyashi, a line 1 tailor, for the support of the workers. Lyashi had a greater density to his set of relationships than Mukubwa. But Mukubwa in contrast to Lyashi was involved in an extensive span of relationships. (Later in the competition Lyashi did extend the span of his relationships and this is seen on table 5.1.) This was one factor which assisted Mukubwa in the *early stage* of the competition to thwart the attempts by Lyashi to undermine Mukubwa's position and to attract support away from him. As the influence of a dense set of ties in mobilising support is modified by the span of the relationships of an opponent so both span and density as predictive indices of the degree of support and influence an individual can exert are dependent on the factor of multiplexity. The assumption which underlies the consideration of multiplexity is, that an individual, when faced with a choice of supporting either one of two competitors, both of whom he is involved with in interactional relationships, will choose to support the individual with whom he has the greater investment. An indication of the degree of an individual's investment in one competitor for his support, relative to his investment in the other, is the extent to which sociational and instrumental transactions are both a feature of the interactional relationship concerned. If both sociational and instrumental transactions occur in an individual's relationships with one competitor (i.e. the relationship is multiplex) whereas only one kind of transaction (sociational or instrumental) occurs in an individual's relationship with the other competitor (i.e. the relationship is simplex) then it is argued that the individual is more likely to support the former competitor.

I now turn to a description of the measures used in the analysis of personal networks.

1 Span By span I refer to the number of relationships out of the total viable interactional relationships operating between actors in the factory captured by Ego as a result of including specific individuals within his direct set or first-order zone of relationships. In my treatment of span I have not taken into account the distinction between sociational and instrumental transactions and only the interactional relationship which they comprise has been used in the measure. The measure of span presented on tables 5.1 and 5.2 was obtained in the following way:

$$100 \frac{(E + Na)}{S}$$

where $E =$ the number of direct links between Ego and other individuals in his personal network, $Na =$ the number of links between each of the

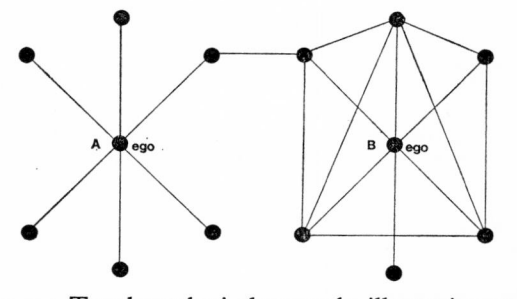

Fig. 5.1 Two hypothetical networks illustrating span

individuals to whom Ego is linked and $S =$ the total number of links between all employees in the factory. For example, take points A and B in the hypothetical personal network on fig. 5.1 to represent all the individuals in a specific context and the lines connecting the points to indicate all the relationships existing between them, which in fig. 5.1 totals twenty. Therefore, the span of A's personal network would be as follows: $N = 6$, $Na = 0$ and $S = 6 \ldots$

$$\text{Span} = 100 \frac{(6 + 0)}{20}$$

$= 30 \cdot 0$; B's span $= 65 \cdot 0$.

My main interest in focusing the measure of span on the number of links involved in a network rather than the number of individuals is to distinguish the differential quality of the span of individual networks. For example, in the two hypothetical networks A and B on fig. 5.1 it is seen that both have the same number of individuals in them but the number of links which each of them includes in his network differs, B's network having a higher percentage span than A's.

2 Density By density I simply refer to the extent to which the individuals to whom Ego is linked are linked to each other. The measure used for network density, is the same as the one used by Kephart (1950: 546) but I have excluded from it Ego's direct relationships to his network members. This particular measure may be regarded as having some similarity with the measure of completeness in graph theory. Network density is found by dividing the actual number of interlinkages between the individuals in a network by the possible number of interlinkages. This is expressed by the formula:

$$\left(\frac{2Na}{N\,(N-1)} \right) 100$$

where $Na =$ the number of actual links and N the total number of persons in the network.

3 Multiplexity[8] There are two dimensions to multiplexity which are measured. The first is *star* multiplexity, or whether one or both transactional contents (sociational and instrumental) are present in each of Ego's direct relationships. The second is *zone* multiplexity, or whether there is one or more transactional contents in each of the relationships between the individuals to whom Ego is directly tied. In this last measure Ego's direct interactional relationships have been excluded. For both star and zone multiplexity the measure is simply obtained by expressing the number of relationships which are multiplex (i.e. sociational plus instrumental transactions as a proportion of the total number of relationships involved (i.e. multiplex relationships and those with only one transactional content or simplex relationships).

The measures for span, density and multiplexity have been used, as indicated on tables 5.1 and 5.2, to typify the individual networks observed in the factory. For each measure the median for the factory

---

[8] The measure of multiplexity used here is different from that I initially devised in an earlier paper (1969: 226). In that paper I broke what I now term sociational and instrumental transactions into a number of further components based on the precise nature of the content, such as general conversation, joking, cash assistance, etc. Where two or more of these contents occurred I then considered that a multi-stranded or multiplex relationship existed. The criteria of multiplexity I now use—i.e. interactional relationships must have sociational and instrumental components and not as before merely two components irrespective of whether they were all sociational or also included instrumental components—is more sensitive as an index of investment and for the type of analysis I pursue.

was taken and those above the median have been indicated by a $+$ and those below by a $-$. Therefore, a pattern of $+++$ indicates that an individual's network is above median for each of the structural properties measured.

On both the relevant tables the individuals and their network types have been ordered according to the pattern of their network. Span and density are the main principles in terms of which the individual networks have been ordered. For the reasons stated earlier, I regard span and density as the major indicators of the degree to which an individual can mobilise support relative to others and the strength of his position in the factory set of relationships. Because the measure of span refers specifically to the extent to which an individual encompasses the total set of relationships in the factory within his personal ties it is the major factor which determines an individual's rank order on the tables. For example, take two individuals both of whom are above the median for span and density in the factory, the individual with the higher span is ranked above the individual with a lower span. The two measures of star and zone multiplexity I regard as mainly relevant in relation to span and density. As star multiplexity applies to the extent of the investments which an individual has in his direct relationships to others, I argue that it will have more influence for an individual's behaviour than zone multiplexity. Therefore, where an individual has a higher measure of star multiplexity than another the former will be ranked higher on the table. In general little significance can be placed on star or zone multiplexity when an individual does not score above the median for either span or density. Star multiplexity is relevant mainly for span as this measure is largely concerned with Ego's direct relationships. Zone multiplexity has its chief relevance for density as it is concerned with the degree of investment which the individuals to whom Ego is directly connected have with each other.[9] The scores on the tables follow this order, highest is $++++$, then $+++-$, $++-+$, $+-+-$, $+--+$, $++--$, etc.

The method for ranking the structural types of networks on the tables is not completely satisfactory but it must be emphasised that the types are only an index.

Analysis: matrices and networks The central problem of the analysis in this section, around which the data I present are organised,

---

[9] There is some degree of overlap. Included in the measure for span are the interactional relationships which individuals directly connected to Ego have with each other. Therefore zone multiplexity has some relevance for span.

generally concerns the extent to which the pattern and structure[10] of interactional relationships for the two time periods I take can be related to changes in worker reaction to strike activity. As stated previously, the September walk-out which occurred just after the period covered by time 1 received most of its support from the senior skilled employees and not from the less skilled junior workers. In contrast, however, in the following February just after the period covered by time 2 a strike was organised which had the united support of all the workers. Two related explanations, the validity of which as explanations can be put to limited test by reference to data on interactional relationships, can account for the change in worker reaction to industrial action against management. These explanations are that by time 2, in contrast to time 1, (a) the actions of members of the work force most likely not to support strike activity were subject to greater control and influence by those whose interests stood to be most benefited by strike action—the line 1 tailors; and (b) the workers, irrespective of such factors as occupational category, tended to share more interests in common.

Fig. 5.2(a) Work positions of factory employees, June 1965

---

10 By 'pattern' I refer to the distribution of interactional relationships, whereas structure refers to such aspects of interactional relationships as the reciprocity or unilaterality of transactions within them, their span, density, etc.

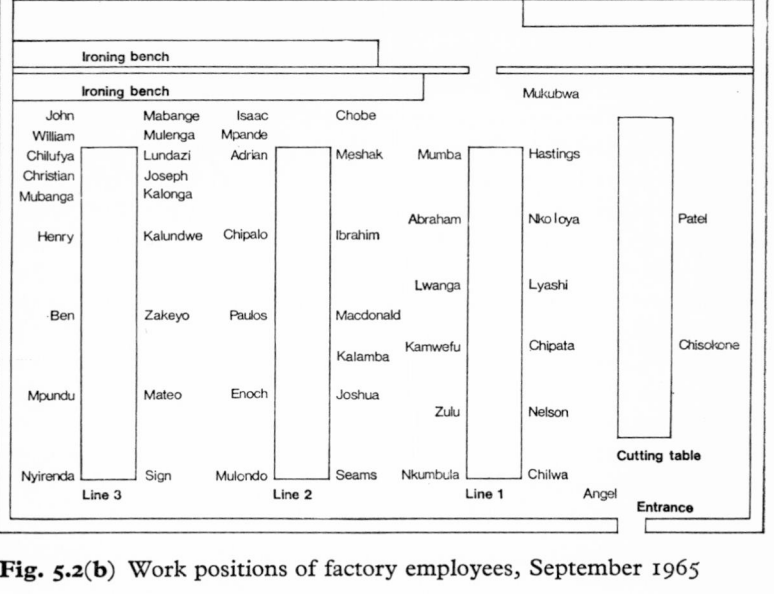

Fig. 5.2(b) Work positions of factory employees, September 1965

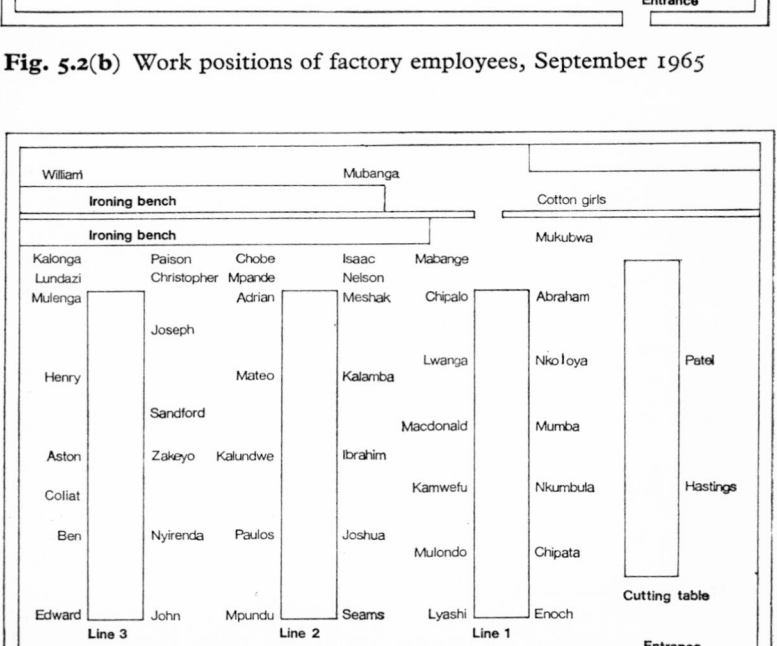

Fig. 5.2(c) Work positions of factory employees, January 1966

	1	2	3	4	5	6	7	8	9	10	11	12	13	14	15	16	17	18	19	20	21	22	23	24	25
1			1	1		1			1			1													
2			1	1								1	1				1								
3	1			1		1	1	1	1	1		1	1	1		1	1			1	1				
4	2											1	1	1	1		1			1					
5							1		1			1	1	1											
6	1		1		1		1	1		1		1	1		1										
7			1									1	1	1			1			1					
8						2				1		1					1								
9																	1		1						
10			1									1			1		1						1		
11													1												
12		1	1	2	1	1		1		1			1	1	1		1			1	1				
13		2	1	2					2			1		1			1		1	1		1			
14			1						2								1								
15	2			2															1	1	1				
16			1														1			1					1
17			3					1		2		1	1	1	2			1		1	1	1			
18																	3								
19																				1	1				
20			2									1	2			2	2				1	1			1
21																3				2			1		1
22																									1
23																									1
24																						1			
25																1				3					
26																	3	3		3		1			2
27			2																						
28																									
29																								1	1
30														3	3					3					
31						3					3											1			
32																		3							
33													3							3					
34																									
35																		3							
36																				3					
37																									
38																									
39																								3	
40																		3							
41																		3		1					
42																									
43																									

Matrix 1 Interactional relationships for time 1.

Key: 1 = reciprocal relationship, 2 = gives more than receives, 3 = receives more than gives. Above diagonal: sociational relationships; below diagonal: instrumental transactions.

Note: (a) As far as possible, only transactions which were

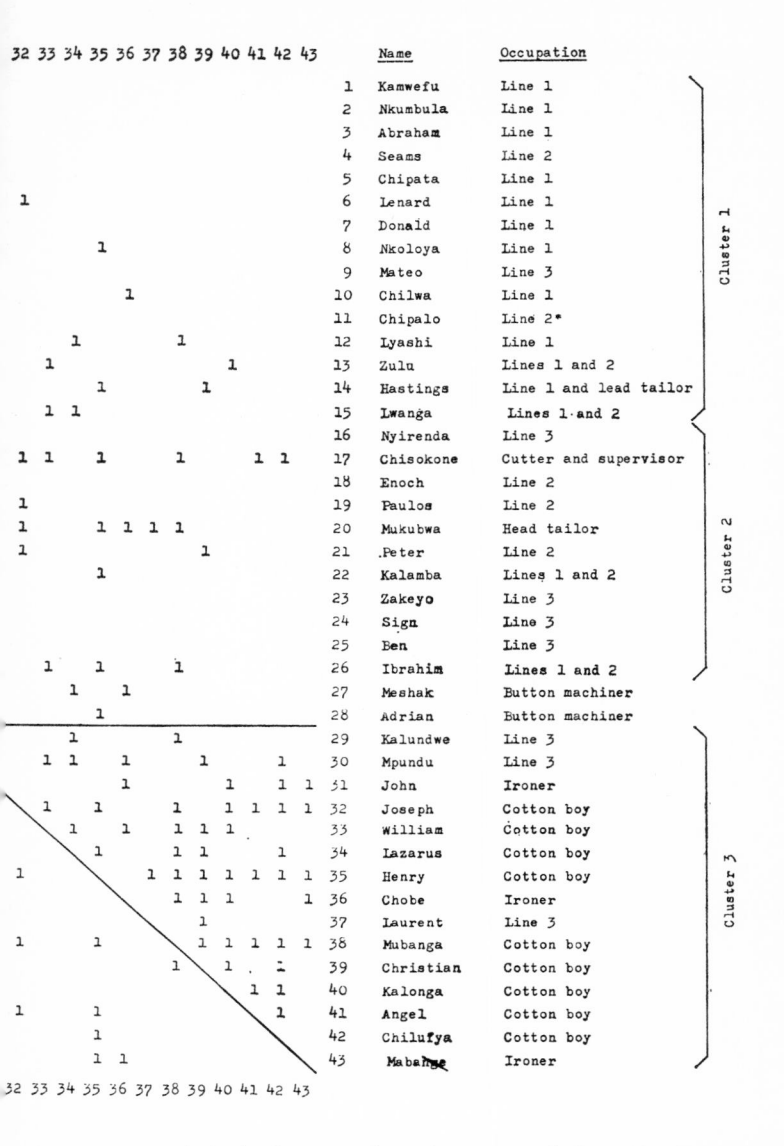

relatively frequent have been recorded on the matrix. For example, instances where I observed only one interaction over the specified time period have been excluded. (b) The reader should be aware that some individuals on the matrix were not present throughout the time period.

* Chipalo joined late in the time period.

Matrix 2: Interactional relationships for time 2.

See notes to matrix 1.

* Donald was re-employed in time 2 for four days.

32	55	38	16	7	33	40	35	36	31	41	43	21	56	57	39	58	42	#	Name	Occupation	Cluster
																		44	Macdonald	Line 1	Cluster 1
																		45	Christopher	Cotton boy	
																		46	Mulondo	Line 1	
																		47	Mpande	Cotton boy	
																		10	Chilwa	Lines 1 and 3	
																		1	Kamwefu	Line 1	
																		19	Paulos	Line 2	
																		11	Chipalo	Line 1	
1	1																	5	Chipata	Line 1	
		1																13	Zulu	Line 1	
1																		8	Nkoloya	Line 1	
	1																	3	Abraham	Line 1	
1			1															15	Lwanga	Line 1	
																		9	Mateo	Line 2	
																		18	Enoch	Line 1	
1					1	1												12	Lyashi	Line 1	
1	1																	48	Mumba	Line 1	
1			1															2	Nkumbula	Line 1	
																		29	Kalundwe	Line 2	Cluster 2
1								1	1									14	Hastings	Lead tailor	
	1	1																49	Lundazi	Cotton boy	
																		4	Seams	Line 2	
		1							1									30	Mpundu	Line 2	
1	1	1					1					1						27	Meshak	Buttons	
	1																	50	Edward	Line 3	
1	1	1			1	1	1											22	Kalamba	Line 2	
1	1						1				1	1				1	1	26	Ibrahim	Line 2	
1		1																51	Sandford	Line 3	
1	1	1	1				1	1	1		1							20	Mukubwa	Head tailor	
	1						1	1										28	Adrian	Buttons	
1		1				1	1											52	Coliat	Line 3	
1		1				1	1	1	1	1		1	1	1	1			17	Chisokone	Cutter	
	1					1												53	Aston	Line 3	
							1		1									54	Paison	Cotton boy	
	1						1					1						25	Ben	Line 3	
	1		1				1											23	Zakeyo	Line 3	
	1					1	1					1		1	1	1	1	32	Joseph	Line 3	
																		55	Isaac	Ironer	
1					1	1	1	1	1				1		1			38	Mubanga	Ironer	Cluster 3
						1		1	1			1						16	Nyirenda	Line 3	
										1								7	Donald	Line 1*	
					1		1	1		1								33	William	Ironer	
					1		1	1		1			1				1	40	Kalonga	Ironer	
1	1							1	1					1	1			35	Henry	Line 3	
		1						1	1									36	Chobe	Ironer	
	1							1	1								1	31	John	Line 3	
								1									1	41	Angel	Cotton boy	
									1	1								43	Mabange	Ironer	
												1					1	21	Sign	Line 3	
																	1	56	Joshua	Line 2	
														1				57	Nelson	Cotton boy	
	1													1			1	39	Christian	Cotton boy	
								1										58	Mulenga	Cotton boy	
																		42	Chilufya	Cotton boy	

A comparison of matrices 1 and 2 reveals both changes and fundamental continuities in the pattern and structure of interactional relationships between the end of time 1 and the close of time 2. At time 1
three major clusters including most of the factory workers can be seen
but with relatively few interactional relationships cross-cutting them.
By the end of time 2, although three major clusters are still discernible,
unlike for time 1, the boundaries between them are less easily established. This is because of the increase in interactional relationships
cross-cutting the respective clusters. At the end of time 2, therefore, the
factory workers are more linked into a common set of interactional
relationships than they were at the end of time 1.

This change receives added significance when the composition of the
clusters for the two time periods is examined. The description in
previous chapters has shown that factors such as skill, length of employment in the factory, occupation, etc., are associated with major divisions
of interest between the employees in the work place. The following
description will show that these factors underlie much of the social
composition of the clusters, and that, in time 1 the tendency towards a
division of interest between the members of the separate clusters, and
particularly cluster 1 and cluster 3, is relatively unmodified by a set of
cross-cutting relationships.

On matrix 1 for time 1, cluster 1 is predominantly composed of line 1
tailors. All these workers are employed on the same bench, possess
similar skills and have been employed for the longest period of time in
the factory. These factors and specifically location on the same bench
and length of employment mean that the individuals concerned have
had greater opportunity to establish interactional relationships with one
another. This partly explains why they should interact together more
than with other factory employees. Similar considerations account for
the social composition of cluster 3. The workers in this cluster are either
line 3 tailors of low skill or of no skill at all such as cotton boys and
ironers. Cluster 2 draws its membership from individuals who are
either supervisors (Chisokone, 17, and Mukubwa, 20) or who are of
medium skill in the factory (line 2 tailors). All these individuals are
engaged in productive activities which tend to bring them into contact
with one another and with members of other clusters. This accounts for
the positioning of this cluster at a point on the matrix midway between
cluster 1 and cluster 3. Thus in the course of their supervisory duties
Chisokone (17) and Mukubwa (20) come into contact with most of the
workers on the factory floor. Ibrahim (26) and Kalamba (22) operate
the overlock machines, which brings them into contact with many of

the other workers. The fact that most of the individuals in this cluster work on line 2 increases their opportunity to interact with one another. The location of the bench between line 1 and 3 also contributes to their tendency to be engaged in interaction with workers on line 1 and workers on or near line 3.

By the end of time 2 there are some alterations both in membership and size of the major interactional clusters. This is partly the result of labour turnover and the promotion of some of the employees who remained. Nevertheless, the factors which underlie the composition of the major clusters for time 1 also account for the composition of those clusters which are represented on matrix 2. In general, therefore, the individuals who comprise cluster 1 on matrix 2 are the skilled, senior factory employees; those in cluster 2 are in supervisory work or occupy a position in the production process which brings them into contact with all categories of workers; and, finally, those in cluster 3 are the unskilled employees. But here the similarity ends. I have already stressed that individuals within the separate clusters, by the end of time 2, are more bound into a set of relationships involving individuals in other clusters. This is important, for I consider that the development of regular interaction with another is impeded if the partners to the interaction do not have, or, at least, cannot develop, some interests in common. If this is accepted, then it follows that the extension of inter-actional relationships linking individuals in the different clusters repre-sented both an expression of the growth of a greater degree of common interest among the workers and the development of channels through which shared interests could be communicated. These aspects alone would explain, at least partly, the greater preparedness of all the factory workers to participate in joint strike action in February 1965.

In addition, the form and content of the interactional relationships at time 2 indicates that the senior workers, especially the line 1 tailors, would be able to exert a greater degree of power and influence over those junior to them. Although, as in time 1, most of the interactional relationships in time 2 are simplex marked by sociational transactions, there is an increase in multiplex relationships. This in itself would indicate an increase in investment in these relationships. An effect of this which could be predicted would be a greater preparedness of partners to these relationships to support each other. This assumes, of course, that individuals act in a way to protect their sets of investments.[11]

---

[11] I have demonstrated the utility of this assumption elsewhere (1969) in a paper which examines processes of social activity among a group of African mine workers.

Table 5.1 Social networks for time 1

Number on matrix	Name	Occupation	Number of direct relation-ships	Network types				Span	Density	Star multi-plexity	Zone multi-plexity
				Span	Density	Star multi-plexity	Zone multi-plexity				
3	Abraham	Line 1	13	+	+	+	+	16.8498	42.3077	0.4444	0.6957
4	Seams	Line 2	9	+	·	+	+	11.3553	61.1111	0.4444	0.6957
35	Henry	Cotton boy	9	+	+	+	-	10.9890	58.3333	0.4375	0.2895
26	Ibrahim	Lines 1 and 2	9	+	+	+	-	9.1575	44.4444	0.6364	0.3478
32	Joseph	Cotton boy	6	+	+	+	-	7.3260	93.3333	0.3333	0.2963
41	Angel	Cotton boy	5	+	+	+	-	5.1282	90.0000	0.4286	0.3889
33	William	Cotton boy	8	+	+	-	-	8.4249	53.5714	0.0833	0.4000
38	Mubanga	Cotton boy	8	+	±	+	-	7.6923	46.4286	0.2500	0.3556
20	Mukubwa	Head tailor	16	+	-	+	+	19.4139	30.8333	0.4545	0.4762
13	Zulu	Lines 1 and 2	12	+	-	+	+	14.2857	40.9091	0.3529	0.4634
6	Lenard	Line 1	8	+	-	+	+	6.9597	39.2859	0.3000	0.4737
21	Peter	Line 2	7	+	-	+	+	5.1282	35.3333	0.3000	0.6000
1	Kamwefu	Line 1	5	+	-	+	+	4.7619	30.0000	0.5000	0.7778
17	Chisokone	Cutter	21	+	-	+	-	29.6703	28.5714	0.4444	0.4906
12	Iyashi	Line 1	16	+	-	+	-	22.3443	37.5000	0.5556	0.3729
30	Mpundu	Line 3	10	+	-	+	-	9.5238	35.5556	0.2727	0.4000
15	Iwanga	Lines 1 and 2	9	-	-	-	-	7.6923	33.3333	0.3846	0.4333
7	Donald	Line 1	7	-	+	-	+	8.7619	30.9524	0.1250	0.8421
10	Chilwa	Line 1	9	+	-	+	+	8.4249	38.8889	0.2500	0.6250

No.	Name	Role	n										
14	Hastings	Lead tailor	6	+	–	–	+	–	–	+	4.3956	40.0000	0.1818	0.6087
31	John	Ironer	7	+	–	–	–	–	–	+	4.3956	23.8095	0.1667	0.3500
2	Nkumbula	Line 1	4	+	–	–	–	–	–	–	3.6630	100.0000	0.4000	0.8000
16	Nyirenda	Line 3	5	+	–	–	+	–	–	+	3.6630	50.0000	0.8000	0.6667
43	Mabange	Ironer	4	+	–	–	+	–	–	+	2.9304	66.6667	0.4000	0.6000
18	Enoch	Line 2	2	+	–	–	+	–	–	+	1.0989	100.0000	1.0000	1.0000
8	Nicoloya	Line 1	4	+	–	–	+	–	–	+	2.9304	66.6667	0.2222	0.6875
24	Sign	Line 3	2	+	–	–	+	+	+	–	1.0989	100.0000	1.0000	0.0000
34	Lazarus	Cotton boy	4	+	–	–	+	–	–	–	3.6630	100.0000	0.0000	0.3333
36	Chobe	Ironer.	5	+	–	–	+	–	–	–	3.6630	50.0000	0.2000	0.1429
39	Christian	Cotton boy	5	+	–·	–	+	–	–	–	3.6630	50.0000	0.0769	0.1250
40	Kalonga	Cotton boy	4	+	–	–	+	–	–	–	3.2967	83.3333	0.0909	0.3548
5	Chipata	Line 1	4	+	–	–	+	–	–	–	2.9304	66.6667	0.1667	0.4444
37	Laurent	Line 3	2	+	–	–	+	–	–	–	1.0989	100.0000	0.0000	0.0000
23	Zakeyo	Line 3	2	+	–	–	+	+	+	–	1.0989	100.0000	0.0000	0.0000
25	Ben	Line 3	6	+	–	–	+	–	–	–	4.0293	100.0000	0.0000	0.0000
19	Paulos	Line 2	4	+	–	–	+	+	+	+	2.1978	33.3333	0.0000	0.5556
22	Kalamba	Lines 1 and 2	4	+	–	–	+	–	+	+	2.1978	33.3333	0.2500	0.7143
27	Meshak	Buttons	4	+	–	–	+	–	+	+	1.8315	16.6667	0.0000	0.5000
9	Mateo	Line 3	2	+	–	–	+	–	+	+	0.7326	0.0000	1.0000	1.0000
28	Adrian	Buttons	1	+	–	–	+	–	+	+	0.3663	0.0000	0.0000	1.0000
29	Kalundwe	Line 3	3	+	–	–	+	–	+	+	1.4652	33.3333	0.2500	0.2000
42	Chilufya	Cotton boy	1	–	–	–	–	–	–	–	0.3663	0.0000	0.1000	0.4167
11	Chipalo	Line 2	1	–	–	–	–	–	–	–	0.3663	0.0000	0.0000	0.0000

Moreover, many of the instrumental transactions in these relationships were unilateral, line 1 tailors, for example, distributing services and benefits to less skilled employees which in large part were unreciprocated.

The suggestion contained here, that the power and influence of the senior workers over those less skilled than themselves increased in the period covered by time 2, receives greater force when the structure of the individual networks is examined. As stated earlier, the network structural measures (see tables 5.1 and 5.2), when viewed in conjunction with the matrices, present some indication of the extent to which individuals can exert power and influence over others in the factory and perhaps mobilise their support.

During time 1 the two supervisors, Chisokone (17) and Mukubwa (20) had high measures of span and star multiplexity to their networks. The interactional relationships which formed their networks were also characterised by unilateral instrumental transactions which involved their distributing unreciprocated benefits and services. These aspects indicate that the supervisors concerned could exert considerable power and influence over others as a function of the structure of their relationships. This accords generally with my observations in the factory over the same period. Other workers in time 1, even though they had high scores for the various network structural measures, had their interactional relationships restricted mainly to individuals of similar skill and work position (see matrix 1).

Even so the network structural measures indicate some differentiation in terms of power and influence within the major clusters. Thus in cluster 1 Lyashi (12), Nkoloya (8), Abraham (3) and Lwanga (15) score highly for the network structural measures. This agrees with my general observations during time 1 of the prominent part which these individuals played in forming opinions and mobilising support for political action. Nkumbula (2) and Lenard (6) in the same cluster also have high network structural measures, but unlike the others, did not play a major political role in the factory. Nevertheless, both were influential and the support which quickly mobilised around Lenard, for example, on the occasion of a dispute he had with Patel and Mukubwa, is to some extent demonstrative of the effectiveness of his set of interactional relationships.[12] Similar differentiation in terms of the structure of personal networks is evident in other clusters for the same time period. Henry (9), William (33), Mubanga (38) and Joseph (32) in cluster 3 all have relatively high structural measures for their networks. All these men were influential in activities centred on

[12] See 'The case of the badly stitched trousers', chapter 6.

the factory particularly within the ranks of the unskilled workers to whom their relationships were largely limited.

Table 5.2 shows that, with the exception of Lenard who had left employment, those individuals whose network structural measures indicate that they could exert some power and influence over the activities of others in the factory during time 1, in time 2 continue to score highly for the various network structural measures. Moreover, these individuals are less restricted in their personal networks to individuals of similar skill and work position (see matrix 2). But by the end of time 2 other individuals, in addition to those discussed in relation to time 1, are also notable for the high scores which they receive for the network structural measures. Thus, Mumba (48), a newcomer to the factory employed on line 1, scores highly for all the network structural properties. Kamwefu (1) also scores highly for all the measures in time 2 compared with his lower scores in time 1, as too do Chipata (5) and Meshak (27). The networks of these individuals indicate that in time 2 they would be prominent in factory politics and from my observations, recounted in some detail in the following chapters, this was indeed the case. Furthermore, that the networks of these individuals were less restricted to peers and included other individuals from different occupational categories supports the earlier statement that the range of power and influence of the senior employees had been extended by the end of time 2 compared with the period covered by time 1.

Before I conclude this description, however, it is important to note that many of the relationships which cross-cut the different clusters at the end of time 2 connect individuals who occupy central positions in the sets of relationships involving mainly their peers. Lyashi (12), for example, as well as being a central figure in cluster 1 (matrix 2), in his relationships outside this cluster is connected to individuals, such as Joseph (32), Mubanga (38) and John (31), who are themselves central in the sets of relationships with their own peers. An individual who can develop a relationship with another who is already influential in a set of relationships different from his own, stands to increase the range of his power and influence to include those who are already subject to the influence of that individual with whom he establishes the relationship. This observation suggests, therefore, that an index of the increase in the range of power and influence of the senior workers over those less skilled than themselves *must not be seen simply in terms of a gross increase in cross-cutting relationships*. An index of the increase in the power and influence of the senior employees should also be seen in terms of the specific individuals to whom these workers extend their interactional

o

Table 5.2 Social networks for time 2

Number on matrix 2	Name	Occupation	Number of direct relation-ships	Network types							
				Span	Density	Star multi-plexity	Zone multi-plexity	Span	Density	Star multi-plexity	Zone multi-plexity
3	Abraham	line 1	17	+	+	+	+	23.6952	58.8235	0.5000	0.3619
5	Chipata	line 1	16	+	+	+	+	17.6190	48.3333	0.3636	0.5793
8	Nkoloya	line 1	14	+	+	+	+	16.9048	62.6374	0.4706	0.3913
48	Mumba	line 1	12	+	+	+	+	13.0952	65.1515	0.3333	0.4444
1	Kamwefu	line 1	10	+	+	+	+	10.9524	80.0000	0.2667	0.4906
15	Iwanga	line 1	11	+	+	+	+	10.0000	56.3636	0.4000	0.4583
13	Zulu	line 1	10	+	+	+	+	9.2857	64.4444	0.3333	0.4464
10	Chilwa	line 1	10	+	+	+	+	9.2857	64.4444	0.4000	0.6000
11	Chipalo	line 1	7	+	+	+	+	5.4762	76.1905	0.2500	0.4706
9	Mateo	line 2	6	+	+	+	+	3.5714	60.0000	0.6667	0.4444
20	Mukubwa	Head tailor	20	+	+	-	+	24.0476	42.6316	0.2500	0.2866
2	Nkumbula	line 1	13	+	+	-	-	11.9048	47.4359	0.3529	0.3437
32	Joseph	line 3	12	+	+	+	-	9.7619	43.9394	0.2857	0.2967
31	John	line 3	11	+	+	+	-	8.3333	43.6364	0.2353	0.2000
35	Henry	line 3	7	+	+	+	-	5.0000	66.6667	0.3125	0.2586
14	Hastings	lead tailor	15	+	+	+	+	15.9524	49.5238	0.1600	0.3652
27	Meshak	Buttons	11	+	+	-	+	8.0952	41.8182	0.1154	0.3723
52	Coliat	line 3	8	+	+	-	+	5.9524	60.7143	0.0000	0.5152
19	Paulos	line 2	8	+	+	-	+	5.2381	50.0000	0.2857	0.4000
22	Kalamba	line 2	11	+	+	-	-	7.8571	40.0000	0.3579	0.3600
26	Ibrahim	line 2	18	+	+	-	-	17.8571	37.2549	0.3600	0.3604
18	Enoch	line 1	9	+	+	+	+	5.2381	36.1111	0.5556	0.4286
12	Iyashi	line 1	21	-	+	+	+	23.0952	36.1905	0.5217	0.3417
17	Chiaokone	Cutter	18	-	-	+	-	13.8095	26.1458	0.3333	0.3271

No.	Name	Job	n							
38	Mabanga	Ironer	13		+		+	10.4762	39.7436	0.2273	0.2697
49	Lundazi	Cotton boy	12		+		+	8.3333	34.8485	0.0769	0.4000
40	Kalonga	Ironer	8	+	–	+	–	4.0476	32.1429	0.0769	0.3125
25	Ben	Line 3	4	+	–	+	–	1.9048	66.6667	0.3000	0.2308
41	Angel	Cotton boy	6	+	–	+	–	3.0952	46.6667	0.2000	0.4400
46	Muiondo	Line 1	6	–	–	–	–	2.8571	40.0000	0.0000	0.6667
54	Paison	Cotton boy	4	–	+	–	+	2.1429	83.3333	0.0000	0.4167
23	Zakeyo	Line 3	4	–	+	–	+	1.9048	66.6667	0.0909	0.3333
29	Kalundwe	Line 2	4	–	–	–	–	1.6667	50.0000	0.0000	0.3333
55	Isaac	Ironer	2	–	+	–	–	0.7143	100.0000	0.0000	0.0000
50	Edward	Line 3	3	+	+	+	+	0.9524	33.3333	0.2500	0.5000
16	Nyirenda	Line 3	6	–	+	–	–	2.3810	26.6667	0.3333	0.2273
4	Seams	Line 2	3	+	+	+	–	0.9524	33.3333	0.6667	0.0000
44	Macdonald	Line 1	4	+	+	+	–	0.4762	0.0000	0.5000	0.0000
45	Christopher	Cotton boy	2	–	+	+	–	0.4762	0.0000	0.5000	0.5000
30	Mpundu	Line 2	8	–	–	+	–	3.3333	21.4286	0.1333	0.0000
28	Adrian	Buttons	4	+	+	+	+	1.4286	33.3333	0.0000	0.3824
58	Milenga	Cotton boy	3	–	+	+	+	0.7143	0.0000	0.2000	0.6250
39	Christian	Cotton boy	3	–	+	+	+	0.4762	0.0000	0.0000	0.5000
57	Nelson	Cotton boy	1	–	–	–	+	0.2381	0.0000	0.0000	0.6667
33	William	Ironer	5	–	–	–		1.9048	30.0000	0.0769	0.2333
21	Sign	Line 3	4	–	–	–		1.4286	33.3333	0.0000	0.3333
51	Sandford	Line 3	3	–	–	–		0.9524	33.3333	0.0000	0.1905
53	Aston	Line 3	3	–	–	–		0.9524	33.3333	0.0909	0.0909
43	Mabange	Ironer	2	–	–	–		0.9524	33.3333	0.1000	0.1667
56	Joshua	Line 2	3	–	–	–		0.7143	0.0000	0.2500	0.3333
42	Chilufya	Cotton boy	2	–	–	–		0.4762	0.0000	0.2500	0.3333
7	Donald	Line 1	2	–	–	–		0.4762	0.0000	0.0000	0.0000
47	Mpande.	Cotton boy	2	–	–	–		0.4762	0.0000	0.5000	0.0000
36	Chobe	Ironer	1	–	–	–	–	0.2381	0.0000	0.0909	0.2174

relationships. Indeed the ability of senior skilled employees to develop relationships with a few less skilled and junior employees who are nonetheless influential in their own sets of relationships, a pattern which in fact is evident on matrix 2, can have the same effect as might be achieved by developing relationships with more, but less influential, junior workers.

This description only broadly sketches the pattern and structure of interactional relationships at the two time periods and the changes which occurred. The description has focused primarily on individuals who, as will be illustrated in the description in later chapters, played a prominent part in factory politics. Generally, however, the description and the evidence presented on the matrices and tables for the two time periods explains partly the greater preparedness of all the factory workers to engage in strike activity after the close of time 2 than at the end of time 1. The extension of relationships connecting individuals of different skill, work position, etc., at the end of time 2 indicates a growth in the degree to which the workers are linked by common interests. Perhaps of more importance, at the end of time 2 the individuals who played a leading part in organising strike activity, such as Lyashi, Nkoloya, Lwanga, etc., had established relationships with workers less skilled than themselves. Moreover, because these relationships were frequently characterised by unilateral instrumental transactions, it can be inferred that these workers could exert greater control over the activities of those junior to them than at the end of time 1 when the latter showed an unwillingness to acquiesce to the line 1 tailor's demands to support strike action.

Principles underlying interactional choice and change

I have used the change in the pattern and structure of interactions between the two periods as an explanation for the different worker reaction to strike action at the close of the two time periods. An explanation was presented for *why* behaviour should be different at these two periods, but only limited understanding was achieved as to *how* it was that the pattern and structure of interactions should take the form they did, and *how* they changed. The solution to these problems rests largely on a detailed examination of my empirical material over time, and this I will do in the following chapters. Nevertheless, a consideration of some abstract principles drawn from social exchange theory can yield some understanding of how the pattern and structure of interactional relationships represented in the matrices can be expected to take the form they do. Furthermore, I will suggest how these same principles explain the broad directions changes in social relationships may be expected to take. The brief setting out of some of these principles as they relate to some of the data I collected will also serve as useful background to the reader for the analysis presented in later chapters.

The basic proposition upon which this analysis rests is that regular interactional relationships will develop between individuals when the expected or experienced gains from the transaction of resources in the relationship are equal to or greater than the costs from the perspective of the individuals concerned.[13] Where this is not the case, interaction will be restricted or will tend not to take place. Gains are held to be equal to or greater than costs when the value of resources used in transaction is equal to or exceeded by the value of the resources received in return.[14]

I consider that this proposition explains the general pattern and structure of interactional relationships throughout the fieldwork period. In order to demonstrate this, some statement is required about the distribution of resources in the factory, and the value attached to them *in transaction* by various categories of workers.

Certain resources are unequally distributed throughout the factory. These resources include skill, expertise, importance in the production system and prestige. Supervisors and tailors (particularly those on line 1

[13] This proposition lies at the root of most exchange theories of which I am aware. It is most explicit, however, in Barth (1966: 4–13). The proposition as it stands is true by definition and hence a tautology. The empirical determination of what is valued in the factory context, which I do in this analysis, and the rough preferences which various categories of worker have for certain benefits and services, reduce the tautology and exposes the proposition to a degree of empirical test. The proposition can be viewed as a version of the maximisation hypothesis common in economics and game theory. I stress that in my application of the proposition I do not require individuals to take the best possible choice among a set of alternatives.

[14] I find it difficult to arrive at acceptable abstract definitions of gains and costs. These, I consider, can be adequately determined only by empirical study. Should the reader, however, still require abstract definition, then Homans (1961: 37–82) makes the best attempt in terms of the analysis I apply here. Broadly, then, following Homans, an individual gains when he receives through his transactions valued benefits and services. Costs cover those benefits and services which an individual must give out in order to receive valued benefits and services. Also counted as costs are the time, energy, etc., which are expended in the course of making certain choices, which have the effect of reducing the time, energy, etc., which an individual can devote in the pursuit of other alternatives. Related to this, costs also comprise those valued benefits and services foregone as a consequence of adopting specific courses of action.

and some on line 2 in particular the overlock and elasticating machine operators) have greatest access to and control over these resources. Other workers (like the unskilled ironers and cotton boys) have little access to or control over the same resources. There are other resources which are equally distributed across the factory in the sense that the employees have the same potential quantities of them. These resources include approval, support and willing compliance. By the resource of 'willing compliance' I refer to the potential ability of an individual to defer to the demands and instructions of another. Although in essence these kinds of resources will be equally distributed, their value in transaction both for givers and receivers will vary, depending on who the givers and receivers are. It is this factor which differentiates the factory workers from one another in terms of these resources. What causes individuals to value the same resource differently, among other reasons, is the extent to which its use in transaction also implies the use of other valued resources. In social life it is difficult, except for analytical purposes, for individuals to separate the use in transaction of one resource from the use of others. For instance a line 1 tailor who gives his support to an unskilled employee during a dispute will be using not only resources of support but also resources of prestige. It is this which may make a line 1 tailor's support during a dispute more valuable to an unskilled worker than support from one of the latter's peers. Alternatively, a line 1 tailor is likely to place considerably less value on the support of an unskilled worker because the latter is offering *only* support. The general point which I stress here is that the value of one resource cannot and should not be considered independently of other resources which individuals may possess and of which they are aware. The degree to which various resources are interlinked and the extent to which their value in transaction is a product of their interdependence with other resources affects the way individuals will choose to distribute their resources and therefore the way their interactions will develop.

Of course, the value of resources in transaction cannot be assessed in relation to the one relationship in which these transactions take place. The conditions which facilitate or restrict the use of resources gained in transactions in one sphere of transactions (e.g. between line 1 tailors and cotton boys) in another sphere of transactions will affect the value of resources transacted in the initial sphere.[15] The value of resources,

---

[15] I use the phrase 'transactional sphere' or 'sphere of transactions' to refer to a set of individuals involved in transactional activity who place similar value on the benefits and services transacted. Transactional sphere in the sense in which I use the phrase should be distinguished from the phrase sphere of exchange in economic anthropology (Firth, 1958: 69). This relates to an area

although relatively low when limited to one set of relationships, may be increased in value if the resources gained in transactions in the initial sphere can be used in transactions in other sets of relationships. For example, the value of support given by a cotton boy to a line 1 tailor is low if the latter cannot use this support to gain increased status among his peers. In conditions where a line 1 tailor can increase his status among peers by using resources gained from transactional activity with cotton boys, then the value of entering into transactions with cotton boys is substantially increased.

Some further considerations are required before the above principles can be applied to the general patterns represented on the matrices. An important assumption which is consistent with the basic proposition which began this analysis is that individuals will organise their trans-actional activity in order to reduce risk and uncertainty.[16] All social interaction to some extent involves risk and uncertainty. Individuals participate in conditions of varying information and knowledge, and because of this the costs which they incur may only be realised after they have embarked on certain kinds of transactional activity. Further-more, as Blau states;

In contrast to economic transactions, in which an explicit or implicit contract stipulates in advance precise obligations incurred by both parties social exchange entails unspecified obligations. There is no con-tract and there is no exact price. A person to whom others are indebted for favours performed has the general expectation that they will discharge their obligations by doing things for him, but he must leave the exact nature of the return up to them. He cannot bargain with them over how much his favours are worth, and he has no recourse if they fail to recipro-cate altogether, except of course, that he can, and probably will, discon-tinue to do favours for them [1969: 315]

The above points suggest that every new transactional relationship which an individual enters constitutes a risk. Much of the activity

---

of transaction in which only certain types of goods and services can be trans-acted with certain other types of goods and services.

[16] A distinction can be drawn between risk and uncertainty, and in this I broadly follow Knight's now classic definitions (1921: 197–232). By 'risk' I refer to those costs which an individual has some idea he must expose himself to as a result of taking specified courses of action. In the case of risk an in-dividual has an idea of the costs to which he becomes subject both from his own past experience and from his observations of the activity of others. 'Uncertainty', in contrast to risk, refers to costs the specific or even rough nature of which are unknown. Uncertainty emerges where the factors affect-ing social action are to a degree unique, i.e. have not been experienced by any of the individuals partner to the social activity. It will be obvious that risk and uncertainty are present, in varying degrees, in all social activity.

observed on the factory floor, and certainly the change in the pattern and structure of interactional relationships between the two time periods, involved the initiating of new relationships. In order to understand these processes, therefore, some statements as to the conditions which must be present before individuals engage in risk-taking are required. There are, I consider, three basic conditions which must apply, either separately or in combination. First, individuals will take risks or initiate new transactions when the costs in their current sets of relationships, as perceived by them, begin to exceed the gains. Second, individuals will initiate new transactions when they perceive that failure to do so will endanger the continuation of benefits incurred from their current set of transactions, or when the benefits received from a current set of transactions are dependent on their taking risks. Finally, individuals will tend to take risks or initiate new transactions should the failure to successfully establish new relationships result in no cost or at least minimum cost to their investments in their current set of relationships.

At this stage some of the general patterns represented on matrices 1 and 2 can be explained. In particular, the above discussion should yield some insight into the distributional pattern of supervisor's relationships as broadly indicated on the matrices for both time periods, and also those of the senior skilled tailors. In addition, some understanding will be achieved of the changes in the distributional pattern of interaction between the two time periods. I begin with a brief consideration of the supervisors' pattern of interactional relationships.

As described at the outset of this discussion supervisors have the greatest access to and control over such resources as skill, expertise, importance in the production system and prestige, etc. The supervisors are desirable persons with whom to develop interactional relationships in so far as benefits based on these resources can be distributed to others in the factory and are valued by these others. It is important to note that the establishment of interactional activity with as many of the workers as possible is to the benefit of the supervisor as long as the units he receives in transaction are units of compliance. An advantage of developing transactional relationships not strictly part of supervisory duties but nonetheless supportive of the supervisory role is that it eases the task of supervision. At the same time the compliance of the other workers increases the supervisors' value to Patel and thus their influence with him. By obligating other workers to him as a result of his distribution of resources the supervisor minimises various costs which could be experienced as the result of his performance of the supervisory role. For example, he reduces the degree to which he is identified as a management stooge, which in itself may register a loss in terms of the esteem or approval in which the supervisor is held by his co-workers. Furthermore, such identification may restrict the successful performance of supervisory duties which in turn could reduce the supervisor's value to management, having the additional effect of reducing the benefits he receives in the management–supervisor sphere of transactions. In other words, successful performance of the supervisory role requires the supervisor to take risks and initiate and develop as many relationships as possible. Moreover, the successful development of transactional relationships whereby others become obligated to the supervisors and as a result comply with their demands, can be considered profitable activity not only in terms of each separate relationship but also because of the benefits it brings in the supervisors' activities in other transactional spheres. In accordance with the above discussion, I would expect the supervisors to engage in a large span of interactional relationships, involving individuals from all occupational categories. That this is in fact the case is well demonstrated on matrices 1 and 2.

The strength of the above considerations in explanation receives further support when the relationships of the one slight exception to the general pattern, Hastings (14) are examined. At time 1 his interactions were relatively restricted to tailors working on line 1. During much of this period his activities as lead tailor were largely limited to specialist work such as the making up of suits and his duties did not require him to engage in much direct supervision of other workers. His job, therefore, did not require him to engage in risk-taking activity by initiating new relationships. Additionally, the benefits he received in transaction with Patel derived purely from his skill and expertise and did not depend on his creation of other resources such as the ready compliance of others to him through the development of a wide span of interactional relationships. In the light of this it is significant that the span of his interactional relationships is more extensive in time 2. In the period covered by time 2 Hastings took on many of the duties of Chisokone (17), who left employment. This required him to engage in more supervisory activity among all workers. Furthermore, Patel began to withhold certain benefits from Hastings. In order to increase the value of the benefits and services Hastings performed for Patel, and perhaps to force Patel into giving him the benefits he required, it became increasingly necessary for Hastings to extend his sets of interactional relationships. Clearly, the factors underlying the change in Hastings' distribution of activity over the two time periods are more complex than I have indicated here and will be treated in greater detail in subsequent chapters.

As the distributional pattern of the supervisors' relationships can be understood in terms of the principles outlined above, so also can aspects of the rate at which supervisors transact benefits and services with others, and the contents of these relationships. The transactional value of resources and the extent to which individuals can expect to experience an excess of gains over costs in their transactional activity with supervisors varies according to occupational category. The fewer resources an individual has access to or control over in relation to supervisors, the more he will value interaction with a supervisor, and the less a supervisor will value interaction with him. As explained earlier, supervisors have access to and control over most resources which unskilled workers are likely to require in order to participate effectively in the factory context. A supervisor can shield an unskilled worker from the threats of dismissal issued on numerous occasions by Patel and can assist these workers in learning a skill. Even sociational activity with a supervisor, such as general conversation and the sharing of gossip, can be valued, for it involves mutual activity with an individual high in prestige— which could have the effect of raising the unskilled worker's own standing among his peers. The receipt of compliance to his demands and instructions from an unskilled worker is less valued by the supervisor than are the benefits and services he gives out by the unskilled worker. Because of this it can be expected that the unskilled worker would be prepared to give out a higher proportion of compliant activity to various benefits and services he receives from supervisors. Furthermore, it is to be expected that the supervisor need not use all the resources he has at his disposal in his interaction with unskilled workers. In many instances it can be expected that he would restrict his interactional activity with these workers to the transaction of resources which would minimise cost to himself. For example, instruction in learning a skill involves a heavy cost in time. Time is a valued resource in itself and would be more profitably used in developing obligations and winning compliance from workers like the line 1 tailors, who, for reasons I shall shortly discuss, are likely to place less value on interaction with supervisors and will consequently demand a higher input of activity on the supervisors' part in relation to their own.

The ratio at which supervisors give and receive services and benefits from the line 1 tailors and the content of the relationships developed are likely to be considerably different from those between supervisors and unskilled workers. Line 1 tailors in general have more or less equal access to and control over various valued resources available to the supervisors. There is really only one resource which the supervisors can present themselves as having greater access to, and this is influence with Patel. Because supervisors and line 1 tailors have access to and control over similar resources, it follows that the gains received from interaction with supervisors by line 1 tailors can be expected to equal, or at the very most only slightly exceed, costs. Should supervisors demand compliance with their demands and instructions from line 1 tailors in return for entering into transactions with them, the line 1 tailors could be expected to incur an excess of costs over gains. Regular compliance with another implies at the very least a cost in status, as recurrent subordination to the will of another is likely to result in the one who complies being viewed by others participating in the same context as being lower in prestige than the person who elicits the compliant activity. This factor explains why it may be expected that line 1 tailors would restrict giving out compliant activity to the supervisors. A problem is thereby presented to the supervisors, especially given the value they place on winning the compliance of the line 1 tailors. As I will describe in the analysis of case material in the following chapters the line 1 tailors are able considerably to influence opinion and action in the factory. The gaining of the compliance of the line 1 tailors by the supervisors thus would not only aid the latter in the performance of their supervisory duties but might restrict the participation of the line 1 tailors in opinion forming activity, and competition for other resources (like the support and compliance of more junior workers), which could militate against the interests of the supervisors. A solution to the problem of winning compliance from the line 1 tailors by the supervisors rests in overwhelming the line 1 tailors with benefits and services.[17] In order to overwhelm the line 1 tailors the supervisors would have to enter into transactions with such a form involving a wide variety of benefits and services. Additionally, supervisors would be expected to emit a higher rate of activity than they would receive from line 1 tailors.

The expected difference, in accordance with the above argument, between the relationships of the supervisors and unskilled workers, and between the supervisors and the line 1 tailors can be summarised as follows: between supervisors and unskilled workers can be expected relationships which show a general tendency to have a low degree of transactional content in terms of the variety of benefits and services

---

[17] See Blau (1964: 106–12) for a general discussion of the role of overwhelming benefactions in securing superiority over others in interactional relationships.

exchanged, and a high rate of activity emitted by unskilled workers in relation to a low rate emitted by supervisors in return. Broadly, the reason for this is the disparity in value of the benefits and services given out by supervisors relative to those received by them from unskilled workers. Here it should be emphasised that the resources used in transaction are of different and unequal value. But in the transactional sphere involving supervisors and line 1 tailors the resources, with the exception of influence with Patel, which can be used in transaction are of more or less equal value. Disparities in the input of one party which could yield an imbalance of obligations are only likely to occur where the *quantity* of one exchange partner's input is greater than the other's. On the basis of these considerations I would expect supervisors to enter into a wide variety of transactions with line 1 tailors involving all kinds of benefits and services and direct proportionately more activity towards the line 1 tailors than the latter direct towards the supervisors in return.

Generally the pattern and structure of interaction between supervisors and unskilled workers on the one hand and line 1 tailors on the other, follows the expected pattern. Some indication of this is shown on the matrices. The greater multiplexity of interactional relationships between supervisors and line 1 tailors than between supervisors and unskilled workers (most of which are simplex) supports the argument that supervisors are likely to interact with line 1 tailors using a larger variety of resources than they do with unskilled workers. In addition, supervisors' interactions with unskilled workers tend to be sociational rather than instrumental, indicating that they are using resources which involve them in less cost, at least in time. Other observations, not shown on the matrices, also support my general conclusions reached in the preceding analysis. Supervisors had much more activity directed towards them by unskilled workers than they gave out in return, whereas the opposite was the case in their relationships with line 1 tailors.[18] Indeed, I often observed unskilled workers go out of their way to strike up conversation with a supervisor, and almost encourage a supervisor to give them an opportunity to comply with some demand or other of his. On the other hand, supervisors engaged senior tailors in

18 The pattern described here, of the supervisors emitting a greater quantity of transactional activity than they receive in return, can be seen as the price, in Homans' (1961: 106–12) sense of the word, which the supervisors must pay in order to receive compliance. This pattern would also appear to be an illustration of Homans' third fundamental proposition, that 'The more valuable to a man a unit of activity another gives him, the more often he will emit activity rewarded by the activity of the other' (*ibid.*).

conversation regularly and went out of their way to be of assistance in their work.

The various principles I have used to explain the pattern and structure of the supervisors' relationships can be used to explain those of the line 1 tailors. The nature of their work does not require the line 1 tailors (unlike the supervisors) to develop an extensive set of relationships. For this reason alone it can be expected that the line 1 tailors would show a tendency to have a more restricted set of relationships. The force of this tendency and the categories of individuals to whom such relationships are likely to be restricted, are dependent on a number of other considerations. The development of interactional relationships by a line 1 tailor with his peers or the supervisors can be expected to be the most attractive of the alternatives open to him. It is in these transactional spheres that a line 1 tailor can gain access to the most valued resources of support, approval, esteem or prestige. A line 1 tailor can gain access to similar resources by entering into interaction with workers in less skilled occupational categories. Indeed, a line 1 tailor will also find it easier to earn the compliance of workers in these other categories, if only because of the disparity in value between those resources they distribute and those they receive from the less skilled workers. But the risks entailed in developing relationships with less skilled workers are high. First, the line 1 tailors are at a competitive disadvantage to the supervisors, whom the less skilled workers, for much of the fieldwork period perceived as offering more benefits and services. In addition the supervisors had greater opportunity, by the very nature of their work, to build up relationships with the less skilled workers. Second, by attempting to develop relationships with individuals who are considered by others to be low in prestige, and who often see themselves in this way, the line 1 tailors would risk a devaluation of their own prestige and standing in the factory. This risk is increased, I suggest, if the individuals who seek the association of those junior to them are not secure in their own positions of prestige. Throughout much of the fieldwork period, and particularly during time 1, although the line 1 tailors considered themselves superior in prestige to most of the other workers, they were not uniformly so regarded by other workers. On many occasions, some of which I will recount in later chapters, members of other occupational categories drew their attention to this. Table 2.3 indicates that the line 2 and 3 tailors ranked the line 1 tailors lower than the latter ranked themselves. It should be noted here that while the line 1 tailors risk a loss in prestige by associating with less skilled employees, they at least stand to cancel out the costs of subordinating themselves to supervisors by gaining greater security in prestige. Over most of the research period, supervisors were accorded the highest prestige by all workers. The line 1 tailors by entering into regular transactional activity with the supervisors, stood to secure their position of prestige in the eyes of the other workers. This is provided, of course, the supervisors did not devalue the prestige of the line 1 tailors below the level which the latter regarded as their due. For much of the fieldwork period this was the case, and table 2.3 shows that the line 1 tailors received a rank prestige score from the supervisors which was about the same as that which the line 1 tailors gave themselves.

In terms of the above argument I have explained why it can be expected that line 1 tailors would tend to restrict their interactional relationships to peers and supervisors. Further, because the number of individuals with whom they come into regular contact must therefore be limited, and because they have access to and control over similar resources it would also be expected that a dense set of relationships linking these individuals to one another would tend to develop. Finally, because they have access to similar resources, it is to be expected that transactions would be characterised by reciprocity.

As described in an earlier section and presented in the matrices, what is to be expected from the preceding discussion is borne out by the interactional data collected over the two time periods. However, as previously described, there are changes in the distributional pattern of interactional relationships between time 1 and time 2. It can be shown, and I do so in greater detail in the following chapters, that this was partly due to processes which resulted in (1) increased costs relative to gains of the line 1 tailors in their then current transactional relationships; (2) a reduction in some of the risks attendant on initiating and developing relationships with less skilled employees, and (3) the development of the necessity to take risks by extending interactional relationships in order to preserve benefits achieved from other transactional activity.

A cost which the line 1 tailors began to experience in time 1 was a devaluing of their prestige by the supervisors. While the supervisors continued to give the line 1 tailors prestige in accordance with the latter's self-evaluation the line 1 tailors stood to balance some of the costs incurred by complying willingly with the supervisors' authority. But the supervisors, not content with a mere withdrawal of their recognition of the prestige of the line 1 tailors, proceeded to ridicule them and impugn their skill and expertise—factors on which the line 1 tailors considered their prestige to rest. In addition, it became apparent to the line 1 tailors, through a series of occurrences at work, that the supervisors would not support them in dispute with Patel and would not assist them in their claims for improved wage and work conditions. These increased costs alone made it necessary for the line 1 tailors to pursue alternative lines of action in a bid to secure benefits previously obtained through transactions with the supervisors.

During the period covered by time 1 competitive behaviour developed among the line 1 tailors, and Lyashi (12) in particular tried to achieve dominance in his set of relationships. This behaviour began before the supervisors had engaged in activity costly to the line 1 tailors. However, competition among the tailors increased once the latter began to incur an excess in costs relative to gains in their transactions with the supervisors. This increase in competition was partly because of the necessity for the line 1 tailors to pursue alternative lines of action in order to bolster their prestige in the eyes of the other workers. An important consequence of this competition, which I will examine more extensively in the following chapters, in terms of Blau's model of the differentiation of status and power in small groups, was the emergence of a more differentiated structure among the line 1 tailors, with workers such as Lyashi (12), Nkoloya (8), Lwanga (15) and Chipata (5) achieving positions of limited dominance. This emergence of a more differentiated structure in addition to other factors such as the identification of the supervisors with management interests, reduced the risks incurred by line 1 tailors initiating relationships with less skilled employees. Earlier, it will be recalled, I noted that the unattractiveness for line 1 tailors of initiating or developing relationships with less skilled workers lay in the risks such interaction involved. Much of this risk rested on the ability of the less skilled workers to transfer their interaction to other individuals providing the same or more benefits, thus escaping having to discharge their obligations in terms of compliance—perhaps, for the line 1 tailors, the most valuable resource which the less skilled workers could distribute. The process of differentiation within the ranks of the line 1 tailors, coupled with the fall from grace of the supervisors, reduced the risks encountered by at least some of the line 1 tailors in developing interactional relationships with the less skilled employees.

Even so much of the risk and uncertainty remained. But the line 1 tailors were now placed in a position where they had to take increased risks if they were to consolidate or maintain the benefits control over which they had secured in past and current transactions. Thus the few who had managed to differentiate themselves from their peers, at least in terms of the esteem and prestige in which they came to be held, such as Lyashi, Lwanga, Chipata and Abraham, were far from secure. This was largely a consequence of the similarity of the resources which they had access to or control over in relation to their peers. This factor enabled the line 1 tailors to take any one or a combination of the following courses of action to prevent any one or a number of their peers becoming firmly established in a superior position of power and prestige. Such an occurrence would cause those who did not achieve such a position, but who were of the same occupational category, to experience considerable cost. For they would be seen by other workers in the factory as subordinate to their peers and therefore inferior in prestige and power. The main courses of action which line 1 tailors could take to avoid such an occurrence included: the reciprocation of benefits and services received from a peer; the development of alternative transactional relationships; or refusing or limiting interaction with those individuals who were attempting to achieve a position of dominance.[19]

Owing to the ability of the line 1 tailors to take these courses of action, no individual among them could firmly establish himself in a position of dominance as long as his activity was *restricted to this set of relationships*. A solution to this difficulty was for the line 1 tailors concerned to build up stocks of power and influence in other sets of relationships and to use this to more firmly establish a position of dominance in those relationships involving their peers. The ability to achieve this successfully would have a feed back effect further reducing competition which provides a threat to an individual's dominance. Consequent on this reduction of competition would be the increased attractiveness of those line 1 tailors concerned and therefore the greater preparedness of more junior workers to establish interactional relationships with them. Thus the power and influence of particular line 1 tailors are further extended. Power or the ability of an individual *recurrently* to impose his will on another is emergent from a process whereby one individual is able to win another's obligation to him normally as a result of the development of unilateral or unreciprocated transactions which can only be discharged by the latter's willing compliance with the demands and instructions of the former. Such relationships could be established with less skilled workers and particu-

---

[19] These courses of action or strategies are derivative from the conditions which should be present for the differentiation in power and status (see Blau, 1964: 118–19; also chapter 6, pp. 208–12).

larly the ironers and cotton boys. Various factors relating to this sector of the factory work force which facilitated the development of relationships characterised by unilateral transactions and an imbalance in obligations with them, with the line 1 tailors involved being the dominant partners. There were few individuals, apart from other line 1 tailors competing for increased status and power, who provided attractive alternatives as individuals with whom the less skilled employees could establish relationships. This factor in addition to the disparity in value between the resources provided by the line 1 tailors and those less skilled increased the ability of the former to engender relationships in which they were dominant to those workers junior to them.

It should be emphasised here that the ability to control and influence the activities of the less skilled workers had in itself increased in value by the beginning of time 2 relative to the period covered by time 1. The September 1965 strike owed much of its failure to the inability of the line 1 tailors to command the support of the less skilled workers. As I shall show in a later description, the line 1 tailors were aware of this. A worker who could demonstrate to his peers that he had such control was likely, therefore, to win increased prestige and influence among his peers.

I have confined much of this discussion to an examination of why some of the line 1 tailors could be expected to extend their relationships into the ranks of the less skilled. It can be expected also that others among the senior workers and not just those competing for increased resources of influence and power would also develop relationships among the less skilled workers. The emergence of competition among the line 1 tailors and the development of some differentiation in terms of prestige and power among them would force other line 1 tailors who were not necessarily competing to extend their sets of interactional relationships. This is so because such competition and resulting differentiation would have the consequence of a prestige loss for the non-competing tailors. Some reduction in this loss would be achieved, however, by winning recognition of superior prestige and status from junior workers by engaging in interaction with them.

The above analysis has explained in broad theoretical terms why certain changes should take place between the ends of time 1 and time 2. However, one aspect of the changes in interactional relationships I described, although already implicit in the analysis, has not been clearly accounted for. This concerns why factors generating change in the overall pattern and structure of interactional relationships should originate mainly within the ranks of the senior skilled employees—the supervisors and the line 1 tailors. My emphasis in description on these senior workers is not just to provide information on the nature of interactional relationships of individuals who were prominent in factory politics and who are the focus of the description in the following chapters. The emphasis is such precisely because it was largely as a result of the activities of these individuals that changes in the general pattern and structure of interactional relationships were generated.

I consider that the direction of interactional changes in the factory and the emergence of them from within the ranks of the senior workers conforms to a general proposition implicit in the various exchange theory principles discussed previously. This proposition is that interactional relationships in which transactions tend to be reciprocal and the obligations balanced will be more unstable and show a greater tendency to change than interactional relationships in which the transactions are unilateral and represent an imbalance in obligations. This proposition is suggested by the conditions which give rise to the above forms of interaction in the first place. For example, recurrent reciprocated transactions involving benefits and services of equivalent value tend to occur between individuals who have access to and control over similar resources. Because of this, individuals in these kinds of relationship are less dependent on each other for the supply of benefits and services than they are on individuals who control resources to which they do not have direct access. I am definitely not stating that interactional relationships which show a tendency towards reciprocity in transactions and a balancing out of obligations are necessarily unstable. Indeed, the very fact that many valued resources such as approval, respect, support, etc., are created only in the course of interaction and that individuals may wish to have secure supplies of these resources can cause them to maintain and stabilise their relationships. The development of intrinsic attachments likewise can lead to stable relationships irrespective of factors such as reciprocity and balance. The emergence of a dense set of relationships linking a set of individuals together can have the effect of stabilising any single relationship within this common set.[20] An individual, for instance, by breaking off his relationship to another may risk his ability to establish or maintain relationships with other persons with whom the latter individual is engaged in interactional activity. The generation of trust in relationships can also lead to increased stability. Here it is interesting to note that the emergence of trust in relationships establishes the conditions for

[20] I have argued this point at greater depth in an article on conjugal role relationships (1971). This article also takes cognisance of other stabilising factors, such as trust.

receiving benefits and services on credit. This results in the development of unilateral transactions and imbalanced obligations which may further stabilise a relationship. But, these considerations aside, the general point I emphasise is that even though relationships which are reciprocal and balanced can be stable *in comparison with* those relationships where the transactions are unilateral and unequal in value they are relatively unstable.

The stability of an interactional relationship, its continuity over time, is a function of its emergent form. Those relationships which are unilateral and imbalanced are relatively stable *because* of their unilaterality and imbalance. Processes which lead to reciprocity in transactions and a balancing out of obligations lead to the progressive generation of instability within a relationship. Once debts are discharged individuals are no longer obligated and are presented with new choice opportunities. They can now choose to continue the relationship on the same terms as before, negotiate and redefine the bases for continued transactional activity, or else break off the relationship and search around for new interactional partners.[21]

In essence most interactional relationships which individuals enter represent, at particular points in time, varying degrees of unilaterality and imbalance. It is this which gives them their durabilty. In much social activity there is no exact price (in an economic sense) for benefits and services performed. This fact in itself, I suggest, may lead individuals to discharge their obligations with interest, if only to reduce the risk of failing to have the value of a transactional contribution recognised. A consequence of this is that a relationship may never be exactly balanced out but rather in the process of the balancing of obligations new imbalances are created.

It has long been recognised by anthropologists that a degree of unilaterality and imbalance promotes a stability over time in both interactional relationships and broader systems of social and economic action. The continuity through time of the *kula* trading system of the Trobriand Islanders (Malinowski, 1922) is partly ensured by the unilaterality in the flow of transactions and imbalances in obligations produced by the operation of the *kula* trade itself. The flow of the major *kula* objects, *soulava* and *mwali*, in opposite directions and the fact that these gifts cannot be returned immediately stabilise the *kula* system over time. The form of transactional activity termed delayed exchange by anthropologists (Sahlins, 1965; Harding, 1968) involves

---

[21] McClements (1970), in a re-analysis of Firth's work on Tikopia, has cogently demonstrated this process.

both unilateral transactions and an imbalance in obligations and has been observed to stabilise relationships and promote further transactional activity.

My data on the direction of change in the factory would seem to conform to the general proposition as originally stated. The main changes in interactional relationships occurred first among the supervisors and line 1 tailors who were involved in sets of relationships which showed the smallest degrees of unilaterality and imbalance. This set up a snowball effect which eventually led to an overall change in the pattern and structure of interactional relationships in the factory.

In this chapter I have described the interactional relationships and the changes which occurred over the two time periods. These changes were then specifically related to observable changes in the industrial activity of the employees and the development of unified support for strike action. This description did not provide sufficient explanation for why the changes in interactional relationships should occur. A central thesis, therefore, was that the changes in interactional relationships could be explained in terms of various exchange theory principles.

The analysis as it stands has necessarily been limited. Thus the discussion of the interactional relationships has obscured continual changes in the relationships *within* the time periods. By presenting a broad description of the pattern and structure of interactional relationships at the end of each time period I have obscured the fact that many of the relationships crucial to the type of analysis I make were in varying stages of growth and decay. Although I refer to the importance of perceived costs and gains in interaction little description has been made as yet of the perceptions of the employees and the processes leading to the changes in these perceptions. The following chapters, which examine in chronological sequence a series of events which occurred in the factory, will be directed at overcoming some of these limitations. Thus through the analysis of events I shall examine processes of change in interactional relationships within the two time periods. Furthermore, aspects connected with the perceptions of the workers governing their interactional activity and changes in these perceptions will be handled in greater detail. Finally, because of my concern in this chapter to describe the factory interactional relationships and the basic exchange principles which govern them, I have found it necessary to restrict discussion of other factors influencing behaviour over the research period. In subsequent chapters, therefore, I shall place the changes in the factory workers' behaviour in the wider context of relevant changes occurring in Kabwe and Zambia.

6   Strategy in dispute, structural change and the quest for power and leadership I

> We *perceive* the world before we react to it, and we react not to what we perceive, but always to what we *infer*—F. Knight, (1921: 201)

> We social scientists talk as if 'society' were the big thing. But an institution is functional for society only because it is functional for men—G. C. Homans, (1961: 384)

General introduction

In this and succeeding chapters I shall examine a number of processes relating to the change in social relationships among and between management and employees through a close analysis of a series of events which occurred in the factory context. I argue that the processes underlying these changes and the patterning of relationships emergent from these processes themselves explain many of the features of behaviour I observed on the factory floor. Important problems which dominate the analysis concern the interrelationship of the constructs, images or perceptions which individual participants have of the elements or resources (i.e. other individuals or groups, social relationships, statuses, organisations, institutions, etc., and also such perceptions themselves) located in the environment of their action with the observed behaviour of the participants. Concomitantly I am also concerned with the processes which lead and allow certain individuals to control the perceptions of and the behaviour of others, and with the processes which generate changes in their perceptions and related social activity. In pursuing these general aims I intend to develop and demonstrate the value of an approach which makes use of concepts directed towards the analysis of social behaviour as process. By so doing I depart from a tendency current in much anthropological and sociological analysis to treat social process through conceptual constructs which are better suited to the study of social statics and which view process as a special and separate problem.

Themes It is basic to my conception of social process that individuals are, in varying degrees, able to shape their own destinies and the destinies of others. Social structures and social systems as far as they are the analytical constructs of anthropologists and sociologists are also the creations, though by no means necessarily identical, of the individuals and groups these social scientists observe. The constructs which individuals and groups make of the contexts of their participation are as important, and perhaps more so, in understanding why individuals behave the way they do as are the constructs made by the social scientist. The latter often includes contextual components and relations between them which lie outside the comprehension, knowledge and experience of the individual participant. For this reason I emphasise the role played by individuals and groups in changing or maintaining the structure of relationships in specified contexts and the norms and values related to them. Individuals through the exercise of power and influence are both able to control the way in which aspects of the context are situationally defined by other participants in the same context and consequently the social activity of these other participants. An individual's behaviour is not only governed by the structure of the context in which he acts (as this is depicted in abstract form by the social scientist as observer, this structure being seen as an emergent property derived from his observation of a particular set of interrelationships between the contextual components at a specific point in time). Individual behaviour is also channelled in certain directions and not others in accordance with the particular constructs or perceptions of relevant aspects of the context made by individual participants.

At any specific time individual and group constructs, images and perceptions include only certain elements located in the arena of their action and exclude others. Furthermore, only particular relational properties of these elements and therefore relationships between them are defined by the participants as relevant to their activity. Central to my orientation will be the thesis that individuals attempt to arrange the elements of these constructs in particular ways and define specific relational properties of them as significant in bids to safeguard and further their own interests and the interests of others. My concern is to isolate the processes which lead to the maintenance and change of specific constructs, these constructs being seen as guidelines whereby participants acting in context orient their behaviour and arrive at understandings of the behaviour of others.

The analytical focus of this chapter and those following is centred in the emergence and decline of power and status in inter-personal relationships. Processes underlying power, involving its emergence and decline, account for changes in the patterning of social relationships and associated behaviour. Also the extent to which an individual is powerful enables him to maintain or change constructs and images current in the context of his participation as these affect the performance of his activities and the pursuit of his interests and those of others. Competition between individuals is seen as a process in which individuals pit their strength against each other to try to undermine the often powerful positions of others. The weapons of such contests are those resources which individuals have at hand and can manipulate, such as ties of friendship, relationships of indebtedness and even constructs and images they or others hold of various elements in the context of action. For example, images and perceptions of statuses and the roles associated with them can be manipulated and reorganised in attempts to arrive at accepted situational definitions which support their interests. Thus I view statuses and roles as forms of address through which individuals attempt to present themselves and others to an interested audience. In doing this they select certain relational properties of their own status or that of others, and this selection demands of their audience that it sees them as occupying a particular position within the context. The degree to which their 'presentation of self' is accepted by the audience—and to gain this acceptance individuals must vie with others—may have implications for the extent to which such individuals are able to direct the course of social action and thereby structure it. The idea I am putting forward here bears some similarity to that developed by Boulding in *The Image*.[1] I emphasise the activity of individuals whereby they communicate messages or convey information aimed at maintaining or destroying particular images. In so far as they do this they attempt to convey information which is critical to the maintenance or destruction of an image. My emphasis here is on the goal-oriented activity of individuals. It is also an integral part of my analysis that individuals may unintentionally convey messages which can destroy images. One reason for this

---

[1] According to Boulding, 'messages consist of *information* in the sense that they are structured experiences. *The meaning of the message is the change which it produces in the image*' (1966: 7). He states that when a message hits an image one of three things can happen. The message need have no effect on the image, it can add to or support an image yet not substantially alter it, or, it can produce a revolutionary change in the image. 'A spectacular instance of such a change is conversion. A man, for instance, may think himself a pretty good fellow and then may hear a preacher who convinces him that, in fact, his life is worthless and shallow as he is at present living it. The words of the preacher cause a radical reformulation of the man's image of himself in the world, and his behaviour changes accordingly' (1966: 8).

which I pursue later is that such messages may occur as the unintended consequence of action which arises from the failure of individuals to resolve basic dilemmas and paradoxes contained in their activity and in the structure of their interpersonal relationships.

Status and power in small groups   A model which is basic to the analysis in accordance with the approach outlined here is that put forward by P. M. Blau for the differentiation of power and status in small groups (1964: 115–42).[2] Some of the main principles relating to this model have already been outlined and applied to the analysis in chapter 5 of the interactional patterns in the factory. Structural change in so far as this relates to shifting patterns of alliance and opposition in the factory is a major theme of my analysis. Shifts in the distribution of power and status often correspond with changes in the structure of interpersonal relationships and a model such as Blau's which suggests some of the basic principles whereby differentiation and change in the distribution of power and status are engendered provides an explanatory framework in which such process can be examined.

In Blau's model individuals become differentiated from each other in terms of power and status in the course of competing for scarce resources. This competition emerges from the process of social integration whereby individuals seek to establish relationships with others. The model in its simplest form relates to a context in which all the participants have newly arrived and have not yet established relationships with each other. A basic assumption which underlies the model is that individuals wish to establish relationships with others both because of the intrinsic benefits which accrue from a relationship (e.g. friendship viewed as an end in itself), and because of the extrinsic benefits derived from relationships with others (e.g. friendship with another viewed as a means to an end such as when money is borrowed or assistance is sought at a time of personal crisis). But in the early stage of social integration individuals must present themselves as being attractive in order to

[2] Homans (1961, especially 283–315) developed an approach to the differentiation of power and status which includes many of the same principles used by Blau. Broadly, however, Homans did not work out the implications of his approach to the same extent as Blau. An appreciation of Blau's approach in relation to Homans', with which I generally agree, can be found in Buckley (1967: 143–4, 201–5). It should be stressed that Homans and Blau were preceded by Thibaut and Kelley (1959), and that this work had an influence on both their studies. A useful comparison of the work of Thibaut and Kelley with that of Homans and others appears in Petersen (1970). Harsanyi (1968), using game theory, has developed an approach to status differentiation similar to Blau.

establish relationships with others. That is, they must be able to show that they have qualities which are valued by others and which will attract others to establish relationships with them. The presentation of certain personal attributes or qualities which are valued makes certain individuals more attractive than others as persons with whom to establish relationships. As sociologists have repeatedly shown much of the early stage of the process of forming relationships is taken up with individuals displaying the various 'wares' which they have to offer.[3]

In Blau's analysis, time is at first the major commodity about which the competition is focused. Time is scarce but is a generalised means through which relationships with others can be established. That some individuals can secure a greater proportion of the time available results in their having more opportunity to present themselves as attractive to others and therefore opportunity to enter into more relationships. Blau states that 'the group allocates time among various members in accordance with their estimated abilities to make contributions to its welfare based on initial impressions' (1964: 125).[4]

In the process of social integration individuals become differentiated from each other on the basis of the time allotted to them. Some individuals are seen as having better access to certain rewards than others and the interaction becomes focused on them. Individuals who have been relatively unsuccessful in the early competition over the allocation of time withdraw from the competition and enter into social transactions with each other. These social transactions tend to be reciprocal or exchange relationships. In the course of opting out of the competition they acknowledge the superiority of those more successful in the competition and also enter into transactions with certain among them. Here the transaction tends to be unilateral. That is, they will receive specific

[3] Malinowski's work on the Trobriand Islanders shows numerous examples of this (see Malinowski, 1922), as does the more recent work of anthropologists in the New Guinea highlands, e.g. Meggitt (1965) and Salisbury (1962). Goffman (1959) devotes a complete book to this process. These are only a few examples, but the literature of sociology and anthropology abounds with such instances.

[4] Here the simplicity of Blau's model does not make it necessary for him to consider other aspects which may lead to the unequal allocation of time among individuals in a context. If we turned to the development of relationships among individuals who had entered a context which has a basic structure regulating their activities, other considerations would have to be taken into account. Thus at Narayan Bros. the task or occupation to which an individual is assigned in the framework of the production system will mean that he will have a differential amount of time at his disposal relative to others. The supervisors, for instance, because of their ability to move throughout the factory have more time and therefore opportunity to establish relationships with other workers.

benefits such as advice, aid in learning a skill or even assistance in securing higher wages or improvements in working conditions. Because they do
not have similar benefits which they can bestow in return, they reward
their benefactor by granting him their approval and respect. However,

since the value of a person's approval and respect is a function of his own
social standing, the process of recurrently paying respect to others
depreciates its value. Hence, respect often does not remain an adequate
compensation for contributions that entail costs in time and effort to the
one who makes them, such as assistance with complex problems. Those
who benefit from such instrumental help, therefore, become obligated to
reciprocate in some other way, and deferring to the wishes of the group
member who supplies the help is typically the only thing the others can
do to repay him. As a result of these processes in which the contributions
of some come to command the compliance of others, a differentiated
power structure develops. [Blau, 1964: 127]

Competition continues among those who have emerged successfully
in the process of social integration and these individuals continue to
struggle with each other for power and leadership. Those who withdraw from the competition become tools in the struggle, for without
their support an individual who is competing for the rewards of power
and leadership is placed at a considerable disadvantage. This competition is likely to be intense as success in achieving the subordination
of other powerful individuals in the context will increase considerably
the power of the person concerned as he may gain not only the support
of the individual who submits but also those who were subordinate to
that individual.

Central to the analysis of the process of the differentiation of power
and status in small groups is the principle that power and status are
expended in use and increased at risk. Power is founded in the unilaterality of social transactions and a resulting unbalance in obligations.
The latter emerges when one individual is able to render another services and benefits which are of a value generally recognised as greater
than those received in return. I emphasise, however, that power is
only emergent in social relationships when individuals cannot receive
various benefits and services regarded by them as essential except
through their willing compliance with the demands of another. The
unilaterality of transactions and the imbalance of obligations are *necessary* but not *sufficient* conditions for the achievement of power. Four
other conditions must also apply.[5] These are (1) an individual cannot

[5] Blau's approach to the various conditions which must be present for an individual to exert power over another is heavily dependent on a paper of
Emerson (1962).

reciprocate with benefits and services regarded as equivalent in value, (2) an individual does not have alternative sources of essential benefits and services, (3) an individual cannot coerce the person who controls or has access to essential benefits and services and (4) an individual cannot do without the benefits and services supplied. The absence of any one of these conditions would reduce the necessity for an individual to experience the cost of subordinating himself to the will of another.

The above conditions in most contexts will vary in the degree to which they are present or absent and much of their importance, I consider, rests in their being used to differentiate between individuals in terms of their potential to exert power and influence over others. But for present purposes, the essential feature of Blau's model which should be noted in relation to the above conditions is that individuals by using their power will threaten the continuity of those very conditions upon which their power initially rested. When an individual causes another to comply with his demands or instructions, he reduces his power as a result of giving the individual subordinate to him an opportunity to discharge part of the debt incurred from previous transactions. An act of compliance itself marks an occasion when an individual is able to reciprocate for benefits and services received and produces a tendency for the balancing out of obligations. 'The power of accumulated obligations is depleted by asking others to repay their debts, because doing so transforms, at least in part, the power relations into exchange relations, which presume relative equality of status' (Blau 1964: 135). Repeated demands on another's resources of willing compliance will also threaten an individual's resources of power as such demands will demonstrate the latter's dependence on this compliance which will correspondingly greatly increase its value. The increased value of compliance will tend to balance the value in transaction of resources received which, in turn, will reduce the imbalance of obligations and thus the power in the relationship. Furthermore, regular exercise of power reduces the attractiveness of remaining subordinate to the particular individual concerned and other individuals, for example, may become increasingly more attractive as alternatives to whom allegiance can be transferred.

The various conditions I have outlined for the emergence of power in social relationships also define the strategies required not only for the attainment of power but also to sustain it (see Blau, 1964: 121). Individuals in order to maintain or increase their power, for example, must restrict the extent to which they demand the compliance of those subordinate to them, should block individuals from seeking out alternative sources of essential benefits and services and discourage the growth of coalitions among subordinates which may lead the latter to coerce an individual in a position of power to supply needed services.

Clearly, the abstract principles outlined above require exploration in relation to empirical material. It can be expected that aspects connected with them will be expanded and modified as they are applied to the activities of individuals in a specific context. Before I extend the analysis to an examination of social behaviour within the factory, it is necessary that I clarify for the reader my use of certain terms in accordance with which I organise the material to be analysed.

Context, situation and events   The data presented and analysed in this and following chapters trace major interconnections between context, situation and events. I use *context* to refer not just to a specific location in which a collection of individuals participate together in regular activity, but also to my understanding of the way these individuals are interrelated with one another within this location. *Situation*[6] and the related phrase 'definition of the situation' applies to that set of understandings which the individual participants acting within a context have of one another's behaviour, interactional relationships, relevant norms and values as well as other resources located in the context and the arena of which the context is a part. The changes which I observed in the structure of the factory context and behaviour within it are both causes and effects of changes in the way individual participants situationally define aspects of this context. My concern is to isolate those processes which are part of the structure of the context, as I observe and describe this, which lead to the maintenence or change in definitions of the situation made by the participants in the context. Likewise, it is my aim to show how the maintenence or change in definitions of the situation themselves lead to new structural arrangements of the context in which the individuals of this study participate. *Events* are major sequences of

---

[6] Garbett (1970) makes some extremely important observations regarding the use of the concept 'situation' in the work of various social scientists. He distinguishes between the use of the concept by anthropologists (e.g. Gluckman, 1958; Devons and Gluckman, 1964; 158 *ff.*) and that by many sociologists (see Thomas, 1958: 68; 1967: 43; Goffman, 1961; Waller, 1965; McHugh, 1969). Garbett states that anthropologists have generally used the concept situation to refer to a 'temporally and spatially bounded series of events abstracted by the observer from an ongoing flow of social life' (1970: 215), whereas sociologists and particularly those of the ethnomethodology and symbolic interactionist schools have applied the concept situation and the associated phrase 'definition of the situation' to apply to the constructs which actors place on activities within their environment. It should be evident to the reader that the sense in which I use situation is more in accord with the latter usage.

social activity which I subject to analysis. An event constitutes a bounded sequence of social activity which I have abstracted from the continuous and on-going social behaviour observed in the factory context. Any one event is closely interrelated with all other events which occur in the factory. In this sense the boundaries I establish around events are arbitrary. However, the major criterion by which I have established boundaries around particular sequences of social activity relates to the extent to which the activity is oriented about a common focus, such as a strike or a complaint made about the poor workmanship of one of the factory employees. My analysis[7] is oriented around specific sequences of activity as events because they contain important definitions of the situation and changes in these definitions made by participants in the context as these relate to significant points in the structural development of social relationships in the factory, as I observed this. Appendix 2 presents some thirty events and the date of their occurrence which I recorded over the field work period. The events which I analyse in depth are those I consider to be of greatest significance in understanding the structural development of the factory context.

My use of the concept of event and the importance it achieves in the analysis is similar to the concept of social drama developed and applied by Turner in his analysis of the Ndembu. For Turner, a social drama 'is a limited area of transparency on the otherwise opaque surface of regular, uneventful social life. Through it we are enabled to observe the crucial principles of the social structure in their operation, and their relative dominance at successive points in time' (1957: 93). Unlike social dramas, the sequences of activity I term events do not have an essential 'processional form' of the type isolated by Turner as the phases of breach, crisis, redressive action and re-integration or recognition of schism (1957: 92). Aspects such as these may be emergent from a number of linked events and are not necessary phases of any particular event.

Background to events   Through an analysis of the following events, I will show how various individuals, and one man in particular, presented themselves in relation to others in bids either to support their

[7] The type of analysis I adopt through the detailed examination of a series of events is the same as that known as 'situational analysis' or 'the extended case method', the latter having developed out of the former. General discussions of analytical approaches are found in Gluckman, 1961; Van Velsen, 1964, 1967; Garbett, 1970. Notable applications of the method are made by Gluckman, 1958; Mitchell, 1956; Epstein, 1958; Turner, 1957; Van Velsen, 1964 and Long, 1968.

claims to exert authority and power over others or to impress others
with their qualities so as to attract followers in an attempt to increase or
achieve power and status. An important recurrent theme throughout
the analysis will be to demonstrate how norms relating to behaviour
which are part of individuals' experience in their everyday participation
in urban life, are used selectively, often thereby acquiring new meanings
in their usage for the achievement of specific ends.

The events examined are viewed mainly from the perspective of one
employee's attempt to achieve a position of power and leadership, and
the processes which both aid and inhibit his various attempts will be
analysed. I have set the events surrounding the progress of Lyashi, the
central figure of the analysis, into three phases. The first phase deals
basically with Lyashi's competition with others in the factory to present
himself in such a way as to gain others' acceptance of his status. Con-
currently, it is the phase in which Lyashi tries to attract followers and to
win support for his particular definition of the structure of the factory
context and the position of others within it. The second phase sees
Lyashi, having been relatively successful in the competition, consolidating his position. Lyashi reaches the summit of his power at the
September walk-out during which he plays a prominent part in the strategy pursued by the workers. However, it is also the period in which
new challenges for power and leadership begin to emerge. The failure
of the workers to achieve generally satisfactory results from the September walk-out contributes partly to Lyashi's gradual decline in power and
influence, although he continues to be significant in the factory's social
and political relationships. Workers who lost out in much of the competition in the first phase begin to re-assert themselves. This pattern
emerges clearly in the third phase.

Lvashi's background has already been sketched in chapter 3[8] with
reference to his labour and urban experience. Briefly, he is 43, an age
which places him among the older workers in the factory. He is a Bemba,
married with four children and lives in a semi-detached house in
Bwacha township. An enlarged photograph of himself as a Deacon in the
Lumpa Church, accompanied by Alice Lenshina, is proudly displayed
in his home. He dissociated himself from the Church at the time of the
Lumpa disturbances in the Northern and Eastern Provinces and states
that he is no longer a member. Although the Lumpa Church is banned,
which is reason enough for such a statement, he maintains a vast network of ties with other 'erstwhile' members of the movement. Lyashi
owns a sewing machine, and after work he is frequently occupied

[8] See p. 75.

making clothes which he sells to supplement his income. Further aspects of Lyashi's background will be discussed in the course of analysis. The salient characteristics of other personalities who figure in the events are given in appendix 1.

Phase I: the ascendance of Lyashi

Like many of the other small events which will be discussed in this chapter, the following dispute grew out of a conversation held among a group of workers at tea break. Those whom it immediately concerned were Mukubwa and Hastings, the head and lead tailors respectively, Kalamba, Abraham, Lyashi, all of whom at this time were tailors on line 1 and Paulos and Mpundu, line 2 and line 3 tailors, respectively. Before the following event is described, it must be emphasised that although these employees were the major participants in the conversation, they were in close ear-shot of the other factory workers. The area in which the employees group themselves outside the factory at tea break is restricted in space. The significance of this is that the conversation between any group of workers can very quickly attract an extended and interested audience.

Event 5[9]   The dream village dispute
June 9 1965

At break Hastings began what was to become a heated discussion by asking his work companions to make a choice between three types of village as an ideal place for retirement. Those gathered were asked to make a choice between (a) a village of women, (b) a village composed entirely of men with large quantities of beer, and (c) a village which had extensive resources of *ibange* (Indian hemp). Mukubwa responded by choosing a village of women. Kalamba opposed Mukubwa and declared his preference for a village of men adequately supplied with beer. Abraham, however, sided with Mukubwa against Kalamba, accusing the latter of being a *chakolwa* (drunkard), at the same time reminding Kalamba that a man's prime concern is to have many children and therefore a village of women should be preferred. Kalamba was supported by Mpundu, who reminded Abraham that he should not be calling Kalamba a drunkard, as he (Mpundu) sees Abraham regularly at the beer hall. But it was apparent that the opinions of Kalamba and Mpundu were considerably outnumbered when Paulos agreed with Abraham's statements.

[9] All the events discussed in the text are numbered in accordance with their appearance in appendix 2.

Up to this point in the discussion the conversation had been friendly, but Lyashi now gave his opinion. Rather than opt for any particular village, he proceeded to attack Mukubwa's original preference for a village of women. Lyashi stated that people who prefer women are similar to Indians, who like them so much that their homes are filled with children. Mukubwa reacted angrily against Lyashi's suggestion and claimed that Lyashi had no right to behave in such a way. All the workers taking tea now turned their attention to Lyashi's confrontation with Mukubwa. However, with the obvious agreement of other participants in the conversation, Mukubwa cut Lyashi short and accused him of provoking needless argument. Lyashi withdrew from the action and shortly afterwards Patel called his employees back to work.

Analysis. One tactic which can be adopted in an attempt to achieve power is to threaten the basis in terms of which a powerful man presents himself to others. The prime interest in this event for the ensuing analysis rests on Lyashi's selection of one relational property of Mukubwa's occupational position in the factory, his association with the Indian management by virtue of his work as a supervisor. I shall now explore this in greater detail.

The nature of Lyashi's opposition to Mukubwa is clearly different from that of men like Kalamba and Mpundu. Their opposition was merely a friendly difference of opinion and factors such as membership of different ethnic and cultural categories or youth (in the case of Kalamba) or low skill and occupational status (in the instance of Mpundu) in relation to those who differed from them was of little relevance.[10] Lyashi, however, differed not only with Mukubwa, the person against whom his attack was most openly delivered, but in his opposition also clearly attempted to emphasise one aspect of Mukubwa's relationships in the factory. This he did by suggesting that a person who wished to retire to a village of women with the intention of fathering many children was behaving like an Indian. It could easily have been construed—and judging by Mukubwa's reaction it was—that Mukubwa, whose work in

[10] This does not imply that factors such as youth and low occupational status were not underlying considerations in the opposition of Kalamba and Mpundu and the reaction to their opposition by the other workers present. Youth, in one sense, for instance, may have been a factor important to Abraham's criticism of Kalamba. Many older workers, Abraham among them, are not loth to remark that young men have lost contact with the 'traditional' ways of the village. Older men in the factory often present an idealised picture of village life and when in the company of younger men frequently take the opportunity to express their disapproval of what they consider to be town customs. In some circles to be branded a *chakolwa*, as Abraham accused Kalamba of being, can be a mark of high approval indicating one's ability to act according to the standards of expected urban behaviour. On this occasion, however, Abraham used the term disapprovingly.

the factory often demands that he acts in the interest of management, also has values in common with his Indian employers.

Further description is required as to why Mukubwa so quickly stopped Lyashi from elaborating his point. Two factors need to be discussed and these refer first, to the way Mukubwa had at this stage in the development of social relationships been able to present himself to the factory workers, and second, to the overall patterning of relationships among the workers at the time and the particular structure of Mukubwa's relationships and others within this overall pattern.

Most of the workers were involved in relationships of limited span, the supervisors, line 1 tailors and Zulu on line 2 generally being the only exceptions. It was among these workers also that any marked degree of multiplexity of transactional content in relationships was apparent. The period just prior to my entry into the factory had been one of considerable labour turnover, especially within the ranks of the less skilled and unskilled workers. Because supervisors were the individuals with whom persons in these occupations initially had the most regular contact and to whom they often owed their employment in the factory in the first place, it tended to be only with supervisors that relationships of any marked multiplexity of content were developed. The two supervisors most noticeably involved in relationships of this kind were Mukubwa and Chisokone.[11] Transactions which these two employees had with the more junior workers were, in the main, instrumental and unilateral; services which could not be repaid, except in terms of respect or compliance, flowing from Mukubwa and Chisokone to these junior workers. Mukubwa and Chisokone also tended to dominate the reasonably close-knit set of relationships which linked them and most of the line 1 tailors to each other. Of the two, Mukubwa was clearly the more dominant but the basis of his superiority was less secure—as also in the case of Chisokone—than were his relationships with the more junior workers. Mukubwa's skill is only marginally superior to that of the line 1 tailors and such advice concerning work which he occasionally offers can often be just as easily supplied by a co-worker seated nearby.

It is a more difficult task to achieve the compliance of the more skilled and senior workers of line 1 than to gain the compliance of junior workers. The line 1 tailors have considerable claim to status by virtue of such factors as their skill, age, urban experience and frequently extended length of service in the factory. If one criterion of prestige is the amount

[11] Hastings, although in a supervisory position, worked at line 1 (see fig. 5.2(a)) and had little opportunity to move around the factory floor establishing relationships, unlike his fellow supervisors Chisokone and Mukubwa.

of respect in which a person is held by virtue of such qualities as skill, age, etc., and if it can be accepted that such qualities were taken into account by the factory workers when asked to rank the factory occupations in accordance with the prestige in which they are held,[12] then it can be stated that these line 1 tailors, together with the supervisors and overlock machiner, are generally held in respect and have high prestige in the factory (see table 2.3). Not only do others in the factory perceive the line 1 tailors as being high in prestige, but the line 1 tailors also perceive themselves in this way. Furthermore, they have an interest in preserving their prestige. One means by which it can be reduced is by subordinating oneself to another. For example, I discussed that some individuals ranked the ironers high because their work freed them from supervision,[13] which in most instances meant that an individual had to behave in a subordinate manner to another. Similarly, some of the junior factory workers ranked the line 1 tailors low because of their constant subordination to Patel. Compliance implies subordination and because of their prestige and status, line 1 tailors and others such as the overlock machiner have an interest in restricting the degree to which they comply with the demands or authority of another.[14] Because they generally perceive themselves and are perceived by others as being low in prestige and status, the junior workers are more willing to comply with another's demands or authority. This is especially so as compliance is invariably the only resource which they can use in transactions for various other services and benefits. Line 1 tailors have few needs in the work place and they can enter into transactions with others for benefits

[12] See the discussion of occupational prestige in chapter 2, p. pp. 54–9.
[13] See chapter 2, p. 57.
[14] Heath (1968) points to what he considers an inconsistency in Blau, who argues at first that 'a man's resources of willing compliance were *inversely* proportional to his status but then goes on ... to imply that the expert receives compliance in return for advice and that this increases both his status and his resources of willing compliance' (p. 278). In my view, Heath has failed to realise an implicit distinction made by Blau between an individual who has a large resource of personal willing compliance and an individual who commands the willing compliance of others. Individuals of high status will have fewer resources of personal willing compliance than individuals of low status because there are obviously fewer individuals of higher status above them than in the case of those of low status, to whom compliance or subordination would not result in a reduction of status. Increase of status reduces the number of individuals to whom a person could personally willingly comply but may increase the number of individuals over whom he commands willing compliance. With reference to the above analysis, the line 1 tailors and even more the supervisors have very limited resources of personal willing compliance but large resources of willing compliance in the sense that they command the willing compliance of a number of others.

they do not have without using such a resource as compliance which would imply their subordination.

However, given the difficulty encountered by the supervisors in achieving the compliance of the senior workers such as the line 1 tailors, one resource which Chisokone and Mukubwa can distribute among these workers is their influence with Patel. This influence can be presented by the supervisors as being used in the interests of the line 1 tailors to obtain such benefits for them as wage increases and protection against Patel's threats of dismissal. In return for the expectation of these rewards, the supervisors can induce the compliance of the senior workers to their demands and authority. But the maintenance of this relationship of the expression of willing compliance from the senior workers to the supervisors is dependent not only on the furnishing of benefits such as those stated above but also on the supervisors' successfully presenting themselves as individuals whose attitudes and interests coincide with those of the senior workers.

A major reason why Hastings did not receive much overt expression of willing compliance—his awareness of which perhaps influenced him not to become embroiled too often in heated discussion—was because of the difficulties he faced in presenting himself in a favourable way to others. In fact, throughout most of the period of my observations in the factory, he was viewed with extreme hostility by most of the workers. Apart from the restrictions on his movement around the factory floor which reduced his opportunity to establish relationships with others, his regular association with Patel frequently based on their joint participation on work such as the making of suits, conveyed the impression to the factory employees that Hastings was Patel's main offsider. Hastings' failure to develop many relationships with others in which he was the superior partner and to present himself as acting in the interests of the employees made it difficult for him to exert authority over the employees at the request of Patel. On the occasions when he was instructed to do so by Patel, workers often refused to comply with his demands and Patel had to come to his aid or more usually Patel asked one of the other supervisors to take over.

This is significant as it reveals the importance of a supervisor's achieving the compliance of others through his own personal relationships. By using his own personal relationships he can, in fact, demand the compliance of others to his authority on the basis, not of his position in an organisational framework which delegates authority to him, but on the basis that those over whom he wishes to exert authority are in some way obligated to comply with his demands in order to discharge aspects of their personal debt to him. A supervisor who can do this limits the extent to which he is seen as acting purely in the interests of management. Hastings who could not operate this way was seen as acting in management's interest and using authority which received the support of management but which was not agreed to by the person over whom it was used. In contrast to Hastings, at this stage in the development of factory relations, Chisokone and Mukubwa were able to use their personal relationships in the exercise of their authority as they had won the acceptance of most of the factory employees that these latter were in certain ways obligated to them.

The danger of Chisokone and Mukubwa becoming the focus of conflict arising from their intercalary position as supervisors, which exposes them to the contradictory expectations of management and worker was reduced by their dominance in the set of factory relationships. This was evidenced by their ability to win the compliance of others to themselves as a result to their either supplying various benefits or holding out the promise of future benefits. In addition, the overall patterning of relationships in the factory at the time also reduced the degree to which the supervisors became a focus of conflict because of their intercalary position. As stated earlier, with the exception of the line 1 tailors in whose set of relationships the supervisors tended to be dominant, most of the workers were involved in relationships of limited span. Thus there were few individuals other than the supervisors who had enough influence or commanded sufficient compliance to mobilise opinion against Mukubwa or Chisokone and challenge their presentation of themselves as acting in the interests of the workers. Furthermore, there was no individual who had yet presented himself as an alternative to Mukubwa and Chisokone and who offered the attainment of benefits attractive to would-be followers. Finally, there was no connected set of individuals representative of a body of opinion who saw their interests as opposed to the supervisors and who could thus threaten the powerful position of the latter.

Now to return to the discussion of the implications of Lyashi's action. In particular, what was the threat of Lyashi's behaviour to Mukubwa's position? Why did Lyashi's statement receive so little support from the others gathered? First, by emphasising one facet of Mukubwa's relationships, Lyashi challenged Mukubwa's presentation of himself as an individual who was acting in the general interests of the employees. The bite in Lyashi's comment was contained in his implication that Mukubwa had values and standards in common with Indians, and by extension Indian employers. Second, on this occasion as well as at previous times (see events 1 and 4, appendix 2) Lyashi had been presenting himself both as a man of status deserving the respect of others and as an individual who could offer some solution to the problems which confronted the workers. In effect, on this occasion and in earlier events he had been projecting himself as a leader of opinion and, as such, an attractive alternative to others like Mukubwa and Chisokone. Thus in event 1 it was Lyashi who had suggested to Kalundwe, a line 3 tailor as well as to other junior workers present, that the workers' inadequate wage and work conditions could only be rectified by militant action. During event 4 it was again Lyashi who played a leading role in a general address of the workers suggesting that they should be paid for the tea break period and that Patel should not be allowed to count it as time lost. In the same address, he argued that the lack of strength of their union was the main reason why the workers were not able to win concessions from the management. In neither one of these two events did Lyashi receive much overt approval for his opinions. At the close of event 4, for example, after he had finished his address, he referred to a small group of line 2 and 3 tailors as *baiche* (young men). Implicit in the use of this term was that Lyashi was superior in status to these men. One individual in particular, Paulos, objected to being called *baiche*. Paulos is considerably younger than Lyashi but had been employed in the factory for the same period as the latter, though on line 2. Paulos stated that as a skilled tailor he had as much right to respect as Lyashi.

Nevertheless, despite Lyashi's relative lack of success in gaining the approval of others either in previous events or in the one under discussion, he was presenting himself as a candidate for power and leadership and was thus threatening the position of others. In the conversation focused upon the ideal village for retirement, by transforming the basis of the discussion from a general plane unrelated to the discussants' position as factory workers to the more contextually relevant level of equating Mukubwa with the Indian employers, Lyashi had openly challenged Mukubwa's presentation of himself. Moreover, in this event and in others he had declared himself as an individual interested in guiding opinion and attracting the approval of others for his opinions. Because of this, and aided by the fact that Lyashi was a line 1 tailor already enmeshed in a close-knit set of relationships largely composed of his fellow workers on the line, it was understandable that Mukubwa should feel threatened by him. Lyashi could stir opinion among the workers and others to the realisation that the expected benefits from their support of Mukubwa were not forthcoming because of the latter's attachment to the Indian management. As already explained, an inability of Mukubwa to maintain the employees' expectations that he would work in their interests would reduce his power and make his task of supervision all the more difficult.

Mukubwa, no doubt encouraged by such observations as Lyashi's failure to win approval on previous occasions, used his power and influence to stop Lyashi from elaborating any further. Lyashi, at this stage in the development of factory relations, had little power and influence, and even if he had wished to pursue his strategy in undermining Mukubwa's position, the evident antagonism of the other workers present towards him would have prevented him from doing so. Here the paradox which involves all those who set out on the road to power is revealed, which is '. . . the impressive qualities that make a person a particularly attractive and valuable group member also constitute a status threat to the rest' (Blau, 1964: 44). Lyashi was not only challenging the position of Mukubwa but also contained in his attempt to assume a leading part was the subordination of other workers to himself. Many of them, such as the line 1 tailors, were of equal if not of higher status. The subordination of the line 1 tailors, for example, to Mukubwa did not entail as great a threat to their status, in the sense that it would be reduced in the eyes of the other employees, as subordination to Lyashi. Mukubwa, at least in terms of the organisational framework of the factory, was placed in a position above the line 1 tailors and the other factory workers. But, especially for the line 1 tailors, subordination to Lyashi, an equal, would reduce their status, and support of him, at least at this stage, would have been against their interests; it being assumed that they did not wish a reduction in their status. Therefore, in the light of this argument, I suggest that the others present and in particular the line 1 tailors such as Abraham who took part in the discussion—and who before Lyashi had added his comments, had supported Mukubwa's opinion and therefore could have construed Lyashi's statement as a criticism of himself—and Nkoloya, Chipata, Chilwa, Lenard, etc., who had come to the outskirts of the conversational group, would have opposed Lyashi. At any rate, judging from the nods of approval at Mukubwa's reaction to Lyashi, it was clear that Mukubwa had considerable support.

By halting Lyashi, Mukubwa protected his image from damage at the hands of Lyashi. But even though the others present may have had interests at stake in opposing Lyashi, Mukubwa by using his power expended some of his resources of willing compliance. No statement implying that his power was greatly reduced as a result of his action in this event is made here but this event taken in conjunction with later ones shortly to be recounted, when Mukubwa again used his power, did result in a reduction of his power.

Before I extend the argument of this chapter into the analysis of subsequent events, a number of points relating to the above discussion should be emphasised. Lyashi's threat was multifaceted. He had attacked Mukubwa's presentation of himself by stressing the latter's close association with the Indian management. Furthermore, on this occasion and on others before it, Lyashi had been projecting himself as an individual concerned with workers' problems who realised the source of their difficulties. Lyashi was trying to influence opinion and as such was attempting to aspire to power and leadership. Lyashi's entry into competition for power and leadership in general and with reference to this one event had a number of effects. First, it is argued that the supervisors depend for their exertion of authority on the factory workers in various ways being obligated to them. Dependence for support on their position within an organisational framework defined by management, as in the case of Hastings, makes it difficult for them to discharge their duties as supervisors. However, supervisory authority can be more easily exercised if the person towards whom it is directed views his acquiescence to it as part of the discharge of a personal debt to the supervisor. Lyashi in his behaviour threatened an exposure of the ephemerality of the expectation among the workers that subordination to Mukubwa would result in various benefits. It had been suggested by Lyashi that Mukubwa had interests in common with the Indian management. Moreover, Lyashi by attempting to present himself as attractive to others, offered an alternative on to whom individuals could transfer their allegiance. If Lyashi was successful, the continued subordination of the workers to Mukubwa was endangered. Mukubwa chose to use his power to minimise the success of Lyashi's presentation of him as an individual in league with management in opposition to the factory employees. But by using it, and thus depending on the support of others present, he gave those who had agreed to subordinate themselves to him an opportunity to discharge part of their obligation by complying with his demands.

Mukubwa was not the only individual who was victim of a paradox. Lyashi, by entering into competition for leadership and power threatened the status of others. It will be a major theme of later analysis that his action demanded that others also must enter the competition to maintain their own status against the threat of Lyashi. The entry of others into the competition for power not only presents an impediment to Lyashi's achievement of power but will also have an important effect determining the changing structure of relationships in the factory. The paradox for Lyashi is that in the pursuit of his ambition to achieve power he sets in motion processes which could lead ultimately to failure.

In the following events, as in the one already discussed, Lyashi again plays a prominent part. Two events are taken together not only because they occurred on two successive days but because they also demonstrate clearly other aspects of Lyashi's politicking and the idiom in which it is cast in his competition with the other factory employees. The occasion of both these events was again tea break.

The first event initially involves Hastings, Nkumbula, Kalamba, Mpundu and Lyashi as the main participants but later in the process Mukubwa, Chisokone and Abraham were to play important parts.

Event 13   A question of town experience
23 June 1965

Hastings opened the discussion by enquiring of Mpundu why he was not drinking any tea but only seemed content to smoke. Mpundu replied that it was his normal custom to have tea at home before leaving for work and therefore he did not require any at break. Nkumbula broke into the conversation and gibed at Mpundu, saying that all those in the present company had tea at home before departing for work and that his excuse seemed a poor one. Lyashi now added his view and, addressing all those seated with him as *imwe baiche* (young men), said, 'Neither of you can be telling the truth. None of you could have lived long enough on the Copperbelt to have become accustomed to the habit of drinking tea in the mornings.' Here Lyashi had suggested that only individuals who can be regarded as town men and specifically those with Copperbelt experience are used to drinking tea at their homes. The implication which could be drawn from such a statement was that those seated with Lyashi were not town men. Adam Kalamba accepted the challenge and claimed that he had been in town for fifteen years and had drunk tea every morning. This claim drew a disbelieving laugh from Lyashi and he snorted in reply, 'Even though you may have been in town for fifteen years you could never have been earning sufficient money to buy the ingredients for tea. Why, you are only a young man and tea is a rich man's drink.' Angered, Kalamba jumped to his feet and said that Lyashi should not disbelieve him. 'Unlike your relatives, Lyashi, many of mine are successful townsmen. My father even owned a store and we always had tea in our house.' Lyashi responded by reciting at length his own town experience. He made special reference to his work as a miner on the Copperbelt and how the wage he earned there enabled him to live in a civilised manner. Others at the break group queried his claims and Mpundu in particular wondered if Lyashi's claims to be a townsman could be greater than those of Hastings, whom everyone knew had been in town most of his life. Lyashi replied that it was not so much town experience that was important but the kind of town a man had been working in and the way of life he had been following in town which was crucial. 'As for myself,' said Lyashi, 'I have been living the life of a true townsman.'

A large number of other factory employees who had been seated elsewhere now came to the outskirts of Lyashi's group. Chisokone in particular joined in the attack against Lyashi. 'Why do you praise yourself like this? I probably drink tea more regularly at home than any of you seated here, yet you do not find me boasting like you, Lyashi, or any of you others for that matter.' At this moment Hastings turned the tables on all those who had been vying with each other as to their respective status as townsmen, by stating that those who boasted about their status as townsmen were behaving in a most untownsmanlike fashion. 'You, Chisokone, should also be careful for by praising yourself in this way you are making the same mistake as Lyashi or Kalamba.' Abraham supported Hastings by adding that those who considered themselves to be townsmen should keep quiet. 'Indians and Europeans who have spent all their lives in town and who are very wealthy and civilised do not boast as you do. I think your boasting shows that you are poor and don't drink tea regularly.' Discussion ended when Patel called his employees back to work. Nkumbula complained that Patel treated them like dogs and did not even give his workers time to talk with each other. Lyashi told Nkumbula to be quiet or else Patel might give him the sack. 'We must show each other respect even though Patel does not give us respect.'

The next event in terms of content has much in common with the above for it, too, is concerned with what constitutes proper civilised behaviour. However, the nature of Lyashi's participation on this occasion is different for he chooses to state his opposition to those with whom he is competing in the idiom of ethnic and national divisions.

Event 14   Malawians and Zambians
24 June 1965

On the following day at break, Mukubwa approached John, a cotton boy, and accused him of taking too large a share of the bread available. Adam Kalamba who was also present jocularly supported Mukubwa and stated that the only way John could hope to become fat was by eating well at break time. John was annoyed at Kalamba's suggestion and replied that he did not like the implication that he did not eat well at home. 'Do you think that I would die if I didn't eat bread here?' Joseph, a working companion of John, saw the humour in the situation and asked, 'Why then can't you stop eating?' John replied good humouredly, 'This is Company's bread. Why shouldn't I eat as much bread as possible at Patel's expense?' Lyashi by this time had joined the small gathering but when he saw Hastings approaching spoke to John in Bemba, 'Be quiet or you will be reported.' Hastings heard Lyashi but did not fully understand what the latter had said as Lyashi had used Bemba words which he as a Nyanja speaker did not understand. He was further interested in what Lyashi had said as the group had suddenly fallen silent and Lyashi and John in particular were eyeing him with suspicion. Hastings, on en-quiring of Lyashi what he had spoken, was met with the sharp reply, 'It doesn't matter. You couldn't understand what I said, unless of course, you took the time to learn Bemba.' Slightly irritated, Hastings replied, 'I am not interested in learning that language of yours.' Seizing his oppor-tunity, Lyashi exclaimed, 'Oh, if that's the case you had better consider learning it. You're in Zambia now.' Chisokone supported Lyashi, 'This is Zambia not Malawi.' Removing himself from the group, Hastings claimed that he possessed Zambian citizenship and that the mention of his Malawian connections was irrelevant. After Hastings had left the group all those present, with the exception of Kalamba, who by this time had gone back inside the factory, stated various complaints to the effect that it was Malawians who took the jobs which Zambians should have and that it was Malawians who played the part of *chichawa* (informer) to European and Indian employers.

Analysis. In the above events, Lyashi is again seen attempting to turn the discussion at tea break to his own advantage. The first event shows Lyashi trying to win the acceptance of others to a particular definition of a civilised townsman suitable to his own interests. In the process he displays some of his qualities in a bid to impress others in order to receive acknowledgment of his high prestige and status. The second event sees Lyashi using to his own advantage the ethnic–national division between the factory workers in the course of excluding Hastings from the conversation, and highlights the latter's association with the management. The outcome of each event sees Lyashi emerging with more success than he did on previous occasions.

Lyashi, in the first event, by opposing Mpundu's claims to being a townsman acquainted with such town customs as tea drinking, was able to enter the discussion with some approval of the others present. Mpundu, a line 3 tailor who had been working in the factory for eigh-teen months, was regarded by the other individuals participating in the discussions as of relatively low status in relation to themselves. With the exception of Mpundu, all the discussants in the tea group were tailors on line 1 and as table 2.3 shows,[15] workers on this line generally regard line 3 tailors as inferior in prestige. Hastings, by making comments about Mpundu's apparent inability to join his companions in the drink-ing of tea, had, in fact, implied that Mpundu was not as 'civilised' or as accustomed to town ways as his fellows. Lyashi, however, transformed

[15] Also see chapter 2, p. 55.

the discussion to a new plane by not only questioning Mpundu's claims to be civilised in his reply to Hastings but also implying that the others participating in the discussions were also not accustomed to civilised town behaviour. Lyashi was aware, as were the others, that some of those present, such as Hastings, had considerable town experience behind them. He thus made his definition of a townsman contingent on Copperbelt experience—an experience which he himself had but which he was aware the others present had not. As a further proviso to his definition of a civilised townsman, he added the condition of wealth, a requirement generally agreed by Africans living in town as necessary for the procurement of material goods which allows people to behave in a civilised manner. Again, unlike those seated with Lyashi, the latter had been employed as a miner which had earned him an income considerably above that in the past experience of the others gathered.[16] In additon, Lyashi, in presenting his opinion, addressed his companions as *imwe baiche*—you young men.[17] The overall connotation imparted here was that those addressed by Lyashi were lower in prestige and status than he, the basis for this being his past experience on the Copperbelt as a miner which gave him claim to consideration as a civilised townsman above all the others. This was not the only occasion, as the earlier reference to event 4 (appendix 2) shows upon which Lyashi had addressed his work companions in such a manner. Similarly, as in event 4, Lyashi's assumption of higher status was not agreed to by the others gathered. Lyashi had biased his definition of a 'civilised' townsman in the light of his own previous experience, and it could have been expected that the challenge to him would have been framed in terms of what constituted the proper definition of a townsman.

Kalamba, a younger man than Lyashi, took up the challenge and introduced the factor of length of town experience as an important criterion for judging whether an individual was a townsman accustomed to town ways or not. When Lyashi insisted that income was a more critical indicator, he excluded such individuals as Hastings from his definition even though Mpundu later tried to question Lyashi's claims by referring to Hastings. Kalamba claimed his own right to be regarded as a townsman on the basis that his relatives were successful townsmen, i.e. wealthy, and that he had been brought up in an environment which accustomed him to town behaviour. New definitional criteria had been

[16] See Lyashi's employment history, chapter 3, pp. 75–6.
[17] There are other meanings which can be attached to the term *mwaiche* (pl. *ba*). Thus used this way, it can have the connotation of 'child'. On this occasion I have chosen to translate the term as 'young man' as I consider it to be the sense most relevant to the context.

introduced and, in response to Kalamba, Lyashi recited his own labour experience and attempted to re-emphasise the importance of Copperbelt residence and the earning of a high income as crucial to his definition.

If Lyashi had presented his definition of a civilised townsman only in opposition to Kalamba and Mpundu, it is conceivable that he would have received support for his claims in accordance with his definition. This need not imply that the content of Lyashi's definition was more accurate than that of either Kalamba or Mpundu. In general terms, aspects of Lyashi's definition would have met with a wide degree of agreement both among the factory workers and individuals elsewhere employed in Kabwe. For example, most Africans I knew in Kabwe, the Narayan Bros. workers included, regard the Copperbelt towns and the life pursued in them as providing a major reference in terms of which behaviour according to town customs is gauged. To them the Copperbelt towns are seen as places of high wages, tall, modern buildings, numerous bars and an exciting night life.[18] Men who can demonstrate extensive experience in these towns or in the other large urban centres outside Zambia such as Salisbury and Bulawayo in Rhodesia or Johannesburg and Cape Town in South Africa can lay greater claim to being townsmen than those who have spent most of their labour experience in such towns as Kabwe, Livingstone or Chipata. Another definitional content which Lyashi emphasised was income. Most Africans with whom I came into contact generally agreed that a high wage is almost an essential prerequisite for a man to be regarded as a civilised townsman. A high income gives access to material goods such as smart clothing and new furniture which in their consumption and display can symbolise an individual's standing as a civilised townsman in the eyes of his peers and in the eyes of those less fortunate. But other factors which are no less important indices used to gauge an individual's claim to civilised townsman status are those mentioned by Mpundu and Kalamba. These include length of urban residence and the standing of one's relatives in urban life. Other indicators not mentioned by any of the three participants can also be important such as education or the type of occupation.

There are clearly many factors which might be included in the definition of a civilised townsman. I suggest, however, that it is the standing of the individual in the company where he makes his definition and the nature and structure of his personal relationships in comparison with those against whom he is opposed, which determine the acceptance or

[18] The European residents of Kabwe view the Copperbelt towns in much the same way as the African residents.

rejection of his definition. It is in terms of considerations such as these that I consider that if Lyashi had only presented himself in opposition to Kalamba and Mpundu he would have received the support of the others in the tea group. Mpundu, as a line 3 tailor, was accorded low respect by the line 1 tailors in the group. Again, Kalamba, because of his relative youth, was considered inferior in status by the line 1 tailors to themselves.[19] Agreement by the other line 1 tailors with Lyashi would have been a vehicle for the re-emphasis of what they considered to be their respective status positions in the context. There were many other occasions when the senior workers lost no time in demonstrating to Mpundu and Kalamba their inferiority of status. Kalamba, in particular, was the object of much jesting on the part of his working companions on line 1 and this was one factor, together with his friendship with Ibraham, which influenced him to join the latter on line 2 in August 1965.

The cause of much of the fun being directed towards Kalamba was the apparent incongruity contained in the employment of a man of Kalamba's age (33) on line 1, a line which consisted of most of the older workers. As event 6 shows (see appendix 2), for example, great play was made of Kalamba's name. *Kalamba* is a term used frequently in town to address old and respected men.[20] In this event a number of line 1 tailors, including Lyashi, knelt before Kalamba at tea break and waited on him with bread and tea. They were showing him a mock respect, implying in their behaviour that the respect they were demonstrating towards him was more in keeping with behaviour which Kalamba should show towards them.[21] This behaviour also had a retributive

[19] Age is a factor to which individuals attach great importance in assessing their prestige, status and behaviour relative to others. I have witnessed long and extremely animated arguments between drinking companions in beer halls, for instance, over their precise dates of birth and therefore the proper address term which should be used in reference to them.

[20] I refer here to the most general meaning of the term *Kalamba*. A reasonable translation of the term is 'big man' for it is often used to refer to men who are generally regarded as senior, be it because of age, political importance or economic wealth. Used between equals or towards those who are considered junior, it takes the form of a jest. Frequently in such cases as the latter it is not taken in good humour and can lead to bitter argument. *Mudala*, which also can be translated as 'big man', is a term similarly used. *Kalamba* is from the Bemba meaning adult, or elder. *Mudala* derives from Zulu via Chila-palapa, meaning 'old man'.

[21] To kneel before someone as a mark of respect is behaviour more consistent with the respect shown towards a chief. Normally, in showing respect to another person, the knees may be slightly bent. The behaviour of the line 1 tailors was therefore exaggerated. In that the behaviour of the line 1 tailors had the function of putting Kalamba in his place, it has some similarity with

purpose as Kalamba, evidenced in his behaviour towards Lyashi, was constantly challenging the claims which his companions on line 1 made to their status in the factory.

Apart from their relatively low status, which might have influenced opinion to go against what Kalamba and Mpundu considered to be the definitional characteristics of a townsman in comparison with Lyashi, these two employees had entered into few transactions with the other workers present. For example, Lyashi and Mkumbula regularly shared cigarettes at work and often met in the beer hall after work. Likewise, Lyashi had a similar relationship with Abraham and Nkoloya, both of whom were seated with Lyashi on the occasion of this tea break but as yet had not participated in the conversation. Kalamba and Mpundu had little contact with these workers either in the factory or outside except occasionally at tea break. Because Lyashi was already involved in transactional relationships of both a sociational and instrumental nature with many of the workers seated with him, whereas Kalamba and Mpundu had few relationships of this kind, it might reasonably have been expected that the other workers, because of their greater investment in their relationship with Lyashi, would have supported him.

But, as stated earlier, Lyashi, in the process of laying down certain definitional prerequisites for being a civilised townsman had implied that he had greater claim to status than all those present. The main focus upon which the definition of a civilised townsman hinged and to which the discussants had continually referred was not the various social attributes such as wealth, length of urban residence or Copperbelt experience but the actual behaviour deemed essential for a townsman to be regarded as civilised.[22] It was, after all, Hastings' charge

the institution of 'binging' in the bank wiring room. See Roethlisberger and Dickson (1941: 501–2) and the instructive re-analysis of Roethlisberger's and Dickson's research by Homans (1951: 60–1).

[22] In most areas of urban life I have observed where arguments have arisen about the relative claims which individuals have to civilised townsmen status, the discussion has focused on expected forms of behaviour. It is unlikely that in any conversation group two individuals would have the same urban and labour experience. The only basis in terms of which some common agreement could be forged is in terms of behaviour. The word *fontini* refers to the behaviour displayed by individuals and indicates that an individual is uncivilised and unacquainted with town customs. Although the application of the term verges on the insulting, it is pointed out that it can be applied in reference to an individual irrespective of his long urban residence, high occupational prestige or large income, etc. One headmaster of a primary school in Kabwe, for example, who had lived most of his life in town and was of a relatively high occupational standing, was regarded by his fellow teachers as a *fontini* because in their eyes he did not behave in a town way. He did not use knives and forks at the table, a form of behaviour which his fellow teachers

against Mpundu to the effect that the latter was not accustomed with town ways of behaviour such as tea drinking which had triggered off the discussion.

Chisokone, who had been standing behind Hastings facing Lyashi, brought the conversation back within the bounds of behavioural relevance and denied the claims of any of the three discussants to civilised townsman status. As an individual who regarded himself as superior in status to the others in the group, in the process of denying Lyashi and his companions' claims to civilised townsman status, Chisokone advanced his own claims. But rather than receiving the support of the others, he found himself under attack. Hastings seized on Chisokone's own statement that a civilised townsman should not boast and pointed out that by claiming to be civilised, Chisokone was just as guilty as Lyashi and Kalamba of boasting. Abraham, with the approval of others nearby, such as Nkoloya and Nkumbula, supported Hastings in the condemnation of Chisokone and also Lyashi, Kalamba and Mpundu. Abraham's point was the non-self-praising behaviour of Indians and Europeans who are often referred to as presenting the archetype of civilised town behaviour.[23] The most significant feature of this last part of the event was not only the failure of Lyashi to receive support for his definition and thus some acceptance of the value of the qualities he displayed but also, the unity of the workers in opposition to Chisokone. Two factors gave rise to this unity, both of these in turn indicative of underlying changes taking place in the structure of social relationships within the factory context.

First, in a series of events which had occurred earlier Chisokone and Mukubwa in their behaviour had been markedly overreaching the accepted limits of their status. Moreover, they had been repeatedly emphasising to the other workers the subordination of the latter to them. By continually presenting their status for approval, they demanded that others had repeatedly to devalue their own. This was particularly galling to the line 1 tailors who had an interest in preserving their own status and viewed themselves as being almost on a par in status with the supervisors. One general pattern which seems to be true of the management of status in many contexts, not least in Narayan Bros., is that once their status had been accepted, individuals protect their

felt could be expected from a man of his occupational position, and in con-versation he continually extolled the values of tribal life to the detriment of urban living.

[23] Mitchell (1956: 13–18) has discussed at some length the position of Euro-peans as a reference group in terms of which urban Africans assess each other's behaviour.

resources of approval by modest and self-deprecating behaviour.[24] This certainly was not evident in the behaviour of Chisokone or Mukubwa.

It is supportive of my argument that it was precisely because Chisokone was not modest in the event discussed above that the opposition to him occurred. But individuals whose prestige and status are secure are more likely to engage in self-deprecatory behaviour—they have much to gain and little to lose—than persons whose prestige and status are insecure. Lyashi's competition for power and leadership was one factor which precipitated the entry of others into the competition, partially at least as a necessary function of protecting their own status. Thus as a result of Lyashi's competition, the status, and concomitant with it the power and leadership, of Chisokone and Mukubwa was exposed to threat. Their immodest behaviour produced an effect contrary to their interests for it made subordination to them less attractive. Other employees felt threatened by Mukubwa and Chisokone's repeated demands on them to show their approval. Furthermore, Chisokone and Mukubwa on a few occasions totally mismanaged their behaviour to the point of almost ridiculing the other employees. A feature of the events in which Chiskone and Mukubwa emphasised their status to the detriment of others, which reveals the magnitude of their mismanagement of their behaviour was the way they chose to act in reference to a complaint initiated by Patel that some of the tea cups were stolen.

Event 7 (see appendix 2) describes an occasion on which Patel came up to Chisokone and Mukubwa at tea break and within hearing distance of the other employees informed them that some of the tea cups had been stolen. Neither Chisokone nor Mukubwa did anything about it at the time for a furious debate broke out among some of the workers, who included Meshak, the button machiner, Kalamba, Kamwefu, Chilwa, who were line 1 tailors, and Paulos and Zulu, a tailor and overlock machiner respectively on line 2. They were all extremely annoyed that Patel should make such a suggestion and complained that he treated them like children. But a few days later (see event 8, appendix 2) Mukubwa and Chisokone who had been detained a few minutes in the factory after the beginning of tea break joined the workers outside to

---

[24] Blau (1964: 47–50) has an extensive discussion of the way individuals adopt modest behaviour once they have impressed others with their qualities and gained social approval. 'Having first impressed us with his Harvard accent and Beacon Hill friends, he may later tell a story that reveals his immigrant background. After having talked only of the successes in his career, he may let us in on the defeats he has suffered. He no longer carefully protects himself against the slightest ridicule but may now tell jokes at his own expense' (*op. cit.*, p. 48).

discover that there were no cups available for them to use. Chisokone complained that at work everyone had to fend for themselves. Nearby a conversation was in progress among a group of line 1 tailors, the general gist of it being whether the size of cup an individual was using or the amount of bread he was eating was in accordance with his status. Mukubwa broke in and mentioned angrily that all the eagerness to drink tea and eat the bread provided was indicative that the line 1 tailors did not eat properly at home. Lwanga reacted most strongly against Mukubwa's remark and with the approval of his other work companions lectured Mukubwa to be careful or else his ties of friendship with them would be threatened. 'All of us here are big men with wives and children. We rent our own houses. It is not good that some people should laugh at their friends as if they are children.'

The following day (event 9, appendix 2) a similar incident occurred when Chisokone complained to all the workers about the shortage of cups. Nkoloya jokingly suggested that Chisokone must have stolen them. Chisokone retorted that he had better tea cups at his home than any of the workers, Nkoloya included. He went on to state that among the workers, Nkoloya could most reasonably be suspected of stealing the factory's cups.

Needless to say, such behaviour of Mukubwa and Chisokone's did not receive the strong appreciation of the workers, least of all the line 1 tailors against whom it was frequently directed. Moreover, the attitudes expressed by Mukubwa and Chisokone appeared to echo the sentiments of management inplicit in Patel's suggestion to these two supervisors that some of the tea cups had been stolen. Mukubwa and Chisokone's mismanagement of their behaviour, often immodest and subjecting the line 1 tailors to ridicule, which in turn was largely produced by Mukubwa and Chisokone's insecurity of status, was creating a unity of feeling among the line 1 tailors in opposition to the supervisors. Others in the factory were not unaffected by the behaviour of the supervisors and began to deny them approval of various kinds. Thus on one occasion (event 10, appendix 2) when many workers were still smarting under Patel's accusation that tea cups had been stolen and Mukubwa and Chisokone's apparent association with him, Sign, a tailor on line 3, ruled Chisokone's presentation of himself as a political leader irrelevant to the factory context. Chisokone had generally called the workers' attention to the plight of fellow Africans in Rhodesia beleagured by Ian Smith's Rhodesian Front. By denying the relevance of Chisokone's statements to the factory, Sign had, in effect, withheld approval of Chisokone's position of political importance in Kabwe.

R

(Chisokone was a township UNIP branch secretary.) It was partly through the use of his political position that Chisokone had initially attracted the support and approval of the factory workers and achieved status, power and leadership in the work place. A considerable amount of the opposition to Chisokone was an example of the growing disaffection being shown towards him.

The threat to the status of the line 1 tailors came not only from the supervisors but also from the competition for power and leadership of a member within their ranks, Lyashi. Lyashi's action in itself demanded some unity among the line 1 tailors to prevent any success on his part. Thus opinion among the line 1 tailors was galvanised to protect themselves from threats to their status emanating from within their ranks as well as from outside.

Given therefore, the different threats to their status, it was predictable that the line 1 tailors would seek a definition of the behaviour of a civilised townsman which would withhold approval from Chisokone or Lyashi—or, for that matter, Mpundu and Kalamba. This they did by supporting Abraham's statement, initiated by a remark from Hastings, that people who boast are not acting in accordance with behaviour expected of civilised townsmen.[25] In effect, also, the line 1 tailors expressed their disapproval of individuals who attempted to present their impressive qualities to others, thereby threatening their status. Competitive behaviour of the kind presented by Lyashi seeks a redistribution of the available resources of approval and respect. A redistribution in Lyashi's favour could have had the effect of reducing the status of his workmates on line 1.

Lyashi, however, did not emerge from the event totally unsuccessful. By warning Nkumbula to desist from criticising Patel or else risk dismissal from work Lyashi again stressed an image of himself which he sought to convey to others as a man who militantly opposed management and had the protection of the workers' interests at heart. At the same time, he expressed his approval of one result of the discussion that the senior workers in the factory should not attempt to differentiate themselves from each other in terms of status. It is not unreasonable to assume that the supervisors, in view of the mismanagement of their

[25] It must be emphasised that although Hastings had little power in the factory and often received expressions of active dislike from many of the workers because of his association with Patel, he was respected. The general respect in which he was held derived from such factors as his being the oldest worker in the factory and the fact that he was the most skilled and longest employed factory worker. He was the first tailor employed by Patel and worked in Narayan Bros.' store as a tailor before the clothing factory was established.

behaviour in other events where they strove to emphasise their superiority and betrayed their association with management, were implicitly included in Lyashi's remark. In one brief moment, therefore, Lyashi had both reaffirmed his support of the line 1 tailors' interests and his opposition to management and the individuals representative of it. Furthermore—and this is probably more significant—Nkumbula agreed with Lyashi and followed his advice, by stopping his complaints against Patel. Nkumbula had thus shown his approval of Lyashi and, although the former was not a powerful figure in the factory and in fact remained outside much of the competition which subsequently took place, he was a respected employee in the factory. This respect he owed to the high regard which most workers had of his tailoring skill, his age as one of the oldest factory workers and the fact that he had worked continually in the factory for twenty years making him, after Hastings, the longest served employee. His approval of Lyashi undoubtedly stemmed partly from his friendship with him, but his acknowledgment of Lyashi's opinions in the company of his fellow employees was to influence the emergence of a growing support for Lyashi's views among the factory workers.

Chisokone's entry into the discussion was also fortunate for Lyashi. Although Lyashi's behaviour was also condemned in Abraham's statement, Chisokone had made himself the focus of the attack and had thus drawn attention away from Lyashi.

In this event I have shown how the definition of a civilised townsman arrived at was emergent from the way in which the workers defined their relationships to one another. A concern of the analysis has been to show how the line 1 tailors were both subjected to threats to their status from individuals outside and inside their ranks. The definition of a civilised townsman, therefore, arose from the line 1 tailors' agreeing on a definition which at the same time preserved their status and denied approval to those who threatened them. Correspondingly, I also showed how through mismanagement of behaviour partly engendered by the insecurity of their status caused partly by the competition of Lyashi, the two supervisors used up their resources of approval and of willing compliance thereby weakening their position of power and status in the factory. The action of the supervisors was beginning to alienate them from the support of the line 1 tailors and this, together with Lyashi's behaviour, saw the development of a greater unity among the line 1 tailors to protect their own interests. Thus the structure of interactional relationships in the factory and the meaning attached to them was beginning to change.

Hitherto, Lyashi's participation in various events, although having an effect on a changing definition of the situation, bore few obvious results favourable to his own interests. In the event which occurred the next day following the discussions focused on the definition of behaviour appropriate to a civilised townsman, Lyashi was to be more successful in the mobilising of approval and support.

The next event with which I am concerned in this discussion was initiated by Mukubwa who admonished John, an ironer, for taking a very large piece of bread. This occasion like the foregoing event and others examined in relation to it is another example of a supervisor, this time Mukubwa, using his status both to impress his superiority over and to control the behaviour of another. Also, like Hastings' comment to Mpundu in the preceding event, implicit in it was reference to the uncivilised behaviour of John. Other workers present also joined in support of Mukubwa, such as Kalamba and Joseph (a cotton boy). An atmosphere of good humour surrounded the event. Nevertheless, the contributions to the discussion could at the same time be viewed as examples of individuals, both defining their own status with reference to John and according approval to Mukubwa for his criticism of John's behaviour. However, it is not this aspect of the event which is emphasised here, but rather Lyashi's manipulation of the ethnic and national identities which differentiate the workers from each other, for the furtherance of his own interests.

In chapter 3 the ethnic and cultural categories to which the workers belong and their areas of origin were described.[26] Throughout the fieldwork period, at least twenty different ethnic categories were represented among the factory workers. The degree of ethnic diversity within the factory labour force is highlighted when it is realised that the number of workers employed in the factory for most months barely exceeded forty. Within the factory, the specific ethnic identities of the workers, for example, Bemba, Bisa, Soli, Ngoni, etc., were not a frequent basis in terms of which interaction was framed. There are two reasons for this. First, workers who belong to the one ethnic category are separated by such factors as work position, skill and occupation. Expression of affiliation to others with whom an individual has interests in common in terms of specific ethnic identity provides more of a barrier than an avenue for the expression of such attachment. For although it may serve to associate an individual with a few other employees, it can exclude many more with whom an individual has interests in common or at least to whom he wishes to convey a sense of common

[26] See pp. 91–2.

interest. Second, and connected with the above, in a context such as Narayan Bros. where individuals are continually competing for the support and approval of others, to seek this on the basis of a specific ethnic identity would greatly limit the extent of support and approval an individual can achieve.

The ethnic categories represented in the factory can be grouped in terms of their cultural and linguistic affinity and area or country of origin. Ethnic categories which are associated on the basis of one criterion will not be associated on the basis of another. Furthermore, certain criteria are more exclusive than others. Culture and province or area of origin as criteria will combine different assortments of ethnic groups into various categories but both criteria will be more exclusive than if language is the major criterion considered. The two languages spoken most frequently in the factory, and as in the above event could form the basis of alliance, were Nyanja, spoken mainly by the employees from the Eastern Province and Malawi, and Bemba which was mutually intelligible to most individual workers whose home areas were in the Northern, Central and Luapula provinces. It must be stressed at this stage, however, that for the majority of time the workers, irrespective of the language group to which they belonged, could communicate through the medium of CiCopperbelti.[27] This is the language of the town and incorporates Bemba, Nyanja and sometimes English and Afrikaans words.

These criteria of culture, province or area of origin and language were the most regular bases upon which individual workers categorised themselves and others. Individuals who spoke varying dialects of Bemba, for example, tended to class themselves as Bemba even though their specific ethnic identity may have been Bisa, Lala or Ambo. It was in terms of these broad categories that relationships with others were established. Thus individuals by classing themselves as Bemba were able to justify the establishment of joking relationships with others whom they categorised as Ngoni, even though they may have belonged to another ethnic category, on the basis of the institutionalised joking relationship which exists in town between Bemba and Ngoni.[28]

A more inclusive basis than any of the above by which individuals

[27] Epstein (1959: 235–52) gives a fascinating account of CiCopperbelti and the derivation of many words still in use at the time of my fieldwork.
[28] My description in this section follows closely the analysis of 'tribalism' among urban Africans which was thoroughly examined in the Zambian context, first by Mitchell (1956) and later by Epstein (1958). Mitchell gives a full discussion of the institutionalised sets of joking ties which exist between various tribal categories (1956: 35–42).

can be categorised in opposition to others is with reference to the
Zambian–non-Zambian distinction. A division represented in the
factory to which individuals occasionally referred to gain support for
their actions, was that between Zambians and Malawians. Mukubwa,
for example, to assure himself of support in the using of his authority
to exhort Nyirenda, a line 3 tailor, to apply himself more actively to his
task referred to Nyirenda's status as a Malawian in stating, 'Malawians
boast that they are townspeople but they are too lazy to be called such'
(see event 12, appendix 2).

The presence of Malawians as a significant category in the factory
was most noticeable in the months June to September inclusive (see
table 3.10). In addition, most of the Malawians were occupied in skilled
work and this in itself was a factor which generated considerable
hostility, particularly among the younger and unskilled workers. Some
of these latter employees were interested in learning the skill of tailoring
and felt that if Patel did not hire Malawians, they might be given the
opportunity to learn tailoring. More generally, most workers felt that
work in the factory should be offered to Zambians in preference to
Malawians. A widespread sentiment, largely engendered by the intense
political and nationalistic feeling of the time, was that Zambia was for
the Zambians and that expatriates irrespective of their nationality had
done little for the country to merit reward and were interested only in
feathering their own nests. Many Malawians because of the often better
education they had received tended to be disproportionately represented
in the skilled and better paid jobs not only in Kabwe but also in other
towns.[29] In the pre-Independence period their tendency to be heavily
represented in clerical work and in junior civil service positions led to
their being associated with the colonial government and other perceived
agencies of colonial interest such as the mining companies. Viewed as
having no commitment to Northern Rhodesia (as Zambia was then),
except to their jobs, they were often suspected of being informers to
the authorities on nationalist activities. Aspects of this feeling carried
through into the post-independence period. UNIP political officials as
well as government politicians frequently blamed some of the problems
which faced the country, such as industrial unrest, on Malawians.

[29] Epstein (1958: 236), for example, states that in Luanshya, Malawians (then
Nyasas) formed an obvious elite holding down of the best paid jobs and
tending, with the Lozi, to predominate in clerical work. My 1964 survey
material on the Kabwe municipal African townships shows a marked tendency
for Malawians to be heavily represented in skilled or clerical work. Also
survey material collected in the Kabwe mine township shows a marked
representation of Malawians in better paid work.

Some Malawians, for example, held high official posts in at least two major unions, the Zambia Mineworkers' Union and the Railway Workers' Union. Both these unions during 1965 were pressing for considerable improvements in wage and work conditions and were threatening strike action.

But the major point which I wish to emphasise is that the broader the base in terms of which appeal is made for support and approval of action, both in the sense that it allows for a wide degree of agreement and provides the opportunity for a considerable number of individuals to identify themselves with it, the more successful the individual who appeals for such support and approval is likely to be. It is the failure to take account of this factor which handicaps individuals in their achievement of status and power. To impress others with the qualities which one displays often means that the individual concerned must select attributes and characteristics specific to himself marking him out as superior to others. Unless the various characteristics which he presents for the approval of others are valued in that they are demonstrated as benefiting their interests, then it is highly probable that the individual who presents these characteristics will fail to win approval. Previous events described in which Lyashi played a part illustrate this point. For example, in the discussion centring on the definition of a civilised townsman Lyashi partly failed to win approval for his particular definition because he based it on specific characteristics which he himself possessed but which were not relevant to the experience of the other participants. The definition which finally gained approval was that a civilised townsman is one who does not boast of his status: a definition to which many of those gathered could lay claim.

The analysis now returns to the event in which John was accused of gluttony by Mukubwa and others. On this occasion, Lyashi framed his action in terms which allowed both for a wide area of agreement and permitted the identification of most of the workers present with the sentiments expressed. John defended himself against criticism by stating that it was company (meaning management) bread and that his heavy consumption of it puts Patel to some expense. This remark in itself was geared to meet with approval, for, as repeatedly stressed, the workers were bitter at the poor wages they received. John's remark gave Lyashi, who was standing ready, an opportunity to present himself as the protector of workers' interests. His objective was assisted by the approach of Hastings. Lyashi, casting his eyes in Hastings' direction, spoke in Bemba to John warning him of the danger of making such statements.

Two aspects of Lyashi's action must be noted. First, Lyashi by signalling the approach of Hastings was making clear reference to the belief widely accepted in the factory that Hastings' interests were identical with those of management. Second, by speaking in Bemba, rather than, for instance, CiCopperbelti, he excluded Hastings, a Nyanja speaker, from participation in the discussion but allowed for the inclusion of the others present. Mukubwa is a Lala, Chisokone a Bemba, John a Lala and Joseph a Bisa. All could understand Bemba. Kalamba, who is a Yao, could not but prior to Lyashi's utterance had gone back inside the factory. The basis, therefore, upon which Lyashi sought approval for his action was broad and allowed for the association with him of all those participating, except Hastings.

Hastings further alienated himself from the company concerned and strengthened the bonds of their association on the basis of their sharing a common language by his expression of annoyance and opposition to Lyashi's behaviour. This is illustrated by the reaction of Hastings to Lyashi's statement that he should learn Bemba if he wanted to understand what had been said, as Hastings had requested. Hastings stated that he had no interest in learning Bemba. Immediately, Lyashi followed up his advantage by referring to Hastings' non-Zambian status as a Malawian, including the implication that Bemba is the language of Zambians. Although Lyashi's reference to Bemba as the language of Zambians could have risked the disapproval and antagonism of other non-Bemba speaking Zambians, his reference to Hastings as a foreigner provided an acceptable medium for the inclusion of others in opposition to Hastings. This is important, as there were other workers seated or standing nearby who, though Zambians, were not Bemba-speaking. In any case, Chisokone extricated Lyashi from the possible antagonism of other workers by clearly defining the basis of the opposition to Hastings in terms of Zambians versus Malawians. At this point in the discussion, Chisokone played the part of a go-between translating 'the differences between speakers and listeners into a view . . . more acceptable collectively than the original projection' (Goffman, 1959: 150). With Hastings' departure from the scene and the development of a general discussion among the workers—and especially among those in the immediate company of Lyashi—with reference to the various qualities of Malawians, it was clear that Lyashi and also Chisokone had won considerable support and approval from the employees for their action. Lyashi, in particular, had succeeded for the first time during my observations in winning a large amount of approval. On this occasion he had successfully presented himself as a defender of employee interest and a militant opponent to those perceived to be in Patel's favour.

But why should Lyashi have been successful? Why did Chisokone apparently support him? True, the idiom in which Lyashi's appeal was cast allowed others greater opportunity to ally with him. He did not present qualities specific to himself only, in a bid to impress others thereby risking the alienation of support and approval. Previous events described have shown Lyashi in opposition to the supervisors, Mukubwa and Chisokone, and it has been emphasised that the competition of Lyashi for power and leadership in turn threatened the power of the supervisors. For Lyashi, in his presentation, was both attempting to undermine the image which the supervisors presented of themselves to the workers, and trying to influence individuals to transfer their approval and support away from the supervisors to himself.

However, I suggest that the best strategy for them on this occasion was support of Lyashi. The confrontation with Hastings, initiated on the basis of management–worker opposition, was expressed in the idiom first of the linguistic cleavage which exists in the factory and then the Zambian–Malawian opposition, also relevant to the factory context. To have sided with Hastings against Lyashi would have been to run the risk of damage to their image, as it could have been perceived by the other factory workers as evidence of their support of management against the interests of the workers. It has already been stressed that there was wide agreement among the employees that Hastings operated in management's interest against that of the employees. Furthermore, Chisokone, as discussed with reference to the previous event already had evidence of a hostility emerging among the workers towards him. To maintain what power and status among the employees he continued to possess, it was in his interest to follow the line of least resistance and thus assure himself of renewed support and approval. During the event Mukubwa showed only tacit support for the action of Lyashi and Chisokone. No event in which he had been involved to date had demonstrated any marked weakness of his position, unlike events concerning Chisokone, although his behaviour had been called into question. Mukubwa, in fact, had used his power effectively on a previous occasion to stop Lyashi from elaborating to his disadvantage on the nature of his connection with management. Moreover, Mukubwa, outside the factory context, was friendly with Hastings, both often visiting each other's homes and occasionally assisting one another with private orders for tailoring work. To have openly participated in expressing hostility towards Hastings would have threatened this friendship. Alternatively, to have supported Hastings could have endangered Mukubwa's position in the factory, for reasons previously described for Chisokone.

Finally, in comparing Lyashi's behaviour with Chisokone's on this occasion, cognisance must be taken of the fact that the roots of Mukubwa's power were stronger than were Chisokone's. The latter had no skill and therefore, unlike Mukubwa, was unable to distribute advice and assistance concerning tailoring work. This advice and assistance which Mukubwa could distribute and which was valued among the employees, though less in the case of the line 1 tailors, to a limited extent provided protection against assaults on his position by others. Chisokone, therefore, was more vulnerable to the effects of competition than Mukubwa.

Both the above event and the previous one discussed relating to the definition of a civilised townsman have shown how individuals in the factory, with special reference to Lyashi, have selected characteristics and qualities perceived as relevant to themselves and to others. They have done this in a bid to present themselves as having claim to superior status and thus the right to the approval and respect of the factory workers or to stress their superiority in the context. The success or failure of an individual's presentation of himself has largely rested, first, on the way the presentation has been made and, second, on his position within a set of relationships. For example, Lyashi, in defining a civilised townsman mainly in terms of his own personal characteristics not generally shared by others with whom he interacted on the occasion, made his definition too exclusive for others to identify themselves with it. Also, he made his definition largely in the company of fellow line 1 tailors who considered themselves equal if not superior to him. To have agreed with Lyashi's definition could have implied an acceptance of their inferiority of status to him. Finally, a major theme in the analysis has been that the behaviour of Lyashi and others had various consequences for the process of social relations in the factory, a fundamental change in the factory being the growing opposition of the employees to the supervisors. In the following event, this process reaches a climax with the general agreement of the line 1 tailors that the supervisors, and in particular Mukubwa, are opposed to their interests.

Event 16   The case of the badly stitched trousers
7 July 1965

Lenard, a tailor on line 1, was approached ¡by Mukubwa and told that the short trousers which he was working on were badly stitched. Lenard denied that the poor workmanship was his fault but rather that of the overlock machiner on line 2, Zulu. Mukubwa refused to accept Lenard's denial. It was then that Patel came to the support of Mukubwa and joined him in continuing to accuse Lenard of shoddy workmanship. Lenard was now clearly extremely upset and threatened to fight Mukubwa. The latter added insult to injury for, in refusing to accept the challenge, Mukubwa stated that Lenard was too weak to fight. 'Everyone here knows that you suffer from TB.' Lenard was now infuriated (possibly because he also feared being dismissed from his job if Patel believed Mukubwa's accusation that Lenard suffered from TB.). Patel shouted at Lenard to shut up or he would be fired but Lenard was far too angry to take any notice of Patel's warning. Patel now demanded that Lenard leave his work and accompany him to the cutting table to see Chisokone. Once at the cutting table, Patel told Chisokone to explain to Lenard that unless he calmed down and admitted his error he would be sacked. Chisokone complied with Patel's demand and quietly repeated Patel's threat. In doing so, he played the part of an interpreter; unlike Mukubwa, he made it clear in his action that this threat was Patel's and that Chisokone did not associate himself with it. Lenard took no notice of the threat, and Chisokone told Patel that the dispute was his problem. Patel was now told by Lenard that he must not support Mukubwa in this way. 'If you continue to treat us like animals you will find your work in this factory becoming very difficult. We are not animals to be treated without any respect. We are human beings. I have been a tailor with Narayan Bros. for over seven years and have never during this time sewn short trousers like that pair we are talking about now.'

Meanwhile some of the line 1 tailors, all of the tailors on this line having stopped work since the start of the dispute, left their stools and joined Lenard at the cutting table. The tailors who gathered in support of Lenard at the cutting table were Lyashi, Nkoloya, Lwanga and Abraham. In their support of Lenard, they stressed to both Patel and Mukubwa that, as line 1 tailors, they should not be treated like learners. Threat was now added to give weight to their demands that the line 1 tailors should be shown respect. Lyashi, in particular, received considerable approval for his vehement statement, 'If you [Patel] and Mukubwa do not stop treating us like learner tailors we will walk out. Now! Now!' Hostility focused specifically on Mukubwa. Many of the tailors gathered round Lenard, shouting '*Chichawa!*' at Mukubwa and stating that he was trying to be a *makobo*[30] to Patel. It was now apparent that Patel was growing concerned about the possibility of a walk-out and together with Mukubwa walked away. Lenard and those who had joined him at the cutting table returned to their line where they entered into short discussions with the other line 1 tailors. Lyashi mentioned to his fellow workers how Mukubwa had been responsible for many a tailor's sacking from Narayan Bros. Lyashi then went on to implicate Hastings, even though he was not present at the time having gone on a shopping errand for Patel, and stated that if Hastings had been present, he would have behaved in a similar way

[30] In this context the best English equivalent of the word *makobo* is the phrase 'sucking up' or 'brown nose'. It derives from the Bemba, meaning 'white fish' and was most regularly used by non-staff African mineworkers to African mine staff employees, the latter being accused of siding with white management or being the instruments of white management.

to Mukubwa. 'We all know that Hastings wishes to become the factory manager.' This comment of Lyashi's caused Nkoloya to reminisce. 'Any little mistake we make is reported to Patel. Even as far back as 1955 when Edward Mutundu was working as a tailor here and we used to attend the Union meetings presided over by Paul Kalichini, Hastings used to inform Patel of what was being said.' Tempers in the factory subsided and the tailors got on with their work.

Analysis. This event marks one point in the culmination of a process whereby the supervisors and, in particular Mukubwa, are faced with the full opposition of the line 1 tailors. To understand the significance of the behaviour displayed in this event, a restatement of some of the points made in the preceding analysis is necessary.

The position of the supervisors is extremely delicate. As supervisors, they must comply with management demands to control the work behaviour of the other employees. In addition, their closeness in status to the line 1 tailors makes it difficult for them to adopt behaviour which is not threatening to the status of the line 1 tailors. This is all the more difficult as others besides the supervisors are interested in gaining the acquiescence of the factory employees to their power and leadership. Competition from other workers may force them into behaving immodestly to reassert their claims to status and power in the factory. Incessant competition, such as that displayed by Lyashi, may require them repeatedly to adopt immodest behaviour in order to impress their attractiveness anew on the factory workers. Recurrent immodest behaviour uses up an individual's resources of approval for his status. Others must continually devalue their own status if they are to accord an individual approval and this becomes increasingly unattractive to them. This is particularly so for the line 1 tailors, who view their status as being only slightly less than that of the supervisors. Therefore the supervisors are exposed to various pressures which, dependent on their reaction to them, can damage the image they present of themselves to induce the compliance of the workers, and specifically of the line 1 tailors, to their commands and directives.

In the exercise of authority, the supervisors use their power. But power is expended in use, for by complying with the will of a supervisor, an individual is given the opportunity to discharge part of his debt. Transactions which were characterised by their imbalance now tend towards balance. To restore his position of power, an individual must continually supply needed services and benefits. This supervisors can do in their relationships with junior employees. But to maintain an imbalance in obligations with senior workers such as the line 1 tailors is a much different matter. It was explained that the compliance of these workers is largely obtained on credit. Every act of compliance which a supervisor demands in exercising his authority extends the credit margin and increases the pressure placed on him to fulfil expectations of himself. Thus, any evidence that the line 1 tailors may have which leads them to suspect that their expectations will not be fulfilled may result in their withholding compliance and the denial of the right of a supervisor to exercise authority over them. Of course, as I have already described, supervisors can use their power in other spheres of activity not immediately related to their exercise of authority in controlling the behaviour of the employees at work. Action such as Mukubwa's, where he used his power to prevent Lyashi from revealing certain aspects of his participation in the factory, is an example of this. The position in which the supervisors are placed, which means that they must continually use their power to exercise authority together with the fact that they must use it in other areas as well to discourage competition against them for power and leadership, necessitates that they must find ways to replenish the power they use. Failure to do this causes them to lose their power and results in the inability to control the actions of others in the factory.

I have discussed the gradual process whereby Mukubwa and Chisokone began to lose their position of power and leadership in the factory. This reduction in their power resulted from the mismanagement of their own behaviour partly caused by the pressures to which they were exposed forcing them to act in certain ways. Also, their failure to influence Patel to consider basic demands for wage improvements did not help their position. Chisokone because of his greater sensitivity to his own vulnerability to changes in opinion began to recoup some of his losses as evidenced in his support of Lyashi. Chisokone's greater sensitivity, I suggest, was engendered basically by the difficulty of his position as an individual with supervisory responsibilities but no skill. This deficiency in skill was partly offset by the general knowledge in the factory of his importance as a senior political branch official in Kabwe but, nevertheless, his lack of skill did produce tensions in his everyday interaction with the highly-skilled employees such as the line 1 tailors. It was Chisokone's sensitivity which undoubtedly assisted him in escaping the sort of hostility which Mukubwa found directed towards himself in reaction to his accusing Lenard of poor workmanship.

Mukubwa, by levelling such an accusation, struck at one of the major qualities, skill, on which the line 1 tailors base much of their claim to prestige and status. The enormity of Mukubwa's criticism was well reflected in Lenard's statement that in all his seven years of employment in the factory, his work had never been called into question. Lenard's blaming of Zulu was not so much a case of passing the buck as a deliberate attempt to have the accusation immediately referred to an appropriate authority. Zulu had not machined any section of the shorts on which Lenard had been working. However, Zulu was the union shop steward and also a key political official in the party branch where Mukubwa himself was a section official. Rather than drop the issue, which would have been the best action, given the outcome of the dispute, Mukubwa persevered in his accusation. With the arrival of Patel in support of Mukubwa, nothing could prevent the dispute from assuming major proportions. But Mukubwa did not merely question a line 1 tailors' skill; he then began to ridicule Lenard, not only in front of his work companions but before all the factory workers. It was not Mukubwa's refusal to fight Lenard so much as the way his refusal was phrased which was so injurious. Considerable store is placed by the workers on physical strength and individuals phrase much of their competition with each other in terms of it. Mukubwa, by implying that Lenard was a weakling, submitted him to ridicule. Moreover, in giving as his reason for making this statement that Lenard had tuberculosis (*ntanda bwanga*), he had implicitly included all the tailors. One of the frequently expressed beliefs of the tailors, usually stated with reference to complaints about working conditions, is that the oil fumes given off by the sewing machines once they have become hot causes TB, in addition to other chest conditions. Tension was further exacerbated by Patel's threatening Lenard with the sack.

Patel's support of Mukubwa's action clearly associated the latter with the management. Finally, Patel's threat of giving Lenard the sack with Mukubwa's apparent approval symbolised to the line 1 tailors the emptiness of Mukubwa's presentation of himself as a protector of the employees' interests.

With Lenard now becoming more angry, Patel tried to involve Chisokone, who had hitherto remained in the background. Chisokone did not involve himself wholeheartedly and passively interpreted Patel's threat of dismissal to Lenard. His non-committal behaviour made it clear that he did not wish to associate himself with Patel's or Mukubwa's action. His behaviour was noted with approval by some of the line 1 tailors. While Lenard was at the cutting table, where Patel had taken him to see Chisokone, he was shortly joined by four of the line 1 tailors. All these workers (i.e. Lyashi, Nkoloya, Lwanga and Abraham) were friends of Lenard. Lyashi and Abraham helped Lenard with small sums of money and this was reciprocated. All regularly indulged in conversation with him both in the work place and outside during tea break. With the exception of Joseph, a cotton boy, all Lenard's friends were senior workers in the factory who were interconnected by a dense set of exchange relationships. Lenard's membership of a dense set of ties mainly involving the line 1 tailors, contributed towards the extent of the mobilisation of support to him in addition to such considerations as Mukubwa's offence against one of the basic principles, skill, upon which the line 1 tailors laid their claims to the receipt of respect.

But, perhaps even more significant than the support given to Lenard and the general anger at the lack of respect shown towards them, was the refusal first of Lenard and then the remainder of the line 1 tailors to comply with Mukubwa's authority. The unity in opposition to Mukubwa generated by their perception that Mukubwa was behaving in a way contrary to their interests and in co-operation with management was expressed in their open accusation of Mukubwa being a *chichawa* and *makobo* to Patel. After work, most of the line 1 tailors and Zulu, the overlock machiner, met at Bwacha beer hall to discuss Mukubwa's action. Here it was generally agreed that Mukubwa had no right to exercise authority over them in his position as supervisor. Lyashi received general approval for his statement that 'Mukubwa thinks he is our *capitao* but in reality he is nothing of the kind'.

This event, however, reveals much more than the importance which the line 1 tailors placed on their status and the dangers to a supervisor's position of power and ability to exercise authority should he abuse their status. For the first time during my observations, the line 1 tailors, as a result of their mobilisation in support of Lenard and in defence of their interests, realised the power they could command if they united in opposition to management. At the beer hall after work, much emphasis was placed on their success in making Patel drop his threats of sacking Lenard by their threat of a walk-out.

But while the line 1 tailors gloried in the realisation of the power they possessed through their unity, individuals among them were trying to exploit this power in their own interests. Foremost among them was Lyashi who did not hesitate to point out to his companions that it had been he who had been continually stressing the opposition of Mukubwa and Hastings to the interests of the factory workers. At last he considered that his opinions which had not found support and were, in fact, quashed by Mukubwa's action, for instance, during the 'Dream village dispute', had been vindicated. Even during the dispute, Lyashi had played a prominent part. Not only did he present himself to Patel and to the factory workers as a leader of employee opinion along with Abraham, Lwanga and Nkoloya, but also it was Lyashi who made the threat of a walk-out which received the support of his work companions. Furthermore, it was Lyashi who emphasised the threat of Mukubwa to the employees' interests by presenting Mukubwa as an individual who had influenced Patel to sack previous factory workers. Mukubwa who had presented himself as an individual who could protect workers against the fear of dismissal was now cast in the part of an individual who was responsible for sacking workers. It was Lyashi also who included Hastings with Mukubwa as an individual worthy of the line 1 tailors' antagonism. Now with the full support of the other workers, Lyashi had emerged as the major spokesman for their interests.

In the leading part they took Lwanga, Abraham and Nkoloya like Lyashi, I suggest, were not just motivated in their action by their friendship with Lenard and the implicit assault made on their status by Mukubwa. Nkoloya, in particular, was beginning to emerge as a competitor against Lyashi for power and leadership in the factory. Nkoloya, in his support of Lyashi's attack on Hastings, alluded to the latter's activities ten years previously, before Lyashi had commenced work in the factory. Through his mention of Paul Kalichini who had a high reputation for considerable militancy in the spheres of political and industrial action, Nkoloya identified himself as a militant protagonist of employees' interests. The start of competition between Lyashi and Nkoloya became more open later at the beer hall where they vied with each other in attempting to impress on the other workers present the extent of their militancy. Nkoloya claimed, for example, that he would have walked out before Lyashi should Patel not have backed down before the workers' threats.

In this first phase I have examined the early stages of Lyashi's entry into the competition for leadership and power. He combines two strategies. First, he aims his attack at the supervisors, two of whom, Mukubwa and Chisokone, are the most powerful individuals in the factory. Second, Lyashi attempts to present himself to the other employees as an individual worthy of their esteem and approval. In his attack on the supervisors Lyashi attempted to undermine the image which they projected of themselves as individuals protective of the workers' interests. Lyashi, therefore, selected various relational properties of the supervisors which carried with them the implication that the supervisors were in fact opposed to the employees' interests. Thus in 'The dream village dispute' Lyashi made the suggestion that Mukubwa held values in common with the Indian management. Again, in the event 'Malawians and Zambians' Lyashi selected Hastings' status as a foreigner to Zambia as the basis upon which opposition could be framed towards the latter. In these events Lyashi presented himself as a man concerned with the employees' interests and militantly opposed to the supervisors, but in other events, such as 'A question of town experience', Lyashi presented qualities specific to himself for approval.

By pursuing these strategies Lyashi stood to benefit in a number of ways. If he succeeded in destroying the image which the supervisors presented of themselves he increased his chances of securing a position of power and leadership as he would endanger the supervisors' resources of support and approval. Provided Lyashi was able to present himself as a suitable alternative to whom the support and approval of the workers could be transferred, he could develop a position of power and leadership in the factory.

At first Lyashi's attempts to increase his power appeared relatively unsuccessful. But, nevertheless, his competition forced Mukubwa and Chisokone in particular to use their power in order to stave off the threat which Lyashi presented. However, it was not only the threat to their dominating command over resources of support and approval which caused the supervisors to use up their power. Other factors also contributed towards the diminution of the supervisors' resources of support and approval such as their mismanagement of their behaviour, which was partly engendered, paradoxically enough, by the demands placed upon them to strive for the acceptance of their superiority in the factory. This behaviour resulted in increased costs being incurred by those who accorded the supervisors support and approval. The senior workers on line I were the employees particularly affected, for by continually having to affirm their approval of the supervisors' superior status they necessarily devalued their own. As a result of the increased costs which they incurred the line I tailors began withdrawing their recognition of the supervisors' superior status. This process reached a peak at the time of 'The case of the badly stitched trousers'.

The principle whereby the demand on the line I tailors to accord superior status to another individual involves a cost in terms of the devaluation of their own status, was also used an an explanation for some of the line I tailors' opposition to Lyashi in the event 'A Question of Town Experience'.

The behaviour of the supervisors, notably Mukubwa and Chisokone, and the entry of Lyashi into the competition for power and leadership had some important consequences leading to significant changes in the structure of the factory relationships. Mukubwa's and to a lesser extent

S

Chisokone's threat to the status of the line 1 tailors combines with their failure to be instrumental in the distribution of rewards favourable to the line 1 tailors' interests, resulted in the development of a clear opposition to the supervisors. Lyashi's entry into the competition first had the result of his fellow line 1 tailors uniting in opposition to him, and second some of them, largely because Lyashi began to achieve success in his efforts, also entered the competition partly in response to the pressures placed on them at least to preserve their status in the face of Lyashi's competition.

The various processes outlined above involved a redistribution of power and status in the factory. As will be described in the following chapter the competition which revolved about the re-allocation of power and status was connected with the growth of increased militancy on the part of some of the senior workers towards management. This found its most frequent expression in the form of more active demands for wage and work improvements.

Strategy in dispute, structural change and
     the quest for power and leadership II

Phase II: the walk-out

In the analysis of the second phase of events, I continue with an examination of the consequences of the processes discussed in Phase I for the
development of social relations in the factory. Three themes already
evident in the preceding analysis will be extended, these are (a) the
growth of Lyashi's power in the factory, (b) concurrent with this, the
more definite emergence of rivals and competitors to Lyashi, and (c) the
continued decline in power of the supervisors, notably Mukubwa and
Chisokone. Three events will be examined in detail but other aspects
connected with them, not discussed in Phase I, become relevant to
analysis. In the preceding description, I confined myself largely to
explaining the process of events mainly with reference to the factory
context. But to understand the process of which some of the following
events are a part, and in particular 'The five-day working week dispute',
events outside the factory context become an important consideration
for an understanding of the developing social relations inside the factory.

Event 25   Chisokone revealed

At tea break Chisokone addressed all the workers on the weakness of
the union and the failure of the union organising secretary either to visit
them at their work place or to take an interest in their complaints.
Nkoloya supported Chisokone's statements and added that because of
the failure of the union to take an interest in their difficulties, it was right
that they should withhold payment of union dues. Lyashi moved to a
position beside Nkoloya and upheld the latter's opinion. However,
Lyashi was given little time to expand on Nkoloya's statement, as Chisokone now directed the attention of the workers to their more specific
complaints and called attention to the reluctance of Patel to advance wage
increments to his employees. 'Look at Hastings. He has been working
here for over thirty years and is still working for 1s 9d per hour!' At this
example, Lyashi muttered that perhaps if Hastings had fought for a wage
increase, he would have got one. Chisokone then broadened the base of
reference to a general attack on the practices of Indian employers.
'Indians don't think of anyone but themselves. They are much worse
than European employers. European employers at least give regular wage

increases and give more money to long service employees.' Nkoloya disagreed with the favourable picture painted by Chisokone of European employers and jokingly reminded Chisokone that it was members from both communities, Indians and Europeans, who supported the Federal government and stood in the way of Zambian independence. All present showed approval of Nkoloya's statement, and Lyashi asked Chisokone whether he had forgotten the struggle for independence. 'Don't you realise that both Indians and Europeans give wages according to the colour of our skins ? Both are Federal in outlook.' In response to this, Chisokone laughed and stated that he would continue pressing the government to take notice of the poor conditions under which they worked. 'All employers must realise that we are living under a Zambian government and not under Smith.' Patel now called to his workers to recommence work and the discussions ended.

After work at the railway beer hall. When work ended, Chisokone and a number of tailors went to the railway beer hall. The tailors were Ibrahim, a line 2 tailor, Kamwefu, Chipata, Lyashi, Nkoloya, Abraham and Lwanga, all line 1 tailors, and Meshak, a button machiner.

At the beer hall Lyashi asked Chisokone bluntly when he was going to ask Patel to increase their wages. Chisokone maintained that it was very difficult to convince Patel that he should increase their wages without the active support of the factory workers. Lyashi, with the support of the others present, refused to accept Chisokone's evasive attitude. 'You cannot expect our support unless we see you take our case to Patel. We all know that you represent our government in the factory. If our government is strong, it should be easy to convince Patel to raise our wages.' Chipata, together with Ibrahim, emphasised that it was not only a general increase in wages which they wanted but also other securities such as leave pay, long service benefits and compensation for illness caused by work in the factory. With reference to this last demand, Kamwefu raised the issue of a worker who had been forced to leave Narayan Bros. to enter hospital because he had contracted tuberculosis. He mentioned a worker who had been employed in the factory some three years earlier stating that on this man's departure from the factory, Patel had given him £5 only. 'This man had to send his wife and children home because he could no longer pay his house rent.' Lyashi now suggested that Chisokone's failure to press their demands on Patel was evidence that Chisokone was afraid of losing his job and, in consequence, preferred to support management against the interests of his work companions. Chisokone was now annoyed and declared that he was leaving the factory shortly anyhow as Zulu and he were getting a government grant to set up a farming co-operative. This was the first time that Chisokone had revealed his future plans to his work mates and all present were astonished. Chisokone followed this statement up by saying, 'When I leave employment, I am going to fight for what I want without any Indians to stop me. However, I will try and influence the government to improve your work conditions.' He then left the drinking group stating that he had important business to attend to at the Bwacha UNIP branch offices.

With Chisokone's departure, a heated discussion broke out among the workers remaining about the effect Chisokone's leaving the factory would have on their attempts to secure wage and work improvements. Lyashi, in particular, mentioned that whenever the question of wage increments arose, Patel always consulted the three supervisors. 'They always tell Patel which person is to have an increment. But we never get what we want as Chisokone, Mukubwa and Hastings are *makobo* to Patel.' All the workers present agreed with Lyashi. Nkoloya gave weight to Lyashi's views by citing an occasion when Paul Kalichini was head of the union in Kabwe and a strike had been called at Narayan Bros. Nkoloya stated that he had been sacked because Mukubwa and Chisokone had informed Patel that he was the ringleader. 'After a few days Patel changed his mind and Chisokone and Mukubwa came to my house to call me back to work. To this day, Mukubwa and Chisokone hate me.' Meshak and Lwanga both vouched for the truth of Nkoloya's statements. Shortly after this, the workers went their various ways.

The focus of the conversations in this event which began in the factory and continued after work at the railway beer hall illustrates a number of aspects relating to the work context discussed in earlier chapters. Chisokone's comments in the weakness of the union and the widespread acceptance of his statement by those present exemplified the general dissatisfaction felt among the workers about the union's failure to satisfy their demands. Nkoloya's statement of support for Chisokone, where he added that the inactivity by the union warranted their with-holding of union dues, refers to the sanction which all the employees were then operating against the union.[1] Other features of the context at the time are also illustrated by various items of the conversation. Specific examples are the general concern of the workers for the secure-ment of wage improvements and long service and end of employment benefits. These latter concerns were more in the interest of the senior employees than the junior workers.

But there are three aspects illustrated by the event which deserve fuller comment. First, there is the pressure placed on Chisokone to discuss some of the doubts which the workers had of the extent of his support for their various objectives. I include in the discussion of this aspect a general analysis of the continued decline of the power of the supervisors in the factory. Second, I shall be concerned with an examin-ation of the continued rise to power of Lyashi in addition to the clear evidence of the emergence for the first time of new rivals in competition with Lyashi. Third, closely related to these two aspects is the interest of viewing the above event in relation to the development of an

[1] See chapter 4, p. 139.

alternative strategy to that already being pursued in the workers' competition with management for wage and work improvements.

This event demonstrates that mere presentation without substance is not enough. By drawing attention to the weakness of the union, Chisokone was playing on a general feeling expressed by the employees. In view of his previous activities—though not as damaging to his image as the behaviour of Mukubwa—Chisokone had to do more than this to reinforce the image he presented. His choice of the case of Hastings as an example of the inequities of the system in which the employees participated, given the current strength of the hostility shown by the workers to Hastings, could not have been expected to win overwhelming support from them. Lyashi certainly lost no time in taking advantage of Chisokone's tactical error by muttering his disapproval. Moreover, the use of Hastings as an example referred to the specific interests of a small section of the more senior employees who were interested in securing additional increments for their length of service in the factory. I suggest that it was because of his own awareness of the restricted appeal of his statement that Chisokone shifted the emphasis of his argument on to the broader basis of the workers' common opposition to the Indian management. But Chisokone's favourable comparison of European employers with Indian employers was not accepted, in particular by Lyashi and Nkoloya. Both the latter took Chisokone's statement as an opportunity to remind him of the joint opposition of Europeans and Indians to African interests. In reminding the workers of the weakness of the union and then excluding Europeans from his attack on employers, Chisokone had not presented one crucial aspect of his identity upon which his claims to power and influence rested. This was his position as a senior political official in the locally powerful and influential Bwacha UNIP branch.

A basic argument emphasised in the preceding analysis is that the supervisors—and, in this instance, Chisokone—had largely obtained their power on credit. Chisokone was now implicitly asked to show evidence that he would discharge some of his debt to the factory workers by using his political influence to the benefit of the factory employees. Throughout the period of observation up to this time, Chisokone had given no indication to the workers that he would use his political influence on their behalf, and the workers were growing increasingly impatient at their failure to achieve any wage and work improvements. What had been implicit at the tea break became explicit during the conversations at the beer hall after work when Lyashi queried Chisokone whether he was going to ask Patel for a wage increase.

Chisokone did not reply to Lyashi but remained silent while the others voiced their grievances. However, he was finally goaded into replying when Lyashi suggested that Chisokone's failure to press their demands on Patel showed that he sided with management. A suggestion had thus been made which cast Chisokone in a part contrary to the image of himself which he wished to present. In his angry retort, Chisokone revealed his intention to leave the factory employment. Thus, by giving evidence that he had no interest in supporting management, Chisokone also showed his work mates the futility of their continued support of him as a means of achieving their objectives. By the time he left the beer hall, Chisokone's promise to continue working in the interests of the workers seemed empty, given the fact that he would shortly be leaving.

The hostility now expressed towards Chisokone is well illustrated by the comments of the workers who remained in the drinking group that he was a *makobo* and allied with the other supervisors in opposition to the rest of the employees. Largely in response to the pressure exerted on him by Lyashi in the company of other workers, Chisokone had been led into a tactical error. It could be argued that Chisokone's statement was of little concern to him as he was leaving employment and, therefore, that it was not an error of judgment on his part. But this is not consistent with his behaviour during this and previous events which clearly show that he had been attempting to present an image of himself to others in a bid to win their approval.

Furthermore, unbeknown to his work mates, he had been negotiating since June for a government grant to establish a farming co-operative. The ability of Chisokone to present a favourable image to his work mates and to win their support and compliance has a significance beyond his need to exercise effective authority as a supervisor. Chisokone, a senior branch official in Bwacha whose influence extends beyond the limits of this township,[2] is subject to the competition of other branch officials and members for his position. As a local party branch official, Chisokone is in an intercalary position. He is at the focus of contradictory expectations flowing from his party branch members on the one hand, and from higher ranking political party officials in the regional office and the government on the other.[3]

[2] In the municipality the Bwacha UNIP branch is regarded by residents of all the townships (i.e. Bwacha, Chimaninine and Ngungu) and by more senior political party and government officials as the most important party branch. Action taken by the officials of this branch frequently influences the policies and decisions followed by members and officials of other township branches.
[3] The UNIP branch official as an occupant of an intercalary position is one result of the achievement of independence whereby the party of which he is a

At the time of fieldwork Chisokone's position as a branch official was particularly vulnerable. In Bwacha there was considerable feeling that some of the older branch officials, of whom Chisokone was one, were doing little to advance the interests of the Bwacha residents. The attack against the older officials was currently being spearheaded by members of the branch youth wing who held that more educated officials—an attribute which they themselves possessed—would act more in the interests of the residents. Information that a branch official is acting against the interests of his members can be used against the official to remove him from office. Moreover, information to this effect which comes from influential party members is especially dangerous. Tailors and other residents who engage in extensive small trading and business enterprises, such as carpenters, fish salesmen and clothes hawkers, etc., are extremely influential in township political life.[4] Two related reasons for this are both their comparative stability of residence (this is particularly so for individuals engaged in such occupations as tailoring and carpentry) and the extensive network of ties developed in response to the demands of their occupations. Concern on Chisokone's part, therefore, that information damaging to his presentation of himself in his relationships outside his work context might be leaked by factory workers, gave additional point to his projection of a favourable image at work apart from the needs arising out of his duties as a supervisor. The danger to his political image in the township being damaged by adverse reports from the factory workers, receives added weight when it is realised that three section officials of the Bwacha branch are working in the factory. These are Abraham, a section chairman in Bwacha and a line 1 tailor, who was present at the railway beer hall, and Chipalo and Isaac, section trustee and publicity secretary, respectively, in Bwacha. Chipalo, at the time of this event, had only just arrived in the factory and was a tailor on line 2, whilst Isaac was an ironer. Each was an official in different sections in Bwacha.

Further indication of the importance to Chisokone of the projection of a favourable image to his work mates despite the imminence of his

member is also the party in government office. As explained in chapter 4, government interests often run counter to the interests of the governed, and the branch official is faced with the problem of conveying sometimes unpopular government directives to branch members while in turn being entrusted with the responsibility to his members of conveying their demands to government.

[4] From my general observations, officials in the constituency, branches and sections of Kabwe who were occupied in trades such as carpentry and tailoring seemed to be markedly over-represented in proportion to the officials engaged in other occupations.

departure from employment was his subsequent attempt a few weeks later to exert pressure on Patel to improve wages and work conditions.

In the light of the above analysis, it is evident that Chisokone had made a tactical error in his statement. Undoubtedly his attitude was generated largely by the heat of the moment and the pressure to which he was subjected by his fellows. But this does not explain the extremely evasive attitude which he took to numerous proddings throughout the event. A reasonable explanation of his evasion and of his refusal to commit himself to present the workers' claims to Patel might have been his awareness of the difficulties of the overall position in which he was placed. As a senior branch official, he was conscious of government policy towards militant industrial action by African employees. Government had made it clear that wage and work improvements would come in due course, but at the same time had emphasised that the workers must not take matters into their own hands. Chisokone did not wish to face retribution at the hands of more senior government politicians. His position was further complicated by his application for a government loan. Arrangements for the loan had not been finalised, and he was worried lest it should be withheld. Chisokone's dilemma and much of his evasiveness arose out of his placement in a typical 'mixed motive' position. It was in his interest to present a favourable image of himself to his work companions, but it was also in his interest to refrain from committing himself categorically to a specific line of action which might well damage his chances of receiving the government loan. Nevertheless, the nett effect of Chisokone's behaviour was to lead the factory workers to perceive him as aligned with Hastings and Mukubwa on the side of management in opposition to them. Subsequent events in which the supervisors were involved gave them little opportunity to recoup their position.

In one important respect, at least, the supervisors are, in the competition for power and leadership, in a more advantageous position than the other workers. This is because of their freedom to move around the factory floor during working hours which gives them both the time and opportunity to enter into transactions with other employees. Even contact with another employee initiated on the basis of directing him in his work can be turned by the supervisor to good effect. Thus, for example, a supervisor can deepen his personal relationship with a worker by adopting a friendly stance, However, the degree to which regular supervisory contacts can be turned to a supervisor's advantage is dependent on the way he is perceived. Two factors are important here and both relate to the rewards which the individual who is supervised perceives he will incur from such contact. First, if the supervisor is generally seen as powerful and influential, then regular contact with him will be viewed as rewarding by the person who is supervised. Two corollaries to this statement are essential for it to hold. In the first place, the contact with the supervisor must be friendly, that is, the content of the contact must not be purely directive or impersonal. In the second place, association with the supervisor must be generally valued by the workers. Provided these conditions are present, the reward which an individual gains from association with a supervisor increases the former's prestige and status among his peers. The basic assumption which is relevant here is that individuals increase their status by associating with powerful and influential persons. Obviously, however, the higher the accepted status of a worker, and the closer he is perceived in status by others to a powerful and influential person such as a supervisor, the less will be the benefit gained from association with the supervisor than if he were of low status and socially distant from the supervisor. But in fact the mode of behaviour which the supervisors in Narayan Bros. generally adopted towards junior workers in the factory was not friendly. On the contrary, it was usually characterised by a directive and impersonal manner. Although an individual of low status can increase his prestige and status by association with a person of high status, the opposite can be true of the latter. By associating regularly with persons markedly lower in status than himself, an individual risks the reduction of his status and approval in the eyes of his peers. I suggest that this was a major reason why, as protection against this negative effect, the supervisors generally adopted impersonal modes of behaviour towards the junior factory employees. The contacts of supervisors which most regularly evidenced modes of familiarity and friendship were more often directed towards individuals closer in status to themselves such as line 1 tailors.[5]

Second, once it is perceived that association with a supervisor may result in the attainment of rewards such as increased skill or protection from management threats, then regular contact with a supervisor may be desired. The greater the contact, the greater the opportunity to demonstrate willing compliance, and therefore the higher the probability of attaining such rewards. Willing compliance to supervisors was regularly engaged in by junior employees as it was the only resource they could exchange for such benefits as learning a skill or protection from management. Senior and more skilled workers had an interest in restricting the extent to which they regularly complied with the demands of a super-

[5] The ideas presented here are formally discussed by Blau (1964: 132–40).

visor for, as previously explained, such behaviour threatened a reduction of their status in the eyes of their fellows.

The central point of this part of the analysis is that so long as the supervisor has successfully projected an image which shows that he is concerned with employees' interests and can furnish them with various kinds of rewards, then his freedom of movement and his ability to establish contacts will have the result of increasing his power and influence. But as soon as the supervisor evinces behaviour which suggests that interaction will not be rewarding, the expansion of his power and influence approaches a threshold. Each contact with a supervisor must be reinforced with evidence of the supply of a reward. Promise of reward which is sufficient to sustain the relationship at the early stage of interaction must actually become rewarding at later stages of interaction for relationships supportive of the supervisor's power and influence to be sustained. Both the failure of a supervisor to produce rewards—such as assistance in learning a skill or protection from management—and behaviour which sees him as acting in a manner contrary to employee interest, will damage the image which a supervisor presents as an individual with whom association is rewarding. Once a point is reached where the supervisor is seen as a person with whom association is not rewarding, each occasion upon which he attempts to exercise his authority results in his using up resources of power without these resources being replenished. By complying with a supervisor's demands, individuals discharge whatever obligations they may have had towards him and begin to experience only cost in their contact with him. A supervisor who comes to be viewed as opposed to employee interest has approval withheld from him, and anyone who regularly comes into contact with him particularly on friendly or familiar lines will also consequently suffer cost in the sense of the loss of approval from his fellows. In addition, those who have previously valued the opportunity to demonstrate their compliance with a supervisor's demands in the expectation of receiving certain rewards from him, will only incur costs without the possibility of future gain when it becomes clear that no rewards are forthcoming.

In order to cut their costs, individuals will restrict their contact with a supervisor and will frequently oppose any attempts by the supervisor to exercise authority over them. Such action can not only cut their costs but may also be positively rewarding in that opposition to the supervisor, who in turn has become generally viewed as opposed to employee interests, receives approval from the other workers. At the point when workers begin to view the supervisor in an unfavourable light, contacts which had hitherto been rewarding to the inferior in terms of extending his power and influence, have an opposite effect and his power becomes steadily reduced.

Later events in which the Narayan Bros. supervisors were engaged, demonstrate the clear opposition which had developed towards them and the refusal of the workers to agree to their exercise of authority over them. In event 23 (see appendix 2) Mubanga, a cotton boy, was involved in a short dispute with Patel. Patel had been asking Mubanga to move around the work floor continually doing a variety of small chores for him. Every movement of Mubanga's was followed by Patel's cursing and urging him to hurry up. After a while, Mubanga refused to do any more of Patel's bidding. Patel then sent Mukubwa to reprimand Mubanga, with the effect that Mubanga walked away from Mukubwa calling him a *makobo*. Other cotton boys supported Mubanga and Mukubwa failed to influence Mubanga's return to the various chores which Patel had demanded of him. Patel then reported the matter to Chisokone, but the latter likewise had no success. The result of the supervisors' failure to exercise their authority on this occasion and the obvious support given to Mubanga by his peers was that Patel dropped making additional demands on Mubanga. Patel permitted him to return to his more regular duties of filling cotton bobbins and picking loose cotton ends off finished clothing.

On another occasion (see event 24, appendix 2) Mukubwa and Chisokone again ran into opposition, this time from Adrian, a button machiner. Adrian had been working in the factory for over ten years and during Phase 1 of the observation period was on familiar and friendly terms with Mukubwa. This he valued as, in general, he was held in low respect even by workers junior to him, who regarded Adrian as a *fontini*. He was often raggedly dressed, and it was held that he was unaccustomed with the ways of town. Thus on one occasion when he returned four days late after two weeks' leave, most of the workers stated that it could only have been expected, as Adrian did not know that there are fourteen days in a fortnight. However, his association with Mukubwa did guarantee him some respect, and the two often conversed during working hours. Although he had done so on many occasions previously, Mukubwa's jocular comment to Adrian that he looked dirty evoked an unexpectedly hostile response. In fact Adrian created such a disturbance that Patel asked Chisokone to enquire what was the matter. Chisokone tried to cool Adrian down by mentioning that Adrian had a joking relationship with Mukubwa as the latter was a Bemba and Adrian was Ngoni.[6] Adrian

---

[6] Actually, however, the specific ethnic identity of Mukubwa is Lala, whilst Adrian is Nsenga.

denied that such a joking relationship existed between them, and Meshak, Adrian's working companion, supported him in this claim.

These two events not only illustrate the sharp opposition which had developed towards the supervisors, but also indicate a new change in the structure of factory relationships. Hitherto, the analysis has primarily focused on the relationships between the supervisors and the senior and more skilled workers in the factory. An important basis of power for the supervisors was their extensive set of relationships into the unskilled and less skilled employees, but as these two events exemplify, the super-ordinate position which the supervisors had up till now enjoyed in their relationships with these workers was now altering. In terms of the fore-going analysis, two explanations are evident. First, partly through the mismanagement of their own behaviour and the effective competition of others in the factory, the supervisors were now seen as individuals who were opposed to the employees' interests. Friendly or familiar associa-tion with a supervisor, because of the general antagonism now emerging towards them, was no longer rewarding. Events in the factory had shown the supervisors as not being a source of rewards such as promotion and the opportunity of learning a skill which the junior employees valued. For example, in July and early August a number of tailors left the factory. For five days three cotton boys, Henry, Joseph and Kalonga had been employed on sewing machines and were given instruction in tailoring work by Mukubwa. But with Patel's hiring of new tailors, Henry, Joseph and Kalonga returned to their previous duties. The three cotton boys concerned were angry at having at first received such rewards only to have them withdrawn. All were relatives of Chisokone, and they made their disappointment known to him. As a reprisal, one sanction which they operated against Mukubwa and Chisokone, whom they held respon-sible for their disappointment and whom they considered did not use their influence with Patel sufficiently, was their withholding of compli-ance with the supervisors' demands. These three were with William, the most influential among the cotton boys. It was Patel's knowledge of Chisokone's kinship with them which, perhaps, partly prompted his seeking Chisokone's aid in dealing with Mubanga's intransigence. The refusal of any of the cotton boys to exert pressure on Mubanga to com-ply with Chisokone and Mukubwa's demands is not only an example of their withholding compliance but is an illustration also of the loss in power of the supervisors over the junior workers. But the momentary promotion of the three cotton boys coupled with the latter hiring of new tailors also offended other sections of the factory work force.

Thus some of the line 3 tailors expressed annoyance that their promotion to a higher line—for it was on line 2 that the cotton boys concerned had been placed—meant that they (the line 3 tailors) had been passed over in favour of workers generally regarded as junior in status to them. Although anger was expressed towards Patel for this, a considerable amount of it was deflected to the supervisors for failing to press on the factory manager the primacy of their claims. One feeling that was vented by the line 3 tailors was that Mukubwa and Chisokone were favouring fellow tribesmen.

The event in which Chisokone was openly asked if he intended to use his influence in the factory employees' interests marks a point when all the supervisors are finally seen as aligned with management against the rest of the Narayan Bros. workers. Occasions upon which Patel called on his supervisors to exercise their authority meant that they expended their power without replenishing it. In particular, this led to the intensification of opposition to them. Most importantly, considerable reduction in the power of the supervisors was evidenced in their relationships with the junior factory workers.

With the rapid decline in power of the supervisors, others were experiencing a corresponding rise to power. Lyashi was the most noticeable of these. He had been the most vocal in presenting all three supervisors as being aligned with management against the interests of the workers. Lyashi, as in the specific event under discussion, was also becoming the most open and regular spokesman of employee interest. For example, in event 18 (appendix 2), by making a general appeal for a loan of money, pleading that he had no food at his home, Lyashi drew general attention to the poor wages which the majority of workers considered they were receiving. Again, in event 15, Lyashi was the most vocal spokesman against the inequities of the wage and work conditions which Patel had imposed on the employees. Not only was Lyashi being shown considerable general approval for his views but also individuals were demonstrating the increased esteem in which they held him by consulting Lyashi in their personal difficulties. Thus, for instance, Lenard took his problem of the difficulty of obtaining suitable paid leave to Lyashi.

The virtual eclipse of the supervisors' power had some important consequences for the continuing process of social relations in the factory. In Phase I, I described how increasing unity among the line 1 tailors had been forged both in response to the assaults on their status by the supervisors and from individuals within their ranks, especially Lyashi. However, Lyashi, unlike the supervisors, altered his early strategy by not presenting himself as a status threat. Lyashi changed his strategy from emphasising the value of his individual qualities above those of his fellows to that of presenting himself as a defender of his companions' interests. But with the successful opposition to the supervisors and the deterioration in the general acceptance of their position of power and leadership, Lyashi again emerges as a status threat. Through his continual presentation of himself as a spokesman of employee interest, he was the most obvious alternative to whom the workers could transfer their allegiance. In particular, he was a status threat to the senior employees on line 1, for acceptance of his power and leadership would, in effect, result in a greater loss of status to them than in their previous subordination to the supervisors.

Obviously, the most effective strategy which the line 1 tailors and other senior employees could adopt to prevent Lyashi's succession to a position of power and leadership would be to unite in opposition to him. But a number of factors intervened to prevent the pursuit of this strategy. First, as previously described, a few workers, some of them influential such as Nkumbula and Lenard, had already demonstrated their preparedness to shift their allegiance to Lyashi. Second, the senior workers were in a 'mixed motive' situation. Although one of their interests was to preserve their status, another interest was to increase it. One way this latter interest could be achieved was by themselves entering the competition for power and leadership. Such an opportunity was now presented with the removal of the supervisors from an accepted position of power. Furthermore, by the achievement of power, other interests could be furthered. Thus, it was explained earlier that the securement of a position of power and influence combined with the ability to make Patel aware of it would lead to the attainment of other rewards—apart from power and increased status—such as promotion and wage increments. Another event in the period July and August in addition to the decline in power of the supervisors also gave opportunity for the achievement of power and this was the employment of a number of new workers for whose support the senior employees could compete.

But of greatest significance to the present argument is that with the reduction of the supervisors' power, the path was now cleared for the pursuit by senior individuals of power and leadership. A new pattern, therefore, clearly emerges which is the growth of intense competition between the senior factory employees. In both 'The case of the badly stitched trousers' and 'Chisokone revealed' some evidence of the competition of others is given. Thus, Nkoloya, within the accepted frame that the supervisors were acting contrary to employees' interests, vied with Lyashi in attempting to present himself as the more militant individual, and hence the more attractive employee to whom support should be given. He attempted to impart the impression that he was the more likely to achieve general rewards for the factory workers from management.

Individuals do not normally know the extent of their power and influence until they put it to the test. One method by which an individual can test his power is by attempting to control the behaviour of others. Moreover, by the successful control of the behaviour of others, an individual demonstrates his power. Two important effects of this for the context I describe are relevant. First, through the effective demonstration of power, an individual comes to the notice of Patel which, in turn, can lead to Patel's bestowing additional benefits on him. Second, an individual's superiority in the effective use of power may lead to the attraction of other individuals to him and therefore increase the range of his power and influence.

A number of events observed at the work place see Lyashi trying to control the behaviour of others. Also in these events other individuals, usually fellow line 1 tailors, are seen vying with him in attempting to control social action. Thus in event 28 (see appendix 2) a general *mêlée* had assembled around the bread and tea at tea break. Lyashi told the workers to behave themselves and not to grab the bread and tea. The workers he addressed were mainly line 2 and 3 tailors and the unskilled employees. These workers complied with Lyashi's demands and the tea and bread was distributed in a more orderly fashion. But two other companions of Lyashi, Nkoloya and Lwanga, came to the forefront and seemingly supported him by stating that the general behaviour of the junior workers at tea break was sufficient reason why Patel should not show them respect at work. At another time (see event 27, appendix 2) during work a violent argument broke out between Meshak, a button machiner and Zakeyo, a line 3 tailor, concerning the former's address of the latter as *mudala* (old man). On this occasion Meshak addressed Zakeyo in a joking way, implying that the latter was senile and not quite in command of his faculties. Mukubwa attempted to legitimate Meshak's use of the term *mudala* by trying to establish Zakeyo's date of birth.[7] Mukubwa attempted this by stating that the two men (Meshak and Zakeyo) were *mbuya* (i.e. had a tribal joking relationship, Meshak being Ambo and categorised as a Bemba and Zakeyo being a Nsenga and categorised as Ngoni). Zakeyo refused to accept Mukubwa's rationalisation of Meshak's behaviour. Zakeyo held that Meshak as a younger man should show him respect, and he was further angered with the added support

[7] Zakeyo is fourteen years older than Meshak.

given to Meshak by Ibrahim and Kalamba, who at this time were working in positions alongside Meshak (see fig. 5.2 (*b*)), and were also classed by him as young men in the factory. Lyashi left his work place and admonished Kalamba and Ibrahim for apparently supporting Mukubwa. He pointed out that old workers in the room should be shown respect and that everyone in the factory knew that Meshak is an Ambo and as such does not have a joking relationship with Nsenga people. Mukubwa, Ibrahim and Kalamba withdrew from the action and the argument stopped.

Various aspects are relevant to a discussion of the two events. First, Lyashi's success in both the events demonstrated that he could effectively control the behaviour of others. Nevertheless, in these two events any risk which may have been incurred from a failure to exercise power was minimised. Thus, unlike the behaviour of Mukubwa and Chisokone described for earlier events, Lyashi directed his call for more orderly behaviour at tea break towards the junior workers and not towards his fellow senior employees. His action, therefore, was geared to receiving support from these latter workers, for, if nothing else, it gave the senior workers an opportunity to impress their superior status on the junior employees. Even though they suffered some cost in according Lyashi approval, giving the latter a chance effectively to 'flex his muscles', the senior workers achieved some reward. In the second event, for reasons which will shortly become evident, Lyashi incurred slightly more risk. But even so, he was assured of considerable support, at least from his peers. Mukubwa had already been discredited in the eyes of most of the workers, and in his support of Zakeyo, Lyashi upheld the interests of an older worker against the opposition of younger employees, i.e. Meshak, Kalamba and Ibrahim.

Second, in the above events, as in others previously discussed, Lyashi's competition with others for power and leadership is evident. The support given Lyashi by Nkoloya and Lwanga in controlling the disorderly conduct of the junior employees at tea break, which no doubt assisted Lyashi in his action, did not arise from any intention on the part of the latter to discharge any obligation to Lyashi. Lwanga's action, for example, in 'The case of the badly stitched trousers' and Nkoloya's behaviour both in the latter event and on the occasion of 'Chisokone revealed' were considerably motivated by attempts to establish their own claims to power and leadership in the factory.

Lyashi's opposition to Mukubwa and Meshak involved more than the mere opportunity for Lyashi to win the allegiance and perhaps compliance of Zakeyo, though this is an important consideration. After this

T

event, the relationship between the two men became closer than had previously been observed. Zakeyo, for instance, gave Lyashi a lift on his bicycle back to Bwacha after work, and the two men frequently joined each other drinking at the beer hall. But more than being a basis for establishing a relationship with a comparative newcomer to the factory (up to this time Zakeyo had only been working in the factory for a little over six months), Lyashi's behaviour was also aimed at discrediting Meshak, who was seen by Lyashi as an important competitor and obstacle to the consolidation of his power and leadership.

Although, relative to most of the senior workers, Meshak was a young man, he had been employed for over eleven years in the factory. Patel often engaged him in friendly conversation, and he was seen by many of the workers as an individual who could exert some influence on the manager. (He was the only worker below the occupation of supervisor and line 1 tailor who had sponsored workers successfully to employment in the factory; see table 3.11). Meshak was perceived as a person of influence mainly by the lesser and unskilled employees with whom he had developed a number of relationships. That Meshak had such relationships with these workers was, no doubt, facilitated by his position in the production process as a button machiner which brought him into contact with tailors and unskilled workers alike. Particularly, in his relationships with unskilled employees, Meshak tended to be the dominant partner. He frequently gave unskilled employees who were interested the opportunity to use the button machine, thus familiarising them with one aspect of tailoring work. Because it was access to a resource which the unskilled workers could not repay except by giving approval and complying with Meshak's directives and commands, Meshak commanded a position of some power.

By opposing Meshak in support of Zakeyo, Lyashi subjected Meshak to a 'trial of strength'. On this occasion Lyashi had the weight of more powerful and influential opinion behind him, that of the line 1 tailors, and was able effectively to demonstrate his superiority over Meshak.

Lwanga, Nkoloya and Meshak were not the only individuals in the context who competed with Lyashi. Others such as Chipata and Abraham also vied with him. It will be shown subsequently with specific reference to Chipata that Lyashi was to lose out in a later phase of the development of social relations in the factory partly as a result of his lack of access to the kind of resources which an individual like Chipata could tap.

But the important point of the analysis at this stage is that Lyashi in his competition with others and in his efforts to control workers' behaviour to demonstrate and test his power was involved in the same paradox which I described earlier for Chisokone and Mukubwa. Lyashi's behaviour meant that he used his power and by using it, he expended it. He either began using up his resources of approval which he had achieved through his participation in previous events or at the very least began to accrue debts, in so far that individuals began complying with his demands, for which they had as yet received little return. If Lyashi were to maintain his power and to consolidate his position as a leader instead of only criticising the behaviour of others, it was necessary that he now should propose a positive strategy for action which would result in the rectifying of some of the employees' grievances.

Therefore it was predictable that Lyashi should devote himself to guiding the workers' opinion in supporting a course of action which would be seen by them as holding out reasonable hope of changing the factory wage and work conditions to their benefit. The way was now clear for the presentation of a strategy for action. Chisokone's declaration that he would shortly be leaving the factory had removed, for the time being, the effective use of outside political pressure for the achievement of the workers' objectives. The following event describes an occasion when Lyashi puts forward a proposal for action.

Event 29 Lyashi outlines a strategy for action
6 August

At break Hastings and Chisokone became involved in a political argument which absorbed the interest of most of the workers. Hastings registered concern at the fate which seemed to be overtaking many African governments. 'Look what has recently happened in Algeria. Ben Bella has been arrested by his opponents.' Chisokone shared Hastings' concern and mentioned that similar processes seemed to be going on in Kenya, where some of the senior government officials had openly declared their opposition to each other. At this point Paulos, a line 2 tailor, intervened and suggested that Chisokone and Hastings did not fully comprehend the political scene. 'You people don't know the trouble. The trouble is that the Eastern and Western powers are struggling against each other to win the confidence of Africans. Many people are receiving money from representatives of these powers to oppose their own governments.' Many of the workers now took the opportunity to comment on Paulos' statement as well as on the opinions of Chisokone and Hastings. One general opinion which emerged from the discussions was that Chisokone and Hastings were not aware of political realities and appeared to be too ready to blame Africans for the internal problems of their countries. Lyashi, for example, stated that if it were not for the Indians in Zambia, many of the difficulties confronted by Africans at present would not exist.

A heated discussion followed concerning Patel's refusal to improve the workers' wage and work conditions. Zulu, the overlock machiner, suggested that the union should be called in to place their demands before Patel. At this, Lyashi expressed considerable horror. 'We all know that the union has never done anything for us. All union officials are like our area organising secretary, who keeps promising us that things will improve but then forgets to do any more. If conditions are to improve, then we must go on strike.' Nkoloya backed Lyashi up which led to the latter's elaboration. 'Matters must be taken into our own hands and we must prevent any interference from the union!' Loud exclamations of approval for Lyashi's statement followed from the majority of the employees and excited discussion broke out among them as to the possibility of strike action.

The conversation on this occasion illustrates the deep interest which the factory workers have in the progress of political events in Africa generally. More especially the event demonstrates further the inability of Chisokone to express views on politics consistent with the general image which the workers had of a political official. The tenor of Hastings' and Chisokone's comments was 'conservative' in that they blamed the difficulties of the newly independent African States on the inability of Africans to govern themselves—a charge regularly made by Europeans in Zambia. Paulos' correction of the views of Chisokone and Hastings received the approval of the other workers present.

However, for the present analysis the most important aspect of the event is Lyashi's outline of a plan for action whereby wage and work improvements could be won. The general level of discussion in the event had been transformed to the more specific level of angry criticism being directed towards the factory's Indian management through the cue provided by Paulos. In response to the general anger expressed by the workers towards the Indian management, Zulu, the factory's union shop steward, suggested that the union should be called in. This gave Lyashi his opportunity to outline an alternative plan of action.

At the time Zulu's suggestion was impolitic. The workers, by withholding their payment of union dues, had already registered their disapproval of union inactivity. Furthermore, most of the workers were well aware that Zulu was a close friend of Chisokone. Zulu was also a senior UNIP branch official, but in Chimaninine, and by now it was general knowledge that Zulu was to be Chisokone's partner in a farming co-operative and would also be shortly leaving employment. Lyashi, taking advantage of this knowledge and the current tide of anti-union opinion, presented his strategy by which the employees could secure their objectives for wage and work improvements. His declared strategy, whereby the factory employees should resort to strike action while excluding the union from participation in negotiations, met with widespread approval from the employees.

In the days immediately following the event the general topic of conversation which regularly concerned the workers was how they were going to cope with the inconveniences produced by strike action. It became clear that as a result of strike action some workers were exposed to greater risk and cost than were others. Because of their skill and, in many instances, the ownership of their own sewing machines, tailors would incur less risk and would be better able to withstand a loss in wages through strike action than the unskilled workers. Many of the tailors emphasised their ability to fall back on the income derived from tailoring work done in the township, though it must be stressed here that some of the less skilled tailors on lines 2 and 3 did not have sewing machines (see table 3.6). Also, the tailors were aware that punitive action in the form of dismissal was less of a risk for them, than for the unskilled workers, as they realised that Patel valued their skill, partly because it was difficult to find replacements for them. Most of the tailors, therefore, continued to hold out strongly for strike action. But the enthusiasm which had been expressed by many of the unskilled workers cooled as they realised the greater predicament in which they would be placed in the event of a strike. Some of the cotton boys, for example, conveyed the disadvantageous position in which they were placed to the tailors. Thus Kalonga on one occasion asked Mulondo, who had just joined the factory as a tailor on line 2, what he intended doing in the event of a strike. Mulondo informed Kalonga that he would find no problem, as he ran a lucrative fishing business in the nearby Lukanga swamps. Kalonga expressed surprise at this, adding that he saw no reason why Mulondo should contemplate supporting a strike. It was through encounters such as these that the tailors, most of whom were for strike action, realised that they could not count on the whole-hearted support of many of the unskilled employees.

Partly as a result of this awareness, the senior and more skilled tailors who had been most militant for strike action agreed that the immediate resort should not be to a strike but that instead a threat of a strike should be used towards Patel. In this way they could conceal from Patel the emerging divisions between the workers over a suitable strategy for action while at the same time keeping a semblance of unity. Some attempt to maintain a semblance of support for strike action was made by the senior tailors. They gave declarations—these being most often voiced by Nkoloya and Lyashi—to the effect that they would seek a wage increment for all the workers and the introduction of a lunch break to replace the current ten-minute break.

The tailors and, in particular those on line 1, were mainly instrumental in selecting the representatives to negotiate with Patel. Lyashi's new position of leadership received general acknowledgment with his selection as a spokesman on the employees' behalf. But the power of some of Lyashi's rivals also received recognition with the selection by the workers of Nkoloya and Abraham to be the employees' representatives. It has been shown in previous events that Nkoloya and Abraham often played leading parts and were the recipients of much approval from the other factory workers. Their selection as representatives was not surprising. What *is*, however, is that it was also agreed by the workers that Chisokone, Zulu and Chipata, should act as their representatives.

The opposition to Chisokone largely grew out of his failure to live up to the expectations which the workers had of a senior political branch official. That the factory workers had become disillusioned with Chisokone as a man who might act in their interests did not mean that they still did not believe that pressure exerted through the political party would be effective in winning concessions from Patel. It was the man, not the office, with whom the factory employees were disaffected. As explained earlier, the opposition to Chisokone not only reduced the extent to which he could effectively exert authority in the factory but also threatened his political position in the sphere of township politics. I suggest that it was this latter aspect more than anything else which influenced him to retrieve some of his lost ground. He did this by responding to the pressure placed on him by the general opposition of the workers and confiding to the line 1 tailors that he was prepared to use his political influence on their behalf.

Zulu and Chipata, unlike Chisokone, did not offer their services but were approached by Nkoloya to give their support. As senior branch officials in Chimaninine it was expected that their presence among the factory representatives would be of assistance in pressuring Patel to grant the employees' demands. Zulu was also the union shop steward, and this was influential in his selection. But it must be emphasised here that Nkoloya, as well as the other line 1 tailors, including Lyashi, remained adamant that higher union officials should not be allowed to enter into the negotiations. In effect, therefore, the workers were trying to use Zulu's office as the factory shop steward to impart the impression to Patel that the union stood behind the employees' action without, in fact, implicating the union in their deliberations. It was felt that the introduction of higher-ranking union officials would result in compromises being reached contrary to the employees' interests. No doubt similar motives were involved in the use of Chisokone, Zulu and Chipata in their positions as political party officials, as they could be presented as representatives of the political party without involving higher party officials in these negotiations. Nevertheless, as later events were to show, should Patel fail to yield under threat the workers were prepared to manipulate their ties into the political party to place greater pressure on Patel. At the time the belief was firm that the party and government, though not the union, would support their cause. By including Chisokone, Zulu and Chipata in the group of workers' representatives, the employees considered that their threat of strike action would receive added weight as it was made to look as if the political party and to a lesser extent the union supported their action.

After tea break on 9 August 1965 all six representatives took the workers' demands before Patel for a 1*d* increment to be awarded to all workers and the introduction of a lunch break. Lyashi and Nkoloya were the major spokesmen and openly threatened Patel with a strike by all the factory employees if he did not agree to introduce these changes. Patel laughed at their threat and said he did not believe them. He was just as aware as the employees themselves that there were divisions among the workers as to the extent to which strike action was in their interests. Owing to the confined area of the factory, Patel had overheard and grasped the general meaning of many of the discussions between the workers. In his refusal to be intimidated by this threat Patel called his employees' bluff. Some face was saved, however, with the intervention of Chisokone, who threatened to take the matter before the Resident Minister. Patel, as described earlier,[8] was sufficiently troubled by the political uncertainties of the time to adopt a more conciliatory manner in response to this new threat. After some discussion it was agreed that the workers should have a $1\frac{1}{2}$ hour break from 12.30 p.m. to 2.00 p.m., and instead of breaking off work at 3.30 p.m. they were now to work through to 5.00 p.m. Patel called his partners into the discussions, and it was largely because of their agreement to the above changes that Patel gave in to the demand for a lunch break. Although the workers' objective to achieve a lunch break had been granted, Patel and his partners gave only assurances that an increment would be awarded, stating that in all probability a wage increase would be given by the end of August.

For the moment the workers were jubilant, and Chisokone's stock especially had risen. But it was soon realised that no real concessions had been granted by Patel. The workers had achieved their lunch break,

[8] See chapter 4, p. 153.

but they had not achieved a wage increase and growing doubt was now being expressed as to the likelihood of achieving it. Under pressure from Lyashi and Nkoloya, Chisokone was urged to ask Patel what had become of his assurances to award a general $1d$ increment. Patel now stated that he could do nothing without consulting the government and union officials. As Lyashi's and Nkoloya's bluff had been called with reference to strike action, so now had Chisokone been challenged to act out his threat of political intervention.

At the time the general feeling—now also expressed among the line 1 tailors—was that the most expedient course of action was the manipulation of their political ties into government. Strike action which had appeared as the best course now was the least attractive alternative with Chisokone's stated preparedness to use his political influence. Even though such factors as skill and the existence of supplementary sources of income made strike action less of a cost and a risk to the tailors in comparison with the unskilled employees, strike action still meant that some cost must be incurred. With Patel's failure to honour assurances, Chisokone and the other senior political branch officials employed in the factory (Zulu and Chipata) could do little else than act upon their threat. Their image as political party leaders was at stake if they did not live up to the employees' expectation of them, a danger already experienced by Chisokone. Moreover, Lyashi and Nkoloya did not allow them to forget it, continually urging upon them in their (i.e. Lyashi's and Nkoloya's) parts as the major spokesmen of worker interest to take the employees' demands before the Resident Minister.

Chisokone, Zulu and Chipata complied with the demands placed on them by the workers and went to see the Resident Minister. Although the latter listened sympathetically to their grievances, no action was taken. Many of the workers expressed anger with this news, and some were beginning to suggest that the new lunch break should never have been introduced. In fact there was a growing realisation that Patel had, in effect, conceded nothing. As one worker stated, Patel did not even have to go to the expense of providing tea and bread, as at lunch the workers left the factory premises. If what they had achieved in terms of an accepted position of power and leadership in the factory was not to be lost, it was essential that Lyashi as well as his competitors should win a wage increment for the employees. It was, after all, a wage increase, not a lunch break, which was at the heart of every worker's interest.

Lyashi again took much of the initiative. He stated that the only recourse open to the workers was to walk-out. This was opposed by the less skilled and unskilled workers, most of whom were concerned lest Patel should dismiss them from work. But perhaps more importantly, they were aware, in spite of assurances to the contrary from Lyashi, Nkoloya and other senior workers, that the more skilled workers would place greater emphasis on the securement of an increment for themselves before they presented the interests of those junior to them. It was common knowledge that the more skilled workers wanted to increase the wage differential between themselves and the less skilled and unskilled employees. Nevertheless, the tailors on line 1 especially were concerned that unless they achieved the support of the junior workers for a strike, they would be at a disadvantage in their negotiation with Patel. Although a stoppage of work by them would be costly to Patel in that they were normally employed on tailoring work which demanded skill, it would not completely disrupt the production process.

Despite the growing concern among the senior employees that they would not have the support of all the workers, on 1 September Lyashi, supported by the workers on line 1, staged a walk-out. Universal support was not achieved, and the cotton boys, ironers and a few of the tailors on lines 2 and 3 stayed in the factory. Considerable anger was expressed by those who had walked out towards those who remained at work, and accusations of *chichawa* and *makobo* were levelled. However, Patel immediately responded and, together with his business associates, whom he informed of the dispute, he entered into negotiations with the strikers. After an hour's discussion no agreement had been reached, and it was reluctantly agreed by the employees concerned that the union area organising secretary should be called in. The latter suggested that the matter should be taken to the labour officer, and Lyashi, Chisokone and Chipata and one of Patel's partners accompanied the area organising secretary to the labour office. Here it was agreed that an increment should be awarded the factory employees, the precise nature of the terms to be worked out between the union and Patel. The representatives of the workers returned to inform their fellows of the result, and those who had walked out returned to work. In the afternoon Patel informed his employees that a 1*d* increment was to be awarded to the supervisors, the line 1 tailors and some of the tailors on the other lines, notably line 2, and to a few other senior workers. Mukubwa went around the factory informing those workers who were to receive an increment.

A worthwhile concession had at last been achieved, but not all in the factory were satisfied. Although the junior workers had not supported the strike, their fears had been upheld, and the fact that it was only the senior and more skilled workers who received increments (see table 2.2) emphasised the status differences in the factory. Even some of those who had received an increment were not completely satisfied as Mukubwa and Hastings, both of whom had not supported the action received increments. These aspects aside, however, Lyashi had considerably consolidated his position of power among his peers for he had been largely instrumental in securing them rewards in return for their earlier approval of his opinions and compliance with his suggested line of action. Nevertheless, Lyashi was not the only individual to emerge successfully from this series of events. Although I have not stressed the parts they played in these events, Nkoloya, Abraham, Chipata and Meshak also achieved prominence in the proceedings. While Lyashi was at the labour office it was they who directed much of the negotiations with Patel and kept the workers on strike. Patel, assisted by Hastings and Mukubwa, had been trying to convince the workers that as the matter was in the hands of the union and labour officer, they should return to work.

Before I continue with a description and analysis of the event which followed, 'The five-day working week dispute', two points should be emphasised. First Lyashi had largely succeeded in consolidating his position of leadership and power. But if he were to continue receiving the approval and compliance of his peers, it was necessary for him to furnish additional rewards. The increment which had just been awarded was only a start, and most of those whom the increment involved considered that a $1d$ per hour increase was nowhere near their true deserts. Moreover, there were many other grievances which the employees felt needed righting, in particular, with reference to leave pay, long service and end of employment benefits. But perhaps most important, in the sense that it was a general demand expressed by all the workers, was the removal of the system of hourly pay and its replacement by a monthly pay system. Second, rivals to Lyashi's new found position of power remained, not the least because those concerned realised that to accord him approval and compliance devalued their own status, a status which in their view was greater than, or at least on a par with, Lyashi's. It is basic to the argument that however much Lyashi was successful in presenting himself as the major instrument in achieving various rewards, his position of power and leadership would continually be open to threat and thus be insecure. His place could just as easily be taken by one of his rivals such as Nkoloya or Chipata. In fact the more he assumed a stable position of power and leadership the greater the cost to his peers in terms of their status. This cost could be minimised by transferring allegiance to others who presented themselves in a similar way to Lyashi.

Among a group of equals, the less a definite leader emerges the less clearly differentiated in terms of power they would be seen by other individuals and, therefore, the less the cost to them in the sense of a reduction in status. By constantly transferring allegiance, the more the cost in status would be minimised, especially among the senior workers, for they would thereby not be seen as regularly subordinated to the will of one man. The preparedness of the senior workers constantly to change their allegiance and to redistribute their resources of support and approval was a regular feature of the factory context. However, the presence of this regularity must not be seen in the simple terms of its being in the self interest of the senior workers. They were able to shift allegiances because of the inability of any one man to supply them rewards which either could not be guaranteed by others among them or which they did not already possess. As long as the roots of Lyashi's power and leadership lay in the support and approval of his peers, this was reason enough for his position to be insecure. To stabilise and consolidate his power further—and this applies equally to Lyashi's rivals—it was essential that Lyashi should gain the support and approval of individuals to whom he could supply rewards which they could not easily acquire from others or provide themselves. The individuals which provided Lyashi with the best opportunity for further consolidating and stabilising his power were those junior to him. In return for their compliance, he could both supply them rewards connected with wage and work improvements and others such as the opportunity to learn a skill. It was expected, therefore, that Lyashi, and others who competed with him, should try to extend into the ranks of the less and unskilled workers, relationships in which they were clearly accepted as dominant. The development of this pattern is important for the understanding of the processes of later events.

Of course, not all the events in a particular context can be related only to the processes occurring within it, many also have their roots in processes going on outside. This is the case with the following event. In September the Employment Act was finally passed by the Zambian National Assembly, an Act which was specifically intended to protect the interests of Africans in employment.[9] The various provisions of the

[9] As the Minister of Labour and Social Development stated before the Act had been passed and while it was in its second reading, '. . . it was designed to replace the "Employment of Natives Ordinance" which is racial and discriminatory in nature . . .'—Second reading of the employment Bill, *Daily Hansard*, 27 July 1965, p. 313.

Act were widely reported in the national newspapers and particular clauses of the Act dominated much of the workers' conversation. Most regularly discussed were those provisions relating to the requirement of an employer to grant thirty-six days' paid holiday leave after three years' service, the providing of twenty-six days' paid sick leave per year, and the requirement of the employer to assist an employee with travelling expenses to his rural area upon the termination of employment.[10] A new provision which received most comment was the clause which stated that employees should be paid for a five-day week. Any time worked in excess of five days was to be paid according to overtime rates.[11] However, the most significant aspect of the new Act was that it indicated to the factory employees a positive attempt by the government to institute regulations protective of their interests. Narayan Bros.' employees now felt they had the complete support of the government, and so saw their opportunity to press once again for the righting of their grievances. The legitimation for their action was the clause in the Act relating to the provision that employees should be paid according to a five-day working week. The reason for selecting this clause was that they saw it as an opportunity to remove the hourly pay system and to replace it with a system whereby they would be paid on a monthly basis.

Event 32   The five-day working week dispute
11 September

The dispute occurred on a Saturday morning during work. Lyashi and a number of his companions on line 1 (Chipata, Nkoloya, Abraham and Lwanga) and Meshak, the button machiner, left their work places and asked Patel whether they were going to be paid for that day. Patel asked his employees what they meant by this, and they responded by informing him that according to the new Act they should be paid for a five-day working week and that Saturday morning was overtime. In reply, Patel stated that he was well aware of the provisions of the new Act and that he had already consulted the labour officer, who had told him that the Act did not apply to those on hourly pay. There was general disbelief as to the truth of Patel's statement. Lyashi wanted to know why they had not been informed if this was the case. Chipata and Meshak were then prevailed

[10] For these and other provisions of the Employment Act see *Republic of Zambia Government Gazette*, Acts (1966), pp. 449–86.

[11] Details of the clause relating to the introduction of a five-day week are in Statutory Instrument No. 413 of 1965. It was also stated in the relevant clause that the duration of each shift or working day should not exceed eight hours.

upon by the line 1 tailors to go and check with the labour officer. At this suggestion, Patel stated that they could not leave work unless they were accompanied by the union area organising secretary. After some debate, this was generally agreed to and the organising secretary was called. Patel's statement was affirmed by the labour officer, and Meshak and Chipata returned to the factory to inform the employees.

With the news considerable annoyance was expressed by the workers. Hastings now intervened and explained to them on behalf of Patel that if they did not work on Saturday morning they could not expect to be paid. Lyashi now assumed the part of chief spokesman and turned his attention to the union organising secretary, who had been relatively silent in the proceedings. 'Why have we been exempted from the law ?' The organising secretary then re-stated the point that workers on hourly pay were excluded. This brought a storm of protest, during the course of which the union was accused of being weak and not working in the employees' interests. Hastings now intervened once again with a general plea that the employees should agree to work, otherwise they would only lose their pay. 'We are all here for money and it won't pay us to refuse to work.' With this, Ibrahim admonished Hastings by stating 'We all know this, but despite the fact, old man [*mudala*], that we come from different countries we must all abide by the law. By saying all this you are supporting the manager against us.' Lyashi now stepped in and stated that no headway would be achieved unless they walked out. This was backed up by Nkoloya, Chipata and Meshak. All the line 1 and 2 tailors now left the factory. Some of the less skilled tailors on line 3 and most of the unskilled workers remained at their benches. However, Patel told the latter to leave also as most of the morning had now gone and there was little work to be done.

For a brief period of time most of the workers gathered around Lyashi who was outside the factory, demanding that the union organising secretary tell them properly about the new law. He was unable to do so, and the workers then dispersed to their homes in the townships.

Later in the afternoon. Mukubwa was visited at his house in Chimaninine by Ibrahim. The latter asked what Mukubwa thought about the morning's activities. Mukubwa's reply was to state that nothing could be settled as the workers did not have strong trade unionists supporting them who could argue and explain their case with Patel. Ibrahim agreed and reiterated with great pride his attack on Hastings in the morning. Mukubwa explained why he did not say or do anything during the discussions at the factory, as he realised that nothing could be achieved. Lyashi now arrived at the home and again asked Mukubwa's opinion as to the walk-out. Before the latter could answer, Lyashi stated, 'I for one think we did the right thing. After all, the tailors at Badat & Co. (the rival clothing factory to Narayan Bros.) were not at work this morning. There was some short disagreement about the validity of this statement, but Lyashi now pressed harder to elicit some comment from Mukubwa regarding the morning's activities. After a short time Mukubwa stated that he could neither say nor do much. 'I can only do what I am told by

Patel.' Lyashi then explained to Mukubwa that this attitude was why the
workers considered him and Hastings to be on management's side. At
this point Chipata entered the house and, like Lyashi, asked Mukubwa
whether he supported the walk-out or not. Mukubwa continued to be
evasive, and Chipata became so annoyed that he threatened to leave the
house unless Mukubwa stated his position clearly. The atmosphere in the
house became more heated when Mukubwa, in trying to defend his
evasive behaviour, stated that there was little that any of them could do
until the following Monday when they would be able to see Patel's reaction to the walk-out. Even then, Mukubwa went on to add, it would be
better for them to wait until the end of the month when they were to be
paid to see if they had received additional wages for Saturday work.
Lyashi erupted angrily at this suggestion. 'If we do this and find out that
we have lost our pay, then we must admit defeat. We will have shown
Patel that we are afraid of him.' Lyashi and Chipata now left the house.
Both went their different ways, Lyashi to Bwacha township where he
hoped to find some of the cotton boys to test their opinions, and Chipata
to Bwacha beer hall, where he knew some of the tailors were gathered with
whom he wished to discuss the morning's walk-out.

At Bwacha beer hall. Seated in the beer hall were Nkoloya, Abraham,
Chipata and Enoch. The latter two were line 2 tailors. Abraham stated
that the workers had done the right thing by telling Hastings not to
interfere in their negotiations with Patel. Earlier in the week Abraham
reported that Hastings had asked him to demand that Patel begin a pension
scheme for his longer service workers. When Abraham had enquired why
he should ask him to do this, Hastings reportedly had said, 'Only you
Zambians can do anything to improve work conditions. This just goes to
show that Malawians are afraid to go against management.' Chipata stated
that this applied not only to Hastings but also to Mukubwa. He went on,
'Even the labour officer is frightened of being fined by Patel, and this is
why he didn't come back with me in the morning to explain the law to
us.' Some general comments now ensued regarding the apparent failure
of the government to support their cause. Abraham added to these
statements by mentioning that the union organising secretary was also
against them and appeared to be backing up Patel in cutting their Saturday pay. Nkoloya got up to leave for his home in the mine farms and stated
that their only option was to beat some sense into the union organising
secretary. This sentiment received loud acclaim from his drinking companions. Others now also rose to return to their homes and Chipata
assured them that if they did not receive their Saturday pay he would
take their claims to President Kaunda.

Chipata visits Lyashi. On his way home Chipata called in at Lyashi's
house. Lyashi told him that he felt that the cotton boys would refuse to
go out on strike. 'I even told them that we will all have more wages if we
are paid for Saturdays.' Chipata stated that he would consult the leaders
of the UNIP Youth Brigade in the various township branches to see if
some pressure could be brought to bear on them.

Monday morning. Most of the workers milled around outside the factory. Some of the employees, particularly a few of the line 3 tailors and the majority of the unskilled workers, showed signs that they were anxious to start work by moving in and out of the factory. Patel called Chipata inside the factory and told him that the labour officer had written to the Ministry of Labour and Social Development to obtain confirmation that the factory workers were exempt from the Act. When asked by Chipata if he had consulted the union, Patel stated that he had phoned through to the Kitwe union headquarters, which had given him no definite reply. Chipata now went outside and repeated what Patel had told him. Lyashi expressed considerable hostility that those bodies should be consulted without the employees' knowledge, and in this he was ardently supported by the majority of the tailors. Patel now came outside and informed Chipata that he was wanted at the labour office. When Chipata returned he told his companions that they should now return to work, as the government would reach some agreement with Patel. He was greeted with silence until Lyashi demanded that Chipata give some indication that they would be paid according to a five-day week. But some of the workers, and noticeably the junior tailors on lines 2 and 3, began moving into the factory. The walk-out now appeared to have come to an end, but in order to convince the line 1 tailors Patel addressed them, stating that he had since phoned through to the Ministry of Labour and Social Development and had been informed that the Ministry was phoning the Kabwe labour office to tell the labour officer that the new Act did not apply to employees on hourly pay. He also added that he had phoned an Indian clothing factory in Lusaka and had been told likewise. Nkoloya, Lyashi and Abraham reiterated once again the concern shown earlier by Lyashi that Patel should have done this without the knowledge of the workers. Once the employees had returned to work, Patel entered negotiations with the union for a settlement. Later in the week the employees were notified that from now on they would be paid for a five-day week and that there would not be any regular Saturday morning work.

The resort to a walk-out in the dispute over whether according to the new Act the workers' wages should be based on a five-day working week was, no doubt, influenced by their earlier success at gaining concessions from similar action on the previous Monday when the more senior factory employees achieved a $1d$ increment to their hourly rate. Apart from the above event in this sense having a connection with the workers' earlier success, in terms of strategy it was also similar. Thus a walk-out was combined with the manipulation of the workers' political ties into the government. The union was also an important element in the strategy and, for various reasons which I will explain subsequently, initially at least, the workers expected it to act more effectively on their behalf than they did during the previous walk-out when they were reluctant for Patel to include it in the negotiations.

Three aspects of 'The five-day working week dispute' will be discussed. First, the strategies pursued by the various parties to the dispute and the basis upon which the major initiators of the dispute attempted to mobilise and maintain support. This leads to the question why there was a marked failure of the leaders of the dispute to secure the support of the less skilled and unskilled workers? Second, the part played by the major spokesmen in the dispute and its effect on their social relationships in the factory. Third, the consequences of the walk-out for the future action of the employees.

The above event was in essence a conflict between workers and management over the definition of the employees' contract with management, with specific reference to whether the factory workers should be defined as being engaged on a monthly or daily basis. The terms of the Act were clear, that is, those whose wages were calculated according to the number of hours worked were deemed to be on daily contract whereas those whose wages were calculated on a daily basis or above were deemed to be on a monthly contract. In its provisions the Act also attempted to account for any areas of possible uncertainty. Thus, for example, it was made clear that an employee who received his wages at the end of each month but whose pay was calculated in terms of the number of hours worked, was regarded as being on daily contract. Although, in abstract the Act was clear as to its terms of reference, this was not so at the level of the factory context. At Narayan Bros. both management and worker were unclear as to the precise meaning of the Act as applied to them, and they sought to negotiate a definition of the Act in a way which best suited their separate interests. Of course, that new employment regulations had been introduced with the Act demanded that management and worker re-define their relationship to each other. The action surrounding the 'Five-day working week dispute', therefore, was a process whereby both management and worker were bargaining and negotiating as to an accepted definition of their relationship to each other under the terms of the Act. The various interests of management and worker were dependent on the definition of the Act achieved. From the employees' perspective, if they were able to gain a definition of their terms of contract as monthly rather than daily, then a number of additional benefits would accrue to them. For example, workers on monthly contract under the terms of the Act were entitled to holiday pay and paid sick leave. Both these benefits the employees considered were inadequately provided for by management. The basis upon which they presented their definition was by their demand to be paid additionally for Saturday morning work. The Act stated that those on a monthly contract should be paid according to a five-day working-week, and any time worked in excess of this was to be counted as overtime. If it were agreed by management that they should receive additional payment for Saturday morning work, then the employees would, in effect, not only have increased their pay but also would have achieved a definition of their contract of employment as monthly rather than daily. By accepting this Patel would, in fact, be stating that he calculated his employees' wages on the basis of a five-day week, not in terms of the number of hours worked.

Although such a definition was seen by the factory employees as beneficial to them, Patel did not view it in the same way. Patel considered that if he paid his workers on the basis of a five-day working week, then he would experience considerable cost in terms of production time lost. He believed that the only way he could curb the loss in working hours through absenteeism and illness and also receive the best return on capital laid out in wages was to keep the hourly pay system. Obviously, too, if Patel accepted his employees' definition, he would be obliged to pay them more wages for Saturday work and would be liable for the payment of increased holiday and sick leave allowances. As Patel saw it, therefore, it was in his interest to maintain his definition of the contract that his employees were paid on an hourly basis.

Given their opposed interests, what were the strategies pursued by the two parties to the dispute and what were the factors constraining their action? How were management and worker placed in regard to each other in the dispute for the securement of their particular definitions of the new legislation? To a large extent Patel was able to control the field of action relevant to the dispute. Patel had anticipated a dispute over the new Act and had already consulted the labour officer, who, he claimed, supported his position. If the employees were to be successful in their demands, then they were more or less forced to demonstrate the falsity of Patel's claims. However, as their strategy on a subsequent occasion which involved strike action was to show, they could have resisted the inclusion of the labour officer in the negotiations. But on this occasion the employees had reason to expect that they would receive the support of the labour officer and the government. A number of factors explain this. In the first place, they viewed the new legislation as a positive attempt by the government to improve the wage and work conditions of Africans in employment. The aim of the employees being to improve their wage conditions, they then felt assured of the support of the government and its representatives, in this case, the labour office. Furthermore, the belief that they would receive the support of

U

the labour officer was strengthened with his support of the award of the 1*d* wage increment on a previous occasion. Finally, present in the factory was Chipata (Chisokone and Zulu were both away at the time inspecting possible farms where they could begin their co-operative farming enterprise), who was a senior UNIP branch official in Chimaninine. It was expected by the workers that he would use his influence in local government circles to win acceptance of the employees' particular definition of the Act. These factors, therefore, were instrumental to the factory workers' agreeing to the inclusion of the labour officer in these negotiations.

But Patel was influential in extending the field of action in yet another direction. He did this by not permitting Chipata and Meshak leave of absence to see the labour officer unless they were accompanied by the union area organising secretary. Here, too, the factory workers were faced with a choice. In fact, there was little Patel could do to prevent Chipata and Meshak going to the labour office. Not only were they well within their rights, but by staging a walk-out immediately the employees conceivably could have forced Patel into permitting the two workers concerned to visit the labour office. But the employees immediately agreed with Patel's demand. Up to this time the factory workers had shown considerable hostility towards the union, and particularly the area organising secretary, as an agency which did not work in their best interests. Why, therefore, did the workers have this apparent change of attitude? The factor which contributed most to this was the part played by the union in gaining the 1*d* increment for the senior factory workers. But of almost equal importance was the arrival of the union president from Kitwe in Kabwe. Before the 'Five-day working week dispute' he had made a visit to the factory and had assured the employees that should any matter arise which needed the union's support, this would be given. It was the president's visit, coupled with the circumstances which led to the award of a 1*d* increment, which had been instrumental in the factory workers' paying their September union dues. Because of the earlier assistance given them by the union and the assurances given by the union president, the factory employees felt confident that they would receive the union's support.

Contrary, however, to their expectations, Patel was better placed with respect to these bodies, given the agreement of the workers that the labour office and the union should be included in the field of action. Patel could amass more information in support of his definition than his employees could. He had already informed himself of the exact terms of reference of the Act, and also felt assured of the support of the labour officer and the union. That his confidence was well founded was borne out with Meshak's and Chipata's return. In one moment the high expectations which the employees had that they would be supported by the union and the labour office dissolved.

Lyashi now openly challenged the union area organising secretary to explain the Act to the workers. There was only one course of action remaining to the factory workers if they hoped to gain any chance of an acceptance of their particular definition of the Act. This was recourse to a walk-out. The platform upon which the dispute was based had a general appeal to all the employees in the factory. If agreement was reached that the employees should receive additional payment for Saturday morning work, then all the workers stood to benefit irrespective of skill or seniority in the work place. Lyashi, with the support of the other leaders, Nkoloya, Chipata and Meshak, called for a walk-out. But, as in the 1 September walk-out, this action received only partial support. Once again the senior and more skilled employees came out but some of the line 3 tailors and most of the unskilled workers remained at their work places. As in the previous instance mentioned above, similar factors explain the pattern of response to Lyashi's suggested line of action. The less skilled and unskilled workers who refused to participate in the walk-out stood to incur a greater risk and cost than their more senior and skilled working companions as a result of such action. Some of the reasons for this are already familiar both from the description in relation to the previous walk-out and from the analysis in chapter 2. The workers who remained in the factory had much sympathy with the viewpoint expressed by Hastings that a walk-out could only cause a loss in wages.

It was clear that an appeal to the attainment of general wage and work improvements was not sufficient to gain the support of the less skilled and unskilled employees. They had, at least, to have some surety that they would be protected from a threat of dismissal by Patel before participating in strike action. Their lack of commitment to the work place and the fact that they tended to be target workers was reason enough why they should not wish to forgo immediate rewards for the sake of some future gain. Moreover, these junior workers were not tied into as close a set of relationships as the line 1 tailors and to a lesser extent some of the line 2 tailors (see matrix 1). The close set of relationships to which most of the senior workers belonged meant that support could be quickly mobilised among them should a threat to their interests arise. It will be recalled that it was partly owing to this factor that Lenard in the 'Case of the badly stitched trousers' received the quick support of his workmates when he was threatened with the sack. But of even greater importance, the senior workers had as yet become involved in few transactions with the junior employees. Thus they could not exert pressure on the junior workers to support them in strike action through the application of such sanctions as the withdrawal of valued goods and services.

In the afternoon following the walk-out and on Sunday many of the senior workers discussed the morning's activities with each other at their homes or in the beer halls. Not only are these workers involved in a close-knit set of relationships with each other at work, but many participate in joint activities such as beer-drinking with each other after work. Most of the senior workers know where the others live and, providing the distances separating their homes are not too great, frequently visit each other's houses. The existence of this set of relationships extending outside the work context facilitates the generation of mutual support and allows for the maintenance of a common commitment to the course of action they have chosen. Moreover, it gives them an opportunity to compare notes and decide on future strategies of action. The conversation between Nkoloya, Abraham, Chipata, Mulondo and Enoch at Bwacha beer hall is an example of this. In the discussion all commented on the opposition of Hastings to their action and the apparent opposition of the labour officer and union. Chipata brought the information that Mukubwa had refused to support them. The general tenor of the conversations emphasised the difficulty of their position and the forces ranged against them; however, Chipata raised their hopes by stating that he was prepared to use his political influence, reassuring them that he would take their claims as far as President Kaunda. Although the senior factory employees met with each other and discussed the walk-out throughout the weekend, they had little contact with any of the less skilled or unskilled workers. None of the latter came into contact with the senior employees socially after working hours. Lyashi's attempt to convince two of them, Joseph and Kalonga, as I later found out, met with considerable antagonism from the two cotton boys. The inability of Lyashi to convince the cotton boys to support the strike was not offset by Chipata, who did not act on his statement to call on the assistance of the UNIP Youth Brigade.[12]

---

[12] In gaining the assistance of the UNIP Youth Brigade, Chipata was considerably handicapped. Most of the cotton boys and other less skilled or unskilled employees lived in townships other than Chimaninine, where Chipata had enough political influence to receive the aid of the Youth Brigade of his branch. Other townships were outside his jurisdiction and it was unlikely that

The position of the strikers was weakened with the refusal of the more junior employees to participate actively in the walk-out. They were much weaker than on the similar occasion of their earlier walk-out. Unlike the previous time, the labour officer and the union area organising secretary had also virtually declared themselves to be in support of Patel's position. However, the workers who had walked out still had one card up their sleeve, namely their link into the government through Chipata. But, undoubtedly, the weakness of their position led some of the ringleaders, notably Lyashi and Chipata, to try to gain added support for their case from another and unexpected source.

This source was Mukubwa, the supervisor against whom Lyashi, in particular, had aimed his attacks in the course of his rise to power. Why did Chipata and Lyashi choose to win Mukubwa to their cause? The reason is plain why they did not seek the support of Hastings. In the morning's activities, the latter had declared himself to be in support of Patel. This action drew the ire of a work friend Ibrahim, a fellow foreigner to Zambia. Ibrahim in his repudiation of Hastings' statements disclaimed his association with Hastings on the basis that they were both foreigners and affirmed his support of the walk-out in terms of the basic opposition between management and worker. The major point, however, is that Mukubwa did not participate one way or the other in the morning's proceedings. There was thus some uncertainty about his feelings in the dispute. Moreover, both Lyashi and Chipata were aware that Mukubwa wielded considerable influence with Patel and they considered that if he could be won over to their side, then pressure could be exerted through him on Patel. Nevertheless, despite Lyashi's and Chipata's attempts to gain the support of Mukubwa in his house in the afternoon, ably supported by Ibrahim, they were unsuccessful.

On Monday morning the senior workers continued the walk-out. But the weakness of their position, coupled with Patel's greater command over informational sources, told. Thus immediately upon the arrival of the employees at the work place Patel was able to inform them that the Ministry of Labour and Social Development was writing to the Kabwe labour office to confirm his position that the workers were not covered by the Act. Moreover, the fact that Patel had access to a telephone, which his workers did not, gave Patel the opportunity to use this channel of communication to his advantage in supporting his definition of the terms of reference of the Act. He had telephoned the

Chipata could have wielded enough influence to have won the support of the respective branch UNIP youth wings concerned.

Ministry of Labour and Social Development and been told that the latter was phoning instructions supporting his position to the labour office and that a clothing factory in Lusaka which employed its workers on an hourly basis was not included under the terms of the Act. This information was a decisive factor in influencing the employees to return to work.

Not only were the cards stacked against the strikers, in terms of Patel's greater command over channels of communication and sources of information, but also the strikers' last remaining hope in the ability of Chipata to exert his influence as a branch political official was dashed. Although Chipata did not reveal this information to his companions when he visited the labour officer at Patel's instruction in the morning, one of the Resident Minister's Political Assistants was present. Chipata was informed that he was acting against the law of the government and was not acting according to the expectations of a political leader. Unlike a later occasion during the February strike (see chapter 4 and event 35, chapter 8), when Chipata was threatened with the loss of office, no threat was issued. In fact, assurances were made, declared by Chipata to his companions at the factory, that the government would look into the employees' complaints. Nevertheless, it was clear to Chipata, at least, that no more support than this could be expected from the government and it was this knowledge which influenced Chipata to press his companions to return to work.

As stated in the account of the walk-out, negotiations were entered into by the union with management with reference to Saturday pay. Irrespective of his victory, Patel sensed that the issue was far from settled and he was concerned lest further walk-outs over the same demands causing a loss to production should arise. It was this consideration which led Patel to remove the grievance in terms of which the senior employees had attempted to win a definition of their employment contract as monthly rather than daily. This he did by ending Saturday morning work.

In the course of the dispute the employees had pursued three main courses of action and these were (a) the manipulation of their political ties into the government through the use of Chipata, (b) an appeal to the union and (c) the use of strike action. The first two courses necessitated an expansion of the relevant field of action beyond the factory context. This expansion arose partly from the strategy set in train by Patel but was nevertheless agreed to by the factory workers. But the expectation of the workers that they would be able effectively to manipulate their links into the bodies concerned was not fulfilled. Given an expanded field of action, Patel was more advantageously placed than his employees, as he had better access to information supportive of his stand and better channels of communication. Moreover, as explained in chapter 4, a dispute which occurs in an expanded field of action makes relevant other pressures and interests which are likely to militate against the specific interests of the workers. It has previously been described that the government was opposed to strike action and was in favour of a more orderly progress towards economic and industrial change. When a government agency such as the labour office was involved in an industrial strike, considerable pressure was likely to be exerted on the workers and the union representative of them to in-fluence the employees to return to work. Only when the employees had returned, as in fact was intimated to Chipata, was it likely to examine the workers' grievances. However, once strike action is called off, the pressure the employees are able to exert on management is reduced with the result that management is in a correspondingly strengthened position should further negotiations eventuate. If the first two elements of the strategy pursued by the workers were ineffective much the same can be said for the senior factory workers' resort to strike action. The refusal of the less skilled and unskilled employees to participate in the walk-out openly displayed before Patel the divisions in the ranks of his workers and the weakness of the strikers' position.

I now examine the 'Five-day working week dispute' from the per-spective of the competition for power and leadership among the senior factory workers. Those who assumed the position of major spokesmen at the beginning of the dispute were Lyashi, Nkoloya, Abraham, Lwanga, Chipata and Meshak. However, most attention was focused by the other workers on Lyashi, Chipata and Meshak, the others dropping more into the background. Earlier I stated that Meshak, a button machiner, had begun to emerge as a major contender for power and leadership. It was explained that he had considerable power and influence among the less skilled tailors and unskilled workers. This was partly due to his position in the production process which brought him into contact with these workers. As an employee with long service in the factory, Meshak's assumption of a leading part was acceptable to the older and senior workers, for in the terms of his length of service, at least, he had some claim to high status in the factory. But the most significant aspect of Meshak's taking a leading part initially was the acceptance of it by the other leading spokesmen of the workers. An explanation for this acceptance and the willingness with which they permitted Meshak to accompany Chipata to the labour office was their awareness of his power and influence among the less skilled and unskilled workers. By going with Chipata to the labour office he represented the interests of the junior workers and thus was able to impart a sense of unity of support given by all the workers to the dispute. However, once the junior workers by their behaviour declared that they were against strike action, Meshak was no longer a dominant figure in the dispute.

With Meshak's withdrawal from a leading part in the dispute possibly because those among whom he had exercised power and influence had withheld their support, only Chipata and Lyashi remained dominant throughout the dispute. For most of the dispute, both co-operated with each other in mobilising and maintaining what support there was for the walk-out. It was only towards the end of the walk-out, when Chipata upon his return from his second visit to the labour office suggested that the strikers go back to work, that Lyashi presented himself in opposition to Chipata, demanding that the latter give some surety that their demands would be met. In doing this, Lyashi maintained the image of himself as a defender of his fellow workers' interests and as militantly opposed to management—an image which he had built up over the preceding weeks.

One feature of the competition for power and leadership in the factory is that not all the individuals who seek it are entirely self-reliant in that they possess access to or control over all the resources necessary for the exercise of power and leadership in the factory. The necessity for an individual to have access to or control over certain resources varies according to the expectations of those who are there to be led as well as according to the field of action in which an aspiring leader must exercise his power and influence. At the time of the 'Five-day working week dispute' Chipata and Lyashi were differentially placed in their access to or control over certain important resources. Chipata was a relative newcomer to the competition for power and leadership in the factory. In comparison with Lyashi (see table 5.1) Chipata's span of ties in the factory was considerably restricted. Furthermore, because he was a recent entrant to the competition for power and leadership, his stocks of approval were low, although as a result of his participation on the occasion of the earlier walk-out, many of the workers were beginning to recognise him as an individual valuable to the pursuit of their interests. The one factor clearly important, however, for Chipata's assumption of a leading part in the dispute was his political position as a branch official, a factor which was of even greater importance with the absence at the time of Zulu and Chisokone from the factory. Because of the extended field of action in which the dispute was cast, Chipata's active participation was crucial as he provided the link as a party branch political official through which the greatest influence could be exerted on the labour office to support the workers' claims. Furthermore, in terms of the immediate confrontation with Patel at the factory, Chipata as a representative of the political party exposed Patel to the uncertainty created by the political climate of the time. But on this occasion, unlike the earlier dispute over the introduction of a lunch break and a 1d increment, Patel failed to be impressed. He evinced no willingness to compromise in the face of his employees' demands.

Assuming that both Lyashi and Chipata were interested in achieving and maintaining a powerful and influential position in the factory both were dependent on each other. For Chipata, the backing which Lyashi gave him brought with it the support and approval of most of the senior and/or skilled workers. Through Lyashi's ability to mobilise the workers to take walk-out action Chipata's hand, as he saw it, was strengthened at the negotiating table at the labour office. Lyashi, alternatively, especially given the extended field of action and the high expectation among many of the senior and more skilled employees as to the efficacy of government pressure on Patel was dependent on the co-operative participation of Chipata, if Lyashi's leadership in the dispute was to have any success.

But the dispute yielded little reward for the employees. What were the results for the factory workers in general of the dispute and more specifically for the positions of those individuals, in terms of leadership and power, who had dominated much of the activities surrounding the dispute? The employees who had supported the dispute against Patel not only failed to win additional payment for Saturday morning work, which would have involved Patel's recognition of them as being on monthly contract, but also with Patel's removal of the basis upon which the dispute was launched—Saturday morning work—the factory employees actually lost out. With the loss of Saturday morning work, the employees now could work only forty hours a week instead of forty-five hours as before. Although this reduction in working hours involved a cost to all the factory workers, those employees who had not received the recent 1d increment were particularly hard hit. The cut in pay which the removal of Saturday morning work involved for the less skilled and unskilled workers generated the emergence of considerable hostility shown by them towards the senior and more skilled employees and particularly the major instigators of the dispute. But despite this hostility, one major effect of Patel's reaction to the dispute was the greater participation by the junior workers in action directed towards the rectification of wage and work conditions. However, that this was not the only cause of their later more militant action will become clear in the analysis of Phase III of the process of social action in the factory.

In the analysis of the dispute it was argued that there was agreement among the workers involved with Patel's extension of the relevant field of action to include other agencies such as the labour office and the union. Contrary to their expectations, the employees now perceived the representatives of the two agencies as working in the interests of management and opposed to them. This was not only expressed during the dispute, for instance by the workers gathered at the beer hall, but also and even more vehemently in the weeks following the dispute. Thus Lyashi, Nkoloya, Paulos, Lwanga, etc., accused the labour officer of acting like his European predecessors despite the fact that he was an African. The same men were even more hostile towards the union area organising secretary, who, they stated, should have at least consulted the workers before entering into negotiations with Patel. They blamed him for the agreement to remove Saturday work, an action to which, they claimed, they would never have consented. The dissatisfaction which the factory workers, in general, had towards the labour office and the union was in a later dispute, the 'February strike', to result in the adoption of a strategy by the employees which involved an attempt to restrict the relevant field of action to the factory, excluding the involvement of the union and labour office.

The failure of the workers to attain their objectives resulted in a cost to all the factory employees, and especially to those who had assumed a leading position in the dispute. Lyashi, in particular, suffered with the outcome of the dispute. Because of his failure in being instrumental for the achievement of wage improvements, he had not discharged his debt to those who had accepted his leadership and complied with his directives. But even more than this, he had not managed to win the support of the junior workers. It was Lyashi who had been chiefly responsible for focusing the dispute on the issue of Saturday pay, and, I suggest, that the choice of this issue was largely motivated by a hope of winning the support of the junior workers, not only to increase the pressure on Patel but also to gain their acceptance of his leadership. Patel's victory in the dispute acted against Lyashi's interests in two ways. First, Lyashi's brand of militancy attracted the hostility of the junior workers because of the costs they incurred through lost wages, and this was to impede his extension of relationships to them which would have the effect of consolidating his power. Second, Lyashi was later criticised by his peers for not focusing the dispute on issues more immediate to their own interests such as length of employment increments, end of service benefits and a greater pay differential in terms of skill. Lyashi's failure to win wage improvements for his peers led to a renewed challenge upon his position by others such as Nkoloya and Abraham on the basis of these more specific issues.

In terms of his ambition to achieve and secure a position of leadership and power, Lyashi lost out in another sense. This can be seen through reference to the rewards received by others, notably Meshak and Chipata, who were prominent at various stages of the dispute. Two points must be stressed. First, a position of power and leadership does not only receive legitimation through the winning of the compliance of others but also can be assisted by the recognition of an individual's power and leadership by those at the apex of the authority structure. Therefore, recognition by Patel of an employee's position of power and leadership can assist in the legitimation of the position of the individual concerned. It will be recalled from earlier discussions that those who are seen to be influential with Patel can present this influence in such a way as to win the support and compliance of their fellow workers. Before their fall from favour, Mukubwa and Chisokone used their influence with Patel to secure the compliance of the employees to their demands. Second, if Patel recognises an individual as being powerful, then there is an increased probability that he will bestow additional benefits on the person concerned, such as the advancement of greater sums of cash on credit, the award of a larger hourly wage or perhaps even promotion.

Following the 'Five-day working week dispute', Patel drew Chipata and Meshak into closer association with him. The amounts of credit which previously he had advanced to them were in the order of £5 to £6. Chipata's credit now rose to £10 and Meshak's to over £18. In addition, aware of the failure of Mukubwa and Hastings to control the workers, Patel began to use Chipata and Meshak in a supervisory capacity, asking them to assist in settling the occasional small disputes which broke out between the workers. Why did Patel choose to recognise Chipata and Meshak and not Lyashi? Perhaps the reasons are obvious. In the first place, their participation in the dispute was more noticeable to Patel than the action of Lyashi. It was Chipata and Meshak who were singled out from the group of disputants to represent them at the labour office, whereas Lyashi, although he was prominent, from Patel's perspective was more subsumed in the group of workers, all of whom were at times pressing their demands. Lyashi's prominence was obscured by the active and vocal participation of others such as Nkoloya, Abraham and

Lwanga. In other ways, too, from Patel's point of view, Chipata and Meshak were clear leaders. Patel was aware of Chipata's official position in the political party and the summons of Chipata to the labour office served to reinforce Patel's opinion that Chipata was an influential and powerful person. With reference to the factory context, Meshak was a more obvious leader in Patel's eyes than Lyashi. Unlike Lyashi, he was virtually unchallenged in his leadership over the less skilled and unskilled employees, and this became more noticeable with the absence of Chisokone from the factory for increasing lengths of time. On the few occasions when Meshak was challenged, as during event 27,[13] by Lyashi he was opposed on the basis that he supported younger workers against their elders. As the majority of the less and unskilled employees tended to be in the lower age categories these challenges made few damaging inroads into the basis upon which much of Meshak's power and influence rested.

But Patel did not choose to bestow his favours on Chipata and Meshak merely because they were obvious to him as leaders. By attempting to 'buy' them over to his side Patel could exert greater control over activities at the work place. In trying to win the support of Chipata, Patel could reduce the threat of political party and governmental intervention against his interests. This was a possibility, despite his success in the various confrontations with his workers, which Patel still viewed with considerable trepidation. Also, Patel by securing the allegiance of Meshak could maintain the division between the senior and junior workers, thereby reducing the chance of the factory workers' becoming united in opposition to him. That Patel attempts to create divisions between his employees in order to reduce the strength of their opposition to him will be more clearly demonstrated in the later description and analysis of the 'February strike'.

The closer association of Patel with Meshak and Chipata and his use of them in a supervisory capacity had some important consequences for the subsequent patterning of social relationships in the factory. This will be explored at length in the analysis in the next chapter. For present purposes it is sufficient to emphasise that in relation to Lyashi, the dispute registered a cost to him in terms of his position of power and leadership. Lyashi had failed to be instrumental in the securement of rewards which would compensate for the costs incurred by individuals as a result of their compliance with his directives.

.   .   .   .   .

[13] See the analysis of this event, pp. 264–5.

Throughout Phase II of the events discussed, the consequences of processes evident in Phase I of the events for the changing structure of the factory set of relationships emerged more clearly. The continued decline of the supervisors' power and influence was exemplified by their increased failure to exert their authority effectively over the workers. Chisokone, however, managed to restore some of his lost status by his action in the August walk-out whereby some of the employees received a 1d wage increment. An explanation for Chisokone's attempts to re-present himself as an individual concerned with the workers' interests was sought in his greater sensitivity to the pressures placed on him in comparison with the other supervisors. The analysis of the event 'Chisokone revealed' showed that Chisokone had more at stake than simply his ability to exert authority in the factory context. His political influence in township politics was also threatened by the possible leakage from the factory of information unfavourable to his political position in the township.

But Chisokone was soon to leave factory employment and with the continued decline in power of the other supervisors, and especially Mukubwa, the struggle between the senior workers over the redistribution of power intensified. Lyashi emerged most successfully from the competition and (as illustrated by the event 'Lyashi outlines a strategy for action') in subsequent events took a prominent part in the organisation of militant action by the employees in opposition to management. The emergence of Lyashi as a powerful figure in the factory is represented by the structure of his network on table 5.2 for the time period up to the beginning of September. The supervisors, Mukubwa and Chisokone, are also represented as powerful individuals in terms of table 5.2, but it must be recalled, as emphasised in chapter 5, that the various structural measures used for networks, and also the presentation of interactional relationships in matrix form, do not take account of the changing processes which have taken place within the time period for which the various indices used are relevant. It is partly to rectify some of the false impressions which these indices may convey and to introduce a greater sense of process into the description that the analysis of the changing structure of relationships in the factory in terms of a number of successive events has been made.

One of the central points of the argument in Phase II was that if the various competitors for power and leadership were to consolidate their positions, they had to demonstrate their effectiveness in gaining rewards in the form of wage and work improvements for the factory employees. Supply of these rewards provided the best opportunity for an individual of winning the compliance of both the senior and junior factory workers. With the intense competition for power and leadership it was expected, therefore, that increased pressure would be placed on management to grant certain concessions. Considerable evidence for this was shown in the description and analysis of the increasingly militant action culminating in the 'Five-day working week dispute'.

But the attainment of general wage and work improvements could not be achieved without the unity of all the workers in opposition to management. Although at first, despite the refusal of the junior workers to support strike action, some small concessions were granted by Patel the failure of the less skilled and unskilled workers to back the walk-out during the 'Five-day working week dispute' contributed to the failure of the strike action. However, other factors were important such as the pressures disadvantageous to their interests to which the workers were exposed as a result of their agreement to negotiate within an extended field of action.

Strategy in dispute, structural change and
        the quest for power and leadership III

Phase III: progress towards strike

Phases I and II were principally concerned with the rise to a position
of power and leadership of Lyashi. A combination of Mukubwa and
Chisokone's mismanagement of their own behaviour and of the strategies pursued by Lyashi and others led to the reduction in power and
influence of the two supervisors. Coupled with the decline in power of
the supervisors was the emergence of a strong unity between the more
senior employees which crystallised into the form of a clear opposition
between them and management and those seen by the senior workers as
representative of it. It was argued that much of this unity and many of
the disputes which arose were engendered by the competition for power
and leadership among the factory workers. However, in their opposition
to management the senior employees did not secure the active support
of those junior to them. Therefore, in the analysis of the final phase of
the development of social relationships in the factory I will examine
the processes which led to the development of more generalised support
for militant action which culminated in the 'February strike'.

But I first concentrate the analysis on the changing allegiances which
characterised the period following the 'Five-day working week dispute'.
The individuals who benefited most from the series of confrontations
with Patel were Chipata and Meshak, at least in terms of Patel's
recognition of their holding positions of leadership and power. Lyashi
and others, such as Nkoloya and Abraham, who had competed for
power and leadership and who had figured prominently in events
preceding and during the 'Five-day working week dispute', continued
in their competition, though a considerable proportion of their energies
was now being directed against Chipata and Meshak. But of equal
significance were the attempts by Hastings and particularly Mukubwa
to replenish their diminished resources of power and to align with the
factory employees in opposition to the management. The reasons for
this new alignment will be explained in the analysis to follow.

I begin with two events which illustrate the difficulties encountered
by Chipata and Meshak in their new found positions of leadership and

power, and the opposition to which they were exposed particularly from the senior workers.

Event 33   The stolen clothing dispute
5 November

Patel suspected that clothing was being stolen from the factory, and ordered a search to be made of all the workers. Meshak, Hastings and Mukubwa were delegated by Patel to stand by the door to search all the workers when they went out. Patel switched off the power to the sewing machines and ordered all the workers out of the factory. As the workers filed outside they were searched but it was Patel who discovered a women's blouse concealed in Adrian's pocket. Patel told Adrian to wait behind him and then addressed his employees in English. 'Anyone who takes clothes made here can leave employment. I will not tolerate clothing being stolen from the factory.' Patel then asked Chipata to interpret his statement to the workers which Chipata did. After some additional warnings Patel then told his employees to return to work.

Suspicion spread among the factory workers that Patel must have been tipped off that Adrian had taken a blouse. Mukubwa in conversation with Lyashi and Nkoloya informed them that it was Meshak who had told Patel of Adrian's felony. When pressed to give additional evidence Mukubwa stated that Meshak had first approached him with the information but that he (Mukubwa) had refused to have anything to do with it.

Once his employees were back at work Patel turned to Adrian and threatened him with the sack. At this point Mukubwa intervened and made excuses for Adrian and asked Patel to grant Adrian another chance. After a short discussion Patel agreed and allowed Adrian to return to work with a reminder that he would sack him the next time he stole clothing. Work now returned more or less to normal but gossip continued to circulate concerning Meshak's part as Patel's major informer. An aftermath of this event is that Patel now required the workers to be searched when they left work.

The following dispute is connected to the one above in that during it, reference is made to Chipata's part in the 'Stolen clothing dispute'. However, the main focus of the next event is an attempt by the senior workers and Nkoloya in particular to identify Chipata as in league with management against the interests of his fellow employees.

Event 34   Chipata is told his nickname
6 November

While at work Nkoloya and Abraham told Chipata that Patel referred to him as 'labour officer'. When Chipata asked them why, Nkoloya stated, 'You are always on Patel's side, that is why he calls you labour officer.'

Chipata now became extremely angry and told Nkoloya to return to work or else he (Chipata) would beat him. Patel noticed the argument and engaged Chipata in conversation asking him why he had been arguing with Nkoloya. To this question Patel was greeted with Chipata's angry retort, 'From now on I do not want you to tell me to go to the labour office to represent these people!' Chipata gestured towards the line 1 tailors, 'These people are disappointing me. If anyone here suggests that I am on the side of the labour officer I will knife him. This applies to anyone who disappoints me'. Patel enquired whether this threat also applied to him and Chipata assured him that it did. Patel laughed and walked away. Nkoloya now renewed his attack on Chipata. 'Why did Patel call you to address us on the occasion of Adrian's stealing of a blouse?' Chipata explained that he was only acting under orders from Patel. But Nkoloya was far from satisfied with Chipata's reply and asked outright how Patel had come to know that Adrian had stolen a blouse. Patel now intervened and stated that if the quarrelling continued the two workers must go outside. Nkoloya, now supported also by Lyashi and Abraham, agreed that the discussion should be continued outside the factory but Chipata showed distinct signs that he wanted to break off the engagement.

The majority of the factory employees had now stopped work and listened attentively to the argument. Chipalo, a Bemba who had joined the factory in August on line 2 as a tailor, called across to Chipata and Nkoloya stating that he was surprised to see two men who both came from the same rural area quarrelling. Mumba, an Nsenga who had begun work in the factory in September as a line 1 tailor agreed with Chipalo, stating that the quarrelling was evidence of the lack of co-operation between the factory employees. 'When Patel sees his workers failing to show respect to each other how can he respect and fear us?' Chipata, appearing to sense some degree of support, threatened all the workers, 'If people continued to threaten me like this no matter how often I am asked by you (meaning the employees) I will refuse to take your demands to the labour office.' As if to give further weight to his position Chipata declared that if anyone insulted him again he would fight him. 'I have lived a long time in Rhodesia and I know how to handle myself in a knife fight.' Chipata spoke first in CiCopperbelti and then repeated the same statement in Shona to demonstrate his facility with one Rhodesian language. Nkoloya and some of the other line 1 tailors including Lyashi and Abraham stated that they were amazed at Chipata's 'uncivilised' behaviour.

Chipata now openly challenged Nkoloya to state what he had done to improve the wage and work conditions of the factory employees. The argument now dissolved into a series of accusations and counter-accusations, Chipata claiming that Nkoloya and Lyashi had achieved nothing but never saying what he himself had achieved, and Nkoloya and Lyashi saying likewise. General interest in the quarrel now subsided and the employees gradually returned to work.

The above event illustrates the use by the factory employees of a number of concepts, many of which were discussed at some length in

Phase I, used either to render meaningful aspects of a dispute or to support their various actions and claims. Thus, Nkoloya, Lyashi and Abraham declared that Chipata's behaviour was 'uncivilised' with reference to Chipata's statement that he would fight anyone who impugned his behaviour, as Nkoloya did by suggesting that Chipata was acting against the employees' interests. Chipalo in mentioning that Chipata and Nkoloya should not be quarrelling referred to a generally expected form of behaviour that men from the same home area should be friends rather than enemies.

In the following analysis, however, the behaviour of the actors in these two events will be examined in order to achieve some insight into the developing process in the workplace both in terms of the individual competition for power and the growing unity which was emerging among all the factory employees, a unity which was expressing itself in the formation of new alliances. A suitable starting point is to explore the various explanations which would solve the problem of Meshak and Chipata's being singled out for attack. These explanations should solve the additional problem of Meshak and Chipata's receiving little support from the other workers. Three factors explain the considerable hostility shown towards Chipata and Meshak expressed particularly by the senior workers. These are, first, the compromising position in which they found themselves as a result of Patel's recognition and the form which this recognition took; second, the fact that Patel placed them in a position which necessitated a greater usage of their resources of power; and third, the threat which their new found power represented to the power and status of other factory workers.

Chipata and Meshak were placed in a compromising position by Patel. Although he used them on occasions in a supervisory capacity, as the 'Stolen clothing dispute' well demonstrates, they were not formally institutionalised into the position of supervisors. Unlike Mukubwa and Hastings,[1] whose work for most of the time involved them in supervisory duties, Chipata and Meshak were occupied for most of the working day in their usual tasks of line 1 tailor and button machiner respectively. The tensions to which Chipata and Meshak were exposed by virtue of their being drawn into an intercalary position as a result of Patel's occasional usage of them as supervisors were greater than those to which Mukubwa and Hastings were exposed. The latter were clearly defined by management and employee alike as supervisors and the

---

[1] Chisokone was now absent from work for longer periods than he was present; Hastings was now being used more regularly by Patel to carry out supervisory duties.

contradictory expectations focused upon them referred mainly to whether their loyalties lay with management or worker. The conflict produced by these contradictory expectations could be reduced either through an appeal of the nature that they were only doing their work and must follow the dictates of management; or through the maintenance of a set of relationships wherein the employees whom they supervised were in some way obligated to them, the workers complying with the supervisors' demands on the basis of their personal relationships with the latter; or a combination of both. An example of a supervisor using the requirements of his job to explain his apparent support of Patel is seen in the account of the 'Five-day working week dispute', where Mukubwa when questioned by Lyashi on his opinion about the walk-out stated, 'I can only do what I am told by Patel.'

In comparison with the supervisors, Chipata and Meshak were not as advantageously placed for reducing the conflict inherent in their new found positions. Neither was clearly defined as a supervisor either by Patel or his fellow workers. From the perspective of the employees, Chipata and Meshak's regular involvement in work similar to their own resulted in the factory workers' firmly classifying them as in the same structural position *vis-à-vis* management as themselves. Therefore, unlike the supervisors they could not as easily explain away some of their actions which could be construed by the workers as supportive of management interests.

Chipata and Meshak often willingly complied with Patel's demands to control the behaviour of the workers. Moreover, on at least two occasions prior to the above events when disputes over wage and work conditions arose, Chipata visited the labour office at Patel's suggestion. The purpose of both visits was to sound the opinions of the authorities concerned—as it turned out on both times these opinions supported Patel's standpoint. Nkoloya's comment to Chipata in event 34 that Patel called Chipata 'labour officer', although untrue, was a clear reference to the opinion held by many of the workers that Chipata was being used by Patel against their interests. Chipata's reply to Patel's enquiry why Chipata and Nkoloya were quarrelling when Chipata stated that he did not wish Patel to send him to the labour office in future, demonstrated his recognition of the implication in Nkoloya's comment. Why did Chipata and Meshak place themselves in the position whereby they were open to such antagonistic criticism from their fellows? An answer to this question will throw into relief an aspect of their position which influenced hostility to be directed towards them, especially when they were used in the part of supervisors.

When Patel recognised Chipata and Meshak as leaders worthy to be wooed he selected those who appeared immediately obvious to him as powerful individuals and not those such as Lyashi, Nkoloya and Abraham who in terms of their relationships with the factory employees and in their ability to affect and direct the behaviour of the workers were considerably more powerful. This is well borne out in table 5.1 for the time period ending at the beginning of September. The table shows that in comparison with Lyashi and to a lesser extent Nkoloya and Abraham, Chipata and Meshak had lower degrees of span, density and star multiplexity—the factors which I take as among the most indicative of the potentiality of an individual to exert power and influence. Moreover, Chipata and Meshak, were generally restricted in the degree to which they had entered into transactions with the other factory employees. Neither had built up an extensive set of relationships whereby they had managed to distribute goods and services to a large number of individuals which could not be repaid except through compliance. In acting occasionally as supervisors they demanded that some workers, who were in no way personally obliged to them, should comply with their demands. The senior workers were the least obliged to Chipata and Meshak in terms of their interactional relationships and they expressed considerable opposition to the attempts of either Chipata or Meshak to exercise authority over them. It will be recalled from an earlier argument that the period when Mukubwa, Chisokone and Hastings encountered difficulty in effectively exercising their authority as supervisors was when they had failed to maintain a degree of obligation to themselves in their personal relationships with the factory employees.

The relative weakness of Chipata's and Meshak's relationships, in terms of the limited extent to which the factory employees were personally obligated to them at the time of Patel's recognition of their leadership, largely explains the intense hostility to which they were subjected in the early stage of their new found positions. But more importantly the weakness of their relationships explains why both readily accepted the new demands, such as assistance in supervision, which Patel placed on them. Chipata and Meshak were faced with a dilemma. Association with Patel as described above generated the belief among the workers that Meshak and Chipata were on management's side. However, not to comply with Patel's demands to assist in supervision could have caused their fall from Patel's favour. There are two related reasons why Meshak and Chipata should have resolved the dilemma by opting for the choice whereby they readily complied with

Patel's demands. First, if they did not comply with Patel's demands they would lose what grip they had on a position of power and leadership in the factory. They would run the risk of Patel's withdrawing his recognition. Two effects could stem from this. In terms of their competition for power and leadership over the workers Chipata and Meshak, because of the relative weakness of their set of relationships, would be in a disadvantagous position especially with reference to those with stronger sets of relationships such as Lyashi, Nkoloya and Abraham. Furthermore, by refusing to comply with Patel's demands they could deny themselves the opportunity of receiving rewards such as a promotion or a wage increment. Although I have no definite evidence to support the following it is possible that Patel was looking for replacements for his supervisors. Patel was aware of Chisokone's imminent departure and he knew that Hastings would shortly retire to his home in Malawi. Patel's occasional use of Chipata and Meshak in a supervisory capacity could be viewed as a transitory phase preparatory to their full promotion to the position of supervisors.

The second reason why Chipata and Meshak should choose willingly to comply with Patel's demands was to strengthen their position of power and leadership in the factory. By demonstrating that they had influence with Patel, Meshak and Chipata could extend the number of relationships in which individual employees felt personally obliged to them. Thus, they could hold out promise that association with them and compliance with their demands would carry with it the promise of rewards such as promotion and protection from the threats of dismissal regularly made by Patel.

Although Chipata and Meshak chose to comply with Patel's demands, this decision placed them in the position where they at first regularly found their authority rejected by the majority of the employees. However, this was not always so. Both individuals and particularly Meshak were able to present their influence with Patel as a basis upon which to extend their relationships among the workers and earn their compliance. This compliance was given in return for the employees' expectation that they would receive at least protection from Patel's threats of dismissal, the opportunity for promotion and the possibility that Chipata and Meshak would use their new found influence with Patel to secure wage and work improvements. But by and large it was only the more junior workers in the factory who evidenced any marked compliance with either Chipata's or Meshak's demands.

However, like Mukubwa and Chisokone before them, Meshak and Chipata by having to exercise authority were placed in the position of using what power they possessed. They did not fulfil the expectations which the employees had of them and criticism of their actions, in the sense that neither Meshak nor Chipata had used their influence with Patel in the employees' interest, had become increasingly expressed by the time of the above two events. The ready acceptance of the employees of the rumour that Meshak had informed on his friend Adrian was a result of the growing belief among the workers that Meshak was opposed to their interests and would not fulfil their expectations of him. Nkoloya's quarrel with Chipata was evidence of this too but was also illustrative of an attempt on the part of Nkoloya and his work mates, Lyashi and Abraham, in particular, to pressure Chipata to fulfil the expectations which they had of him.

Two further aspects connected with the above events must be explored. First, both the gossip concerning Meshak and the attack on Chipata came from the senior workers. Moreover, the supervisors, notably Mukubwa, and the senior tailors on line 1 were apparently allied in their opposition to Meshak and Chipata. Why? Second, and this refers mainly to the dispute between Nkoloya and Chipata, not all the workers registered approval of Nkoloya's action. What were the reasons for this?

The gossip against Meshak and the attack upon Chipata cannot be seen purely in terms of their failure to fulfil their expectations. An earlier argument explained some of the opposition which Lyashi experienced in his rise to power in terms of the status threat which he presented to his peers on line 1. The gossip about Meshak and the attack on Chipata can be viewed in a similar way. Let me examine the gossip concerning Meshak first. Patel in his use of Meshak and Chipata in a supervisory capacity began transferring his dependency for the control of the work behaviour of the factory employees away from Hastings and Mukubwa. This was no doubt engendered by his aware-ness of the employees' opposition to Mukubwa and Hastings, described in the analysis of previous events and the failure of Mukubwa and Hastings effectively to exercise authority over the workers. The eleva-tion of Chipata and Meshak to a quasi-supervisory position and Patel's growing use of them presented a status threat to Mukubwa and Hastings. In effect by his action Patel was withdrawing his recognition of Mukubwa and Hastings and bestowing it upon Chipata and Meshak. Other actions of Patel reinforced this impression and Hastings and Mukubwa themselves were becoming increasingly aware of it. For example, Patel began to adopt a relationship of considerable familiarity with Chipata and Meshak but assumed a greater formality in his association with

Hastings and Mukubwa than had hitherto been evident. Moreover, previously, if relatives had called at the factory asking to see Mukubwa or Hastings, Patel had shown no objection to their leaving the premises and conversing with their visitors. Likewise, Patel would allow Hastings and Mukubwa to go on shopping errands in the town during working hours without any pay being deducted. Benefits such as these Patel now withheld, granting similar favours instead to Chipata and Meshak. Quite severe arguments between Patel and Hastings and Mukubwa now began to occur with increasing frequency. On one occasion, for instance, a relative of Mukubwa's entered the factory to talk with Mukubwa but Patel ordered him off the premises shouting that Mukubwa's relative had not asked permission. Mukubwa expressed his anger vehemently to Patel that a relative of his (i.e. Mukubwa) should receive such rough treatment. In his angry altercation with Patel, Mukubwa referred to what he considered to be his fall from Patel's favour, despite the long period of time he had served him.

Because Patel's recognition of the power and leadership of Meshak and Chipata involved a threat to the supervisors it was expected that they would engage in action to retrieve what they had lost. Furthermore, it was predictable that they should participate in action aimed at undermining the power of Chipata and Meshak while at the same time trying to re-establish a position of power and influence among the factory employees. It is in this light that Mukubwa's initiation of the gossip implying that Meshak was an informer against a workmate can best be understood. By this action he gained in at least two ways. He discredited Meshak among those employees whom the latter was mainly dependent for support. He also dissociated himself from complicity in Patel's decision to search the workers. He thereby indicated that he (Mukubwa) sided with the employees against management.

Other actions of Mukubwa during the 'Stolen clothing dispute' and in the weeks following show Mukubwa attempting to re-establish relationships with the employees on the basis of winning their compliance. Thus in the above dispute it was Mukubwa who interceded on Adrian's behalf in an attempt to influence Patel against acting on his threat to dismiss Adrian. In later weeks Mukubwa presented himself as responsible for a number of promotions. Henry's and Joseph's promotions from cotton boys to line 3 tailors were claimed by Mukubwa to be the result of his good offices and this claim was accepted by the two individuals concerned. Hastings also gave signs that he was concerned with the interests of the factory employees and on more than one occasion surprised the workers by engaging in heated argument with Patel. Hastings' need to achieve a strong position of power and leadership was particularly pressing if he was to be in a good bargaining position in his current negotiations with Patel for end of service pay.[2] At the time Patel failed to be impressed with Hastings' demands.

If Mukubwa and Hastings were to improve their relationship with Patel they had to demonstrate their power and leadership in the factory. In his behaviour Patel was showing signs that he valued the services of Chipata and Meshak above those of his supervisors. Therefore, to re-establish what they had lost in their relationship with Patel it was imperative that Mukubwa and Hastings demonstrate that they had control over resources which Patel valued, resources which they could then use in transaction with him in return for various benefits over which Patel had control. Patel's respect for Mukubwa and Hastings' skill and expertise in tailoring allowed them to continue to exert some influence on Patel. But this was not sufficient either to induce him to stop withholding some benefits which they had previously enjoyed, or, in the case of Hastings, to achieve some statement to the effect that future benefits would be forthcoming. Moreover, Mukubwa and Hastings had to reduce the threat to their status which Patel's recognition of Chipata and Meshak involved.

To return to the gossip concerning Meshak's alleged informing on Adrian: Mukubwa's scandalous comment about Meshak was readily accepted by the line 1 tailors and was used, no doubt as Mukubwa himself intended, to discredit Meshak in the eyes of the other workers. The information was easily digestible for Meshak, who worked opposite Adrian, would have been the person most likely to have observed Adrian stealing the blouse. I have no information which suggests that Meshak did in fact inform on Adrian but the truth or falsity of the gossip is hardly relevant to the argument.

Three effects of the gossip should be noted. First, it was used by individuals to further their specific individual and sectional interests. Second, as expressed in various reactions to it the gossip allowed for the re-affirmation of the workers' unity *vis-à-vis* management and the statement of norms of behaviour related to this unity. Finally, through it pressure was exerted on Meshak to give some evidence that he would discharge expectations which the employees had to him.[3]

[2] See chapter 4, p. 140.

[3] My analysis of gossip is guided by Gluckman's (1963) discussion of this form of behaviour. Gluckman takes account of both individual and community factors in his analysis of gossip and scandal. The following quotation illustrates this: 'Scandalizing is one of the principal means by which the group's

First I will examine the way the gossip against Meshak was used by individuals other than Mukubwa to further their own interests. It was the line 1 tailors who seized on the gossip and were responsible for its dissemination. Like the supervisors the line 1 tailors were presented with a status threat by Patel's recognition of Meshak. Here an employee who worked as a button machiner, an occupation which the line 1 tailors viewed as low in prestige (see table 2.3) was being treated by Patel in a manner which indicated to them that he regarded Meshak as higher in prestige or status than themselves. In terms of their own self-image it was important that Meshak should be put in his place. From this standpoint it is understandable, therefore, that the line 1 tailors should have so readily accepted Mukubwa's information and played a large part in spreading it throughout the factory. However, Meshak was not only a status threat to the senior workers as a whole, and those on line 1 specifically, but in terms of the competition for power and leadership he also presented a threat to the position of power which others such as Lyashi and Nkoloya had achieved. Should Meshak use his new found favour with Patel effectively he could by attracting followers reduce the power of workers like Lyashi and Nkoloya. It was then no surprise that Lyashi and Nkoloya should be main agents for the spread of the gossip. It enabled them to present Meshak as an informer who was actively working against the interests of the employees. By doing this Lyashi and Nkoloya attempted to show that Meshak was an individual with whom association would be unrewarding.

In the circulation of the gossip throughout the factory Meshak's alleged action was communicated and commented on from the standpoint that he had infringed on accepted norm of behaviour. This was, that an employee should never inform on a work mate, even less a friend (Meshak and Adrian being generally regarded as friends). One of the most frequent reactions to the information was that the workers should be united in opposition to management and that their objectives for the achievement of wage and work improvements could never be achieved if individual workers assisted management against the interests of their fellows. Thus the second point concerning the gossip about Meshak is borne out, for here the gossip became a vehicle for the expression of unity among the workers in opposition to the management.

The third point concerning the gossip is that it made Meshak aware

separateness is expressed, even though it is also the principal manner in which internal struggles are fought' (p. 312).

that he could not hope to maintain Patel's recognition of his leadership unless he showed that he could command the approval of the employees and control their actions. Patel was aware of the gossip and the current hostility being directed towards Meshak, and it is reasonable to suppose that unless Meshak could rectify things he would fall from a position of favour as quickly as he had risen to it. An aftermath of the 'Stolen clothing dispute' was that Meshak with greater frequency than previously began presenting the claims for wage and work improvements to Patel.

The attack on Chipata by Nkoloya has some aspects in common with the action surrounding the 'Stolen clothing dispute'. As already stated Nkoloya by accusing Chipata of being used by management against the employees' interests drew Chipata's attention to the expectation which the employees had of him that he would act in their interests. It is also of interest that it was Lyashi and Abraham who supported Nkoloya in his confrontation with Chipata. As in the case of Meshak, Chipata's recognition by Patel represented a status and a power threat to them. Nkoloya's implication that Chipata may also have informed on Adrian, contained in his question as to how Patel came to know of Adrian's theft was clearly aimed at discrediting Chipata before the workers. Chipata's reaction to the implied accusation whereby he threatened to fight anyone who dared insult him in such a way gave the line 1 tailors and notably Abraham and Lyashi an added opportunity to condemn Chipata. This they did on the grounds of his 'uncivilised' behaviour.

But Nkoloya's attack on Chipata did not receive the general support of the workers. To understand this a brief comparison will be made between the action in this event and the action surrounding the 'Stolen clothing dispute'. The gossip about Meshak was communicated and discussed behind his back, he was not openly confronted with it, although both he and Patel were aware of it. The divisions between the workers were not openly aired before Patel; however, in the instance of Nkoloya's quarrel with Chipata the divisions among the workers were overt and, as the description of the event illustrates, Patel himself took part in the quarrel. This explains why some of the workers expressed their disapproval of Nkoloya. As their action on previous occasions demonstrates, the factory employees believed that it was essential for them to present a united front before Patel and to conceal internal divisions. From earlier bitter experience they were all well aware of the advantage which Patel could take of divisions within their ranks. It is this consideration which explains the attempt first by Chipalo and later Mumba, both line 1 tailors, to stop the quarrel by their showing of disapproval.

Broadly, the action surrounding the two events grew out of a process involving various structural changes in the factory connected with earlier events. Patel's recognition of Chipata and Meshak as leaders in the factory following the 'Five-day working week dispute' and his use of them in a supervisory capacity not only had consequences for the relationships which these two employees had with their workmates but also was a major factor contributing towards a shift of the supervisors, Mukubwa and Hastings, from a position of neutrality or apparent alignment with management to an alignment with the other workers in opposition to management. This shift in the supervisors' alignment was probably inevitable, for the failure to win the willing compliance of the employees was making their task as supervisors virtually intolerable. As explained earlier, the change in Hastings and Mukubwa's alignment was accelerated by Patel's elevation of Chipata and Meshak, with its consequent threat to the status of the supervisors. Mukubwa's behaviour in the 'Stolen clothing dispute' is an illustration both of his new alignment with the employees, evidenced in his initiation of the gossip against Meshak, and his attempt to re-establish himself in a position of power, one aspect of which is seen in his successful intervention on behalf of Adrian. Patel's action in recognising Chipata and Meshak as leaders was aimed at increasing his control over the behaviour of the factory employees. But it was to have unintended consequences which were to militate against his interests as the later analysis of the 'February strike' will demonstrate. Far from increasing his control over the workers his action, by forcing Mukubwa and Hastings to join forces with the factory employees, strengthened the workers' bargaining position.

Both the 'Stolen clothing dispute' and the event 'Chipata is told his nickname' reveal an expression among the workers of the need for unity in opposition to management. This is evidenced by the speed with which the gossip concerning Meshak was accepted and by the general condemnation which he incurred. Likewise in Nkoloya's quarrel with Chipata the former met with some disapproval because he revealed before Patel the presence of internal divisions between the workers. The growth of an expression of the need for unity was present among all sections of the factory force and was a response to the new privations which the employees were now feeling as a result of Patel's earlier successes. The reduction of the working week to forty hours following the 'Five-day working week dispute' and the cessation of

Saturday morning work, resulted in a loss of pay, particularly for those who had not received the 1d increment. All workers were now demanding wage increases and were attempting to exert pressure on Patel to initiate some wage improvements. That the more junior workers were now involved in this kind of action whereas prior to September only the more skilled and/or senior workers had been involved was also partly the result of the pressures which were being placed on them by the senior workers. The reasons for this development will become clear subsequently. The development of unity among the employees in opposition to management received added impetus from the increasing awareness that their links to other agencies such as government departments, the political party and the union would be of little assistance to the achievement of their various demands. In his quarrel with Nkoloya, Chipata's threat of discontinuing his representation of their demands to the labour office met with almost no response. The reason for this was the growing belief among the workers that the labour officer would not act in their interests, an attitude sparked off by their failure to win the support of the labour officer during the 'Five-day working week dispute'.

The two events which have been analysed show too the continuation of the competition between the senior employees for power and leadership. The action of Nkoloya especially and Lyashi and Abraham was aimed at their presentation of themselves as the major spokesmen of employee interests. In the weeks prior to and following the two events all three of the above individuals attempted to increase or maintain a position of power and influence in the factory. Lyashi, however, was the most successful despite the setback which he incurred as a result of the 'Five-day working week dispute' and as matrix 2 and table 5.2 indicate was able to extend his relationships in the factory. Furthermore, his relationships now not only embraced the more senior workers but also included some of the junior workers noticeably a number of the cotton boys. Lyashi's extension of his relationships to include the workers junior to him was part of a general pattern observable among the senior employees (see matrix 2). The significance of this for social action in the factory will be discussed later in the analysis.

So far I have set the two events analysed in the context of processes set in motion through action and events which occurred prior to them. I will now briefly consider the influence which both the 'Stolen clothing dispute' and 'Chipata is told his nickname' had on subsequent action in the factory. First, the pressure of opinion expressed in these two events brought to the realisation of Chipata and Meshak the importance of securing the support of the factory employees. If the employees, as they did on these occasions, vented hostility towards them then Chipata and Meshak would run the risk of falling from Patel's favour. Patel's selection of them as leaders stemmed considerably from his belief that they could exercise control over the behaviour of the employees. In order to exercise control then, Chipata and Meshak had to demonstrate to the employees that compliance with their demands could reasonably be expected to furnish future rewards. A direct result of the events, therefore, was that Chipata and Meshak began more openly to declare that they were concerned with assisting the other workers to achieve their demands. Thus Chipata and Meshak were drawn into the position of declaring more positively their alliance with the factory employees in opposition to management.

Second, Patel's action following the 'Stolen clothing dispute' whereby he initiated a daily search of the workers added to their grievances. By such an action he imparted the distinct impression to the employees that he did not trust them. This was particularly galling to the senior workers many of whom had worked for many years in the factory and as older men felt that they were deserving of some respect from Patel. For them to be searched represented an indignity for, as many of them stated, Patel was treating them like children. But of even greater importance the introduction of a daily search represented a tightening of the restriction which Patel now placed on his employees. Prior to the event the factory workers often took small quantities of cotton and material left over from the day's work to their homes. Here they were used either to make up small articles of clothing on the workers' own sewing machines or to patch up clothing which had fallen into disrepair. Patel was aware of this and had hitherto taken no action to prevent the practice.[4] Patel's tacit condoning of this behaviour had, I suggest, arisen in response to his need to control the work behaviour of his employees. It was part of Patel's transactional relationship with his workers that he permitted this practice in return for their compliance with his demands to perform their respective work tasks according to his expectations. The institution of the daily search involved Patel's clamping down on the practice of taking cotton and material from

[4] This form of behaviour has some similarity with an aspect of the indulgency pattern described by Alvin Gouldner (1965: 18–22) in his study of a gypsum plant in the U.S.A. The effects of Patel's new restriction in that it had some connection with increased agitation by the workers for wage and work improvements which reached a head with the 'February strike' also has a marked similarity with the move to strike action by the workers at the gypsum plant following the removal of the indulgency system.

the factory and was symptomatic of the greater control over work activities which he now perceived himself as having. Previous events had indicated to him that the workers were unlikely to receive much support from government, the political party, the labour office or the union; if anything, representatives of these bodies on earlier showings were more likely to support him rather than his employees. However, consideration of this factor must not obscure another possibility which may have influenced him to take such action. In the weeks prior to the 'Stolen clothing dispute' Patel had been subjected to considerable militant action on the part of his employees and especially the senior workers. It was these workers, because they were skilled tailors most of whom possessed their own sewing machines, who stood to lose most through Patel's action to stop the taking of material and clothing from the factory. In the walk-outs which had occurred these employees had withdrawn one most important element of their transactional relationship with Patel, their labour. Patel responded, therefore, by revoking one aspect of his transactional relationship with his employees, the condoning of their taking cotton and material from the work place.

Whatever the reasons behind Patel's putting a stop to this practice his action exacerbated the tensions already present between management and workers and accelerated the inevitable process towards further militant action on the part of the factory employees.

This then was the situation before the 'February strike'. Patel's recognition of the leadership of Chipata and Meshak presented a status threat to Hastings and Mukubwa. This, in combination with his withdrawal of certain benefits which had previously been a feature of his transactions with them, led Mukubwa and Hastings to enter the competition in the factory for power and leadership, in order to re-establish their position in the factory. This necessitated their alignment with the workers in opposition to management. Chipata and Meshak, through the pressure exerted on them by the employees, were also forced into a more open alignment with the other workers. In response to the demands to consolidate their power in the factory some of the employees, notable among them Lyashi, extended their relationships to include workers both skilled and unskilled, junior and senior at the work place. It must also be noted that this was part of a general pattern, involving as well individuals who at the time were not competing for power and leadership in the factory. As a result of this extension of relationships all members of the factory work force became more closely bound into a common set of relationships. Finally, the majority of the workers, irrespective of skill or seniority expressed the desire for unity in opposition to management for the pursuit of common aims in the securement of wage and work improvements.

On 15 February 1966 the factory workers called a strike and demanded a monthly increase of £1 on their present wages. Lyashi, as on earlier occasions, was one of the main protagonists for strike action.

Event 35   The February strike
15 February

On the morning of the 15th Lyashi, Chipata, Nkoloya and Abraham, arrived early at the factory and stated to the incoming workers that they were going on strike for higher wages. By the time work was due to begin all the workers were seated or standing outside the factory. Patel came out of the factory and demanded to know why his employees had not started work, he was met with cries that work would not begin unless he agreed to increase their wages. For a short time Patel entered into discussions with Lyashi, Chipata, Nkoloya and Abraham who had presented themselves as the workers' major spokesmen. It soon became clear to Patel that work would not start and he left to consult his partners at the store. One of the partners, Badat, a younger and more smartly dressed man than Patel, approached the employees and stated that they could not hope for a wage increase if the workers persisted in such action. Badat was greeted with angry shouts of defiance and went to consult with Patel who meanwhile had withdrawn into the background. After a moment Badat returned to where the workers were gathered and informed them that he would now call the labour officer to come to the factory. At this Lyashi shouted that the employees would refuse to deal with the labour office. 'The dispute is between Patel and us.' Nevertheless, despite this protest, Badat left the factory, soon to return in his cream Ford Zephyr, accompanied by the labour officer. This immediately confirmed the workers' impression that the labour officer was in league with management. Upon the arrival of the labour officer the four workers who had presented themselves as the major spokesmen were summoned by Badat to discuss the dispute inside the factory. I was not present at these discussions, but some pressure must have been placed on the workers involved for when they came out some ten minutes later Lyashi stated that Patel would agree to a wage increase and that the employees should return to work.

At this point it is important to state that while the negotiations were taking place inside the factory a few of the workers had begun to move away, ostensibly to do some window shopping in the nearby shops. They were herded back by Nkumbula, Kamwefu and Mumba, all line 1 tailors. Kamwefu and Mumba were especially prominent in the discussions between the workers which went on outside. Mumba particularly attracted attention by intermittently singing out UNIP political slogans, 'United we stand, divided we fall', 'Freedom and labour'.

Lyashi's statement that the employees should return to work met with mingled cries of anger and surprise, nevertheless Lyashi continued in his attempts to convince the workers that they should recommence work. By placing himself at the head of the main body of employees and facing the labour officer Lyashi tried to reduce the extent of the hostility directed at him as a result of making an unpopular suggestion; a suggestion which was all the more unpopular because as yet no definite agreement had been reached. At one and the same time Lyashi was trying to influence action in a direction which was in the interests of management and the labour officer while attempting to impart the impression that he was opposed to them.

At this stage Hastings came to the fore stating that on no account should the employees return to work until a definite agreement for a wage increase had been reached. Mumba supported Hastings. He declared that the four men who had negotiated with the labour officer should not be regarded by the employees as their spokesmen. 'We are all equal and we have no special representatives. We, each and every one of us, speak for the situation here. One Zambia, one nation.'

With Lyashi's failure to influence a return to work, the labour officer now tried his hand. He stated that if work started he would consult the union area organising secretary about a wage increase. This statement met with shouts of protest to the effect that the current dispute in no way involved the union. At this the labour officer went back inside the factory to consult further with Patel and Badat. Shortly all three came out and the labour officer stated he was leaving but that he wanted some of the workers to accompany him to the labour office to continue negotiations. Significantly, the labour officer indicated that he wanted Nkoloya, Lyashi and Abraham to join him. They agreed and left with him in Badat's car. Patel followed soon after in his car which he left parked at the side of the factory. Like the labour officer, Patel was accompanied by three employees: Mumba, who had pressed himself forward as a representative of the employees, Chipata, whom Patel had asked to join him, and Coliat, a new recruit to the factory. Coliat had joined as a line 3 tailor the previous week and like Mumba presented himself as a major spokesman for the employees.[5]

The remaining workers waited at the factory an hour before their six representatives returned. While their representatives were gone the workers joked and talked among themselves about the morning's activities sharing observations concerning the major participants in the dispute. Most of their comments referred to the behaviour of the labour officer. A few examples will suffice to give the general flavour of these comments.

[5] Coliat had been employed in Narayan Bros. before, and was well known to the senior employees and Patel. Patel, in fact, regarded Coliat as a highly skilled tailor. Coliat was employed on line 3, as Patel did not have a place for him on line 1. From evidence I collected it was clear that during his previous employment Coliat had played an important part in factory politics, and his action on this occasion can be interpreted as an attempt to re-establish his former position. Because Coliat was employed only shortly before the February strike and my fieldwork ended soon after I have not been able to make a full assessment of his role in the activities. However, it should be stressed that as far as I could observe he only played a relatively minor part.

Paulos and Mpundu, both line 2 tailors, remarked about the lack of respect which the labour officer showed towards the senior workers in the factory. At one time in the morning's activities the labour officer had singled out Hastings and told him to stop talking. In doing so the labour officer addressed Hastings in the diminutive *iwe* (you) instead of the respectful *imwe*, a term more appropriate to a man of Hastings' age. Paulos commented on this in conversation with Mpundu. 'The labour officer has no respect for big men (*ba mudala*). He was even telling a big man like Hastings, '*Iwe* stop talking.' Paulos then went on to state that he could not understand why the labour officer had not been severe with Patel. 'He [the labour officer] knows very well that if Patel hadn't been in the wrong we shouldn't have gone on strike.'

Mateo, another line 2 tailor who was standing nearby, proffered the explanation that the labour officer was probably in Patel's and Badat's pay. Hastings remarked to a group of cotton boys that African labour officers were no different from the European labour officers before them. 'This is why the Indians boast that our government will not do anything for us.'

Other workers discussed with each other what they would do if the strike was not called off soon. Enoch, a line 1 tailor, stated to his friends that a long period out of work would not bother him. He added that if the strike lasted for any length of time he would take to fish selling. Chipalo and Kamwefu both agreed that their private tailoring business would see them through any immediate financial worries.

The strategy which the workers should adopt in their dispute was also discussed. Most of the employees agreed that they should stay out on strike until a definite wage increase was achieved. Kamwefu addressed his workmates saying that the negotiations should involve only themselves and Patel. He stated that, despite Patel's short temper, if they bargained with him he would soon agree to a wage increase if only to get them back to work.

During the discussions Patel arrived back at the factory—he had only been away approximately five minutes—and bantered with his workers. At one time he shouted at Hastings, 'Hey, *ba kalamba*, you are a sick man—when are you going to leave work?' Shortly after this Hastings was walking towards the factory gate when Patel again shouted to him, 'Where are you going, back to Malawi?'

The general conversations between the workers came to a halt, however, with the return of their representatives. Chipata, Lyashi and Abraham kept a pointed silence while the labour officer addressed the employees. He repeated what he had said earlier, emphasising that if they returned to work the union would be called in to negotiate a wage increase. Nkoloya and Mumba loudly expressed their opposition to this suggestion. 'It is no use to call in the union—we will not listen to it. We have formed our own union here and we are the people who should negotiate the wage increase.' At this the labour officer left. Badat drove him back to his offices. Soon after, Badat returned and stated that despite the employees' opposition the management and the labour officer would discuss the dispute with the union area organsiing secretary. He then told the workers to leave for their homes and return to the factory the next morning to hear the result of the meeting. At this the workers dispersed and went their various ways, some meeting later in the day at the beer hall to discuss the strike.

The next morning—Wednesday. When the employees arrived at the factory they were met by a new labour officer. (He was the assistant of the one who had attempted to settle the strike the previous day.) Accompanying him was the union area organising secretary. The labour officer informed the workers that their strike was illegal unless it had the support of the union. As the employees had not entered into prior negotiations with the management through the union, they could not expect the support of the government. Like his predecessor, the new labour officer suggested that the workers return to their jobs and allow their union to negotiate a wage increase. But the employees stood firm in their opposition. Lyashi addressed the workers, emphasising that they should not be concerned about the illegality of their action. 'We cannot rely on assistance from the union. In the past it has completely failed to achieve our demands.' Lyashi then turned to the union area organising secretary, 'You can leave. This case is in our hands alone.'

Badat, Patel, the labour officer and the union area organising secretary now conferred among themselves. The labour officer turned on the union area organizing secretary and accused him of covertly influencing the workers to stay on strike. Patel suggested that they contact the union president in Kitwe to come down and negotiate.

Meanwhile Hastings addressed all the employees. He stated that no one should return to work unless an agreement for a wage increase was definitely reached. To support his view he recounted the past history of management–worker relations in the factory—how Patel always promised them wage increases but never fulfilled his promises. Hastings gave them evidence of the utility of firm strike action and told them how in 1956 when Paul Kalichini headed the union a strike was called by the Narayan Bros. workers and wage increases won.

The labour officer left soon after he had completed his discussions with Patel and Badat. He was driven to the labour office by Badat. The latter soon returned and informed the workers that either they return to work immediately or else be signed off the next day. Mumba now addressed the workers and declared that they should not be shaken by this threat and should continue with the strike. His statement was met with handclapping and cheers of approval. Pleased with the impression he had made Mumba followed up his statement with a threat of his own, that anyone who returned to work would be beaten. This also met with cheers and handclapping.

The employees now began to move away from the factory. Badat shouted after them that they could not hope for any assistance from the government. None of the workers took much notice, save to shout back at Badat that they would be at the factory at 10.00 a.m. the next day to be signed off and to receive the pay owed them.

The afternoon saw much the same pattern as on the previous day, with the employees visiting each other to discuss the morning's activities. However, on this day Chipata and Lyashi were much more dominant. Chipata, Mulondo and Mumba visited the Mine Farms where they joined Nkoloya to discuss the strike. Chipata shortly left this group of workers and went on a tour of all the township areas checking to see if any worker intended to strike break. He ended at Bwacha beer hall where he joined a large group of workers which included Mukubwa, Edward, a line 2 tailor, Joshua, also on line 2, Ben, a line 3 tailor, Mubanga, a cotton boy and John, an ironer. Later Paulos, a line 2 tailor, joined the beer drinking group. All declared their intention to refuse a return to work until a wage increase of £1 had been granted to all of them. There was considerable gossip about some of the workers who either at the factory or elsewhere had not publicly affirmed their support of the action. Mubanga suggested that the reason Nkumbula, a line 1 tailor, stayed in his home drinking beer and was not joining them in the beer hall was that he was brooding over his lost wages and was worried about the possibility of being given the sack. Joshua said, 'Ya, Ya. Some people haven't said a single word at any of our meetings with the management!' After various comments such as these the drinking group broke up and the workmates returned to their homes.

Like Chipata, Lyashi also did the rounds of the townships checking on the opinions of the employees and receiving reaffirmation of their support for the strike.

The strike enters its third day—Thursday morning. On the previous evening Nkoloya and Lyashi had visited Chipata's house and persuaded him to visit the Resident Minister to secure his support before the employees met management at 10.00 a.m. the following morning. Thus before 10.00 a.m. Chipata went to see the Resident Minister but to his surprise he was lectured by the latter on the irresponsibility of the workers' action. When he arrived at the factory Chipata told his work companions of his failure to win the Resident Minister's support.

The meeting with management was similar to that of the day before and the same workers again played a major part as spokesmen. However, Patel and Badat did not sign off the employees as threatened. Instead they wanted to discuss the matter further with the union and the labour office. They did add, nevertheless, that unless the workers returned to their jobs soon the factory would be closed down completely.

In the afternoon one of the Political Assistants to the Resident Minister visited Chipata at his home to inform him that the Resident Minister wished to address the strikers at his office the next morning.

Chipata immediately left to call on five of his work companions to discuss the line they should adopt in their meeting with the Resident Minister. The individuals he called on were Nkoloya, Lyashi, Lwanga, Kamwefu, Hastings and Mukubwa. Chipata organised that they should meet at Mukubwa's house that evening.

At the evening meeting Chipata explained that no strike committee had yet been formed and that those gathered should regard themselves as being henceforward the members of the strike committee. Chipata then

went on to display his fears. He stated that he expected the Resident
Minister to order them back to work before a definite wage increase had
been arranged. He went on to emphasise that on no account should any
of them agree to this. Lyashi then rose and reiterated what Chipata had
already said. He added, 'There might be some men who will break our
strike. These men should be warned that they will be beaten.' Lwanga
now said his piece and focused his attention on the union. 'I propose that
any intervention by the union should be rejected.' Others rose and re-
stated what had been said. During the meeting a number of other workers
who had heard about it arrived at Mukubwa's house and these included
Paulos, Meshak, Mubanga, Enoch and Abraham. At the close of the
meeting Chipata announced that all the employees were to meet the
Resident Minister at 8.00 a.m. the next day. He asked that those present
should search out their friends from the factory and ask them to be at the
Resident Minister's office by 7.00 a.m. so that general agreement could
be reached about the course of action.

The fourth day of the strike—Friday morning. The workers arrived at the
Resident Minister's office an hour before their scheduled meeting with
the Resident Minister was due to begin. All appeared to be in agreement
that, despite anything the Resident Minister might say, they would
remain on strike until a wage increase had been settled.

Before the Resident Minister arrived Chipata, Lyashi and Nkoloya
were called into the Political Assistant's office. Here Chipata was told that
unless he used his influence to end the strike he risked being stripped of
his official position in the political party.

Later at the meeting with the Resident Minister, the workers were
admonished for their behaviour and as expected were urged to return to
work. The workers all declared their refusal to return unless they achieved
their demands of a £1 increase in their wages. The Resident Minister then
informed them that the President of the union had been summoned from
Kitwe to discuss their demands with them. Some of the workers registered
their disapproval of this information but many felt that the union president might take a stronger stand than the area organising secretary in
negotiation with the factory management. The workers were told that they
should meet their union president at the factory at 10.00 on Saturday
morning.

The strikers meet the president and the strike is called off. On Saturday
morning the union president opened the meeting by explaining his
activities before his arrival at the factory. He told them that he had met
with the Resident Minister, the factory management and the labour
officer and that a compromise agreement had been reached whereby the
workers would receive a 10s increase on their monthly wages instead of
£1. The wage increase, he added, would not become effective until March.
At this Enoch stood up and declared that it was unacceptable as everyone
had sworn that they would not return to work until they received an
immediate wage increase. 'This is just another example of Indian trickery.'

Lyashi supported Enoch, stating that work could not be resumed until the £1 increase had been granted. 'Why should we give in to these Indian foreigners? Let them close the factory.' Hastings demanded that the workers be given a written document to the effect that the 10s increase at least, would be honoured. The union president now repeated the compromise agreement and stated that the government would make things rough for the employees if they did not return to work. Many of the workers now began to express their doubts about continuing the strike. Kamwefu suggested that in view of what the union president had said they should all return to work on Monday and that if the increase did not appear to be forthcoming then they should call another strike. His suggestion met with considerable agreement. But before the meeting broke up some of the senior workers took the opportunity to declare that their demands were not just for a general wage increase. Hastings mentioned that they wanted end of service pay. Lyashi, Abraham and Nkoloya called for some consideration to be made for greater wage differentials according to skill. However, many of the employees were now leaving for their homes and the union president said that they should place their grievances through the normal union channels.

Analysis. The 'February strike' was a dramatic enactment of the new solidarity of the employees *vis à vis* the factory management, the unity of the workers emerging from a series of past choices and actions already discussed in relation to earlier events. The strike was only ended after the application of the strongest governmental, political and union pressure. This illustrates the unity which had developed among the employees as a result of the growth of uniform grievances, the spread of social relationships involving both senior and junior employees in a common set of ties and the emergence of new alignments whereby all the workers including the supervisors were opposed to management. The last two factors are probably of the greatest significance in explaining the unity of support given to the strike action which was maintained over four days in spite of the strength of the forces marshalled against the employees.

The importance of the extension of a set of ties embracing both senior and junior workers alike is highlighted when the state of affairs at the time of the 'February strike' is contrasted with that at the time of the 'Five day working week dispute'. One of the major reasons for the failure of the senior workers effectively to sustain their strike in this latter dispute was their failure to command the support and control the action of the less skilled and unskilled employees. This was directly related to the fact that at this time the senior workers had entered into few transactions with the junior employees. They had few personal ties through which they could pressure them to conform to a specified chosen line of action. Viewed from another perspective, the absence of ties binding the junior workers more closely to the senior employees meant that the junior workers were not afforded the protection against dismissal which the involvement in a set of ties which included the senior workers could bring. After September the senior workers began to extend their relationships into the ranks of the junior employees. This process was not, I argue, so much in response to the general need of the senior workers to control the actions of the workers junior to them so as to be more effective in militant action against Patel, as it was a response of each of the senior workers concerned to consolidate their positions of power and leadership.

Earlier it was argued that there were pressures operating within the ranks of the senior workers which operated against any one individual's achieving the clear recognition by his peers of his dominance in terms of power and leadership. A pattern which was clearly evident among the senior workers was the transference of their support and approval from one of the major competitors for power to another. The main reason explaining this was that for one of the senior workers to receive the clear recognition of his power and leadership from his fellows would result in the status of those who so recognised him being reduced in the eyes of the other factory employees. The regular transference of support and approval was facilitated by the fact that there was little except for the promise of wage and work improvements which a senior worker could offer his peers which the latter did not already have access to or control over. However, the less skilled and especially the unskilled employees did present an opportunity for the senior workers to consolidate their positions of power and leadership. A senior worker could offer various rewards to these employees which he could not offer his peers. These rewards included not only the opportunity to learn or increase one's skill, and perhaps protection from the threats of Patel but also the chance for a junior worker to increase his status among those placed in a similar position to himself. Association by an individual of low status with individuals who are generally regarded as of high status can have the effect of increasing the status of the former among his peers.

The extension of ties into the ranks of the junior workers also had the effect, described in chapter 2, of increasing their conformity to the informal norm restricting the number of hours worked established among the senior employees.

The alignment of all the factory employees against the management placed the workers in the strongest position in which they had yet been over the period of observations. There were no apparent open divisions

among the workers which could be exploited by Patel to his own advantage as he had done on previous occasions. Furthermore, the supervisors'
support of strike action presented these workers with an opportunity to
exert pressures on management which had hitherto not been possible.
It will be recalled that during the walk-out described in 'The five-day
working week dispute' the inability of the employees to gain the support
of Mukubwa considerably weakened their bargaining position. In the
words of Lwanga who commented on Hastings' radical position during
the present strike, 'No matter that Hastings is from Malawi, he has influence with Patel and this could help us to get our wage increase.'
For the factory employees the support of the supervisors was regarded
as a means through which additional pressure could be exerted on Patel
to concede their demands. From Patel's point of view the opposition
of the supervisors to him deprived him of individuals who could present
his opinion to the employees and perhaps influence them to return to
work. It was in this way that Patel used Hastings during 'The five-day
working week dispute'.

I will now examine two aspects of the action surrounding the strike.
First, the conditions which led to the maintenance of the alliance between the strike leaders in opposition to management. Their alliance
was maintained despite pressures which militated against it. These
arose from their competition with each other for a greater share of power
and leadership over the factory employees and the dilemmas which
confronted the strike leaders arising from the mixed motives involved in
their seeking acceptance of their power and leadership. Second, the
various strategies pursued by management and worker in the dispute to
secure the strongest position from which to bargain.

In the period leading up to the strike all those who initially assumed a
position of leadership, Lyashi, Nkoloya, Abraham and Chipata, had been
intense competitors with each other for power and leadership. This
competition did not cease with the strike and there was considerable
evidence, particularly during the initial stages of the strike, of their
competition for a prominent place in the proceedings. The necessarily
shortened account of the strike provides illustration of this. Thus upon
the return of the strike leaders from the first round of negotiations with
the labour officer and management, Lyashi tried to assume the greater
part of the leadership by urging the workers to return to work. That
Lyashi should attempt an action so unpopular, as it turned out, in spite
of the way he presented himself to the workers, points to the other
factor which threatened to bring the strike leaders into opposition.

In this chapter and in chapter 4 I emphasised that the individuals who compete for power and leadership do so in terms of a set of mixed motives. For example, they compete for power and leadership for the increased status which it brings in itself. But they also compete for leadership in an attempt to achieve the recognition of Patel. This recognition may bring rewards such as a wage increment, promotion or increased credit facilities. It is clear also that Patel's acknowledgment of an individual's leadership may feed back assisting the person concerned to further consolidate a position of status and power. It was Patel's recognition of Chipata which was one factor enabling the latter to strengthen his position in the factory.

My information is incomplete as to what happened inside the factory at the time of the first round of negotiations, but I suggest that Lyashi saw his opportunity to receive Patel's recognition in an attempt to use his power and influence to convince the employees to return to work. But the workers' disapproval of Lyashi's behaviour gives some insight into why erstwhile competitors formed an alliance throughout most of the strike. None of the leaders at the initial stage of the strike could by himself control the action of the factory employees. Each in fact was dependent on the other. In terms of their relationships in the factory none of them could claim the clear support of the other employees. Lyashi at the time of the strike had one of the largest spans of relationships in the factory (see table 5.2), Mukubwa, as in September, continuing to have the largest span. But, Lyashi was not alone in having an extensive span of relationships. Many of his competitors also had increased their span of relationships by the time of 'The February strike'. Moreover, many of the individuals with whom Lyashi had the strongest relationships were also strongly connected to those against whom he competed (see matrix 2). Without the support of the other individuals who had assumed leadership of the strike Lyashi could not hope to achieve the unopposed loyalty of the factory workers. Indeed, the momentary withdrawal from the action by Chipata, Nkoloya and Abraham during Lyashi's address of the employees was tantamount to their withholding of support from him. No doubt it contributed to the intensity of the opposition expressed towards Lyashi.

It could be argued that Chipata, Nkoloya and Abraham by withholding their support furthered their interests in terms of their competition with Lyashi for it had the effect of contribution towards Lyashi's loss of approval from the factory employees. But this explanation is not entirely satisfactory in terms of the data collected. If they had supported Lyashi it might not have been against their interests. Chipata, for instance, could have further consolidated his recognition as a leader in the eyes of

Patel, and Nkoloya and Abraham could also have earned Patel's acknowledgment of their leadership. However, at this stage in the development of the factory's social relationships it was uncertain whether even if they had allied to force a return to work they would have had sufficient power to so so. By February other individuals had begun to show prominence in the competition for power and leadership, such as Hastings, Mukubwa, Mumba and Kamwefu. Table 5.2. and Matrix 2 indicate greater strength in a number of individuals' personal relationships. In particular Mumba, Kamwefu and Hastings had extended the span and transactional multiplexity in their relationships by time 2 compared with time 1.

The costs of an alliance of the four individuals who had assumed leadership to force a return to work at the initial stage of the strike far outweighed the possible gains. Assuming that the strikers could have been persuaded to return to work early in the strike only one gain could have been achieved, that is recognition by Patel of the leadership of those instrumental in the return to work. But by engineering a return to work Chipata, Nkoloya and Abraham would have incurred the risk of considerable cost. Their power would have been immediately weakened. They would have exercised it without being instrumental in the distribution of rewards in the form a of wage increase which would have replenished their resources of willing compliance. These resources were already depleted because of their action in organising the strike, which entailed using their power in the first place. In addition failure to supply rewards could have led to the transference of support by the factory employees to the other competitors for power and leadership such as Mumba or Kamwefu. Finally the recognition of Patel did not by any means ensure them of a wage increase on the scale demanded by the strikers.

It is evident then that the best course of action for Chipata, Nkoloya, Abraham and Lyashi was to form an alliance in opposition to management. By thus pooling their resources of power they could more easily secure the compliance of the workers to their demands, for all the workers stood to gain from the action. Such an alliance also provided the best opportunity for maximising their interests. Thus they would reduce the threat to their power emerging from the competition of other workers. Mumba's shouting of the UNIP slogan 'United we stand, divided we fall' was as relevant to the interests of Chipata, Nkoloya, etc., as it was to the furthering of Mumba's own interests. Furthermore, through their alliance Chipata, Nkoloya, Lyashi and Abraham had the possibility of securing general wage increases which would replenish any reduced resources of their power. They could just as effectively secure

Patel's recognition of their leadership by maintaining their control over the strike action, which in itself would be greatly facilitated by their alliance, and ensuring that the strike was not broken or called off until some concessions had been granted.

I now turn to an examination of the broad strategies employed by both management and worker during the strike. There are many aspects which could be discussed but most, I consider, have been sufficiently analysed elsewhere. Thus in chapter 4 I discussed how Patel in major disputes often attempts to transfer the onerous responsibility of negotiation with the employees to one of his partners.[6] Through such an action he is able to salvage some of the personal relationships he has established with his employees necessary for the running of the factory in more peaceful times. Patel's behaviour in the above strike where he transferred the task of negotiation to Badat is illustrative of this. Not all Patel's behaviour, however, is geared towards re-establishing or maintaining his personal relationships with his workers in spite of hostilities. For example, I suggest that Patel's enquiry of Hastings as to whether the latter was returning to Malawi was aimed at creating divisions among the workers. By his reference to Hastings' foreigner status, Patel attempted to manipulate one relational property of Hastings' persona which had been the idiom in terms of which opposition had been expressed by the workers to each other in previous events.

Of central interest to the present analysis, however, is the attempt by the factory employees to restrict the field of action of the negotiations to themselves and the factory management, But the factory management, largely through the offices of Badat, attempted to extend the field by including representatives of the government and the union in an effort to settle the dispute and pressure the employees back to work. From the perspectives of management and worker specific elements located in the arena were viewed as conflict points or trading points.[7] Following Boulding's definitions of these terms, a conflict point is that where one party to a dispute perceives himself as worse off if it is included in the action, whereas a trading point is that where both the parties to a dispute perceive some advantage being derived from its inclusion (1963: 12). This applies almost perfectly to the action surrounding the 'February strike'. From previous experience the factory employees had come to see the labour officer and the local union branch as opposed to their interests. During the strike the arrival of the labour officer in Badat's

---

[6] See chapter 4, p. 148.

[7] It should be emphasised that there is a difference between the use I make of field and Boulding's use of the same term. My usage of the term 'arena' is nearer Boulding's concept of field but they are not strictly identical (1963: 7).

car and Badat's summoning of the union area organising secretary only reinforced the view among the workers that these individuals were in alliance with management and opposed to the factory employees' interests. But unlike the employees the management viewed both the labour office and the union as providing pressure on the workers to management's advantage. Basically, therefore, the labour office and the union were conflict points which one party to the dispute saw necessary to exclude in its interests.

However, in the arena there were a number of trading points which both management and worker could agree to include in the field of action. These were the Resident Minister and the president of the NUCIW. The factory workers had been impressed with the union president on the occasion of an earlier visit of his to Kabwe when he addressed a general meeting of union members. The Resident Minister was a militant speaker on the political party platform, and the factory workers were trepidatious about the degree to which he was likely to support their action, but they felt reasonably assured that he might show some sympathy with their position. Chipata had the most misgivings about the possibility of the Resident Minister's support largely brought on by the cool reception which he had received from the Resident Minister's political assistants during the 'Five-day working week dispute'. It was Chipata's fears about the type of action which the Resident Minister might take that motivated him to call in many of the factory employees and attempt to form a strike commitee.[8] Broadly, however, even though there was a risk that both the Resident Minister and the union president would oppose them, one clear advantage was evident should they be included in the field of action. Through this inclusion notice of the factory workers' demands would be brought to their attention. Furthermore, it was only through an appeal to the Resident Minister and the union president, as the workers perceived it, that pressure could be exerted on the labour office and the area organising secretary to reach an agreement with management more in line with the workers' interests.

But even if the factory employees had opposed the introduction of the Resident Minister and the union president in the field of action there

---

[8] By summoning the meeting which most of the powerful and influential factory workers attended, public commitment to strike action was gained from them. One possible effect of this which I was unable to investigate as my fieldwork ended soon after the strike, was that the main strike leaders, Chipata, Lyashi, Nkoloya and Abraham by receiving agreement for the course of action they had initiated, reduced the costs to themselves in terms of lost approval should the strike fail.

was little they could have done to prevent their entry. As I stated earlier with their inclusion in the field of action increased pressure was brought on the workers to return to work. The threat issued to Chipata by the political assistants before his meeting with the Resident Minister was an example of the new pressures which began to operate. Even so, the workers began to receive a glimpse of some concessions in their favour. Although the union president emphasised the danger of more drastic government action should the employees continue with their strike, he did pacify them with the promise that they would receive a 10s increase.

It was a combination of the pressures applied on the workers through the introduction of the union president and the Resident Minister in the field of action and the promise of a 10s increase which was mainly responsible for the workers' agreement to recommence work. But other factors also contributed to the ending of the strike. Because of the strike the factory employees had lost almost a week's wages and they were beginning to incur heavy costs. It was this factor, rather than the threats issued by Badat that they would be signed off and the factory closed down if the strike continued, which was beginning to generate some feeling among the employees that work should be resumed. Badat's threat of sacking the employees had been proved empty by his failure to carry it out and most of the workers believed that it was as much against management's interests as theirs for the former to close the factory.

Because fieldwork ended shortly after the strike very little can be said about the implications of the event for subsequent action. The behaviour of Kamwefu, Mumba, Mukubwa and Hastings may be indicative of their future greater prominence in the direction and control of the factory employees' actions. The alignment of Mukubwa with the employees might be indicative of a later re-establishment of the power which he exercised in Phase I.

Any analysis along these lines, however, is dependent on a degree of knowledge which could be provided only by data which I do not possess. What might have happened after the 'February strike', therefore, would rest on pure supposition. Instead I propose to set the events which occurred in Phase III in the context of the general argument presented through an analysis of the events in the previous two phases.

Differentiation and change

Each event discussed in the analysis of the three phases marked a point in the development of the factory's changing structure and alignments.

Exchange theory provided a framework in which individual behaviour observed at one point in time could be explained and its consequences for later events assessed. Exchange theory thus provided me with a broad theoretical scheme within which I could analyse the sequence of behaviour in each event as part of an ongoing process.

The analysis of the sequence of events began at a point of time in the factory's social structural development when the workers were divided on the basis of such factors as their position in the production process, their skills and ages. Although the line 1 tailors were involved in a close knit set of interactional relationships they had not yet emerged in the form of a solidary group firmly united in opposition to management and its representatives. Two supervisors, Mukubwa and Chisokone, were able to win the compliance of the workers to their demands and directives. This was explained in terms of their extensive span of relationships linking the majority of the employees to them, their dominance in the set of relationships composed mainly of the senior workers, and their ability to project an image of themselves as individuals who would protect the employment interests of the workers. None of the other factory employees had a span of relationships involving as large a number and range of the factory employees. This meant that the supervisors could mobilise greater support to protect their own interests if their position was threatened. Because they were accepted by the employees concerned as superordinate in the senior workers' set of relationships they received additional support for their position. But of greatest importance for the supervisors' position of power was their successful presentation of themselves as defenders of worker interest. The two supervisors were the only individuals who were seen as being able to distribute rewards such as wage and work improvements and protection from Patel's threats. In return for the expectation of these rewards the employees reciprocated with the one resource valued by the supervisors, their support and compliance.

The supervisors are in an intercalary position subject to contradictory expectations from worker and management. However, because of their position of power Mukubwa and Chisokone were able to keep these contradictory expectations separate and to prevent them from being brought into conflict. An example of this was the 'Dream village dispute'. On this occasion Lyashi selected one relational property of Mukubwa's position and attempted to emphasise his association with management. Mukubwa by using his power prevented any success on Lyashi's part.

This brings me to a basic principle the operation of which was a constant theme in the analysis of the events. Power is expended in use and increased at risk. Mukubwa and Chisokone expended their power. The support and compliance of the workers was essential to the effective exercise of their authority as supervisors. In the course of their factory duties and in preventing behaviour, such as Lyashi's detrimental to their interests, they gave individuals the opportunity to comply with their demands. Power is founded in unilateral transactions and imbalanced obligations. An individual can exercise power if he is able to supply needed benefits which cannot be repaid except by the recipients' compliance. Largely through their successful presentation Chisokone and Mukubwa gained the workers' compliance on 'credit' in the expectation that rewards would be forthcoming. These expectations were not fulfilled, and pressure was applied on the supervisors to discharge their debt. This pressure came predominantly from the senior workers on line 1. It was they who incurred the greatest cost by their compliance.

Here another basic principle became relevant for the analysis. The closer in status an individual perceives himself and is seen by others to be to a person who exercises power over him, the greater the cost he experiences. Each act of compliance he displays reduces his status in the eyes of others and increases the social distance between him and the individual with whose demands he complies. This was exemplified in the event 'A question of town experience'. Here Lyashi in his competition for power and status attempted to define himself as superior in status to his companions on line 1. If they had accepted his claims to superior status they would have reduced the esteem in which they were held by the other workers. This was used as an explanation for their opposition to him. It will be recalled, with reference to the event 'Malawians and Zambians', that Lyashi only received support when his behaviour did not immediately appear as threatening the status of those more or less equal to him.

Because of their failure to distribute rewards and the increased costs which the senior workers incurred, unified opposition to the supervisors and to Mukubwa in particular developed. This received its most complete expression in 'The case of the badly stitched trousers'. Here Mukubwa ridiculed a senior worker. He impugned the very basis on which that worker and his workmates staked one of their greatest claims to status in the factory—their superior skill. Mukubwa also gave clear evidence that the workers' expectations of him would not be realised. Moreover, he showed that he was prepared to participate actively against their interests through his apparent support of Patel's threat of dismissal.

A process has been outlined whereby the power of the supervisors became steadily reduced. With the decline in their power, a process which continued into Phase II illustrated by the analysis of the event 'Chisokone revealed', the contradictory expectations of them which hitherto they had kept separate were brought into conflict. But concomitant with the loss in power of the supervisors was the emergence of both a growing unity among the line 1 tailors and the development of a more clearly defined opposition between management and worker.

At the same time there were other changes. Lyashi's growing success in his bid to achieve power and status in turn affected the status of his peers. In accordance with the basic principle stated earlier any success on Lyashi's part would reduce the status of his fellow workers, who considered themselves to be his equals. With the fall of the supervisors from power the road to increased success for Lyashi was clear. Therefore, to preserve their status against the threat presented by Lyashi some of his workmates also began to compete more openly with him. A struggle ensued focused on the redistribution of power and status. But to achieve or safeguard their power and status all, Lyashi included, had to show that support and compliance with their demands would supply the types of rewards which the supervisors had failed to distribute. From this competition emerged new strategies whereby militant action was proposed for wage and work improvements. Through this the individuals concerned were able to present the possiblilty of the attainment of future rewards in return for support and compliance.

Lyashi continued in his success, despite the competition of others. He was a main protagonist for militant action, as illustrated in 'Lyashi outlines a plan for action', and was a major architect of the walk-out which secured the 1d increment for the senior employees.

But Lyashi's success and the benefits he was partly instrumental in distributing were mainly limited to his peers. As long as Lyashi depended on the support and approval of employees who were more or less his equals his power and newly increased status was insecure. Some basic processes governing individual behaviour described earlier are again relevant. An individual's power and status are most secure when those over whom he exercises power and status cannot easily transfer their allegiances to obtain similar benefits. There was nothing which Lyashi could supply his fellow senior workers which they either could not supply themselves or which could not be provided by others among them. This meant they could easily transfer their allegiances. Also it militated against Lyashi's establishment of an imbalance in obligations through transacting with his peers. This was a factor too explaining the insecurity of the power and status of the supervisors among the senior workers. It was a factor which generated their behaviour which involved repeated attempts to impress their superiority over the senior workers which had the unintended consequence of eventually aligning the latter against them.

The senior workers in fact continually redistributed their resources of support and approval. It was in their interest to do so. By so doing they could restrict the emergence of a clear leader among them who could have the effect of reducing their own status.

Because of Lyashi's and others' inability to establish a firm foundation for their power and status by competing for the support and approval of their equals the area of their competition was extended to include workers junior in status to themselves. Many of these workers were dependent on the types of benefits which could only be supplied by those senior to them. Not only did support of a senior worker give them the opportunity to achieve wage and work improvements but some protection from Patel's threats could be supplied in addition to the chance to learn or increase a skill. The lower in status an individual the less cost he incurs by complying with the demands of an individual generally regarded as being higher in status. In fact it could be positively rewarding, in that association with a high status individual by one of low status could increase the latter's standing among his peers. This was discussed with reference to the relationships the supervisors had with the junior workers. Of vital importance for the argument is that in their relationships with the junior workers these individuals among the senior employees competing for power and status could more easily develop an imbalance in obligations through their transactions.

But to be successful in this new aspect of the competition the senior workers had to present themselves as attractive to those lower in status by demonstrating that they would protect their interests. This was one factor underlying the action surrounding the 'Five day working week dispute', during which Lyashi and others framed their action in terms of the general appeal of their demands.

A number of important consequences resulted from the action surrounding and immediately following the 'Five day working week dispute'. One general effect discussed with reference to the 'February strike' was the attempt by the workers to restrict the field of action to themselves and management. More specifically Patel's reaction to the militancy of his employees had significant effects for the developing structure of social relationships in the factory. In various ways he was to influence the alignment of all his workers in firm opposition to him, contrary to his expectation of the advantage which he apparently considered his action would bring.

By his removal of the grievance—Saturday morning work—in terms of which the strike leaders attempted to define their contract with him as monthly rather than daily he acted against the interests of the less skilled and unskilled employees. They incurred increased costs for by shortening the working week Patel in effect reduced their pay. This was not compensated for by a $1d$ increment as it was for the senior workers. Although initially the junior employees expressed hostility towards the senior workers whom they blamed, the strategy which the senior workers presented to them was now more in their interests. Militant action was a way by which they could recover their losses.

The attempts by the senior workers to develop relationships with the junior employees, engendered, partly at least, by their competition among themselves for power and leadership, now met with greater success, not only because they presented a solution for the loss and unskilled workers' grievance but because they also offered other benefits such as advice in learning a skill. A set of ties cross-cutting divisions in the factory was thus developing which was to influence the emergence of unified support for strike action in February.

But of equal importance for future events and the development of more unified opposition to Patel were his actions whereby he elevated Chipata and Meshak to a position of favour, and withdrew elements of his transactions with his supervisors and other employees.

Patel's development of a more familiar relationship with Chipata and Meshak, and his bestowal of certain benefits on them such as increased credit facilities was an attempt to exert greater control over the behaviour of his workers. Patel now frequently used Chipata and Meshak in a supervisory capacity. At the same time he reduced his dependence on his supervisors and withdrew aspects of his transactions with them. The supervisors because of their lack of power and influence could not effectively exercise their authority over the workers and decreased in their value to Patel. His action whereby he elevated Chipata and Meshak to a position of power had presented a status threat to the supervisors. The necessity for the latter to restore the balance in their favour was only made imperative with Patel's withdrawal of some of the benefits he had supplied them. The supervisors entered the competiton for power and leadership and aligned with the employees in opposition to management in order to increase their value to Patel and to regain access to benefits which he now denied them. Indication of their alignment was given in the analysis of Mukubwa's part on the 'Stolen

z

clothing dispute' and Hastings' militant proposals during the 'February strike'.

However, in choosing to use Chipata and Meshak in a supervisory capacity Patel was inadequately informed as to their power and influence over the workers. There were others more powerful but less obvious to Patel given his perspective onto the factory. Lacking sufficient power and influence Chipata and Meshak could not keep separate the contradictory expectations at which they were now the focus as a result of Patel's drawing them into an intercalary position. They were not clearly defined by management or worker as supervisors. Their actions in a supervisory capacity could not be explained away to the other employees in terms of the nature of their work. The new authority with which Patel had invested them necessitated that they use up what little resources of power and influence they had. Pressures were applied, exemplified in 'The stolen clothing dispute' and 'Chipata is told his nickname', on Meshak and Chipata to conform to the employees' expectations of them. Not yet secure in the position of favour to which they were elevated by Patel they were forced to align with the employees in order to demonstrate their power and influence and thus their value to Patel.

These processes as a result of action during and following the 'Five-day working week dispute' in combination with processes which arose in relation to earlier events, such as the competition between senior employees for power and leadership, explain the development of unified action by all the employees at the time of the 'February Strike'. This unity of opposition to management was intensified with Patel's withdrawal of other elements of his transactions with his workers, exemplified in his tightening up of the indulgency system.

An emergent property of the structural changes which took place in the factory relates to the common alignment of the employees in opposition to management and their involvement in a more cohesive set of ties. The factory workers through the competition of some among them for power and leadership became bound together in a set of relationships which cross-cut divisions noticeable at an earlier period of the observations. The effective mobilisation of the factory workers to the support of one particular individual was not possible without the support of those who competed with him. Although specific individuals could be isolated as powerful and influential none was supremely dominant. Lyashi, for example, was unable to influence a return to work without the support of other powerful and influential employees. Strike action was only broken through management's ability to extend the field of action to the disadvantage of the workers who attempted to restrict it.

Although the set of events I have analysed in all three phases of the structural development of the factory are unique they indicate the operation of basic social processes which generate structural changes and the form which action in specific events takes. Each event marked a point in the structural development of factory social relationships and was an occasion where individuals attempted to define or redefine their position in relation to one another. Some of the processes whereby power and status are won and lost were explored, and the consequences of individual action in the pursuit of power and status for the developing structure of the factory were investigated.

9 Postscript

The theoretical approach I have used in this study has been one based on the orientations of choice and decision-making and most especially on the theory of social exchange.

Individuals are never treated as actors independent of the actions of others. Individual behaviour is framed and moulded in a social matrix of reciprocal influence and interaction which is not confined to activity on the shop floor but extends to the world outside. The approach enables me to range from the description and explanation of the minutiae of the dynamics of interpersonal behaviour within a specific context to a consideration of broader social and political processes occurring within the general environment of the individual participant.

The exploration and description of empirical material in accordance with an abstract theoretical and conceptual scheme was conducted through the examination of two broad problems which appeared relevant and significant in the light of my field experience. The first was related to the difference in employee reactions to work in the factory and their relationships with management. Why was there a difference between certain categories of employee in terms of preparedness, for instance, to engage in militant activity in wage and work negotiations with management? How and why did the change come about whereby workers who were divided at one occasion of strike action against management should be united at a later stage? Second, and closely connected with these themes, was the more general interest of the extent to which social activity observed within the factory was emergent from the circumstances and conditions of factory employment and/or from the past and current participation of the workers in the wider urban and national environment of Kabwe and Zambia.

The explication of these themes through an abstract theory and set of concepts constituted a method by which key variables could be systematically isolated from the mass of complexly interwoven behaviour and apparently relevant data collected during research.

Through the use of such concepts as investment and commitment, arena and field, network and a variety of others connected specifically with exchange theory, like transaction, balance, etc., different aspects of the workers' involvement in the factory and town were examined. The partial views which each of these concepts gave of empirical reality led to the gradual establishment of a composite picture of the influences which shaped the behaviour of the factory employees.

In the early chapters the description and explanation of the social activity and characteristics of the workers was largely presented through concepts like investment and commitment. It was noted that the skilled and senior employees tended to engage more readily in militant action designed to win wage and work improvements than the younger un-skilled workers. It was shown that the factory workers were differen-tiated in terms of the extent of their investment both in the work place and in the town. This pattern was a consequence of a series of choices which individual workers had made over the course of their life and occupational careers. Skilled workers also controlled resources which were influential for others, like the factory manager, to furnish them various valued benefits. This had a feedback effect of further committing them to factory employment. In addition, unlike the unskilled workers, the investments of many of the tailors both at work and in the town were interrelated to the extent that the forfeiture of one set of investments would seriously threaten others. Factors such as these, among others, were used to explain why the skilled workers should tend to opt for action directed towards changing their work conditions to suit their interests, while the younger and unskilled employees were more prepared to change their place of employment in a bid to increase wages and perhaps im-prove work conditions.

The concepts of investment and commitment were also used to trace aspects of the interrelationship of the factory with its general socio-economic environment—as this was seen through the participation of individuals in factory and town life. The concepts of arena and field were applied in the course of examining the nature of the factory's integration into its political environment. It was shown that the type of strategy pursued by the employees in their bargaining and negotiation with management was largely connected to the way they perceived the various elements located in the environment and the organisation of these elements one to the other as these related to worker interest. The fact that Zambia had just gained its independence led the employees to expect that they would have the support of outside individuals represent-ative of the political party and government. The political uncertainties of the time, as far as the Indian manager was concerned, I suggested, influenced him to back down at first before the threats of his workers to exert outside pressure. However, it was shown that when the workers were forced to operate in an extended field of action, the various relevant elements in the arena were aligned in opposition to worker interest. Partly as a result of experiencing the disadvantage of negotiating and bargaining within an extended field, the workers tried to restrict their field of action to the work place.

The dynamic aspect of social action I examined through such concepts as field were also emphasised in the contrast of individual network structures and distribution of transactional relationships for two separate time periods. This indicated that the control and influence of the senior skilled employees over those junior to them had increased by a later time period, and this prepared the way to successful strike action.

The process whereby the pattern and structure of interactional relationships changed was seen in terms of a redistribution of power and status. The direction and nature of this change and the points within the factory set of social and work relationships, from which this change received its impetus, were described and explained through concepts and principles derived from exchange theory. The competition for and rise to power and influence of certain individuals broadly arose in response to such factors as the workers' perception of increased costs in specific sets of relationships. This competition was largely emergent from and framed in terms of dissatisfaction with wage and work conditions. However, among its consequences this competition also increased worker militancy and influenced important changes in strategy. One such change was the growth and acceptance of a feeling among the employees that individuals representative of outside agencies should not be allowed to intrude into management and worker negotiation.

The book generally essays a contribution to a growing debate in the social sciences, a debate relating to the opposition between what have been termed institutional approaches and those which are actor-oriented. Much of the opposition between the protagonists of these orientations arises from their concern to describe and explain behaviour at different levels of abstraction (Mitchell, 1969a; Garbett, 1970). It is my view that the actor-oriented approach seems more relevant to the analysis of the behaviour of a small number of individuals within a comparatively confined context. Other considerations, however, some of which have already been referred to, also influenced my preference.

There is, for example, the much lower level of empirical abstraction at which actor-oriented approaches operate. The factory workers of this study are only representative of a small proportion of the Kabwe population. The full range and diversity in the life and occupational careers of the town residents is not represented by the Narayan Bros. employees. The administration, political party, trade unions, etc., combined in different ways to affect the lives of town residents participant in other spheres of activity, such as those employed on the railway or mine. Choice/decision-making and exchange theoretical orientations, as actor-oriented approaches, enabled me to set my description in the particularity of individual behaviour and experience while at the same time linking it to abstract theoretical principles unlocated in space and time. In this way the principles guiding the analysis of particular cases have been shown to have relevance for the understanding and explanation of a general class of behaviour (e.g. migration, trade union politics, strike activity, competition for leadership, etc.) without my being forced into the position of stating that a particular observed instance was 'typical' of the general class.

Analyses, conducted by the other approach along broad institutional and/or structural–functional lines, seem to me to be prone not just to empirical generalisation based on the observation, I suspect, of a relatively few instances, which is also a feature of many who advocate an actor-oriented approach, but to unjustified generalisation at too high a level of abstraction, which is erroneously assumed to have a wide area of empirical validity. I refer not so much to the assumption often made in an institutionalist approach of homogeniety and a lack of attention to variation from standardised patterns (e.g. Van Velsen, 1964: xxiii–xxv; Long, 1968: 7–8) as to the tendency to infer, from the behaviour of a few individuals, the behaviour of all people within a given society. To a certain extent this might be defensible for those anthropologists who work in small-scale village communities and have observed much of that upon which they base their empirical generalisations. It is more difficult to defend when the observations are made in large scale contexts like the rapidly expanding, densely populated and complex towns and cities of the third world.

The main reason for the application of the specific theoretical and conceptual approach in this study is the attention which such an orientation gives to the study of social behaviour as process, in the sense that it concentrates on the factors which lead to the generation and emergence of social forms. This approach permits an understanding of what is observed as change, and the direction of this change, in addition to answering questions relating to the persistence and stability of behaviour, structures and institutions.

The major and important criticism of so-called structural–functional and institutionalist orientations rests in their failure adequately to explain social change. But the problem may be more deep-seated than this. Not only might such approaches fail to explain change, but they also

fail to explain the *relative persistence or stability* of the structural and institutional forms which are isolated in terms of them. As Homans states,
'Many sociologists spend years describing and analysing social structure
without once asking themselves why it is that behaviour persists long
enough for them to describe and analyse it at all. Structure is not a given:
it is itself the result of social process' (1961: 99).

Although an actor-oriented approach, which emphasises the view of
social behaviour as process, is used in the analysis, I have not relied
exclusively on it in tracing changes and developments which occurred in
the factory. In essence I have combined formal statements contained in
choice/decision-making and exchange theoretical orientations which
state a causal connection between properties of behaviour organised in
some temporal sequence, with a form of micro-historical explanation
and description.

I have not found it necessary to explore some of the most usual anthropological interests in the urban areas of the developing world. Thus,
the extent to which 'traditional' customs and behaviour, more applicable
to rural systems of relationships, change or persist in the town, has not
been a major element of the analysis. Neither have I been concerned
with the ways 'traditional' beliefs and practices have facilitated or impeded participation in a modern urban setting. These interests have not
been treated here because they did not appear as relevant during my
research experience towards achieving an understanding of the social
activity of the workers. Their behaviour was fully capable of being understood in terms of the nature of their past and current life and work
experience, the structure of work and social relationships on the shop
floor, employment and wage conditions, etc. In short the social behaviour I recorded and observed was capable of being comprehended in a
way similar to that by which we may attempt to study behaviour in the
more developed regions of the world. This does not mean to say that
beliefs, customs and practices associated with so-called 'traditional'
ways of life are not important towards an understanding of other areas of
urban activity. But this is another study.

The extensive use I have made of theory and abstract conceptualis-
ation has been motivated above all else by a wish to present as accurately as possible the empirical reality I observed. They way in which I
have attempted to do this and the relation of abstract theoretical formu-
lation with the description I have given can best be expressed through
the words of Ronald Laing.

Our task is both to experience and to conceive the concrete, that is to say,
reality in its fullness and wholeness . . . But this is quite impossible

immediately. Experientially and conceptually, we have fragments . . .
We can begin from concepts of the single person, from relations between
two or more persons, from groups or society at large; or from the material
world, and conceive of individuals as secondary. We can derive the main
determinants of our individual and social behaviour from external
exigencies. All these views are partial vistas and partial concepts.
Theoretically one needs a spiral of expanding and contracting schemata
that enables us to move freely and without discontinuity from varying
degrees of abstraction to greater or lesser degrees of concreteness. Theory
is the articulated vision of experience [1967: 19–20].

Appendix 1 Major social characteristics of factory employees

a Occupation, either at the time the employee left work or at the time I left the field.

b Age.

c Tribe.

d District.

e Place of birth.

f Township in which residing.

g Marital status. Unless otherwise stated, wife is in town.

h Religion.

i Education.

j Length of time employed at Narayan Bros.

Mukubwa *a* Supervisor. *b* 44. *c* Lala. *d* Kabwe. *e* Kabwe. *f* Chimaninine. *g* Married. *h* Roman Catholic. *i* Standard III. *j* 16 years.

Hastings *a* Supervisor. *b* 56. *c* Chewa. *d* Malawi. *e* Village. *f* Chimaninine. *g* Married. *h* Anglican. *i* Standard III. *j* 28·5 years.

Chisokone *a* Supervisor. *b* 41. *c* Bemba. *d* Mpika. *e* Village. *f* Bwacha. *g* Married. *h* Ex-Roman Catholic. *i* Standard II. *j* 12 years.

Nkoloya *a* Line 1 tailor. *b* 42. *c* Kunda. *d* Chipata. *e* Village. *f* Mine farms. *g* Married. *h* Anglican. *i* Standard I. *j* 10 years.

Lyashi *a* Line 1 tailor. *b* 43. *c* Bemba. *d* Chinsali. *e* Village. *f* Bwacha. *g* Married. *h* Pagan (ex-Lenshina). *i* Nil. *j* 2·5 years.

Chipata *a* Line 1 tailor. *b* 43. *c* Ngoni. *d* Chipata. *e* Kabwe. *f* Chimaninine. *g* Married. *h* Roman Catholic. *i* Standard IV. *j* 1·5 years.

Nelson *a* Line 1 tailor. *b* 41. *c* Lakeside Tonga. *d* Malawi. *e* Village. *f* Bwacha. *g* Married. *h* Free Church. *i* Standard I. *j* 2·5 years.

Donald *a* Line 1 tailor. *b* 40. *c* Bemba. *d* Kasama. *e* Village. *f* Bwacha. *g* Married. *h* Roman Catholic. *i* Nil. *j* 0·5 year. (Information incomplete.)

Lenard *a* Line 1 tailor. *b* 39. *c* Bemba. *d* Mpika. *e* Village. *f* Mine farms. *g* Married. *h* Roman Catholic. *i* Standard I. *j* 7 years.

Abraham *a* Line 1 tailor. *b* 48. *c* Bisa. *d* Mpika. *e* Village. *f* Bwacha. *g* Married. *h* Roman Catholic. *i* Standard IV. *j* 12 years.

Kamwefu *a* Line 1 tailor. *b* 48. *c* Bisa. *d* Chipata. *e* Village. *f* Chimaninine. *g* Married. *h* Pagan (ex-Jehovah's Witness). *i* Nil. *j* 4 years.

Nkumbula *a* Line 1 tailor. *b* 50. *c* Soli. *d* Mkushi. *e* Village. *f* Chimaninine. *g* Married. *h* Roman Catholic. *i* Nil. *j* 20 years.

Mumba *a* Line 1 tailor. *b* 33. *c* Nsenga. *d* Petauke. *e* Village. *f* Chimaninine. *g* Married. *h* Anglican. *i* Standard I. *j* 0·5 year.

Zulu *a* Line 1 tailor. *b* 31. *c* Ngoni. *d* Chipata. *e* Village. *f* Chimaninine. *g* Married. *h* African Reform Church. *i* Standard IV. *j* 7 years.

Lwanga *a* Line 1 tailor. *b* 40. *c* Nsenga. *d* Petauke. *e* Village. *f* Chimaninine. *g* Married. *h* Pagan. *i* Nil. *j* 13·5 years.

Enoch *a* Line 1 tailor. *b* 48. *c* Lala. *d* Serenje. *e* Village. *f* Chimaninine single quarters. *g* Married; wife in rural area. *h* Free Church. *i* Standard III. *j* 1·5 years.

Mulondo *a* Line 1 tailor. *b* 40. *c* Lala. *d* Serenje. *e* Village. *f* Bwacha. *g* Married. *h* Jehovah's Witness. *i* Standard II. *j* 0·5 year.

Macdonald *a* Line 1 tailor. *b* 26. *c* Lakeside Tonga. *d* Malawi. *e* Village. *f* Bwacha. *g* Married; wife in rural area. *h* Pagan. *i* Nil. *j* 0·5 year.

Chipalo *a* Line 1 tailor. *b* 48. *c* Bemba. *d* Kasama. *e* Village. *f* Bwacha. *g* Married. *h* Roman Catholic. *i* Nil. *j* 0·5 year.

Kalamba *a* Line 2 tailor. *b* 33. *c* Yao. *d* Malawi. *e* Village. *f* Bwacha. *g* Married. *h* Muslim. *i* Nil. *j* 4 years.

Ibrahim *a* Line 2 tailor. *b* 39. *c* Yao. *d* Mozambique. *e* Village.

Mukomango *a* Line 2 tailor. *b* 34. *c* Bisa. *d* Luwingu. *e* Village. *f* Mine farms. *g* Married. *h* Jehovah's Witness. *i* Standard VI. *j* 0·2 year.

Seams *a* Line 2 tailor. *b* 37. *c* Kabende. *d* Samfya. *e* Village. *f* Mine farms. *g* Married. *h* Roman Catholic. *i* Standard III. *j* 0·9 year.

Paulos *a* Line 2 tailor. *b* 31. *c* Chewa. *d* Lundazi. *e* Village. *f* Bwacha. *g* Married. *h* Roman Catholic. *i* Nil. *j* 2·5 years.

Joshua *a* Line 2 tailor. *b* 33. *c* Lungu. *d* Mbala. *e* Village. *f* Mukobeko. *g* Married. *h* Roman Catholic. *i* Standard IV. *j* 0·5 year.

Kalundwe *a* Line 2 tailor. *b* 37. *c* Lala. *d* Serenje. *e* Kabwe. *f* Mine farms. *g* Married. *h* Pagan. *i* Standard I. *j* 0·75 year.

Mateo *a* Line 2 tailor. *b* 42. *c* Nganja. *d* Malawi. *e* Village. *f* Katondo farms. *g* Married; wife in rural area. *h* Free Church. *i* Standard III. *j* 0·75 year.

Mpundu *a* Line 2 tailor. *b* 47. *c* Nsenga. *d* Petauke. *e* Village. *f* Mine farms. *g* Married. *h* Roman Catholic. *i* Nil. *j* 13 years.

Henry *a* Line 3 tailor. *b* 25. *c* Bisa. *d* Mpika. *e* Village. *f* Bwacha. *g* Married. *h* Roman Catholic. *i* Standard III. *j* 2·5 years.

Joseph *a* Line 3 tailor. *b* 25. *c* Bisa. *d* Mpika. *e* Village. *f* Chimaninine. *g* Married. *h* Free Church. *i* Standard V. *j* 1·25 years.

Zakeyo a Line 3 tailor. *b* 53. *c* Nsenga, *d* Petauke. *e* Village. *f* Bwacha. *g* Married. *h* Pagan. *i* Nil. *j* 0·66 year.

Laurent *a* Line 3 tailor. *b* 34. *c* Bisa. *d* Mpika. *e* Village. *f* Mine farms. *g* Single. *h* Roman Catholic. *i* Nil. *j* 0·33 year.

Sign *a* Line 3 tailor. *b* 32. *c* Nsenga. *d* Petauke. *e* Village. *f* Mine farms. *g* Married. *h* Pagan. *i* Nil. *j* 0·25 year.

Nyirenda *a* Line 3 tailor. *b* 41. *c* Tumbuka. *d* Malawi. *e* Village. *f* Bwacha. *g* Married. *h* Pagan. *i* Standard IV. *j* 1·5 years.

Ben *a* Line 3 tailor. *b* 35. *c* Lala. *d* Serenje. *e* Village. *f* Bwacha. *g* Married. *h* Jehovah's Witness. *i* Nil. *j* 0·66 year.

Aston *a* Line 3 tailor. *b* 30. *c* Kiga. *d* Tanzania. *e* Village. *f* Mine farms. *g* Married. *h* Roman Catholic. *i* Nil. *j* 0·05 year.

Sandford *a* Line 3 tailor. *b* 29. *c* Chewa. *d* Lundazi. *e* Village. *f* D. H. Patel's compound. *g* Married; wife in rural area. *h* African Reform Church. *i* Standard III. *j* 0·1 year.

Edward *a* Line 3 tailor. *b* 47. *c* Chikunda. *d* Feira. *e* Village. *f* Bwacha. *g* Married. *h* Roman Catholic. *i* Standard III. *j* 0·33 year.

John *a* Line 3 tailor. *b* 34. *c* Lala. *d* Kabwe. *e* Kabwe. *f* Bwacha. *g* Married. *h* Watch Tower. *i* Standard III. *j* 0·9 year.

Meshak *a* Button machiner. *b* 39. *c* Ambo. *d* Lusaka. *e* Village. *f* Bwacha. *g* Married. *h* Roman Catholic. *i* Standard II. *j* 11 years.

Adrian *a* Button machiner. *b* 36. *c* Nsenga. *d* Lusaka. *e* Village. *f* Chimaninine. *g* Married. *h* Pagan. *i* Nil. *j* 10 years.

Kalonga *a* Ironer. *b* 25. *c* Bisa. *d* Mpika. *e* Village. *f* Bwacha. *g* Married. *h* Roman Catholic. *i* Nil. *j* 0·8 year.

Chobe *a* Ironer. *b* 31. *c* Tonga. *d* Mazabuka. *e* Village. *f* Mine farms. *g* Married; wife in rural area. *h* Salvation Army. *i* Standard IV. *j* 0·9 year.

Isaac *a* Ironer. *b* 21. *c* Lala. *d* Mkushi. *e* Village. *f* Chimaninine single quarters. *g* Married; wife in rural area. *h* Methodist. *i* Standard V. *j* 0·5 year.

Mabange *a* Ironer. *b* 42. *c* Nyakyusa. *d* Tanzania. *e* Village. *f* Mine farms. *g* Married. *h* Free Church. *i* Standard II. *j* 0·4 year.

William *a* Ironer. *b* 36. *c* Lala. *d* Serenje. *e* Village. *f* Toromboshi. *g* Married. *h* Pagan. *i* Standard II. *j* 1·5 years.

Mubanga *a* Ironer. *b* 28. *c* Nsenga. *d* Lusaka. *e* Village. *f* Chimaninine. *g* Single. *h* Methodist. *i* Standard V. *j* 1·2 years.

Chilufya *a* Cotton boy. *b* 24. *c* Bemba. *d* Kasama. *e* Village. *f* Bwacha. *g* Married. *h*. Nil. *i* Standard V. *j* 0·33 year.

Christian *a* Cotton boy. *b* 19. *c* Soli. *d* Lusaka. *e* Village. *f* Bwacha. *g* Single. *h* Roman Catholic. *i* Standard VI. *j* 0·5 year.

Angel *a* Cotton boy. *b* 23. *c* Ngumbo. *d* Mufulira. *e* Mufulira. *f* Chimaninine. *g* Single. *h* Roman Catholic. *i* Standard VI. *j* 1 year.

Nelson *a* Cotton boy. *b* 22. *c* Tumbuka. *d* Lundazi. *e* Village. *f* Bwacha. *g* Single. *h* Free Church. *i* Standard II. *j* 0·5 year.

Lundazi *a* Cotton boy. *b* 19. *c* Nsenga. *d* Malawi. *e* Village. *f* Bwacha. *g* Married; wife in rural area. *h* Pagan. *i* Nil. *j* 0·4 year.

Christopher *a* Cotton boy. *b* 18. *c* Ambo. *d* Kabwe. *e* Kabwe. *f* Chimaninine. *g* Single. *h* Roman Catholic. *i* Form 1. *j* 0·2 year.

Paison *a* Cotton boy. *b* 35. *c* Lala. *d* Serenje. *e* Village. *f* Katondo farms. *g* Married. *h* Pagan. *i* Standard II. *j* 0·33 year.

Lazarous *a* Cotton boy. *b* 21. *c* Bisa. *d* Mpika. *e* Village. *f* Bwacha. *g* Single. *h* Roman Catholic. *i* Standard III. *j* 0·6 year.

Mulenga *a* Cotton boy. *b* 21. *c* Bemba. *d* Mporokoso. *e* Village *f* Central police station compound. *g* Single. *h* Ex-Watch Tower. *i* Standard V. *j* 0·4 year.

Mpande *a* Cotton boy. *b* 16. *c* Nsenga. *d* Petauke. *e* Village. *f* Bwacha. *g* Single. *h* Watch Tower. *i* Nil. *j* 0·2 year.

Coliat No information recorded.

Chilwa *a* Lines 1 and 3 tailor. *b* 41. *c* Lakeside Tonga. *d* Nkhatia Bay. *e* Village. *f* Bwacha. *g* Married. *h* Pagan. *i* Nil. *j* 2·5 years.

Peter *a* Line 2 tailor. *b* 34. *c* Nsenga. *d* Lundazi. *e* Village. *f* Chimaninine. *g* Divorced. *h* Pagan. *i* Nil. *j* 0·33 year.

Appendix 2 Summary of events in chronological sequence

The events I have presented below are only summaries of what I recorded. Also, not all the events which were noted have been included here. The main reason for the inclusion of this appendix is to set the principal events discussed in the text in the general context of other events, and to show that aspects of these principal events are recurrent themes of other events not discussed in detail. Another reason is to show in a limited way the pattern of social activities as they unfold over the research period.

The reader will note that I have presented more events recorded early in the research than later. There are two reasons for this. First, after August there were no more daily tea breaks. Because the break had been short there was virtually no opportunity for the workers to walk round town or visit their homes, which was the case when the longer lunch break was instituted. Because the workers did not leave the factory premises at tea break, this period not only afforded the workers an opportunity to interact with each other freely but also provided a 'captive' audience before whom various workers could present themselves and compete for approval and support. With the ending of tea break after August there was a reduction in the number of extended sequences of social activity. Most of the extended sequences of activity I recorded occurred at tea break. The second reason for showing a bias towards including events from the early period of my observations relates to a concern to illustrate as much as possible the occasions in which the power and influence of the supervisors was challenged and to illustrate the prominent part which Lyashi and others began to play in activities on the shop floor.

1   2 June 1965 at tea break

A small group of line 2 and 3 tailors discuss their drinking experiences in the townships. Kalundwe (line 3 tailor) tells Mpundu (line 3 tailor) that 'We newcomers to the factory have little say in what goes on here.' Mpundu assents and states that the tailors in stores get more money. 'If our wages don't increase I shall look for another place to work.' A few cotton boys (Kalonga, Joseph and Henry) join the tailors and remark on the attractive job opportunities elsewhere in Zambia. Lyashi (line 1 tailor) comes over to the workers and tells them that wages can be improved only by forcing Patel to grant increases.

2   3 June 1965 at tea break

Cotton boys (Mubanga, Angel, Henry and Christian) comment on the way Patel likes to stand at the factory doorway watching them drink tea.

Another cotton boy, Joseph, joins the group and the others comment on the soiled trousers he is wearing. Joseph retorts that at least he owns a bicycle, which is more than can be said for his companions.

3   3 June 1965 at work

Kalundwe (line 3 tailor) approaches Paulos (line 2 tailor) for a cash loan. Refused. Paulos tells Kalundwe that he should look after his own affairs. Other tailors on line 2 support Paulos.

4   4 June 1965 at tea break

Lyashi, Kamwefu, Chilwa (line 1 tailors), Paulos and Seams (line 2 tailors) complain about the break period and the loss of pay resulting from it. Attitudes are expressed about the union's lack of strength.

During the conversation Lyashi addresses all the factory workers and tells them they must fight Patel and all those who assist him. He stresses that they should be paid for the tea break. Lyashi addresses his comments specifically to the line 2 and 3 tailors but refers to them as *baiche* (young men). The use of this term brings an angry response from workers such as Paulos (line 2 tailor).

5   9 June 1965 at tea break

The 'dream village' dispute: see chapter 6.

6   19 June 1965 at tea break

A number of senior tailors (Lyashi, Nkoloya, Abraham, Lenard, all line 1 tailors, and Lwanga, then on line 2) joke with Kalamba about his name. Lwanga claps his hands in mock respect in front of Kalamba's face. Lyashi and Nkoloya kneel before Kalamba and present him with a cup of tea and some bread. Kalamba angrily refuses their offerings.

7   14 June 1965 at tea break

Patel, within earshot of the other factory workers, tells Mukubwa, the head tailor, and Chisokone, the cutter, that he suspects that some tea cups have been stolen. This is overheard by the other employees and Kalamba, Kamwefu, Chilwa (tailors, line 1), Zulu (overlock machiner), Paulos (tailor, line 2) and Meshak (button machiner) vent their anger against Patel. Many claimed that Patel treated his workers like children. This led into an attack on the system of hourly pay and the hardships which it incurred.

8   16 June 1965 at tea break

Mukubwa, the head tailor, and Chisokone, the cutter, join the other employees late for tea and find no tea cups available. They comment about this lack of thoughtfulness on the part of others and the way many of the tea cups seem to be disappearing. Nearby some of the senior workers are measuring each other's status in accordance with the size of cup being used and the amount of bread being eaten. Mukubwa breaks into the conversation and tells them that they could not eat properly at their homes. This is taken as a slight against their status. Lwanga (tailor, line 2) warns Mukubwa, 'All of us here are big men with wives and children. We rent our own houses. It is not good that some people should laugh at their friends as if they are children.' Mukubwa added, 'We must watch our tongues or else we will find ourselves quarrelling with our friends.'

9   17 June 1965 at tea break

Chisokone, the cutter, compains to all the workers about the shortage of cups. He suggests that someone must be stealing them. Nkoloya jokingly suggests that the culprit is Chisokone. Chisokone reacts by informing Nkoloya that he has a better set of tea cups at home than Nkoloya. He compares the furnishings in his house with those in Nkoloya's home. Chisokone then suggests that Nkoloya's home is so badly furnished that the latter has probably stolen the factory tea cups in order to build up his stock of crockery.

10   21 June 1965 at tea break

Chisokone addresses the employees about the plight of Africans in Rhodesia under the government of Ian Smith. Sign, a line 3 tailor, tells Chisokone that politics should not be discussed at the factory.

11   21 June 1965 at work

Adrian (button machiner) reports for work after taking some leave three days late. Many of his fellow workers hold him up as an example of a *fontini*. Adrian is laughed at particularly by William, an ironer, and John, an ironer. Meshak laughs when Adrian is called a *cipuba* (stupid) by some of his friends. At break a lengthy discussion occurs which is mainly concerned with defining the status of the participants.

11   22 June 1965 at tea break

Lyashi joins a group of cotton boys and ironers and asks them to lend him some money as he has no food in his house. The workers he addresses tell him that they have also spent last month's wages. General discussions follow about the poor wages and work conditions in the factory.

12   22 June 1965 at work

Mukubwa, the head tailor, admonishes Nyirenda, a line 3 tailor, for not working fast enough. He says, 'Malawians boast that they are townspeople

but they are too lazy to be called such.' Nyirenda does not reply but a
number of the other workers nearby laugh at Mukubwa's statement.

13 23 June 1965 at tea break

'A question of town experience': see chapter 6.

14 24 June 1965 at tea break

'Malawians and Zambians': see chapter 6.

15 24 June 1965 at tea break

Ibrahim, a line 2 tailor, complains to Nkoloya about the piece-work rates
which Patel pays. Nkoloya states that piece-work rates would be better if
some of the workers on lines 2 and 3 did not work overtime like the line 1
tailors. 'We should all combine and refuse to work overtime.' Lyashi, a
line 1 tailor, accuses the employees who were prepared to work overtime
as being *makobo*. 'I don't have to work overtime as I run my own business.'
Other line 1 tailors agreed with Nkoloya and Lyashi that there should be a
general embargo on overtime.

16 29 June 1965 at work

'The case of the badly stitched trousers': see chapter 6.

17 30 June 1965 at tea break

Kalamba, a line 1 tailor, is again the object of fun. Lyashi shouts to
Abraham to take Kalamba some bread. 'Come on, *mwaiche*, don't you
know that Kalamba is an old man ?' Later Mukubwa tells Kalamba not to
take such a large cup of tea. 'You must leave the big cups for big people'
(*ba Kalamba*). Kalamba accuses Mukubwa of being selfish. Nkoloya
comes to the support of Kalamba and emphasises that Mukubwa always
wants to bring attention to himself. Lyashi tells the workers that Mukubwa
wants to be the factory manager.

18 5 July 1965 at tea break

Lyashi addresses all the workers at break. He asks everyone to lend him
some money as he has no cash at home for relish. General response along
the line that this was a similar situation which all employees were
experiencing.

19 7 July 1965 at work

Lenard tells Lyashi that he feels that Patel will refuse him leave to visit
his home area. Abraham joins in with anti-Patel comments. Lenard talks
generally about the difficulty of leaving town for any length of time.
Wife would be without proper income and might be evicted.

20   13 July 1965 at work

A joking relationship goes astray between Lyashi and Abraham. Lyashi uses a Bemba word in addressing Abraham which in Nyanja is regarded as obscene. In the argument which follows Lyashi gets no support but Nkoloya rallies to Abraham's aid.

21   14 July 1965 at tea break

There is some general griping about Patel *but* this suddenly becomes explosive when Lyashi openly accuses Mukubwa of being an informer (*chichawa*).

22   15 July 1965 at tea break

Mukubwa asks a group of line 1 tailors whether he can have some bread. He is told to do without by Lyashi.

23   15 July 1965 at work

A small dispute starts between Mubanga and Patel. Patel had been asking Mubanga to move round the work place continually doing small chores for him. As seemed customary, Patel accompanied Mubanga's moves with constant cursing and urging to hurry up. After some time Mubanga refuses to do Patel's bidding any more. Patel asks Mukubwa to go and reprimand Mubanga. Mukubwa meets with no success and Patel then asks Chisokone for his assistance.

24   19 July 1965 at work

Mukubwa accuses Adrian of looking dirty at work. Adrian attempts unsuccessfully to object by appealing to Patel. Patel asks Chisokone to enquire why Adrian is creating such a disturbance. Chisokone tries to calm things down by telling Adrian that he has a joking relationship with Mukubwa and that he should not quarrel. Adrian denies that there is a joking relationship between them. Lyashi sides with Adrian against Mukubwa.

25   22 July 1965 at tea break

'Chisokone revealed': see chapter 7.

26   26 July 1965 at tea break

Ibrahim expresses concern over the harsh working conditions to Lyashi, Nkoloya, Paulos and Meshak. All state that action must be taken to get rid of hourly pay.

27   29 July 1965 at work

Meshak calls Zakeyo *'mudala'*. A heated quarrel breaks out. Lyashi supports Zakeyo against Meshak.

AA

28 2 August 1965 at tea break

A noisy group of junior workers crowd round the tea and bread. Lyashi shouts to them that they should let the senior workers have some food. He is supported by Nkoloya and Abraham. The junior workers comply with their seniors' demands.

29 6 August 1965 at tea break

'Lyashi outlines a plan for action': see chapter 7.

30 9 August 1965 at work

Demands for the introduction of a lunch break and $1d$ increment are taken before Patel. Lunch break given but no pay rise.

31 1 September 1965 at work

Walk-out organised by Lyashi and others for $1d$ increment. Management eventually agrees but awarded only to senior workers.

32 11 September 1965 at work

'The five-day working week dispute': see chapter 7.

33 5 November 1965 at work

The 'stolen clothing' dispute: see chapter 8.

34 6 November 1965 at work

'Mwanza is told his nickname': see chapter 8.

35 15 February 1966 at work

The February Strike: see chapter 8.

Bibliography

Abrahamsson, B. (1970), 'Homans on exchange: hedonism revived', *American Journal of Sociology*, vol. 76, pp. 273–85.

Abegglen, J. (1958), *The Japanese factory*, Glencoe, Ill.: Free Press.

Arensberg, C. M. (1959), *The Irish countryman*, Gloucester, Mass.: Peter Smith.

Bailey, F. G. (1960), *Tribe, caste and nation: a study of political activity and political change in highland Orissa*, Manchester: Manchester University Press.

Baldwin, R. E. (1966), *Economic development and export growth: a study of Northern Rhodesia, 1920–60*, Berkeley and Los Angeles: University of California Press.

Bales, R. F. (1950), *Interaction process analysis*, Cambridge, Mass.: MIT Press.

Barnes, J. A. (1954) 'Class and committees in a Norwegian island parish', *Human Relations*, vol. 7, No. 1.

Barth, F. (1966), *Models of social organisation*, London: Royal Anthropological Institute occasional paper No. 23.

Becker, H. S. (1960), 'Notes on the concept of commitment', *American Journal of Sociology*, vol. LXVI, pp. 32–40.

Bell, E. M. (1963), *Polygons: a survey of the African personnel of a Rhodesian factory*, Salisbury: University College of Rhodesia and Nyasaland occasional paper No. 3.

Berg, E. J. (1961), 'Backward-sloping labour supply functions in dual economics: the African case', *Quarterly Journal of Economics*, vol. LXXV.

Beum, C. O., and Brundage, E. G. (1950), 'A method for analysing the sociomatrix', *Sociometry*, vol. XIII, pp. 141–5.

Blau, P. (1964), *Exchange and power in social life*, New York: John Wiley.

Boissevain, J. (1968), 'Networks, brokers and quasi-groups: some thoughts on the place of non-groups in the social sciences' (translated from the Dutch), Assen: Van Gorcum.

Bott, E. (1957), *Family and social network*, London: Tavistock Publications (new edition 1971).

Boulding, Kenneth E. (1961), *The image*, Ann Arbor, Mich.: University of Michigan Press.

— (1962), *Conflict and defence: a general theory*, New York: Harper & Row.

Buckley, Walter (1967), *Sociology and modern systems theory*, Englewood Cliffs, N. J.: Prentice-Hall.

Cancian, Frank (1966), 'Maximisation as norm, strategy and theory: a comment on programmatic statements in economic anthropology', *American Anthropologist*, vol. 68, pp. 465–70.

Chaplin, D. (1968), 'Labour Turnover in the Peruvian textile industry', *British Journal of Industrial Relations*, vol. VI, No. 1.

Cunnison, Sheila (1966), *Wages and work allocation: a study of social relations in a garment workshop*, London: Tavistock Publications.

Dennis, N. *et al.* (1956), *Coal is our life*, London: Eyre & Spottiswoode.

Devons, E. G. and Gluckman, M. (1964), 'Introduction' and 'Conclusion' in *Closed systems and open minds*, ed. M. Gluckman, Edinburgh: Oliver & Boyd.

Dotson, F., and Dotson, L. O. (1968), *The Indian minority of Zambia, Rhodesia and Malawi*, New Haven, Conn.: Yale University Press.

Downs, Anthony (1957), *An economic theory of democracy*, New York: Harper & Row.

Ekeh, P. (1969), 'Issues in exchange theory', *Berkeley Journal of Sociology*, July, pp. 42–58.

Elkan, W. (1956), *An African labour force*, East African Studies No. 7, Kampala: EAISR.

Emerson, Richard M. (1962), 'Power–dependence relations', *American Sociological Review*, vol. 27, pp. 31–41.

— (1969), 'Operant psychology and exchange theory' in R. L. Burgess and Don Bushell, *Behavioural sociology: the experimental analysis of social process*, London: Columbia University Press.

Epstein, A. L. (1958), *Politics in an Urban African community*, Manchester: Manchester University Press for the Rhodes-Livingstone Institute (now the Institute for African Studies, University of Zambia).

— (1959), 'Linguistic innovation and culture on the Copperbelt, Northern Rhodesia', *Southwestern Journal of Anthropology*, vol. 15, pp. 235–253.

Firth, Raymond (1958), *Human types*, New York: Mentor Books.

Festinger, Leon (1957), *A theory of cognitive dissonance*, Evanston Ill.: Row Peterson.

Garbett, G. Kingsley (1968), 'The application of optical coincidence cards to matrices of digraphs of social networks', *Sociology*, vol. 2, pp. 311–31.

— (1969), 'Directed graphs and social networks: procedures, measures, and the problem of isomorphism' (mimeograph).

— (1970), 'The analysis of social situations', *Man*, vol. 5, No. 2, pp. 214–27.

Garbett, G. Kingsley, and Kapferer, Bruce (1971), 'Theoretical orientations in the study of labour migration', *New Atlantis*, vol. 3.

Garfinkel, Harold (1967), *Studies in ethnomethodology*, Englewood Cliffs, N. J.: Prentice-Hall.

Glass, Yette. (1960), *The black industrial worker: a social psychological study*, Johannesburg.

Gluckman, M. (1949), (with J. C. Mitchell and J. A. Barnes), 'The village headman in British Central Africa', *Africa*, vol. 19, No. 2, pp. 89–106.

— (1958), *Analysis of a social situation in modern Zululand*, Rhodes-Livingstone Paper No. 28, Manchester: Manchester University Press, for the Rhodes-Livingstone Institute (now the Institute for African Studies, University of Zambia).

Gluckman, M. (1961), 'Ethnographic data in British social anthropology', *Sociological Review*, vol. 9, pp. 5–17.

— (1963), 'Gossip and scandal', *Current Anthropology*, vol. 4, pp. 307–16.

— (1969), 'Inter-hierarchical roles: professional and party ethics in tribal areas in South and Central Africa' in *Local-level politics: social and cultural perspectives*, ed. Marc J. Swartz, London: London University Press.

Goffman, E. (1959), *The presentation of self in everyday life*, New York: Doubleday.

— (1961), *Encounters*, Indianapolis: Bobbs-Merrill.

Gouldner, A. W. (1954), *Patterns of industrial bureaucracy*, Glencoe, Ill.: Free Press.

— (1965), *Wildcat strike*, New York: Harper & Row.

Gulliver, P. H. (1955), *Labour migration in a rural economy: a study of the Ngoni and Ndeuli of southern Tanzania*, East African Studies No. 6, Kampala: EAISR.

Gutkind, P. (1968), 'The energy of despair: social organisation of the unemployed in two African cities, Lagos and Nairobi', part 1, *Civilisations*, vol. XVII, No. 3.

Hanson, R. C., and Simmons, O. G. (1968), 'The role path: a concept and procedure for studying migration to urban communities', *Human Organisation*, vol. 27, No. 2.

— (1969), 'Differential experience paths of rural migrants to the city', *American Behavioral Scientist*, vol. 13, pp. 14–35.

Harsanyi, J. C. (1968), 'Individualistic and functionalistic explanations in the light of game theory: the example of social status' in *Problems in the philosophy of science*, ed. I. Lakatos and A. Musgrave, Amsterdam: North Holland Publishing Co.

Hartshorne, E. Y. (1940), 'Metabolism indices and the annexation of Austria: a note on method', *American Journal of Sociology*, vol. XLV, pp. 899–917.

Heath, Anthony (1968a), 'MacIntyre on Blau', *Sociology*, vol. 2, pp. 93–6.

— (1968b), 'Economic theory and sociology: a critique of P. M. Blau's *Exchange and power in social life*', *Sociology*, vol. 2, pp. 273–92.

Heider, Fritz. (1958), *The psychology of interpersonal relations*, New York: John Wiley.

Homans, G. C. (1951), *The human group*, London: Routledge & Kegan Paul.

— (1961), *Social behaviour: its elementary forms*, London: Routledge & Kegan Paul.

Kapferer, B. (1966), *The population of a Zambian municipal township*, Lusaka: Communication No. 1, Institute for Social Research (now the Institute for African Studies), University of Zambia.

— (1969), 'Norms and the manipulation of relationships in a work context', *Social networks in urban situations*, ed. J. C. Mitchell, Manchester: Manchester University Press for the Institute for Social Research (now the Institute for African Studies), University of Zambia.

— (1971), 'Social network and conjugal role in urban Zambia: towards a reformulation of the Bott hypothesis' in *Network approaches*, ed. J. Boissevain and J. C. Mitchell, Leiden (forthcoming).

Katz, F. E. (1966), 'Social participation and social structure', *Social Forces*.

Kay, G. (1967), *A social geography of Zambia*, London: University of London Press.

Kephart, W. M. (1950), 'A quantitative analysis of intragroup relationships', *American Journal of Sociology*, vol. LV.

Kerr, C., and Siegal, A. (1954), 'The interindustry propensity to strike—an international comparison' in *Industrial conflict*, ed. A. Kornhauser *et al.*, New York: McGraw-Hill.

Knight, Frank H. (1921), *Risk, uncertainty and profit*, Boston and New York: Houghton Mifflin.

Kuhn, Alfred (1966), *The study of society: A multi-disciplinary approach*, London: Tavistock Publications.

Laing, R. D. (1967), *The politics of experience and the bird of Paradise*, Harmondsworth: Penguin Books.

Lantz, H. R. (1958), *People of Coal Town*, New York: Columbia University Press.

Leik, Robert, Emerson, Richard, and Burgess, Robert (1968), 'The emergence of stratification in exchange networks' (mimeographed).

Lewin, Kurt (1958), *Field theory in social science*, ed. D. Cartwright, Evanston, Ill., and London: Harper Torchbooks.

Long, Norman (1968), *Social change and the individual*, Manchester: Manchester University Press for the Institute for Social Research (now the Institute for African Studies), University of Zambia.

Lupton, T. (1963), *On the shop floor: two studies of workshop organisation and output*, Oxford: Pergamon Press.

Lupton, T., and Cunnison, S. (1964), 'Workshop behaviour' *in Closed systems and open minds*, ed. M. Gluckman, Edinburgh and London: Oliver & Boyd.

McCall, G. J., and Simmons, J. C. (1966), *Identities and interactions*, New York: Free Press.

McClements, Rosemary (1970), *Tikopia: area-analysis in terms of exchange theory*. M.A. thesis (unpublished).

McCulloch, M. (1956), *A social survey of the African population of Livingstone*, Rhodes-Livingstone Paper No. 26, Manchester: Manchester University Press for the Rhodes-Livingstone Institute (now the Institute for African Studies, Universities of Zambia).

McHugh, Peter (1968), *Defining the situation: the organisation of meaning in social interaction*, Indianapolis and New York: Bobbs-Merrill.

Malinowski, B. (1922), *Argonauts of the western Pacific*, London: Routledge.

Mayer, P. (1961), *Townsmen or tribesmen?* Cape Town: Oxford University Press.

Meggitt, M. (1965), *The lineage system of the Mae-Enga of New Guinea*, Edinburgh and London: Oliver & Boyd.

Mitchell, J. C. (1956), *The kalela dance: aspects of social relationships among urban Africans in Northern Rhodesia*, Rhodes-Livingstone Paper No. 27, Manchester: Manchester University Press for the Rhodes-Livingstone Institute (now the Institute for African Studies, University of Zambia).

Mitchell, J. C. (1956), 'Urbanisation, detribalisation and stabilisation in southern Africa: a problem of definition and measurement' in *Social implications of industrialisation and urbanisation in Africa south of the Sahara*, Paris: UNESCO.

— (1954), *African urbanisation in Luanshya and Ndola*, Rhodes-Livingstone Communication No. 6, Lusaka: Institute for African Studies, University of Zambia.

— (1961), 'The causes of labour migration' in *Migrant labour in Africa south of the Sahara*, publication No. 79, Abidjan: Commission for Technical Co-operation in Africa South of the Sahara.

— (1966), 'Theoretical orientations in African urban studies' in *The social anthropology of complex societies*, ed. M. Barton, London: Tavistock Publications.

— (1969a), 'The concept and use of social networks' in *Social networks in urban situations*, ed. J. C. Mitchell, Manchester: Manchester University Press for the Institute for Social Research (now the Institute for African Studies), University of Zambia.

— (1969b), 'Structural plurality, urbanisation and labour circulation in Southern Rhodesia' in *Migration*, ed. J. A. Jackson *Sociological Studies* vol. 2, Cambridge: Cambridge University Press.

— (1969c), 'Urbanization, detribalization, stabilization and urban commitment in southern Africa' in *Urbanism, urbanization and change*, ed. P. Meadows and E. H. Mizruchi, Reading, Mass.: Addison-Wesley.

— (1971), 'Networks, norms and institutions' in *Network Approaches* ed. J. Boissevain and J. C. Mitchell, Leiden (forthcoming).

Mulford, D. (1967), *Zambia: the politics of independence, 1957-64*, London: Oxford University Press.

Nash, Manning (1967), *Machine-age Maya: the industrialisation of a Guatemalan community*, Chicago and London: University of Chicago Press.

Nelson, P. (1959), 'Migration, real income and information', *Regional Science*, vol. 1, pp. 43-74.

Newcomb, Theodore (1961), *The acquaintance process*, New York: Holt, Rinehart & Winston.

Nicholas, Ralph W. (1969), 'Rules, resources and political activity' in *Local-level politics: social and cultural perspectives*, ed. Marc J. Swartz, London: University of London Press.

Niemejer, Rudo (1971), 'Measures for use in network analysis' in *Network approaches*, ed. J. Boissevain and J. C. Mitchell (in press).

Richards, A. I. (1966), 'Multi-tribalism in African urban areas', *Civilisation*, vol. XVI.

Robson, R. A. H. (1968), 'The present state of theory in sociology' in *Problems in the philosophy of science*, ed. I. Lakatos and A. Musgrave, Amsterdam: North Holland Publishing Company.

Roethlisberger, F. J., and Dickson, W. J. (1941), *Management and the worker*, Cambridge, Mass.: Harvard University Press.

Roy, D. (1952), 'Quota restriction and goldbricking in the machine shop', *American Journal of Sociology*, vol. LVII.

Salisbury, R. F. (1962), *From stone to steel: economic consequences of technological changes in New Guinea*, Melbourne: Melbourne University Press.

Savage, Charles H. Jnr. (1964), *Social Reorganization in a factory in the Andes, Society for Applied Anthropology*, monograph No. 7, New York: Connell University.

Schelling, T. C. (1963), *The strategy of conflict*, New York: Oxford University Press.

Schutzenberger, M. P. (1954), 'A tentative classification of goal-seeking behaviours', *Journal of Mental Science*, vol. 100, pp. 97–102.

Seashore, S. E. (1954), *Group cohesiveness in the industrial work group*, Ann Arbor, Mich.: University of Michigan Press.

Shannon, Lyle. (1969), 'The economic absorption and cultural integration of immigrant workers: characteristics of the individual versus the nature of the system', *American Behavioral Scientist*, vol. 13.

Sheth, Narayan, R. (1968), *The social framework of an Indian factory*. Manchester: Manchester University Press.

Simon, H. A. (1956), 'Rational choice and the structure of the environment', *Psychological Review*, vol. 63, pp. 129–38.

Smith, Willie (1968), 'Industrial sociology in Africa: foundations and prospects', *Journal of Modern African Studies*, vol. 6, pp. 81–95.

Sjaastrad (1962), 'The costs and returns of human migration', *Journal of Political Economy*, vol. 70.

Strauss, A., et al. (1964), *Psychiatric ideologies and institutions*, London: Collier–Macmillan.

Swartz, Marc J. (ed.) (1969), *Local-level politics: social and cultural Perspectives*, London: London University Press.

Taylor, Howard F. (1970), *Balance in small groups*, New York: Van Nostrand–Reinhold.

Thibaut, J. W., and Kelley, H. H. (1959), *The social psychology of groups*, New York: John Wiley.

Thomas, W. I. (1966), *On social organisation and social personality: selected papers*, ed. Jamowitz Morris, Chicago: University of Chicago Press.

Turner, V. W. (1957), *Schism and continuity in an African society: a study of Ndembu village life*, Manchester: Manchester University Press for the Rhodes Livingstone Institute (now the Institute for African Studies, University of Zambia).

Turner, Victor (1969), 'Mukanda: the politics of a non-political ritual' in *Local-level politics: social and cultural perspectives*, ed. Marc J. Swartz, London: London University Press.

Van Velsen, J. (1961), 'Labour migration as a positive factor in the continuity of Tonga tribal society' in *Social change in modern Africa*, ed. A. Southall, London: Oxford University Press for the International African Institute.

— (1964), *The politics of kinship: a study of manipulation among the Lakeside Tonga*, Manchester: Manchester University Press for the Institute for Social Research (now the Institute for African Studies), University of Zambia.

— (1967), 'The extended case method and situational analysis' in *The craft of anthropology*, ed. A. L. Epstein, London: Tavistock Publications.

Walker, C. R. (1950), *Steeltown: an industrial case history of the conflict between progress and industry*, Yale Labor and Management Center series, New York: Harper & Row.
Waller, W. (1965), *The sociology of teaching*, New York: John Wiley.
Warner, W. L., and Low, J. O. (1947), *The social system of the modern factory*, New Haven, Conn.: Yale University Press.
Watson, W. (1958), *Tribal cohesion in a money economy: a study of the Mambwe people of Northern Rhodesia*, Manchester: Manchester University Press for the Rhodes-Livingstone Institute (now the Institute for African Studies, University of Zambia).
Weber, Max (1930), *The Protestant ethic and the rise of capitalism*, London: Routledge & Kegan Paul.
Wilson, G. (1942), *The economics of detribalisation*, part 2, Rhodes-Livingstone Paper No. 6, Rhodes-Livingstone Institute, Livingstone, Northern Rhodesia.

Government and official publications

Copperbelt of Zambia Mining Industry Yearbook, (1964), Kitwe: Copper Industry Service Bureau.
Federation of Rhodesia and Nyasaland (1958), *Economic survey of Broken Hill*, Salisbury: Government Printer.
Government of the Republic of Zambia (1964), *Second report of the May–June 1963 census of Africans*, Lusaka: Ministry of Finance.
— (1965), *Final report of the September 1961 census of non-Africans and employers*, Lusaka: Central Statistical Office.
— (1965), Department of Labour, *Annual report*, Lusaka: Ministry of Labour and Social Development.
— (1965), *Daily Hansard*, Tuesday 27 July, Lusaka: Government Printer.
— (1965), Statutory instrument No. 413, Lusaka: Government Printer.
— (1966), *Gazette Acts*, 1966, Lusaka: Government Printer.

Index